Race in the Jury Box

SUNY series in New Directions in Crime and Justice Studies
Austin T. Turk, *editor*

Race in the Jury Box

AFFIRMATIVE ACTION IN JURY SELECTION

Hiroshi Fukurai
and
Richard Krooth

STATE UNIVERSITY OF NEW YORK PRESS

Published by
State University of New York Press, Albany

© 2003 State University of New York

All rights reserved

Printed in the United States of America

For information, address State University of New York Press,
90 State Street, Suite 700, Albany, NY 12207

Production by Judith Block
Marketing by Michael Campochiaro

Library of Congress Cataloging-in-Publication Data

Fukurai, Hiroshi, 1954–
    Race in the jury box : affirmative action in jury selection / Hiroshi Fukurai and
Richard Krooth.
      p. cm. — (SUNY series in new directions in crime and justice studies)
    Includes bibliographical references and index.
    ISBN 0-7914-5837-7 (hc : acid-free paper) — ISBN 0-7914-5838-5 (pb : acid-free paper)
      1. Jury selection—United States. 2. Race discrimination—Law and legislation—
United States. 3. Criminal procedure—United States. I. Krooth, Richard II. Title III. Series.

KF9680.F85 2003
347.73'752—dc21   2002042633

10 9 8 7 6 5 4 3 2 1

CONTENTS

Preface   ix

Table of Cases   xvii

Chapter 1 INTRODUCTION TO RACIALLY MIXED JURIES   1

Racially mixed juries and jury verdicts   6
The significance of minority jurors in the jury box   14
Reform and its barriers   17
Conclusions   18

Chapter 2 DEFINING AND MEASURING RACE AND
           RACIAL IDENTITY   20

Measuring and identifying race   21
Social deconstruction of race: Social elements and concepts   23
Reliability and validity of race as a measurement   32
Racial identity and ancestral backgrounds   41
Deconstructing race and the importance of
     affirmative action programs   51
Conclusions   59

Chapter 3 RACIALLY MIXED JURIES AND AFFIRMATIVE ACTION   61

Affirmative action in jury selection   63
The jury "de medietate linguae" model   65
The Hennepin County model   69
The social science model   70
Public perceptions of racially balanced juries   72
Results   73
Racially diverse juries, racial quotas, and
     peremptory challenges   83
Conclusions   89

Chapter 4 EUGENE "BEAR" LINCOLN AND THE NATIVE
AMERICAN JURY: AFFIRMATIVE ACTION IN
JURY SELECTION AND PEREMPTORY INCLUSION   90

People v. Eugene "Bear" Lincoln   92

Defense strategies to increase the likelihood
of a racially diverse jury   102

Affirmative jury structures and peremptory inclusion   111

The need for progressive legislative and court action   121

Conclusions   123

Chapter 5 THE SIXTH AMENDMENT AND THE RACIALLY
MIXED JURY   125

Impartiality   126

The fair cross-section requirement   131

Jury of one's peers   138

Conclusions   146

Chapter 6 SHORTCOMINGS OF PROCEDURALLY BASED
REMEDIES: JURY REPRESENTATION FROM
THE BEGINNING TO THE END OF THE JURY
SELECTION PROCESS   149

The goal of random selection and the fair
cross-section doctrine   150

Empirical checkpoints in jury selection   153

Jury representation from the beginning to the
end of jury selection   155

Analyses and findings   156

Partial remedies and their impacts on jury selection   167

Final jury composition: Inequities, remedies,
and future reforms   169

Conclusions   174

Chapter 7 JURY NULLIFICATION AND THE MINORITY-DOMINANT
CRIMINAL JURY: THE O. J. SIMPSON VERDICT AND
ACQUITTAL BY RACE   176

Presumption of innocence, the burden of proof,
and reasonable doubt   180

The Simpson jury and a hypothetical scenario   184
A hypothetical scenario: Results and findings   185
Jury nullification, racial identity, and legal concepts 190
Conclusions   195

Chapter 8   JURY NULLIFICATION AND AFFIRMATIVE
            ACTION JURIES   197
Jury nullification   199
Jury nullification and affirmative action juries   202
Jury nullification and criminal justice concepts   206
Judicial and legislative history of jury nullification 211
Conclusions   213

Chapter 9   RACE AND THE AFFIRMATIVE JURY: CONCLUSIONS 215
The jury and the potential for democracy   215
Distinguishing features of affirmative action in jury selection 217
Conclusions   221

Appendix A   SURVEY AND DATA BASE INFORMATION   224
Community surveys (4 data sets)   224
College student survey (1 data set)   228
Jury panel survey (1 data set)   230
College student experiment (1 data set)   231
Census information   232

Appendix B   METHODOLOGICAL STRATEGIES ON
             HOW TO DETERMINE AND MEASURE RACE
             IN COURTROOMS   233

Notes   235

Bibliography   249

Index   265

PREFACE

This study reflects our own experience in tracking criminal trials. On our own account, we have found that, in almost all of the final juries that have tried criminal defendants of minority race, there has been a shocking failure to adequately represent racially and ethnically diverse communities where the alleged crimes were committed, or from the venues where the cases were finally tried.

We have long recognized the barriers and impediments to overcome the legal system's procedural failings, moral inequities, and judicial injustices. Yet, even today, almost all legally prescribed arguments and defense motions that attempt to mount the claim of racial discrimination have had a limited scope, dealing only with racial disparities in the composition of the jury pool *before* jurors are ultimately chosen for the final criminal jury. Surprisingly, the United States Supreme Court has never discussed or addressed the *necessity* to introduce procedural means or legal arguments to ensure racial equality in the *makeup of final juries*.

In most criminal trials, it is fairly clear that the laws calling for equitable jury selection have been systematically undermined, politically manipulated, and legally entangled in procedures that prohibit defense counsel from initiating actions to compel courts to empanel racially diverse final juries. The result has been the general absence of racial diversity in such juries, leading to discriminatory, racialized trials and convictions. And to date, there have been a litany of abuses, ensuring that final juries will be skewed away from an equitable balance of racial minorities in criminal cases involving minority defendants.

Take prosecutors, for instance, who follow tradition-bound pathways that ensure the overwhelming white composition of the final jury. Realizing that final juries can be shaped to be predominantly white, prosecutors often make race-based trial preparations, knowing that certain types of evidence and certain witnesses can be presented in court imbued with racial overtones that white jurors might be more inclined to accept. And, as commonly recognized, prosecutors frequently overcharge criminal counts against minority defendants, forcing them to plea bargain in a way that, at root, amounts to racialized admission to "lesser" crimes.

Equity in the criminal system will thus require reforms of the methods and mechanisms used in jury selection and the composition of the final jury, together with reestablishing an effective system of checks and balances on the abuse of governmental power.

In this study, we argue that racially diverse tribunals will lead to a growing public awareness that courts need to carefully take account of minority defendants' presumption of innocence and prosecutors' burden of proof beyond a reasonable doubt. In trials monitored by minority jurors today, credibility of evidence and strength of testimony—as well as race-neutral preparation and presentation of such evidence—have become critical concerns of both police and prosecutors. For in the minds of jurors, these matters raise reasonable doubt that the accused may not be guilty.

Police and prosecutors may also be deterred from pursuing racially discriminatory investigations, evidence gathering, and overcharging criminal acts by the public's perception of fairness and by empaneling racially diverse juries.

District attorneys, too, may be compelled to alter their prosecutorial methods to conform with racial-nondiscrimination by placing racial minorities in the final jury box.

When presenting evidence and putting witnesses on the stand, the prosecution's trial strategies may be similarly altered in preparing, introducing, and arguing.

Racially diverse juries may have still another effect: raising the bar for attorneys to pay close attention to the quality of their overall performance, including jury selection strategies, trial preparations, and methods of presentations.

So, too, racially diverse tribunals may exert a significant influence over the judges, including evaluations of racial fairness in peremptory challenges, taking the recommendations of jury forepersons, making assessments of culpability, and sentencing determinations.

To offset so called intimate work-group relations in the courtroom among judges, prosecutors, and public defenders, racially diverse tribunals may even explode traditional alliances rooted in their similarly shaped socio-demographic characteristics, including race, for which there are as yet no effective checks to evaluate the overall fairness and quality of their courtroom performance.

Given all these shortcomings of the enforcement system of law and order and courtroom procedures, jury reform is absolutely essential to the criminal process, establishing norms of social fairness and legal equitability, and engendering a belief in judicial legitimacy among the increasingly diverse communities of our nation.

To reform this system, this book examines the applicability, constitutionality, and public perception of race-conscious affirmative efforts to allocate jury seats in order to build racially diverse juries in criminal trials. The study also attempts to show that racially balanced juries provide an internal check to insure fair and proper performance by governmental agencies, enhance the appearance of justice and fairness in criminal trials, increase the public respect and confidence in jury deliberations and verdicts, and eliminate the possibility of juries ignoring the facts and nullifying the law in criminal trials.

By reviewing census figures and court cases, and making careful statistical surveys and analysis, we have analyzed four specific types of affirmative action jury selection strategies. These affirmative methods reveal the potential for basic jury reform using race, class, ethnicity, gender, and other legally cognizable categories for the wider administration of equity and fairness.

ORGANIZATION OF THIS BOOK

Overall, then, this book offers a critical analysis and systematic examination of possible applications of affirmative jury selection policies in jury trials with the goal of composing racially diverse juries. Chapter 1 is a brief review of differing community responses to two criminal cases in which each has been adjudicated by an all-white jury and then by a racially mixed jury.

Chapter 2 starts off with the central question of what constitutes race and racial definition in modern America, examining the historical components and dynamics of the classification and construction of race and racial categories. As we will review, in order to create and design effective race-conscious jury selection schemes, affirmative action programs in criminal jury proceedings must rely on the clear and well-defined conceptualizations of race and racial classifications. This chapter also examines the most current political and legal definition of race and attempts to analyze the unstable, irregular, and fluid nature of race and racial categories.

Chapter 3 focuses on jury research using three different models of racially mixed juries and presents empirical studies to add substance to the discussion of public attitudes towards using an affirmative action mechanism in jury selection and trials. The discussion focuses on three distinct types of racially diverse juries—the jury "de medietate linguae" (the split jury), the Hennepin model (the proportional jury), and the social science model (the quarter-jury). We argue that the mandatory affirmative action strategies and race-specific jury structures are essential to both the substance and appearance of trial fairness and verdict legitimacy.

Chapter 4 explores the potential use of affirmative jury selection procedures covering the 1997 racially charged criminal trial, *People v. Eugene "Bear" Lincoln*. The trial received extensive national and international attention, in which a Native American defendant was charged for the murder of a white deputy at an Indian reservation in Mendocino County, California. The present authors participated as community surveyors and jury consultants to defense counsel during the course of the trial.

This chapter reviews whether or not the use of affirmative jury selection can lead to greater and broader acceptance of a jury trial and its verdict in a racially sensitive case. It focuses on the function of the jury as an ideal, racially heterogeneous body able to sway both the racial majority and minority to mediate their racial interests during jury deliberations. The chapter also focuses on the affirmative use of inclusive methods by which both defense and prosecution are given affirmative jury selection choices to secure particular members in the final jury and influence its ultimate racial balance. As we will see, this method of affirmative peremptory inclusion facilitates mediation, making possible integrated jury deliberations. By securing the place of minorities in the final jury, the optimum conditions for verdict legitimacy and trial fairness also help elevate the public's potential for accepting jury verdicts in racially sensitive trials.

Chapter 5 examines the relationship between various requirements for the racially mixed jury in a criminal case and the constitutional concepts derived from the Sixth Amendment, covering impartiality, a fair cross section of the community, and a jury of one's peers. An attempt is made to analyze the balancing of these three constitutional requirements, as well as the legal pathway to achieve racially diverse juries.

Chapter 6 sums up the social significance of racial exclusions from jury service and identifies a variety of technical problems and procedural deficiencies of current jury selection procedures that systematically exclude racial minorities from jury service. This chapter also suggests that traditional reforms proposed to create racially representative and diverse juries are fundamentally inadequate to secure racial minorities in the final jury or to prevent racially biased jury verdicts. Certainly, the representative ideal for jury service may be difficult to attain, especially due to racially biased procedural defects inherent in jury selection, racially discriminatory social settings, and economic inequities that also affect the availability and voluntary participation of minority jurors. Thus, the application of affirmative mechanisms in jury selection and the mandated use of racial quotas may be the only potentially unfailing means to compose racially mixed juries, thereby preserving the structure of fairness and creating optimal conditions for trial and verdict legitimacy in criminal proceedings.

Chapter 7 introduces a practical, empirical, and corresponding theoretical analysis of the relationship among the race of defendants and victims, criminal jurors, and jury nullification. Jury nullification refers to the jury's power to acquit the defendant contrary to evidentiary fact and substantive legal provisions. Many observers of the O. J. Simpson trial, for example, suggested that the predominantly black jury rejected overwhelming evidence of guilt in favor of their concept of justice. By contrast, this chapter presents empirical analyses of the O. J. Simpson verdict, arguing that, despite the widely shared images of "untamed" minority juries ignoring facts and nullifying the application of law, the acquittal may have reflected their adherence to the strict application of the law and legal concepts in evaluating testimony and evidence, including a presumption of innocence, the burden of proof, and reasonable doubt.

While the media powerfully reinforced the image of racial minorities' inclination to disrespect and ignore the application of law in criminal trials involving the notion of racism, our empirical analysis demonstrates the opposite tendency: that racial minorities are more likely to exhibit a greater propensity to apply a stricter standard of criminal justice principles in assessing and evaluating the credibility and validity of evidence, especially when presented by traditionally oppressive law enforcement agencies. Finally, this chapter examines recent controversies over racially based jury nullification and how racially diverse juries can respond to their role as the judge of both facts and law.

Chapter 8 continues the discussion of the relationship between jury nullification and affirmative action juries, examining whether or not the distinct types of racially mixed juries, race-based jury box allocations, and race-conscious peremptory inclusive methods are able to prevent harmful instances of jury nullification, that is, racially-based vengeful convictions and acquittals. This chapter also demonstrates that the application of affirmative jury selection has a significant impact on public perceptions of trial fairness and verdict legitimacy, and that the use of racially mixed juries may prevent racially explicit forms of jury nullification. Finally, Chapter 8 reviews the affirmative application of race-based jury selection approaches, asking if they meet the needs of our multicultural society by exploring the future of affirmative action in jury selection.

The final chapter or Chapter 9 of this study attempts to make a strong and unapologetic case for affirmative jury selection procedures. By presenting in-depth comparisons of different models of affirmative action in jury selection and other related areas (including those in education, hiring, and contracting), we focus on the distinct features, approaches, and effective models of race-specific structures. We try to demonstrate how selected juries increase public acceptance of jury verdicts and enhance the legitimacy of jury proceedings and verdicts.

Finally, two appendices are created to provide information on our empirical and methodological analyses. Appendix A provides detailed information on historical and contemporary census data, community-wide surveys, personal interviews, college student experiment and surveys, as well as data collection methods, various survey instruments, and measurements used in our analysis. Appendix B provides our methodological strategies on how to determine and measure race in courtroom.

On the cutting edge of the most recent research on the intertwined relationship between affirmative jury selection and the depth and fairness of jury deliberation by racially diverse juries, this book attempts to offer scientific studies corroborating the possible application of race-conscious affirmative jury structures and peremptory inclusive approaches in order to assess the optimal condition for trial fairness and verdict legitimacy in race-impacted criminal trials. We have attempted to present the most recent research on the intertwined relation between affirmative jury selection and the fairnes of jury deliberations. And we have found that deep-seated reforms to ensure the presence of racial minorities on the jury are absolutely essential, hopefully contributing to the intense debate concerning the present search by legal practitioners and academic researchers for an egalitarian and racially equitable jury system.

Though we have worked hard to bring this study to a successful conclusion, we have also relied on the help and contribution of others. For our manuscript could not have been completed without the support and encouragement from a number of scholars, trial attorneys, colleagues, students, staff members, and our families. So here we wish to express our indebtedness to all those who contributed to this research effort.

Our special gratitude goes to Emeritus Sociology Professor Edgar W. Butler, at the University of California, Riverside, who offered us the first research opportunity to examine racial fairness in the selection of criminal juries in southern California, as well as to Emeritus Sociology Professor John I. Kitsuse, at the University of California, Santa Cruz, who initially introduced us to the discipline of social constructionism.

At various stages of completion, other colleagues and scholars also provided their expertise, support, knowledge, and questions concerning the significance of empaneling racially diverse tribunals in criminal trials. On this account, thanks are due to Deborah Ramirez at Northeastern University School of Law; Dane Archer, John B. Childs, and Dana Takagi of the sociology department at the University of California, Santa Cruz; Craig Haney of the psychology department at the University of California, Santa Cruz; late Emeritus Education Professor Millie Almy, at the University of California, Berkeley; Ann Baxandall Krooth, oral historian and civil rights essayist in Berkeley; and Karl W. Krooth, human rights and criminal trial attorney in San Francisco.

Other trial attorneys we have worked with or observed in attempting to secure racially balanced juries include: in New York City, William Kunstler and Justin Finger; in Washington, D.C., David Krooth; in Atlanta, Georgia, Howard Moore; in Chicago, Gene Hutchinson; in the Virgin Islands, James McWilliams; in Madison, Wisconsin, Mary Kay Baum and Neil Toman; and in San Francisco, Neil Eisenberg and Angela Alioto.

We also have been strongly influenced by two longtime advocates of racially equitable jury structures at the University of Wisconsin Law School: Professors Willard Hirst and William Rice, both now deceased.

In obtaining student survey questionnaires, we appreciate the support and assistance of Professors Alexandra Maryanski of the sociology department at the University of California, Riverside and Tonya Shuster of the sociology department at the University of California, Irvine, both of whom were instrumental in distributing and collecting survey questionnaires on their respective campuses.

At the University of California, Santa Cruz, we are particularly indebted to Lin Weyer, Barbara Lawrence, and Dana Hagler, and other office staffs who were extremely helpful and facilitated the completion of the manuscript. Our appreciation is also extended to Professors Koichi Niitsu, Yoshito Ishio, and Kazuko Tanaka at International Christian University in Mitaka, Japan, and Akiko Kaji, Satoko Fukai, Reiko Sakaba, Nao Nagata, and Maiko Sato at the University of California Study Center in Tokyo, Japan, where the last stages of the manuscript were prepared.

Funding for this study came from a number of sources. We thank, in particular, the following groups: The Faculty Senate at the University of California, Santa Cruz, the University of California, Berkeley sociology department and law library for providing research and library facilities, and superior courts in various California counties, including Los Angeles, San Francisco, Alameda, Santa Clara, Mendocino, Contra Costa, and Santa Cruz.

Our appreciation is extended to Professor Austin Turk, at the University of California, Riverside, who is also a State University of New York series editor for New Directions in Crime and Justice Studies. He remained very patient throughout the editing stages of the manuscript preparation. We are also indebted to Senior Editor Nancy Ellegate, at the State University of New York Press. And we thank those reviewers who, though remaining anonymous, offered their helpful, yet critical and insightful comments and suggestions.

In the end, though, the study is based on our own research, participation in, and observation of trials, and survey analyses and conclusions. So needless to say, we accept full responsibility for the contents and the views presented in this book.

TABLE OF CASES

Akins v. Texas, 131

Apodacca v. Oregon, 17, 18

Ballad v. United States, 236

Ballew v. Georgia, 71, 240

Barry v. Garcia, 12

Batson v. Kentucky, 136–37, 169

Carter v. Kentucky, 182

Castenada v. Partida, 39

City of Richmond v. J.A. Croson Co., 88

Coffin v. United States, 180

Commonwealth v. Alberto Penabriel, 240

Commonwealth v. Richard Acen, Jr., 240

Duncan v. Louisiana, 139, 177

Duren v. Missouri, 132, 236

Estelle v. Williams, 180

Fields v. People, 243

Fleming v. Kemp, 243

Georgia v. McCollum, 236

Glasser v. United States, 131

Goldberg v. Kelly, 242

Harper v. Virginia Bd., 151

Hernandez v. Texas, 39, 129

Holland v. Illinois, 17, 132–33

Hoyt v. Florida, 231–32, 244

Kentucky v. Whorton, 180

Kramer v. Union Free Sch. Dist., 151

Lanprecht v. FCC, 239

Lockhart v. McCree, 18, 131

Lozano v. Florida, 13

Marshall v. Jerric, 242

Minnesota v. Charles, 239

People v. Eugene "Bear" Lincoln, xi, 91, 92

People v. Layhew, 180

People v. McLean, 240
People v. Tervino, 29
Peter v Kiff, 18
Plessy v. Ferguson, 29
Powers v. Ohio, 242
Raynolds v. Sims, 151
Respublica v. Mesca, 240
Richards v. Commonwealth, 240
Saint Francis College v. Al-Khazraji, 23, 24, 236, 237
Smith v. Texas, 18
Sparf and Hansen v. United States, 87, 211, 212
Stokes v. People, 242
Strauder v. West Virginia, 2, 113, 218, 236, 243
Swain v. Alabama, 132, 243
Taylor v. Louisiana, 113, 129, 131, 132, 147, 236
Thiel v. Southern Pacific Co., 131
United States v. Boardman, 212
United States v. Breckenridge, 172
United States v. Burkhart, 211
United States v. David, 243
United States v. Dougherty, 211
United States v. Montgomery, 243
United States v. Spock, 211
United States v. Vaccaro, 243
United States v. Wood, 68, 126
Wendling v. Commonwealth, 240
In re Winship, 180, 183
Withrow v. Larkin, 129

Chapter 1

INTRODUCTION TO RACIALLY MIXED JURIES

"I was stunned by the verdict. It shows that racial profiling seeps so deeply in our society that a wallet in the hand of white man looks like a wallet, and the wallet in the hand of a black man looks like a gun."
—Bill Bradley, former Democratic presidential candidate in reacting to the acquittal verdict of four white police officers in the Amadou Diallo murder trial in 2000.

"Today the system failed us."
—late Los Angeles Mayor Tom Bradley in responding to the acquittal verdict of four white police officers in the Rodney King assault trial in 1992.

"The court system has worked."
—then President George Bush in reacting to the same acquittal verdict in 1992.

"You'd almost have *to be black to understand. All their grievances, all their distrust of the system, all the beliefs people had in the evil of the system. Suddenly, it all turned out to be true."*
—Clarence Dickson, the highest-ranking black administrator in the Miami Police Department, in responding to the 1980 acquittal verdict of four white police officers in the murder trial of Arthur McDuffie, a black motorist, by the all-white jury.

"They kill with love."
—Innocent black death row inmate John Coffery, telling the head guard, Paul Edgecome (played by Tom Hanks), before facing his own electrocution in *The Green Mile.*

The fact that a minority defendant is tried by an all-white jury can be a nightmarish thought for racial and ethnic minorities.[1] In reality, however, a minority defendant in most jurisdictions is often confronted by white police officers, indicted by an all-white grand jury, prosecuted by a team of all-white district attorneys, convicted by a predominantly, if not all, white jury, sentenced by a white judge, denied appeals by white state appellate court jurists and white federal judges, and executed by a team of white prison officials. Such criminal proceeding and jury trials carry a long lasting impression of racial inequality in the criminal justice system. Race, then, becomes a critical emblem which members of minority race carefully assess trial fairness, verdict legitimacy, and the quality and integrity of the criminal justice system.

In the eyes of many marginalized segments of our community, an all-white jury that convicts a black defendant, or acquits a white defendant against overwhelming evidence of his guilt, is deeply disturbing. The fact that a jury is all-white has the powerful effect of racializing the jury proceeding. Even in earlier times in the South, following the Civil War, atrocities continued in the Ku Klux Klan's epidemic of violence against blacks and white Republicans, lynching frenzy gone unpunished by all-white juries. "It is notorious that practically never have white lynching mobs been brought to court in the South, even when the killers are known to all in the community and are mentioned in name in the local press," Gunnar Myrdal's 1944 work on race relations declared (Myrdal 1944, 552–553).

Judicial and political efforts to diversify the jury, however, have been extremely slow. Before the Civil War, Massachusetts was the only state to allow African-American men on the jury (Graber 1997). In 1875, Congress prohibited jurisdictions from excluding qualified citizens of color from jury service, and in 1880, the Supreme Court in *Strauder v. West Virginia* declared that West Virginia law deprived African-American defendants of equal protection of the law. Despite such a judicial pronouncement and the institution of remedial programs that followed the 1880 decision, many legal and extra-legal factors, exclusionary practices, discriminatory procedural mechanisms, and socioeconomic barriers have prevented black residents from effectively serving as jurors (Fukurai, Butler, and Krooth 1993).

Today, issues of racially mixed juries and racial balance in trials involving inter-racial crimes continue to pose unique challenges to our judiciary, the criminal justice system, and the community. Despite the potential benefits of racially diverse tribunals, racial and ethnic minorities continue to be substantially and significantly underrepresented in the vast majority of state and federal criminal courts. The continued lack of minorities' jury participation reduces the chance of ensuring racially diverse juries in criminal trials that involve highly sensitive elements of racism.

To best explain procedural deficiencies and exclusionary practices, we diagram the jury selection method used in most court jurisdictions today and examine selection criteria and exclusionary elements at various jury selection stages—venue selection, source list development, the purging and merging methods to create master files, qualification list questions, jury summons development, jury venires and panels, voir dire selection, trial jurors selection, and even jury foreperson selection in the final jury. Figure 1.1 reveals these eight distinct stages of jury selection procedures. As we will show, each and every stage of jury selection excludes a disproportionate number of racial and ethnic minorities from effectively serving as jurors.

The first stage of jury selection begins with a determination of the place or venue of the trial. In many racially sensitive trials, trial sites have often been moved from minority dominant areas to jurisdictions with very small minority-race residents. The change of venue usually takes place when courts determine that the "media hype" or other improprieties impacting the original trial venue makes the selection of impartial jurors impossible. The

1992 Rodney King assault case, for example, was moved from Los Angeles, where almost two-thirds of residents were racial minorities, to Simi Valley where almost 80 percent of residents were white (Fukurai, Butler, and Krooth 1994).[2] The 2000 Amadou Diallo murder trial of four white defendants was moved from the black- and Hispanic-dominant Bronx (61 percent nonwhite) to Albany, with very small minority populations (11 percent nonwhite) (McShane 1999).

Federal law only requires the use of ROV (Registration of Voters) lists for the selection of potential jurors, though past studies have consistently demonstrated that the lists significantly underrepresent racial minorties (Fukurai, Butler, and Krooth 1993). Even in some state courts where additional source lists are required such as DMV (Drivers Motor Vehicle) records, infrequent updates and technical difficulties in eliminating duplicate names have led to the overrepresentation of white jurors. This is due to the fact that white residents are most likely to be identified in both ROV and DMV lists, and computer scanning programs often fail to correctly purge and merge duplicate names, thereby increasing or even improving the chance of selection of white potential jurors. Jury qualifications such as a residency requirement and no previous felony conviction, as well as jury excuses based on economic and personal hardship have also led to the significant exclusion of the poor and minority jurors (Fukurai, Butler, and Krooth 1991a).

Racial minority jurors are excluded for other reasons, too. Since both jury summonses and qualification questionnaires are mail delivered, geographically mobile groups such as racial minorities and the poor often fail to receive these documents and are thereby excluded from jury service. The lack of systematic follow-up procedures further contributes to the poor response rates by racial minorities. Even when they may receive qualification questionnaires or summonses, many of these recipients, mistrusting white-dominated court and criminal justice institutions, often fail to respond to jury calls, and again are excluded from subsequent jury selection procedures. While some minorities may actually receive jury calls, economically disenfranchised residents hardly display a willingness to appear at the courthouse, largely because jury pay in most jurisdictions remains minimal. In most California courts, jurors are paid $15 for a day's service, hardly enough to cover, for instance, the cost of the care for a baby, children, or a dependent elderly person.

Abuse of peremptory challenges also exacerbates the exclusionary nature of jury selection, especially in criminal trials of minority-race defendants. While attorneys are legally prohibited from exercising race-based peremptory strikes during voir dire, they are often able to come up with apparent race-neutral reasons to rationalize their discriminatory practices. Some legal rationalizations for engaging in race-based peremptory exclusion include minority jurors' knowledge of either close friends, or relatives, of a defendant or a witness, their own prior criminal records, unsatisfactory prior jury service, living near the residence of a defendant or a witness, speaking Spanish, being overweight, being welfare recipients, and having insufficient community ties (see Melilli 1996, for a list of latent race-neutral reasons for rationalizing the practice of race-based peremptory challenges). Such race-implicit peremptory strikes continue to ensure the systematic elimination of racial minorities from the final jury.

Even after twelve final jurors are chosen, selection of a jury foreperson becomes critical, because it is not determined on the basis of random selection or race-neutral reasons or procedures. The judges or bailiffs often nominate or appoint a jury foreperson prior to jury deliberations. On other occasions, the jurors themselves nominate or vote a jury foreperson at the beginning of jury deliberations (Moses 1997). Given the significant underrepresentation of racial minorities in the final jury, it is not uncommon that the jury foreperson nominated or voted by the fellow jurors is less likely to be a member of minority races (Fukurai 2000).

The influence of jury forepersons is not to be discounted. They are often able to alter the unique qualities and characteristics of jury deliberations. Study of small group dynamics suggests, for example, that the foreperson speaks approximately three times as much as the average juror, and the magnitude of difference in jury participation indicates that the foreperson contributes disproportionately to jury deliberations (Hastie 1993).

Discriminatory mechanisms and racially biased practices at each and every stage of the jury selection process also have a cumulative, exclusionary impact on minority participation in the final jury. Since a series of exclusionary, procedural mechanisms have eliminated racial minorities, long before they are even called to appear at the courthouse, it is no wonder that, in the vast majority of both state and federal courts, we hardly see racial minorities sitting in the jury box. While some minority members meet jury qualification requirements, respond to jury summonses, and appear at the courthouse, further screenings for exemptions, personal and economic excuses, and minimal jury remuneration further diminish their chances. Even though some of those minority-race candidates successfully make it to the courtroom for voir dire, the race-based exercise of peremptory challenges can weed out most of those with any remaining chances of serving on the final jury. Even so, a few may finally make it to the trial jury, although discriminatory selection of the jury foreperson can further diminish their participatory contributions to jury deliberations.

Given the overload of discriminatory mechanisms and exclusionary biases built into the jury selection process, racial minorities are most likely to develop strong skepticism and cynicism about legitimacy of the legal system, the ability of the jury selection system to empanel racial minorities in the final jury, and the creation of racially equitable and diverse tribunals to render fair and legitimate jury verdicts in most criminal trials (Fagan and Davies 2000; Tyler 2001).

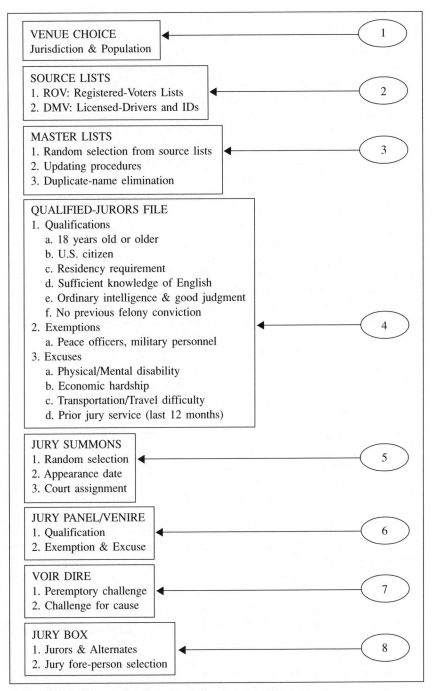

Figure 1.1 Eight Stages of Jury Selection Procedures

Indeed, the problems and biases of racialized justice administration have been well-documented. These include racial profiling in arrest, interrogation, and identification; race-based decisions in filing criminal charges; inequitable pretrial and plea bargaining decisions; insufficient resources for defense representation; sentencing disparities, including erroneous and discriminatory impositions of the death penalty against minority defendants; and racially biased correctional programs and their operations. While such racially discriminatory practices in police and criminal court proceedings raise serious questions about the nation's commitment to democratic principles in the administration of justice, the need for public confidence is extraordinarily high in racially charged jury trials. This is because jury decisions carry important social meanings; they send racialized messages to the marginalized segment of minority communities.

The racial composition of the final jury has thus become one of the most important, if not the most critical, determinants of the public's perception of, and judgment about, legal fairness and verdict legitimacy (Fukurai 1997, 1999b). The lack of minority jurors in racially sensitive trials often leads racial minorities to solidify and express feelings of deep cynicism about the legitimacy of laws, their lack of confidence in the criminal justice system, and the ability of both juries and courts to function fairly in an effective, nondiscriminatory manner (Fukurai 2000). The absence of minority-race jurors in the criminal decision-making process and criminal court system further exacerbates the degree of legal cynicism and the lack of confidence in the system of justice (Farber and Sherry 1997; Sampson and Bartusch 1998).

RACIALLY MIXED JURIES AND JURY VERDICTS

For trials involving blatant racial issues, the degree of jury participation by racial minorities is perceived as an important barometer of equity. Criminal cases tried before all-white juries, with black victims or black defendants, often evoke bitter images of injustice (Fukurai and Davies 1997).

Certainly the Rodney King assault verdict has not been an isolated case. Racial minorities have repeatedly expressed dismay and anger over white juries' verdicts in acquitting white defendants of crimes against racial minorities. For a large number of jury trials have exhibited racial injustices in the jury selection process, inequitability of criminal court proceedings, and a lack of racial minorities' participation in jury panels and trial juries themselves. Although there are great variations in the nature of trials, their background and social milieu, as well as legal or statutory factors that influence jury composition and verdicts, clear evidence of the social mechanisms that allow jury verdicts to perpetuate racial inequalities reaffirms the need to empanel mixed juries in racially sensitive trials.

The social dynamics of the times, reflecting racial and social inequalities in the community, often determine the outcome of jury verdicts, especially when the juries are composed of all-white members. In racially sensitive trials where the evidence of factual guilt has been virtually irresistible—often including either the testimony of eyewitnesses or evidence that the defendant publicly bragged about purposeful violence or killings—the public has sometimes come to demand racially mixed tribunals and shown a willingness to accept their verdicts, either for acquittal or conviction of white defendants.

Taking two tragic but typical cases of racial disenfranchisement in the criminal jury system—in which all-white juries quickly acquitted, or were unable to agree on convicting, white defendants accused of murdering blacks—here we review the facts, evidence, and trial proceedings of Byron de la Beckwith in Mississippi for the murder of Medgar Evers, and the trials in Miami, Florida for the murder of three blacks. The accounts of those two racially explosive cases are important for revealing facts and evidence of racial feelings, for the ways in which the jury system was racially structured, and for the ways the trials themselves were morphed with racial tracings.

The Byron de la Beckwith Trials

On June 12, 1963, Medgar Evers, a highly respected black civil rights activist, was assassinated in the driveway of his home in Jackson, Mississippi. Evers had been working with the Mississippi NAACP. As he was walking into his house with his wife and three children, he was shot in the back by gunmen from a passing pickup truck.

Three days later on June 15, 1963, Byron de la Beckwith,[3] a fertilizer salesman and avowed white supremacist, was arrested by federal officers and charged with violating the 1957 Civil Rights Act for "conspiring to injure, oppress and intimidate Medgar Evers in the free exercise of his Constitutional rights" (Vollers 1995, 151). And soon after his arrest, Beckwith was formally indicted for murder by the Hinds County grand jury. District Attorney Bill Waller announced that the state would seek the death penalty.

Jury selection began on January 27, 1964, after the names of two hundred prospective jurors were drawn from voting rolls of Hinds County. All potential jurors were men, as it would be another four years until women were legally awarded the right to serve on state juries in Mississippi (Vollers 1995, 161). Racial discrimination and oppression against blacks in the Deep South also played a prominent role in the selection of Beckwith's jury. District Attorney Bill Waller began the voir dire, questioning each jury candidate in the pool on their views of lynching blacks in the South. "Do you think it's a crime to kill a nigger in Mississippi?" the prosecutor asked each juror (Vollers 1995, 161). Though one hundred venire-persons were finally assigned to the trial, the jury pool only included seven blacks. None of them had ever served on a final jury, because either they were never interviewed for jury duty, or they were dismissed due to work conflicts or opposition to the death penalty (Vollers 1995, 161).

After four days of jury selection, an all-white male jury emerged (Vollers 1995, 162–163).

The trial began on January 31, 1964. The prosecution witnesses testified that the cause of Evers' death was hemorrhage due to gunshot wounds and that a rifle with the type of bullet that killed Evers was found near the murder scene. The prosecution also revealed that the markings on the recovered rifle matched the markings on a rifle owned by Beckwith, that the scope on the rifle found by police was recently acquired by Beckwith, and that Beckwith's fingerprints were found on the scope.

The defense then presented eyewitnesses who testified that Evers might have been murdered by three men, arguing that Beckwith was ninety miles away from the murder scene when the crime was committed. The trial received extensive media attention and coverage, and Mississippi Governor Ross Barnett made frequent appearances at the defense table. More than once Barnett shook Beckwith's hand and clapped him on the back in full view of the jurors (Vollers 1995, 164). After five days of testimony, both sides rested. The all-white jury deliberated for eleven hours and took twenty ballots before announcing that they were hopelessly deadlocked; the court ordered a mistrial (Vollers 1995, 201).

Jury selection for a second trial began on April 6, 1964, nearly ten months after Evers was murdered. A jury pool of three hundred men were assembled at the Jackson Courthouse. The prosecution accepted the first twelve jurors, one of them a cousin of a key defense witness for Beckwith (Vollers 1995, 204). The jury also included a bookkeeper, a food broker, an IRS employee, and several businessmen and executives. Seven held college degrees and two were born in the North. As in the first trial, all were male and all were white (Vollers 1995, 205).

During the trial proceedings, the prosecution presented essentially the same evidence as they did in the first trial. But the defense introduced one new alibi witness, James Hobby, who was the same height and weight as Beckwith. Hobby testified that he had been living in Jackson in June 1963, and that he owned a car that matched the description of Beckwith's car.

Outside the courtroom, meanwhile, the Ku Klux Klan continued to engage in heated demonstrations and militant activities, offering its support to the defendant. For four days after the trial began, ten crosses were burned by the Klan in and around Jackson, igniting fear of retribution to any who might not subscribe to Klan doctrine (Vollers 1995, 205).

In this climate, the defense closed its case, arguing that the whole matter was a witch hunt with Beckwith being framed by the prosecution. The all-white jury then deliberated for two days, before it announced another deadlock, and the judge declared another mistrial. District Attorney Bill Waller indicated that without new evidence, he would not seek yet another retrial for Beckwith. To celebrate his release, on the night of the second jury's verdict, the Ku Klux Klan burned crosses in nearly half of the eighty-two counties in Mississippi (Vollers 1995, 209).

During the course of next twenty-six years, the political and social climate in the South changed sharply. Both state legislatures and cities had witnessed a significant increase of racial minorities in political office. Miscegenation laws were overturned, and many public facilities and housing had been desegregated. Then, in December 1990, Mississippi prosecutors resubmitted the Beckwith case to a grand jury, and the seventy-one-year-old Beckwith was re-indicted for murder (LaFraniere 1990). Following ten months of resistance, Beckwith was extradited from his home in Signal Mountain, Tennessee, to Jackson, Mississippi, and was incarcerated until his release on bail in December 1992 ("Extradition ordered in Evers murder case" 1991; Stevens 1992; Hansen 1993a, 1993b).

Then in 1994, Beckwith was tried for the third time. There were several notable differences from Beckwith's first two trials. For the jury in the third trial was not composed of only white men, but was a racially mixed—eight blacks and four whites. Four of the black jurors were old enough to remember Medgar Evers and his civil rights activities in Mississippi. The jury also reflected a fair cross section of the blue-collar, working-class community, including factory workers, truck drivers, a cook, a maid, a secretary, a white co-manager of Wendy's restaurant, and a black minister ("Jury chosen in 3d Evers trial" 1994).

The prosecution was now able to locate four new witnesses to testify that they heard Beckwith brag, or indirectly admit to, killing Medgar Evers. Dan Prince, who rented an apartment from Beckwith in 1986, testified that while he and Beckwith were talking about Evers' murder, Beckwith said that he had been tried twice for "killing that nigger" (Vollers 1995, 356-357). He also stated that Beckwith then said, "I had a job to do and I did it and I didn't suffer any more than your wife if she was going to have a baby" (307). Peggy Morgan, who once rode in a car with Beckwith on the way to visit a mutual friend in the penitentiary, testified that Beckwith said "he killed Evers, a nigger, and he wasn't scared to kill again" (358). Delmar Dennis, an FBI informant on Ku Klux Klan activities, testified that Beckwith said, "Killing that nigger did me no more physical harm than your wives have to have when they're having a baby for you" (Vollers 1995, 359). Mark Reiley, a prison guard who met Beckwith while working as a prison guard in Louisiana, also testified that Beckwith once shouted at a black nurse, "If I could get rid of an uppity nigger like Medgar Evers, I would have no problem with a no-account nigger like you" (Vollers 1995, 362).

The defense also suffered a huge procedural setback, when the court ruled that James Hobby could not take the stand in Beckwith's defense. The defense then decided not to call Beckwith to testify, because they feared his unpredictability on the stand and the negative impression of his testimony on the members of the racially mixed jury (Smothers 1994a).

On February 5, 1994, after three trials and the passage of thirty-one years since the killing of the legendary Mississippi civil rights leader, Beckwith was found guilty of murdering Medgar Evers. Beckwith, who wore a Confederate flag pin on his lapel throughout his third trial, was sentenced to life in prison for the killing (Booth 1994; Smothers 1994b).

As a result of the successful prosecution of Beckwith for the murder of Evers, there have been successful calls to press on with other cases of hung all-white juries, including the 1966 firebombing death of Vernon Dahmer who was active in voting rights in Hattiesburg, Mississippi (Harrison 1995; "Mississippi may reopen Klan killing" 1995). Dahmer, a wealthy black businessman and civil rights leader in Hattiesburg, was killed when a gang of Ku Klux Klan White Knights firebombed his home on January 10, 1966. Two all-white juries were deadlocked in the trial of the alleged mastermind of the plot, Klan's Imperial Wizard Samuel Bowers.

Perhaps the worst aspect of comparable race-related crimes is the fact that assailants have rarely been brought to justice. Mississippi authorities prosecuted no one for the murder of the three civil rights workers, Michael Schwerner, Andrew Goodman, and James Chaney, all of whom were found buried under an earthen dam in Neshoba County, Mississippi. Schwerner and Goodman, both white, came from New York City to support civil rights activities in Mississippi; Chaney, black, was a native of Mississippi (Herbert 1994).[4]

In Mississippi, even when bombers confessed, they have escaped appropriate punishment. One Pike County judge gave bombers only suspended sentences and probation. Between 1960 and 1965, just a single man went to a southern state prison for a civil rights killing, and his sentence was a mere ten years. The federal government has had so little faith in the local Mississippi courts that the crimes have been pursued under the United States Code. As murder was not a federal charge unless it took place on government property, the accused killers were charged with conspiracy to deprive the victims of their civil rights, a federal crime. The maximum sentence, however, was ten years in prison (Vollers 1995, 221). This was despite the fact that between early 1961 and the middle of 1964, Mississippi alone was the scene of one hundred fifty incidents of serious racial violence, including at least twenty-six civil rights related murders.[5]

In the first and second Beckwith trials, all-white male juries and their verdicts challenged the democratic and cherished ideal of the jury system—that the cases being tried by an impartial jury of peers and not being predisposed to favor a particular racialized verdict. Even if the first two Mississippi juries might very well have been impartial, the fact that the defense was twice able to manage to secure an all-white jury in a jurisdiction that included a large proportion of black populations raises serious questions about the fairness of the jury selection process in Mississippi, the racial equitability of the jury trial, and the integrity of the judicial decision-making process.

Only the third, racially mixed jury was able to convict the defendant. Supporters of the jury system might protest that the first two trials were exceptions—not representative of jury trials elsewhere in the country. Indeed, the Deep South has had a long history of racial injustice and discrimination against blacks, though, even there, the sensitivity to civil rights issues has increased in recent years. And, yet, as the next Miami cases suggest, these and the Beckwith trials are not an anomaly.

The Miami Trials in 1980s

Miami in Dade County, Florida was in turmoil prior to 1980, beset by a number of racial explosions. From August 1968 through July 1979, at least thirteen significant civil disturbances rocked the city, involving violent confrontations between blacks and whites. The predominantly white police were under attack during many of these riotous episodes—a fact not forgotten by these officers or the black community.[6] In February 1979, police had raided the Miami home of a black school teacher who was mistaken for a cocaine dealer. Officers beat both the teacher and his son and vandalized their home. The police department, however, took no action against the offending officers (Montgomery 1980).

The next year brought a new confrontation, then another two years later, and still a third in 1989. These confrontations were set in motion by all-white juries exonerating all-white police officers, who were accused of killing three African Americans: Arthur McDuffie in 1980, Nevell Johnson in 1982, and Clement Anthony Lloyd in 1989.

The 1980 Miami uprising was fueled by a case in which four white police officers were tried on charges that they had beaten to death a thirty-three-year-old, black insurance executive, Authur McDuffie, who had been arrested for a traffic violation. McDuffie, a divorced father of two small children, was riding a 1973 black and orange Kawasaki 900 motorcycle that he had borrowed from his cousin (Porter and Dunn 1985, 33).

Within three minutes of his apprehension, McDuffie had been set upon by as many as six to twelve police officers who used eighteen-inch Kelite police flashlights to crush his skull, splitting his head wide open. Officers on the scene then had a marked patrol car run over McDuffie's motorcycle to make it look like as if it had been damaged in an accident, reporting that McDuffie had been injured in a fall from his vehicle. Four days later he died from the massive head injuries (Porter and Dunn 1985, 34–35).

As a result of Dade County medical examiner Don Wright's skepticism about the story and, eventually, as some police officers, who had been on the scene began talking with the district attorney, the police coverup began to unravel (Porter and Dunn 1985, 34–36). Investigations by the office of then State Attorney Janet Reno led to her announcement that four of the officers—Ira Diggs, Michael Watts, William Hanlon, and Alex Marrero—had been charged with manslaughter and tampering with evidence, while a fifth, Sergeant Evans, was charged with tampering with evidence and leading the coverup (Porter and Dunn 1985, 36).

Black communities had closely followed each and every step of the trial proceedings. Jury selection began in March 1980. Defense counsel moved carefully, using their thirty-four peremptory challenges to remove all black jurors from the pool, resulting in an all-white six-person jury. As the trial did not involve a first degree murder case, instead of the traditional twelve-member jury, a six-member jury was called into chambers. During the trial proceedings, a police officer, who had been on the scene and was given immunity from prosecution in return for his testimony, stated that Alex Marrero, one of four charged officers, had struck McDuffie as if he was chopping wood with an ax, and that Marrero had ordered other officers who were beating McDuffie, "Easy. One at a time" (Porter and Dunn 1985, 38–39).

"I heard Sergeant Evans say . . . 'The bike needs more damage . . . [G]o get in your car and ride up on it.' . . . [Then] I saw a . . . police unit sitting on top of the motorcycle," the officer testified (Porter and Dunn 1985, 39). The chief medical officer also testified that McDuffie's head injuries were the worst he had seen in thirty-six hundred autopsies (Crewdson 1980), stating that the amount of force necessary to cause the fracture was "equivalent of falling from a four story building and landing head first . . . on concrete" (Porter and Dunn 1985, 38).

Yet, after four weeks of trial, on May 17, 1980, the all-white jury deliberated for less than three hours before finding all police officers not guilty on all charges. To minority communities, the verdicts were political and racialized statements, reaffirming intolerable racial injustice. "We despise the verdict. We hate it and it hurts us to our hearts. I feel like my people are nobody," McDuffie's sister choked with emotion (Blum 1980). "They're guilty, . . . they're guilty in God's sight and they have to live with this," McDuffie's mother, Eula, cried out ("Rage at verdict" 1980).

Immediately after the verdict was announced, eruptions shook neighborhoods throughout the county—lasting three days—leaving eighteen people dead, including whites who were beaten or burned to death in their cars. A dead Guyanan immigrant had been taken for white; blacks were shot by police officers, killed by a security guard, and by roving white motorists driving through black residential neighborhoods; and a police officer died of a heart attack (Porter and Dunn 1985, 71–73). Even in the aftermath, tempers flared, the riot resulting in $800 million in property damage, with 372 total arrests, of which 233 were caught for looting (Pite 1980; "Miami still shows scars of rioting 1980; *Barry v. Garcia,* 573 So.2d 932 933, 1991). A community survey immediately after the riot indicated that 26 percent of black residents participated in the melee (Ladner, 1981).

Two years had passed to December 1982, when another civil disturbance was sparked by Miami police officer Luis Alvarez. Charged with manslaughter in the death of twenty-year-old black motorist, Nevell Johnson, Alvarez had shot and killed Johnson while on patrol (Stuart 1984b). Headed by Janet Reno, the office of the Dade State Attorney prosecuted the police officer. Yet, again, during jury selection, the defense attorney's peremptory challenges produced an all-white, six-member jury of three men and three women. Bill Perry, one of several prominent blacks, called for prosecution of the officer by a racially mixed jury, arguing for an immediate change in state laws to allow the use of affirmative jury selection mechanisms to register racially mixed juries in racially sensitive trials (Stuart 1984a).

The court contest was less than sharply defined on the underlying racial issues. During the trial, defense counsel argued that the defendant deliberately shot Johnson in self-defense, while the prosecution sought to prove that the defendant shot Johnson after committing a series of procedural errors. After a fifty-seven day trial, the all-white jury deliberated less than two hours over the evidence presented, finding that the twenty-four-year-old officer was not guilty in the shooting death of Johnson. "It's a tragic day for the total community," outspoken black activist and radio commentator Les Brown exclaimed. Bill Perry, president of the Miami chapter of Operation PUSH, declared that the acquittal was a "travesty" (Stuart 1984a).

The announcement of the acquittal quickly spread throughout the Miami area, loosing another racial confragration in Miami. In the predominantly black Liberty City area, two police officers were shot, and the police arrested more than two hundred rioters, mostly young black males (Stuart 1984b).

Seven years later, after the fatal shooting of a motorcycle rider, Clement Anthony Lloyd, by police officer William Lozano, riots erupted at the scene, spreading to other parts of Dade County. The death of Allan Blanchard, a black passenger on the motorcycle, fueled three nights of large scale civil disturbances, leaving one man dead, seven others shot, and 136 buildings burned and looted (*Lozano v. Florida,* 584 So.2d 19 20 21, 1991). Extensively covered and reported by both national and international media on the scene, overlapping Martin Luther King's birthday and the Super Bowl week in Miami, the riots were a powerful testimony of unremitting racial discord.

Similar to the previous two Miami trials, local newspapers described the defendant by name as a police officer, though few reports mentioned his Colombian origins. At least one press report described him as white, none described him as Latino, and the media's message seemed clear: Lozano was a "white knight," a protector of the people (Truyol 1994). Meanwhile, evoking negative stereotypes, the media consistently painted the victims darkly: "black men riding motorcycles. . . . The implicit message was that the bad guys were up to no good" (Truyol 1994, 422).

In the wake of the verdict in the Rodney King beating case in Los Angeles, in an effort to reduce the chance of empaneling another all-white jury, the venue was changed to Tallahassee, which had a 24 percent black population (Booth 1993). But then the venue was changed yet again—back to Orlando, a conservative, overwhelming white community, with an only 10 percent black population (Clary 1993). This was because Lozano was found guilty of manslaughter in his initial trial in Miami, but that decision was overturned by a court of appeals, which decided that the defendant had not received a fair trial due to the Miami jurors' fears of more rioting. On remand, the trial was simply transferred from Dade County back to predominantly white Orlando in Orange County.

On March 10, 1993, a six-person jury was finally picked: one black juror, along with three white jurors and two Hispanics (Gilbert 1993, 181). An acquittal was the likely outcome, a close observer of the trial nonetheless suggested, largely because the defense had more practice and experience from the previous mistrial case, and witnesses' memories of the shooting had begun to fade after four years, no longer being perceived as credible or reliable (Rohter 1993). The important divergence of the Lozano jury from previous juries of racially sensitive trials was that the six-member jury was racially mixed, or at least included a juror who shared the same racial background with the victims. There was also greater expectation of trial fairness and verdict legitimacy in the community (Gilbert 1993; Rohter 1993).

Nevertheless, the police and law enforcement officers were apprehensive. In order to prepare for possible riotings in black sections of Miami neighborhoods, National Guard units were called out prior to the verdict. Reaching a decision after less than seven hours of deliberation, on May 28, 1993, an acquittal verdict was announced—followed only by minor and sporadic disturbances in the streets. This time, there were no ensuing racial riots or disturbances after the acquittal verdict (Rohter, 1993).

THE SIGNIFICANCE OF MINORITY JURORS IN THE JURY BOX

The Beckwith and Miami cases illustrate initial jury trials in which the crimes may well have been racially motivated; yet the juries that tried the defendants failed to include any members who shared the race, ethnic, or ideological characteristics of the victims. With changing times and perceptions, the third Beckwith trial in 1994, and the third Miami trial in 1993, provided the exceptions. In both instances, a white defendant was accused of killing a black victim. As there was no widespread racial violence following the trials, the verdicts were largely perceived to be fair and widely accepted by both white and black communities. Though the verdicts were very different in each case—the conviction in the former and the acquittal in the latter—the public's perception of the fairness of the trial and the willingness to accept the jury verdict were apparently much greater for racially mixed tribunals than for all-white juries.

More recently, the verdict of the Amadou Diallo trial in January 2000 provides another example in which a racially diverse jury acquitted four white, unpopular police officers accused of killing a black immigrant; but the public's reaction to the verdict failed to lead to major racial riots. The jury was composed of four black women, a white woman, and seven white men. Street demonstrations and condemnations of both police and their actions preceded the trial and continued during and after the verdict. Minority communities reacted with furor—yet neither burned the Bronx, the site of the killing, nor the site of the trial in Albany.

African-American Reverend Al Sharpton had organized and led the early protests. After the verdict, however, he appealed cautiously to his followers: "We do not want to tarnish his [Amadou's] name with any violence," Sharpton admonished, "not one brick be thrown, not one bottle be thrown. We are fighting violence" (Goldman 2000). The solution appeared different than in years past: the concerted efforts by various minority groups and civil rights organizations were now being directed toward the political and legal arena to pressure the federal government to prosecute the four white police officers under civil rights laws (Knutson 2000).

What common threads can we weave by stepping back to examine the ways in which these major cases reflect the intertwined relationship of race, jury composition, verdicts, and the public's reactions to, and perception of, the integrity of the jury system? Have racially diverse tribunals offered legitimacy to the fairness of the final jury verdict? Does the race of victims, defendants, and accused together play a crucial role in influencing public perceptions, respect, and acceptance of final jury verdicts?

In criminal trials involving sensitive and unmistakable elements of racism, there is widespread consensus that a racially mixed jury offers many benefits. Scholars, judges, and litigants argue that a racially mixed jury may help to overcome racial bias, improve the fairness of trial proceedings, and enhance public respect and acceptance of criminal and civil verdicts (Johnson 1985; "Developments in the law" 1988; Colbert 1990; Fukurai 1999b).[7] Those advocating racially diverse juries posit that minority representation on a jury minimizes the distorting influence of race and increases the likelihood of a fairer and more legitimate verdict (Colbert 1990, 112–115).[8] To the extent that minorities can contribute different viewpoints that may not be readily apparent to majority jurors, the deliberation process may indeed be substantially fairer and wiser (King 1993a; Meyer 1994).

Both the depth of discussion and cogency of exchange are enhanced by racially mixed juries. Racially heterogeneous juries are more likely than single race juries to enhance the quality of deliberations. The quality of the jury's exchange and deliberation is also improved in larger and more diverse groups than in smaller ones (Tindale et al. 1990; Keele 1991).[9] Drawing upon varied experiences of its members, the racially diverse jury is less likely to rely upon complacent and uninformed assumptions in its deliberation, suggesting that impartiality is not self-contained in a single "impartial" juror, but achieved through the diverse representation of a range of views and experiences. Empirical studies of mock and actual juries show that racially mixed juries minimize the distorting risk of bias and prejudice (Johnson 1985; Hans and Vidmar 1986; "Developments in the law" 1988). Racially integrated juries force us to examine, not whether whites, blacks, Hispanics, or Asians exhibit a greater or lesser propensity for impartial decision-making, but whether or not optimum conditions for an impartial deliberative process exist. Participation across racial groups is an important component of the truth-seeking function of the jury system, as the jury is the vehicle through which a fair evaluation of the evidence is consummated.

Racially mixed juries also advance mutual experience and education during jury service, unifying jurors of different racial and ethnic backgrounds to work together as equals (Hastie, Penrod, and Pennington 1983; King 1994). In general, this is one path towards integration, embracing diversity and diverse viewpoints in decision-making bodies.

Besides diverse juries' effects in enhancing the quality of jury deliberation, the realization of racially diverse tribunals also has significant and important social and political ramifications. The realization that racially diverse jurors are in a position to evaluate the credibility and legitimacy of evidence may provide internal checks to insure fair and proper performance of all criminal justice participants, including prosecutors, defense attorneys, judges, law enforcement officers, the jury, and other key players in the judicial system. The empanelment of racially diverse juries, for example, may restrain prosecutors from engaging in prosecutorial misconduct and racially calculated decision makings. Prosecutors may be forced to make conscious efforts to pursue their prosecutorial work in a racially nondiscriminatory manner, including charges to be filed, plea bargaining decisions, pretrial recommendations of defendants' dispositions, and trial strategies including evidence determination, witness and testimony preparations, and the manner in which evidence is introduced and presented.

The emergence of racially diverse tribunals also influence the performance of defense attorneys, including defense motions to be filed, voir dire strategies in jury selection, and trial preparations and presentations. The fact that racially diverse jurors carefully weigh their exchange forces them to be aware of the quality of their trial deliberations, actions, and conduct that will be evaluated by other jurors of diverse backgrounds, as well as by judges, prosecutors, the media, and the public. Their concerns about the collective quality of their performance also influence decisions and presentations of defense attorneys in the courtroom.

Racially diverse tribunals also have an equally powerful impact on the quality of performance by judges in making decisions on pretrial detention of defendants, rulings on motions and evidence, jury selection—including peremptory challenges, challenges for cause, and/or stipulations—recommendations for the selection of jury forepersons, and sentencing when defendants are convicted.

As well, racially diverse tribunals may help eliminate the work-group relations in the courtroom, which are often portrayed as "work-units," harshly criticized by many scholars and legal practitioners. Because of the intimate relations developed among judges, prosecutors, and defense attorneys or public defenders, all whom likely share the same dominant race, there is no effective checks and balances mechanism in evaluating their work performance in the courtroom. The disregard of the defendants' rights to competent and just legal representation also spills into the jury trial, because many minority defendants are likely represented by public defenders or other court-appointed counsels, who have shown an intimate work relationship with prosecutors, judges, and other officers in the criminal justice system (Flowers 2000).

Thus, the pursuit and realization of racially diverse tribunals in jury trials enhance the possibility of changing the qualitative landscape of the criminal justice system. Racially imposed checks and balances influence the performance of the jury, as well as of defense attorneys, prosecutors, judges, law enforcement officers, and other key players in the criminal justice and criminal court system. From a broader social perspective, then, racially diverse juries enhance the legitimacy of jury verdicts, the quality of work performance by criminal justice participants, and the parties' and public's perception of justice and social peace (King 1993a, 1993b; Ramirez 1994).

REFORM AND ITS BARRIERS

Despite the importance of race in jury selection and the potential benefits of racially mixed juries in criminal trials, current jurisprudence offers no affirmative mechanism to guarantee minority representation on the jury. The United States Supreme Court has been reluctant to recognize and accept academic research, mock studies, and empirical findings, showing that juries balanced by racial diversity show a greater propensity to render fairer, more just decisions. The Sixth Amendment's provision for a jury to represent a fair cross section of the community forbids systematic discrimination in the creation of the jury venire and panel; but it does not guarantee that the final jury will actually reflect an accurate cross section of the community.[10] Rather, the Supreme Court has summarily rejected a right to a racially mixed jury (*Apodaca v. Oregon,* 406 U.S. 404, 413, 1972), declaring that there is no right of the accused to the inclusion of jurors racially similar to the defendant. Similarly, the Court has refused to recognize any constitutional right to proportional racial representation on the final jury itself (*Holland v. Illinois,* 493 U.S. 474, 1990). Past jury research substantiates that racial minorities have been systematically excluded from jury service in the vast majority of both state and federal courts (Johnson 1985; Fukurai, Butler, and Krooth 1991b; King 1993b, 1994; Fukurai 1996, 2000). Minorities may also remain underrepresented in the venire or jury box, even without invidious discrimination (Fukurai, Butler, and Krooth, 1993). Yet, the Supreme Court has only stated that a party is entitled to an impartial jury, not necessarily a representative or racially diverse one.[11]

In bringing about reforms in jury diversity, the Supreme Court has been reluctant to recognize the importance of an affirmative action approach to jury selection, though the Court has been willing to reiterate the importance of representative and fair cross sectional ideals for jury composition. The Court once declared that a jury is more likely to fit contemporary notions of unbiased neutrality, if it is composed of representatives of all segments and groups of the community, thereby creating a body that can reflect "the commonsense judgment of a group of laymen" (*Apodaca v. Oregon,* 406 U.S. 404 410, 1972). The Court has also stated that "our democracy itself requires that the jury be a 'body truly representative of the community,' and not the organ of any special group or class. . . . It is part of the established tradition in the use of juries as instruments of public justice that the jury be a body truly representative of the community" (*Smith v. Texas,* 311 U.S. 128, 85–86, 130–131, 1940). In a frequently quoted passage from *Peter v. Kiff,* Justice Thurgood Marshall reiterated the importance of representative and diverse juries:

> When any large and identifiable segment of the community is excluded from jury service, the effect is to remove from the jury room qualities of human nature and varieties of human experience, the range of which is unknown and perhaps unknowable. It is not necessary to assume that the excluded group will consistently vote as a class in order to conclude, as we do, that its exclusion deprives the jury of a perspective on human events that may have unsuspected importance in any case that may be presented (407 U.S. 493, 503–504, 1972).[12]

Resolving the underlying issues of fairness and equity involving race, gender, and social class may well determine how various groups view the legitimacy of the judicial and criminal justice systems. And the Supreme Court has clearly stated that the broader participation by various segments of the community serves to preserve "public confidence in the fairness of the criminal justice system" (*Lockhart v. McCree,* 476 U.S. 162, 174–175, 1986). In order to increase jury participation by minorities and improve the public's respect and confidence in the jury system, this book takes up the challenge by examining important affirmative strategies to ensure the inclusion of racial minorities in the trial jury, proposing a number of deep-seated reforms to correct representative imbalances.

CONCLUSIONS

The public's skepticism of trial fairness and verdict legitimacy, as well as community reactions—whether public protest or demonstrations, race riots, or civil disturbances—all point to the need for drastic reforms in the jury system to allow for and empanel racially diverse juries in criminal trials, especially those involving interracial crimes and highly sensitive elements of racism. How to accomplish this can be best understood by acknowledging the collective shortcomings and deficiencies of the jury system and its selection procedures. Among the system's most glaring faultlines are the systemic and systematic exclusionary policies and practices that have been handed down from the past, and discriminatory selection procedures that continue to exclude large segments of racial minorities in various communities.

Our study points to these frailties that help maintain exclusionary procedures and, at the same time, maps a path to overcome such racially exclusionary practices. We believe that, given the growing racial diversity of our nation's communities and the increased public attention to interracial crimes, dramatic jury selection reforms are needed here and now, with all due speed. Affirmative action in jury selection is an important legal and remedial policy that can overcome exclusionary selection practices and ensure the presence of racially diverse jurors in the final jury box.

While the question of affirmative action in education, employment, and business contracting has divided the nation and even some racial minority communities themselves, affirmative action in jury selection has yet to receive muchdeserved attention. This book attempts to refocus on the nonrepresentative imbalance by examining the possible applicability of affirmative action in criminal jury proceedings. As such, we define alternative jury structures for racially diverse tribunals, focusing a lens on the racialized distribution of jury seats in criminal trials, as well as on the voir dire selection strategy called "peremptory inclusion," in identifying and selecting racial minority jurors for the final jury.

We demonstrate that an affirmative action mechanism to secure racially diverse juries is essential to the appearance, the substance, and the public's perception of trial fairness and verdict legitimacy in criminal jury proceedings; racially diverse tribunals also represent the mechanism of internal checks to insure fair and proper performance by government agencies; and maximizing the essence of the legitimacy and integrity of the judicial decision-making process and trial verdicts is a compelling social, governmental, and judicial interest.

Chapter 2

DEFINING AND MEASURING
RACE AND RACIAL IDENTITY

"Was Babe Ruth black? ... Ty Cobb once refused to share a cabin with Ruth.... 'I've never bedded down with a n——,' said Cobb.... The same repellent epithet was spit at Ruth by opposing bench jockeys, who saw in the Babe's full lips, broad nose and swarthy complexion a visual basis for their vile insults."
—Daniel Okrent in "Background Check."

"Many articles have echoed the view that whites are fast becoming a minority ... because of the growth of the Hispanic population.... [But they] have failed to take account of the fact that nearly half of the Hispanic population is white in every social sense of this term."
—Orlando Patterson, Harvard University Sociology Professor, on race relations.

Race and racial identity are both real and illusionary—real because our society designates certain identities as racial ones, illusionary because there is only one human race. Dealing with such social definitions of race is often mind boggling because historically supposed racial differences have become culturally infused as a way of thinking and reasoning, as well as institutionalized in the social and political domain.

How, then, does one cut through the veil of race, exposing and offsetting the idea that there are different races—when most individuals in a given social milieu identify racially and have their beliefs confirmed by racially differentiated, daily experiences?

The answer has a dual nature. While affirming that there is a single, identifiable human race, one must struggle to overturn those cultural and institutional practices that discriminate unfairly against those historically defined and identified as members of a minority or subordinate race. In an effort to extend civil and human rights, this may ultimately require a dramatic shift in popular thinking and social definitions, everyday practices, and government enforcement. Short of such changes from the grassroots, the executive, legislative, and judicial systems will need to dramatically reform their procedural methods and the substantive applications of law.

In this chapter, our particular concern is focused on people of different "races" being excluded from securing their rights to full, equitable participation in the social and judicial arena. We emphasize the need for an effective race-conscious policy of affirmative action in jury selection and jury representation.

However, we also need to proceed with caution. For such a policy for reform must rely on a clear conceptualization of race, racial classification, and racial identity. Without a precise understanding of how race is identified, conceptualized, defined and measured, race-based remedial programs aimed to eliminate racial inequality may come face-to-face with confusion and ultimate failure. The same fate awaits affirmative action in jury selection aimed at composing racially diverse tribunals—with the danger of unfairness impacting the race-conscious allocation of jury seats and the use of peremptory inclusive methods in jury selection, the subject detailed in subsequent chapters.

MEASURING AND IDENTIFYING RACE

Measuring and identifying one's race is not simple. The ambiguity of racial classification and the amorphous nature of racial identity, designation, and its social construction can be illustrated by the following example. As a university professor, the first author asked approximately one hundred students in an undergraduate course, entitled "Race and Criminal Justice," whether they consider Iraq's Sadam Hussein a member of the white race. Responding to this rather peculiar question, no one in the class responded with a strong affirmative. When asked if Libya's Moammar Kadafi is white, everyone said "no." When the students were also asked if tennis player Andre Agassi is white, almost everyone enthusically said "yes." After disclosing that his father came from Iran, just north of Iraq, approximately half of the students who initially thought he was white said "no," while one exasperated student exclaimed, "he is white, O.K., because his mother is American!"[1]

The student's assertion that Andrei Agassi is white was based on the following three tenuous assumptions: (1) the assertion that "his mother is American" presupposes that the so-called American refers to a person of white race, neglecting the fact that there are other nonwhite Americans; (2) Iranians are considered as members of a dominant racial group, although in other societies Iranians or persons of other Middle Eastern heritage are often regarded as a racial or ethnic minority and have been discriminated against;[2] and (3) the rule of hypodescent (based on the "one-drop of blood" hypothesis) is supposedly only applicable to a "nonwhite" or "non-Iranian" person, while many whites do in fact share nonwhite ancestry, including black, Asian, Hispanic, and Native American.[3]

Another example of the amorphous nature of racial classification and racial identity can be illustrated by the following. An English language instructor at a community college in Northern California once gave the following speech to a group of Afghan refugees in a special course designed for foreign students who spoke English as a second language. On the first day of the class, the instructor declared that "from now on, you will be considered a white in this country. Live with a pride and do your best in a new world." Her statement offers another example of how racial identity, especially identity as "white," is personally attributed, socially designated, and politically ascribed in the United States.

This chapter also examines the current definition of race and racial groups in America and establishes some ground rules on the definition of race and racial classificatory schemes. Given that every society has devised unique categories and definitions of race and/or ethnic-based groups of its own, we will use the United States government's most recent definition of race as the foundation to engage in an intense analysis of the meanings and measurements of race. This matter is critical because the application of race-conscious affirmative jury selection must rely on theoretically valid and methodologically reliable information and data to understand, measure, and identify one's race. Careful analyses of the meanings of, and methodological questions about, governmental definitions of race are also critical to assess racial parity, because government data such as census figures and their racial aggregates provide fairly accurate information on the proportionality of racial subgroups in the community.

A word about our methods of analysis is also necessary. The first section of this chapter attempts to establish the fluid and unsettling nature of race and racial classifications. In our brief analysis of different ethnic and racial classifications outside the United States, we try to demonstrate that race and racial categories are not natural or innate characteristics, but rather are perceived artifacts and socially arranged categories. In other words, racial classifications are not necessarily based on physical differences, but on what people believe about physical or other differences. Since race is a cultural, ideological, and historical construct, this section also tries to trace the history of race and racial categories devised by the United States government from 1790 to 2000. Critical analysis of the governmental definition and designation of race specified in the United States census further substantiates that the concepts of race and racial difference have gone through repeated fulminations and transformations in the context of changing social, cultural, and "scientific" definitions of race.

The second section of this chapter empirically deconstructs race as a social concept based on government-defined racial categories, self-identity of race, and self-reported racial ancestry. Here we also critically examine the reliability and validity of the current racial classification schema and argue that the measurements of race suffer from lack of internal consistency, the failure to classify people of "mixed" race, the absence of empirical verification of racial identity and ancestral race, and the failure to detect those who engage in what is known as "racial passing."

The last section embodies our empirical and methodological strategies designed to overcome many of the shortcomings and problems in considering race as an empirical and scientific measurement. In order for affirmative jury selection to be successful in criminal court, race still needs to be empirically measured and individually identified. For this purpose, we propose two sets of racial-identity questions to classify people in terms of their racial beliefs: self-identity of race, or self-declaration of ancestral race. And, in order to critically assess the relationship between race and self-defined views for affirmative action purposes in the following chapters, we propose a set of socio-demographic and attitudinal questions impacting affirmative action in jury selection—questions that also impact other areas such as education, hiring, and contracting.

SOCIAL DECONSTRUCTION OF RACE:
SOCIAL ELEMENTS AND CONCEPTS

Race dominates our personal lives, our sense of social well-being, and our economic prospects. Race also permeates our politics, acts as a motivating force solidifying political, social, and legal alliances, determines the allocation and distribution of local, state, and federal funds, alters electoral and judicial boundaries, promotes policies and programs shaping affirmative action and antidiscrimination legislation, and even influences the frame and conduct of law enforcement. In fact, from its inception, America has divided people along racial lines in determining the allocation of opportunities and resources (Haney-Lopez 1994, 29).

Despite the pervasive influence of race in our social, economic, and political lives, few seem to understand the unstable nature of racial classification and the fluid concept of race and its classification. From a scientific viewpoint, moreover, the measurement of race is neither a reliable nor a valid scientific instrument or indicator because racial definitions, any set of mono-racial classifications—and even data gathering methods in designating one's race—are all subject to sociopolitical changes over time. Racial definitions also vary with changing governmental standards that turn on administrative efficiency and criteria adopted by different state and federal agencies.[4] Race is thus a socially defined and politically constructed concept; and through the sociopolitical process of historical change, the categorization of race is structured, maintained, reproduced, and periodically destroyed (Omi and Winant 1986).

The general notion that race is a myth and a socially and political derived concept has been widely expressed in the literature of sociology and socio-psychological studies (Haney-Lopez 1994; Karst 1995, 267–281; Wright 1995; Johnson 1996; Payson 1996). For race is neither a biological nor genetic concept; so-called biological races such as Negroid, Mongoloid, and Caucasoid simply do not exit (Haney-Lopez 1994, 13; see also *Saint Francis College v. Al-Khazraji*, 481 U.S. 504, 610, n4, 1987). Scientific critiques of race have shown the fallacies of constructing racial categories, emphasizing that: (1) racial categories are biologically and genetically underinclusive, suggesting that the physical characteristics or genetic traits associated with any particular race are also found in other populations that are designated by other racial categorizations; and (2) racial identifications are overconclusive, meaning that the presence of more physical and genetic variations exists within a racially defined group than between populations assigned to different racial categories (Cavalli-Sforza, Menozzi, and Piazza 1994). Other studies have shown that genetic variations are generally more attributable to geographical separation of populations than any clear division among "racially" identified categories (Nei and Roychoudhury 1982, 18; Tooby and Cosmides 1990, 35).

Historically speaking, biological divisions of race such as white, black, and Asian (or Caucasoid, Negroid, and Mongoloid) are rooted in the Eurocentric knowledge and imagination of the Middle Ages, when known territory only encompassed Europe, Africa, and the Near East, thereby excluding from the three major "races" the people of the North American continent, the South American continent, the Indian subcontinent, East Asia, Southeast Asia, Oceania, and the South Pacific (Haney-Lopez 1994, 12). Even the United States Supreme Court has recognized the sociopolitical conception of race, stating that "[t]he particular traits which have generally been chosen to characterize races have been criticized as having little biological significance. . . . It has been found that differences between individuals of the same race are often greater than the differences between the 'average' individuals of different races. These observations and others led some, but not all, scientists to conclude that racial classifications are for the most part sociopolitical, rather than biological, in nature" (*Saint Francis College v. Al-Khazraji,* 481 US 604, 610 n.4, 1987).

Racial categories derived and used by the United States government also reflect the mythical and ambiguous nature of racial definition and classification. Table 2.1 shows the governmental definition and census classification of race and racial categories between 1790 and 2000.[5] From the first 1790 census, race questions appeared on every census. Analysis of the census classification of race shows that, for more than the last two hundred years, the federal government has continuously categorized individuals into a set of discrete, mono-racial categories, and that the census has constantly adjusted and readjusted the list of available racial classifications and definitions. As table 2.1 reveals, the racial divisions we commonly categorize, such as black, Asian, American Indian, and so forth, are relatively recent inventions and phenomena.

Slavery was the baseline of the classificatory scheme for race relations after the American Revolution. From 1790 to 1810, the census distinguished only white, slave, and others. But there were pockets of free "slaves" in both North and South, and the 1830 census accommodated, dividing "Negro" into slaves and free-colored persons. The term, "black," however, did not appear until the 1850 census when the slaves and the free-colored persons were further divided into Mulatto and black. Following the near-complete defeat of Native American tribes and the import of Chinese labor to build the transcontinental railroad and to work in the California gold fields, the 1870 census added Indian and Chinese. Japanese were added with the United States opening of Japanese ports in 1868, later linked to trade to the west coast in 1890. The 1890 census

TABLE 2.1
Census Classification of Race Between 1790 and 2000

1790 (Pennsylvania)[1]
Free Whites
All other persons
Slaves

1800 (Massachusetts)[1]
Free Whites
All other persons
Slaves

1810 (Massachusetts)[1]
Free Whites
All other free persons
Slaves

1820
Free Whites
All other free persons
Slaves

1830
Free White Persons
Slaves
Free Colored Persons

1840
Free White Persons
Slaves
Free Colored Persons

1850[2]
White
Black
Mulatto

1860[3]
Identical to previous
   Census

1870[4]
White(W.)
Black(B.)
Mulatto (M.)
Chinese(C.)
Indian(I.)

1880[5]
White(W.)

Black(B.)
Mulatto (M.)
Chinese(C.)
Indian(I.)

1890[6]
White
Black
Mulatto
Quadroon
Octoroon
Chinese
Japanese
Indian

1900
White
Black—Negro or of
   Negro descent
Chinese
Japanese
Indian

1910[7]
Identical to previous
   Census

1920[8]
Identical to previous
   Census

1930
White
Negro
Mexican
Indian
Chinese
Japanese
Filipino
Hindu
Korean
Other

1940[9]
White
Negro
Indian
Chinese

Japanese
Filipino
Hindu
Korean
Other

1950
White
Negro
Indian
Chinese
Japanese
Filipino
Other

1960[10]
White
Negro
American Indian
Japanese
Chinese
Filipino
Hawaiian
Part Hawaiian
Aleut
Eskimo

1970[11]
White
Negro or Black
Indian (Amer.)
Japanese
Chinese
Filipino
Hawaiian
Korean
Other

1980[12]
White
Negro or Black
Japanese
Chinese
Filipino
Korean
Vietnamese
Indian (Amer.) Print tribe

TABLE 2.1 (continued)
Census Classification of Race Between 1790 and 2000

Asian Indian	Korean, Guamanian	*(ethnicity)*
Hawaiian	Vietnamese, Other API-*	Hispanic or Latino:
Guamanian	Other race	Cuban, Mexican, Purto
Samoan		Rican, South or
Eskimo	*(ethnicity)*	Central American, or
Aleut	Hispanic	other Spanish culture
Other	Not Hispanic	or origin, regardless
		of race.
1990[13]	*2000[14]*	Not Hispanic or Latino
White	White	
Negro or Black	Black or African	
Indian (Amer.): Eskimo,	American	
Aleut	American Indian or	
Asian or Pacific Islander	Alaska Native	
(API)	Asian	
Chinese, Japanese	Native Hawaiian or	
Filipino, Asian Indian	Other Pacific Islander	
Hawaiian, Samoan	Other race	

Source: U.S. Department of Commerce. 1993. 200 Years of U.S. Census Taking. Washington, D.C.
Notes:

1. The early census acts prescribed the inquiries in each decennial census, but the U.S. Government did not furnish uniform printed schedules until 1830. In 1790, the marshals submitted their returns in whatever form they found convenient (and sometimes with added information); from 1800 to 1820, the States provided schedules of varying size and typeface. There are separate schedules for "taxed or untaxed Indians," depending on Census year.

2. *1850*
Census data includes 2 schedules, Schedule 1-Free Inhabitants . . . " and Schedule 2-Slave Inhabitants . . . " Under heading 6, entitled "Color," in all cases where the person is white, leave the space blank; in all cases where the person is black, insert the letter B; if mulatto, insert M. It is very desirable that these particulars be carefully regarded.

3. *1860* Identical to 1860
Census data includes 2 schedules, Schedule 1-Free Inhabitants . . . " and Schedule 2-Slave Inhabitants . . . "

4. *1870*
Color.—It must not be assumed that, where nothing is written in this column, "White" is to be understood. The column is always to be filled. Be particularly careful in reporting the class Mulatto. The word is here generic, and includes quadroons, octoroons, and all persons having any perceptible trace of African blood. Important scientific results depend upon the correct determination of this class in schedule 1 and 2.

Indians.—"Indians not taxed" are not to be enumerated on schedule 1. Indians out of their tribal relations, and exercising the rights of citizens under State or Territorial laws, will be included. In all cases write "Ind." in the column for "Color." Although no provision is made for the enumeration of "Indians not taxed," it is highly desirable, for statistical purposes, that the number of such persons not living upon reservations should be known.

5. *1880*
By the phrase "Indians not taxed" is meant Indians living on reservations under the care of Government agents, or roaming individually, or in bands, over unsettled tracts of country. Indians not

in tribal relations, whether full-bloods or half-breeds, who are found mingled with the white population, residing in white families, engaged as servants or laborers, or living in huts or wigwams on the outskirts of towns or settlements are to be regarded as a part of the ordinary population of the country for the constitutional purpose of the apportionment of Representatives among the States, and are to be embraced in the enumeration.

Color.—It must not be assumed that, where nothing is written in this column, "white" is to be understood. The column is always to be filled. Be particularly careful in reporting the class mulatto. The word is here generic, and includes quadroons, octoroons, and all persons having any perceptible trace of African blood. Important scientific results depend upon the correct determination of this class in schedules 1 and 5.

"Indian Division"
If this person is of full-blood of this tribe, enter "/" For mixture with another tribe, enter name of latter. For mixture with white, enter "W." with black, "B." with mulatto, "Mu."

6. *1890*
Special Enumeration Of Indians.
The law provided that the Superintendent of Census may employ special agents or other means to make an enumeration of all Indians living within the jurisdiction of the United States, with such information as to their condition as may be obtainable, classifying them as to Indians taxed and Indians not taxed.

By the phrase "Indians not taxed" is meant Indians living on reservations under the care of Government agents, or roaming individually, or in bands, over unsettled tracts of country. Indians not in tribal relations, whether full-bloods or half-breeds, who are found mingled with the white population, residing in white families, engaged as servants or laborers, or living in huts or wigwams on the outskirts of towns or settlements are to be regarded as a part of the ordinary population of the country for the constitutional purpose of the apportionment of Representatives among the States, and are to be embraced in the enumeration.

The enumeration of Indians living on reservations will be made by special agents appointed directly from this office, and supervisors and enumerators will have no responsibility in this connection.

Many Indians, however, have voluntarily abandoned their tribal relations or have quit their reservations and now sustain themselves. When enumerators find Indians off of or living away from reservations, and in no wise dependent upon the agency of Government, such Indians, in addition to their enumeration on the population and supplemental schedules, in the same manner as for the population generally should be noted on a special schedule (7–917) by name, tribe, sex, age, occupation, and whether taxed or not taxed. The object of this is to obtain an accurate census of all Indians living within the jurisdiction of the United States and to prevent double enumeration of certain Indians.

When Indians are temporarily absent from their reservations the census enumerators need not note them, as the special enumerator for the Indian reservation will get their names.

Color, Sex, and Age
Whether white, black, mulatto, quadroon, octoroon, Chinese, Japanese, or Indian, write white, black, mulatto, quadroon, octoroon, Chinese, Japanese, or Indian according to the color or race of the person enumerated. Be particularly careful to distinguish between blacks, mulattos, quadroons, and octoroons. The word "black" should be used to describe those person who have three-fourths or more black blood; "mulatto," those person who have from three-eighths to five-eighths black blood; "quadroon," those persons who have one-eight or any trace of black blood.

7. *1910*
For census purposes, the term "black" (B) includes all persons who are evidently full-blooded negroes, while the term "mulatto" (Mu) includes all other persons having some proportion of perceptible trace of Negro blood.

8. *1930*

There were specific instructions for reporting race. A person of mixed White and Negro blood was to be returned as Negro, no matter how small the percentage of Negro blood; someone part Indian and part Negro also was to be listed as Negro unless the Indian blood predominated and the person was generally accepted as an Indian in the community. A person of mixed White and Indian blood was to be returned as an Indian, except where the percentage of Indian blood was very small or where he or she was regarded as White in the community. For persons reported as American Indian in column 12 (color or race), columns 19 and 20 were to be used to indicate the degree of Indian blood and the tribe, instead of the birthplace of father and mother.

In order to obtain separate figures for Mexican, it was decided that all persons born in Mexico, or having parents born in Mexico, who were not definitely White, Negro, Indian, Chinese, or Japanese, would be returned as Mexicans (Mex).

Any mixture of White and some other race was to be reported according to the race of the parent who was not White; mixtures of colored races were to be listed according to the father's race, except Negro-Indian (discussed above).

9. *1940*

With regard to race, the only change from 1930 was that Mexicans were to be listed as White unless they were definitely Indian or some race other than White.

10. *1960*

The instructions for completing P5 (race or color) by observation directed that Puerto Ricans, Mexicans, or other persons of Latin descent would be classified as "White" unless they were definitely Negro, Indian, or some other race. Southern European and Near Eastern nationalities also were to be considered White. Asian Indians were to be classified as "Other," and "Hindu" written in.

11. *1970*

If "Indian" (American), *also* give tribe
If "Other," also give race

12. *1980*

Enumerators were no longer allowed to enter race (item 4) by observation, but were instructed to ask and mark the race with which the person most closely identified. If a single response was not possible, as in the case of a racial mixture, the mother's race was to be reported. If this was not satisfactory, the first racial group given was to be entered. In further contrast with 1970, "Brown," "," etc., could be entered as "Other" (unless one of the listed categories was chosen). If a person was unable to select a single group in the Spanish-origin question (7), and only part two was Spanish (as in "Irish-Cuban"), the "No, not Spanish/Hispanic" circle was to be filled. If more than one origin was reported in the ancestry question (13), all answers were accepted.

Is this person of Spanish/Hispanic origin or descent?

13. *1990*

What is . . . 's race? For example, White, Black, American Indian, Eskimo, Aleut or an Asian or Pacific Islander group such as Chinese, Filipino, Hawaiian, Korean, Vietnamese, Japanese, Asian Indian, Samoan, Guamanian, and so on. Fill ONE circle for the race the person considers himself/herself to be. If response is "American Indian," ask—What is the name of . . . 's enrolled or principal tribe? If response is an "Other API" group such as Cambodian, Tongan, Laotian, Hmong, Thai, Pakistani, and so on, fill the "Other API" circle and print the name of the group. If response is "Other race," ask—Which group does . . . consider (himself/herself) to be?

14. *2000*

The racial and ethnic categories came 1998 from the Executive Office of the President, Office of Management and Budget (OMB), Office of Information and Regulatory Affairs, in a report entitled "Revision to the Standards for the Classification of Federal Data on Race and Ethnicity."

also extended racial classifications by adding Quadroon and Octoroon to the racial categories of white, black, Mulatto, Chinese, Japanese, and Indian. The definition of "black" now included persons having three-fourths or more black blood. "Mulatto" was reserved for persons having from three-eighths to five-eighths black blood; "Quadroon" included those having one-fourth black blood; and "Octoroon" referred to persons with one-eighth or any trace of black blood (Williamson 1980, xii–xiii).

The 1900 census definitions, however, eliminated Mulatto, Quadroon, and Octoroon and returned to five basic racial categories because of *Plessy v. Ferguson,* (163 U.S. 537, 1896), and the logic of biracial stratification and segregation between Blacks and Whites. In the 1910 and 1920 census, Mulatto reappeared; but it disappeared again in 1930, while four new racial categories were added to the list, including Mexican, Filipino, Hindu, and Korean, along with the undefined category called "other."

The 1940 census then eliminated Mexican, and the 1950 census also deleted Hindu and Korean. The 1960 census then added new racial categories such as Hawaiian, Part Hawaiian, Aleut, and Eskimo and reclassified Indian as American Indian; however, the 1970 census deleted Part Hawaiian, Aleut, and Eskimo and changed Negro to "Negro or black." Both the 1980 and 1990 census added a number of new racial categories such as Guamanian, Samoan, and Vietnamese, reinstated Korean, Eskimo, and Aleut as racially classified groups, and reclassified Indian as Asian Indian. With respect to ethnicity, Hispanics had never been considered as a racial group, though Mexican was once considered a racial category in 1930 but disappeared thereafter. The 2000 census finally recognized Mexicans and other Hispanic categories as distinct ethnic, not racial, groups.

Almost every census since 1790 relied on varying standards of racial classification and different sets of racial categories. The government's continuous struggle to create and redesignate the set of racial categories suggests that there was no universally established, concrete set of discrete, social or cultural characteristics which set people of different "races" apart, and that future racial categories may remain historically influenced, subject to further contestation and revision.

Racial classification and categories used in the 1980, 1990, and 2000 census are no exceptions. The most recent racial definition and racial categories were defined by Directive No. 15, "Race and ethnic standards for federal statistics and administrative reporting," which was promulgated by the Office of Management and Budget (OMB) on May 12, 1977, as well as the revision to Directive No. 15 entitled "Revision to the standards for the classification of federal data on race and ethnicity" issued by OMB in February 1998. Both directives, for example, specify that white refers to "[a] person having origins in any of the original people of Europe, North Africa, or the Middle East."[6] According to this definition, Iraq's Sadam Hussein and Libya's Moammar Kadafi are indeed considered and classified as white by the United States federal government. Similarly, Turkish immigrants, Armenian refugees, so-called Middle

Eastern Zionists and Palestinians, and Moroccans from the northwest coast of Africa can also be considered as white and members of the racial majority in America.

The same groups, however, are often not considered as members of the dominant racial group outside the United States.[7] In Holland, where the general population may be considered white according to the United States governmental standards of racial classification, Turks and Moroccans constitute two of the largest minority groups (de Vries and Pettigrew 1994). They have been discriminated against in employment, education and housing, and affirmative action programs have been specifically established to assist them in attaining equal education and employment opportunities.[8] Turks and their descendants have also been discriminated against in Germany, and they have been subject to continual racial attacks by neo-Nazis and skinheads (Whitney 1992; Fisher 1993; Tomforde 1994, 13; Schafmann 2001). Similarly, in the final five years of Communist rule after forty-two years of Communist domination in Bulgaria, the government began a program of discrimination against ethnic Turks in the midst of declining industrial productivity and increasing economic isolation from the world economy. This discriminatory governmental program was only reversed by the democratic government following the end of Communism (Ludwikowski 1995, 42–44).

In Japan, Iranians and other Middle Easterners are treated as deviant minority groups whose members are often considered to be involved in a variety of criminal activities, including drug trafficking, gambling, and illegal sales of prohibited commodities including handguns (Adrian 1992; Nishimuro 1995). They have also been subject to selective prosecution by Japanese law enforcement agencies and have been discriminated against in housing and employment (Kajita 1995; Mori 1997).

The Kurds, Iran's minority groups, have been discriminated against in Turkey, Iraq, and other Middle Eastern countries (Goldman 1994, 44–45; Krooth and Moallem 1995). Ironically, when members of the Kurds migrate to the United States, they begin to share the same racial identity as Turks, transcending the ethnic and racial differences in their native countries.

Similarly, the category, black, as a supposed distinct racial group, entails no universalistic standard or homogeneous unit. In England, for example, South Asian immigrants from Bangladesh, Pakistan, Sri Lanka, and India are considered as black and placed at the bottom of the social hierarchy, even within the black community, because of their non-Christian religious beliefs and practices (Seabrook 1992; Robinson 1993; Mann 1994; Small 1994). In the United States, on the other hand, the same group is classified by the government as a member of Asian and Pacific Islanders and constitutes an integral part of the so-called model minority group (see generally Takaki 1987).

Physical appearance or visible phrenotypical characteristics are not the only methods of devising race and racial classification. In certain Latin American countries, the acquisition of wealth is most likely to determine one's racial categorization in which one's wealth can make him/her become "white" (Sowell

1983, 101). In the Caribbean, too, economic wealth and demographic conditions have led to the development of a highly defined and sophisticated racial hierarchy based on one's wealth and skin color, while in the United States largely due to the one-drop-of-blood criterion, biracial stratification classified all Blacks as such, rather than falling in some other classification (Sowell 1983, 105). In Mexico, after the Spanish conquest, there were sixteen categorizations of race depending on the degree to which individuals carried Spanish, indigenous, and black-slave blood (Krooth 1995, 30–31).

The term race is also used differently in other societies. In Britain, for example, the court has recently declared that the Scots are a different race from the English because of their separate church and legal and educational systems (Bowditch 1997, 4). In litigation in which a senior English policeman, because he was English, brought a race discrimination case against the police for an assigned senior Scottish post, the unanimous decision of the tribunal affirmed that the English and the Scots are separate racial groups defined by reference to national origin.[9] Similarly, the Burakumin, the largest minority group and historically outcast communities in Japan, are visibly and phrenologically indistinguishable from the "average" Japanese, but they are considered an uniquely different race from the non-Burakumin population (see generally De Vos and Wetherall 1983). Herman Ooms (1996) examined the origins of discrimination against the Burakumin population, concluding that increasingly institutional discrimination, abetted by racial theories designed to justify the emerging practice, transformed a partially segregated, functional status group into a distinct outcast and racial minority.[10]

These are some examples of different social designs of racial classification and civic treatment of different racial groups. A critical analysis of racial classification is of great importance, because societies routinely invent and adopt racial classifications that are closely intertwined with the ways in which wealth, opportunities, legal protections, and freedom are distributed and allocated.[11] Despite the pervasive nature of race and racial classification, however, there has been little research examining the fallacies and fictions on which notions of race depend. Few researchers have asked the critical question of what race is and how racial identity is socially maintained and politically constructed.

The lack of empirical analyses of the assumptions and beliefs about racial identity and ancestral race is further complicated as individuals from different races and with different racial ancestry intermarry with increasing frequency, and as individuals intentionally blur racial lines for economic reasons, political gains, and social advantage. In light of the need to organize the increasingly complex designations of race and racial identity, the next section addresses both theoretical and empirical problems of understanding, defining, and measuring one's race by investigating racial identity and beliefs about one's ancestral race within the context of the government's most recent conception and delineation of race and racial classification.

RELIABILITY AND VALIDITY OF RACE AS A MEASUREMENT

Race cannot be properly understood as falling into civil and legal categories without uncovering the social impact based on their origins and historical evolution. In this sense, racial classification and definitions explained in the Federal Directive No. 15 have failed to provide the inclusive and exhaustive definition of the relationship between race, racial identity, and civil society. Rather, racial and ethnic definitions and governmental standards are rooted in four fallacies and errors, making the measurement of race increasingly unreliable and invalid: For there is (1) no internal consistency among racially classified groups, (2) a lack of comprehensive descriptions and classifications of racially mixed persons, (3) no provision for verification of racial identity and ancestry, and (4) no empirical check for those who "pass " as being members of other races, raising the question of the validity and the efficacy of one's own self-identified race. In the following, we review each of these shortcomings in the logical design and measurement of racial differences and the categories to which races are assigned.

Internal Consistency Among Racially Classified Groups

In order for any qualitative measurement to be valid, reliable, and internally consistent, the attributes or categories used in the measurement must be both exclusive and inclusive in its scope to capture the full range of social phenomena under investigation (Babbie 1995, 135). Exclusiveness means that there is no overlapping among the attributes of the measurement, suggesting that all racial categories are independent of each other in a manner that one racial category does not overlap with any other racial groups (Babbie 1995, 135, 142).

Directive No. 15, for example, enlists five major racial categories: white, black, American Indian, Asian and Pacific Islander (API), and others. The revision of the directive severed the API category into Asian and Native Hawaiian or other Pacific Islander (NHPI). In order for racial categories to be exclusive, racial categories provided by the directive assume that the white as a distinct racial group is uniquely different from and does not overlap with any other racial groups. As noted earlier, however, each of the above racial categories are not a distinctly cohesive, homogeneous unit because some Asians are considered black and, in other racial classification schemes, some whites from Middle East or Northern Africa are not considered whites. Some scholars even argue that Native Hawaiians should be considered as part of American Indians or Native Americans, while the directive requires that they be classified as members of Asian and/or Pacific Islanders. Thus, the exclusive and distinct principle of homogeneous categories for the measurement of race has not been met by the directive's racial definitions and classification scheme.

Inclusiveness means that racial categories are created in a way that every individual can be classified into one of the available racial groups, suggesting that race as an measurement must exhaust all the available categories of major racial groups. Creating the "other" race is an ingenious way of creating a category for those who do not fit into the four existing, major racial categories. The problem with the "other" race category, however, is that many racially mixed persons began to self-identify themselves by choosing this "other" category to resolve the problem of classifying their mixed racial ancestry into a predetermined set of mono-racial categories.

The 1990 census form instructed respondents to "[f]ill one circle for the race that the person considers himself/herself to be." Because the instruction emphasizes that only one box be checked, many mixed race persons wrote in "multiracial," "biracial," "mixed-race," or other names to designate their racially mixed backgrounds (see generally Payson, 1996). If racially mixed persons are unable to choose a mono-racial category, the government uses their mother's race to determine their race (see table 2.1, and notes). If a single race response could not be provided for the person's mother, the first race reported by the person was used. For example, if a person wrote in multiple racial categories such as white/Hawaiian, then the person will be classified as white, while those who wrote Hawaiian/white will be classified as Hawaiian and become a member of Asian and Pacific Islanders (Payson 1996). Similarly, in all cases where occupied housing units, households, or families are classified by race, the federal government uses the race of the householder as the person's race.[12] Further, in situations where no race is available to identify one's race, race of the closest neighbor is used to determine his/her race (Payson 1996, 1270).

Such specific reclassification procedures are also recent inventions; for over time, the governmental method of reclassifying racially mixed persons went through dramatic changes. In 1930, for example, for those who were unable to obtain a mono-racial identity, father's race, rather than race of a mother, was used to determine one's race (see table 2.1, for example). Tiger Woods, the youngest grand slam champion in golf, who is racially mixed, exemplifies that different classification methods may affect how his racial identity is determined. Tiger Woods once called himself "Cabliasian" because his ancestral race includes Caucasian, black, American Indian, and Asian (see Morse 1997). According to the 1990 census classification scheme, if Woods declined to provide his racial identity, he might be classified as a member of the Asian society, because his mother, who came from Thailand, is classified as Asian—half Thai and half Chinese (McLead 1997; Morse 1997). If he then provided no racial identity of his mother, he might be reclassified as white, because his nearest neighbor, Mark O'Meara, is a white professional golfer (Nevius, 1997). If he was born prior to 1930, he might well have been classified black as his father is a self-identified black—half-black, a quarter white and Native American, respectively (McLead 1997). In 1870, he could have been classified as Quadroon, because of his mixed racial heritage under the rule of hypodescent (the "one-drop" rule).

Those are some examples of how different reclassification methods can lead to different racial identity. Such inconsistent methods of reclassifying the person of mixed race pose serious problems in terms of data comparability and reliability across time and space. Since Directive No. 15 has failed to keep pace with changing social conditions, shaping ambivalence in the representation and the construction of race, the mixed race person can be easily reclassified into more than one racial category because of different reclassification methods used by the federal government.

Self-Reporting of Race and Lack of Verification

One's race can be identified in two ways: self-reported race and other-reported race. Directive No. 15, however, failed to specify which method of data collection to use. The lack of standardized identification methods creates obvious problems of data comparability and consistency. For example, the guideline of the Equal Employment Opportunity Commission (EEOC), which is the enforcer of the civil rights program and relies on census data to assess racial representation in employment, only stipulates that employers may not directly elicit race from their employees and they are to make their racial evaluation only by visual inspection (see 29 CFRs 1602. 13, 1995; see also EEOC Standard Form 100 Instruction Booklet 5, 1992). Such racial identification through third-party observations was used because of the fear that asking one's race could be offensive, insensitive, or even misleading, suggesting that one may be reluctant to choose and determine his or her race from the predetermined set of racial categories.

The Census Bureau, by contrast, currently relies on self-reported data, though it was not until the 1960 census that self-reported data were exclusively used. Prior to 1960, so-called census enumerators collected race information by observation (Goyer and Domschke, 1983, 398). The two different approaches do not necessarily produce the same racial classification, as research on reporting biases shows that there exists a huge discrepancy between self-identified and third-party determination of race, creating problematic methodological discrepancies in evaluating possible racial discrimination by comparing the census data with EEOC information. For example, a recent study of birth and death certificates of infants has revealed that 43 percent of Asian and Native American babies were classified by race differently at death than at birth, demonstrating that differences between self-identified race and third-party evaluations of one's race can arise and that such differences can undermine racial comparisons for data collected by different agencies (Payson 1996, 1268). Similarly, the above example illustrates that third parties are increasingly unable to classify individuals of mixed race accurately when their choices are limited to a set of discrete mono-racial categories. While the agencies that use third-party reported data may have raised legitimate issues relating to privacy concerns, asking the third party to guess whether a person is mixed race, and if so, what the person's component race is, suffers from the lack of consistency and empirical accuracy. Thus, different data gathering techniques and the lack of standardized procedures in verifying one's self-reported race in case of third party identification may lead to incorrect assessments of one's racial identity and thus fail to evaluate the extent of true racial discrimination and unequal treatment.

Lack of Classifications for Racially Mixed Persons

Various reclassification schemes used by the Census Bureau, including mother's race, first race mentioned, race of the head of household or the nearest neighbor, among others, were adopted for administrative purposes without carefully examining whether racial reclassifications make initial sense in categorizing racially mixed persons into a mono-racial group on the given criteria. As people are becoming more multiracial in their backgrounds, the ambiguity of race is exacerbated and racial identification becomes increasingly problematic.

Research shows that mono-racial categorizations may not be appropriate in assessing individuals' racial identity. Children of mixed parents represent approximately 3 percent of all births in the United States (Barringer 1989). As of 1989, one million persons of racially mixed parentage had been born in the prior twenty years, in which 39 percent of the mixed-race children were from black-white parents, 36 percent from Asian-white, 18 percent from Native American-white, and 6 percent from Asian-black or Native American-black (Barringer 1989).[13] Similarly, the number of interracial married couples almost quadrupled between 1970 and 1993, from 310,000 in 1970 to approximately 1.2 million in 1993, suggesting a dramatic increase from less than 1 percent of all reported marriages in 1970 to more than 2 percent (see generally Funderburg, 1994). Among all interracial marriages, white and black couples accounted for 242,000, compared with 920,000 for whites and non-blacks.[14] Research also suggests that 40 percent of all multiracial births in 1990 (excluding births for which the race of parents was unknown) were mixed black-and-white, up from 32 percent in 1970. According to the National Center for Health Statistics (NCHS) that has tracked mixed race births since 1968, birthrates of children with one black and one white parent have been increasing— 52,232 of such births being recorded in 1991, compared to 26,968 in 1981, and 8,758 in 1968 (Funderburg 1989).

Given the exponential increase of so-called mixed race individuals, the problem of Directive No. 15 becomes even more acute, because the directive's racial classification has failed to indicate whether and to what extent multiracial persons are, or are not classified into mono-racial categories. The 1990 census shows that 9.8 million people were classified into the "other" racial category which accounted for 4 percent of the entire United States population (U.S. Department of Commerce 1991). Similarly, the racial classification used for the evaluation of possible employment discrimination often enlists only major racial categories defined by the national census, excluding "other" races from the questionnaire, with the expectation that racially mixed people will somehow determine their mono-racial identity from a predetermined set of racial classifications. The employment form used at Human Resources of the University of California, Santa Cruz, by contrast, does not have the "other" race group on the application, but enlists the following groups instead: (1) white, (2) black, (3) Native American, (4) Asian and Pacific Islander, and (5) Hispanic (UCSC Employment Application Form 1997, 1). In the absence of data on multiracial persons and a lack of empirical analyses of both racial identifications and ancestral race, the Federal Directive's racial classification thus failed to show whether and to what extent multiracial individuals are the victims of discrimination.

Similarly, given the recent increase of racially mixed populations and the frequent changes in the definition of racial categories by the federal government, Directive No. 15 remains unable to indicate how to meaningfully classify and reclassify racially mixed persons, or if such classification is even advisable.

While the 1998 revision to Directive No. 15 recommends allowing individuals to freely identify themselves and check more than one racial category, the problem still exists with respect to the accuracy, consistency, and lack of empirical verification of identified races. For the year 2000 census to obtain self-identification of race, OMB recommended the use of methods for reporting more than one race from the categories of (1) white, (2) black or African American, (3) American Indian or Alaska Native, (4) Asian, (5) Native Hawaiian or other Pacific Islander, and (6) other. As we will demonstrate in part II, many individuals may identify themselves as white, for example, while their ancestry does not include white. Similar patterns of racial identification have been observed in other racial groups. In other words, while multiracial categories in the 2000 census allowed individuals to identify more than one racial category, it is not entirely clear whether their identified races accurately reflect their knowledge of their ancestral history. Perhaps they may choose the most desired racial identity based on their physical appearance, familiar cultures, or religious beliefs, suggesting that multiracial categories do not necessarily offer the desired validity and empirical reliability of measuring one's race and identity.

As past research on the identification of one's social class positions in NORC surveys has shown, people have exhibited a tendency to claim their social class position different from their own class position because of their strong desire to belong to and be perceived as members of the higher and different social class (Archer et al. 2001). Similarly, since whiteness is perceived to possess distinct racial privilege and property values in our society, it is not surprising that some individuals have a strong desire to be perceived and accepted as members of the white race, particularly when their physical appearance allows them to pass or "inhabit" more than one racial identity.

"Passing" and the Factual Accuracy of Component Race as One's Self-Identified Race

The problem of racial classification is further exacerbated by racially mixed persons who are counted as minorities but socially and politically treated as if they are white, suggesting that the classification problem may award affirmative benefits and minority-group allotments to individuals who may be functionally white. For example, since some persons of mixed Asian/white descent may be accepted by the public and society as white or at least "white enough," should racially mixed persons who look white and are treated as white by society be counted as members of racial minority groups?[15] Since it is not uncommon for persons of very remote African ancestry to claim that they are black, should they also be counted as members of the black race, despite that they may be treated and accepted as white in our society? Because the racial data of the census are mostly derived from individual self-reportings, it is possible that some individuals can pass as one race and can possibly change or shift personal identity between different racial groups for social advantage and economic gain.

Gunnar Myrdal's 1944 study of race relations provides a definition of passing. According to Myrdal, passing "means that a Negro becomes a white man, that is, moves from the lower to the higher caste. In the American caste order, this can be accomplished only by the deception of the white people with whom the passer comes to associate and by a conspiracy of silence on the part of other Negroes who might know about it" (Myrdal 1944, 683).

The controversy over passing offers the basis for an important inquiry about individuals of mixed race, because substantial numbers of self-identified black Americans do pass, that is, live important parts of their public lives as if they are white. Passing stems from the social reality of whiteness offering a valuable social and economic advantage, a theme that has not lost its value in our time (Bell 1989, 1602; Williams 1991, 124; Harris, 1993, 1714). Clearly, the persistence of passing is also closely related to the historical and continuing pattern of white racial domination and economic exploitation that has given passing a certain political edge and economic logic. While past research offered no precise count of people who pass, Joel Williamson (1980) provides rough guesses for the period 1900–1920, ranging from ten thousand to twenty-five thousand persons each year who crossed the color line from black to white (100–126).

The irony of passing is that, in the contemporary era of affirmative action, "reverse passing" becomes a social phenomenon—as Whites attempt to be reclassified as racial minorities for purposes of affirmative action program. In 1975, for example, Paul and Philip Malone took part in civil service competition for jobs with the Boston Fire Department. They scored poorly and were not accepted by the department. Though they initially identified as white in the 1975 test application, when they applied again in 1977, they identified as black and were hired, because of a court-ordered affirmative action program under which the city maintained separate minority candidate lists for firefighter vacancies (Ford 1994).

This presents a problem for empirically measuring those who pass as white, as they may declare to be a member of the dominant racial group, while they are fully aware of their nonwhite ancestry which they might claim for some purposes. Affirmative action programs are based on such empirical identification of inclusion or exclusion. For the rule of hypodescent assumes that those who have shared the blood of nonwhite ancestors such as black are branded and labeled as black, no matter how remote their black ancestral backgrounds may be. Yet, the large number of racially mixed individuals and multiracial groups in today's society may make it difficult, if not impossible, to trace the blood line—to apply the one-drop rule—as effective or functional in classifying racial minorities.

The question of the passing becomes even more problematic when Hispanics are introduced as a racial minority in affirmative action programs. For instance, the EEOC, as an enforcer of civil rights programs relies on census data to assess the population's racial distribution in employment, yet still uses language such as "non-Hispanic white" (or white with "non-Hispanic origin") or "non-Hispanic black" (or black with "non-Hispanic origin"), asserting that the Hispanic category is a multiracial classification tied to Spanish heritage and that Hispanics can be white, black, Asian, or even Native American (Tienda and Jensen 1988, 23–61). While the census specifies Hispanic as a distinct ethnic, not racial group, the problem of treating Hispanics as one among distinct racial groups is that a large proportion of individuals from Central and South America are indistinguishable physically and phrenotypically from the "average" white person in the United States, though they are classified as Hispanic by the census and other criteria employed by different federal agencies. As noted earlier, in affirmative action programs, Hispanics are routinely considered as one among racial groups based on Spanish culture or national origin regardless of racial ancestry, and the term Hispanic remains problematic, because the term generally encompasses immigrants from Spain, Cuba, Mexico, Central and South America, and on occasion, Italy and Portugal, showing that the term includes those classified as white by the census (Saragoza et al. 1992, 1).

If we introduce figures for comparative self-identity of race, we gain a clearer picture of the problem. Table 2.2 shows 1990 United States census information on the population breakdown by race and ethnicity. There were more than twenty-two million people who identified themselves as Hispanic in the United States, and the majority of the Hispanics were classified as white (51.7 percent), closely followed by others (42.8 percent). Though Hispanics can be of any race, the number of Hispanics who identified their race as black, Native American, or Asian was very small (3.4 percent, 0.7 percent, 1.4 percent, respectively). Similarly, 5.8 percent of whites identified as Hispanics and 97.5 percent of those in other racial groups said that they were members of Hispanic populations. However, when Hispanics are added as a separate group to existing racial categories—as done routinely in the evaluation of racial discrimination and the effectiveness of affirmative action programs—Hispanics accounted for 9 percent of the total United States population. When Hispanic whites are excluded from white racial groups, the addition of Hispanic as a separate and distinct racial group then reduced the white population from 80.2 percent to 75.6 percent (see the last column in table 2.2). The potential addition of Hispanic populations as a distinct and separate racial group reduced the white population by almost five percentage points. Nevertheless, the proportion of blacks, Native Americans, and Asians almost remained the same (12.0 percent to 11.8 percent for black, 0.8 percent to 0.7 percent for Native American, and 2.9 to 2.8 percent for Asian) after Hispanics are introduced as one of six distinct racial categories. The 2000 census also provides similar figures with respect to the percentage of Hispanic whites—48 percent of Hispanics classified themselves as solely white. Furthermore, if Hispanic whites are included as members of the white race, whites constituted 75.1 percent of the total population, down by only 5 percent from the 1990 census (Patterson 2001).

These findings suggest that, if passing can be defined as those who are classified as racial minorities but who act and are treated as members of the racial majority, nearly half of the Hispanic population is passing (51.7 percent of them identified themselves as white in the 1990 census and 48 percent in the 2000 census), creating even greater problems in terms of data comparability and consistency. Clearly, the census is unable to socially distinguish people based on their physical appearances and how they are socially and economically treated.

One cautionary note, however, needs to be mentioned and stressed concerning race-ethnic identification of Hispanics, that is, the regional variation of the proportion of Hispanic populations and Hispanic-white identification. For instance, while the overwhelming majority of Hispanics in Florida identified as whites (81.5 percent), less than half of California's Hispanics identified as whites (45.8 percent), suggesting that unique regional history and specific migratory patterns of ethnic minorities also affect local race relations and the construction of racial identification of community members.

Furthermore, the Supreme Court has ruled that Hispanics can include persons with Spanish surnames, suggesting that spouses of interracial marriages, their children, and immigrants from the Philippines and their descendants can be legally included as Hispanic, though the census specifically classifies Filipinos as either members of Asian and Pacific Islanders (API) in the 1990 census, or Native Hawaiian or other Pacific Islanders in the 2000 census. In jury compositional challenge cases, for instance, the Court has stated that Hispanics are a distinct racial group in the community and would include those with Spanish surnames. *Hernandez v. Texas* (347 U.S. 475, 1954) became the first case in which the United States Supreme Court considered discrimination against Hispanics as evidenced by the exclusion of Mexican jurors. The Hernandez court determined that Spanish names provide ready identification of members of Hispanic communities (347 U.S. 475 481, 1954). In *Castaneda v. Partida* (430 U.S. 482, 1977), the court also asserted that Mexican Americans were a clearly identifiable class and used the terms "Spanish-surnamed" and "Mexican American" as synonymous. Similarly, in 1985, the California Supreme Court in *People v. Tervino* held that "'Spanish surnamed' is sufficiently descriptive of a cognizable group" for purposes of determining abuses of peremptory challenges by

TABLE 2.2

1990 U.S. Census: Race and Ethnicity With and Without Hispanic Origin

Response	No.	%	Hispanic Origin No.	%	Non-Hispanic Origin No.	%	Hispanic as Race No.	%
Total Population	248.709[1]	100.0	22.354	100.0	226.364	100.0		
White	199.686	80.2	11.557	51.7(5.8)[2]	188.128	83.1	188.128	75.6
Black	29.986	12.0	.769	3.4(2.6)	29.216	12.9	29.216	11.8
Native American	1.959	0.8	.165	0.7(8.4)	1.793	0.8	1.793	0.7
Asian/PI	7.273	2.9	.305	1.4(4.2)	6.968	3.1	6.968	2.8
Others	9.804	4.0	9.555	42.8(97.5)	.249	0.1	.249	0.1
Hispanic	—	—	—	—	—	—	22.354	9.0

Total

Source: Bureau of the U.S. Census. 1990. *Race and Ethnicity.* Washington, D.C.
Notes:
1. The figure shows in million.
2. The figure in parentheses shows the percentage of Hispanics for a given racial group. For example, 5.8 percent of whites identified as Hispanic.

the prosecution, concluding that "Spanish-surnamed" describes Hispanics in general (704 P.2d 719 721 [Cal. 1985]).

In the absence of empirical data on racial identity and ancestry of individuals, especially multiracial individuals and their mixed heritage and backgrounds, past census, court cases, and research have failed to examine the validity and reliability of the government's racial classification and specification in showing whether and to what extent racially mixed persons and the "passer" are victims of discrimination. The predominant views on passing still assume that one's component racial identity belongs to that of the racial minority, but the person acts as if he/she is a member of the racial majority. Race research has been unable to show which of a mixed race person's component races should be more meaningfully reclassified. Since persons of different racial mixtures may be classified differently by self-determination, society, and federal agencies, there may not be a single method that will result in meaningful classification for all the various combinations of racially mixed individuals.

Classification becomes even more convoluted as multiple specification of racial identity may allow individuals to specify more than one racial designation.

It is still not clear that identified race will reflect their racial identity based on beliefs in their ancestral race; or identified race may be based on their passing status; or it may even stem from one's desire of a certain racial membership and affiliation, regardless of whether or not one can pass as a member of the desired racial group.

In the following section, we examine the internal inconsistency of the government's racial classification and specification. In order to design race-specific programs to eliminate racial discrimination in jury proceedings, we need not only to examine whether or not mixed race persons' treatment comports with the treatment of one of their component racial groups, but also to analyze whether passing occurs with greater frequency because of the way society defines racial identity, as well as the lack of empirical verification of self-reported race. That is, we attempt to deconstruct race on the basis of government-defined racial categories, racial identity, and reported ancestral race by carefully examining how racially mixed ancestry affects one's personal determination to design and construct a self-identified race.

RACIAL IDENTITY AND ANCESTRAL BACKGROUNDS

In 1996, a representative group of college students at four University of California campuses (Berkeley, Irvine, Riverside, and Santa Cruz) were contacted to provide their responses to various questions involving racial identity, ancestral history, and their views on affirmative action in jury selection (see appendix A for more detailed explanations on the University of California wide survey).

Self-identified race and ancestral race may not match, as table 2.3 shows in survey results of the respondents. The first three columns of table 2.3 show (1) the six different racial categories, (2) the total number of self-identified respondents for different racial groups, and (3) percentages of respondents in each racial group. For example, of 911 total respondents, 344 respondents identified themselves as white, which is 37.8 percent of the total sample. Similarly, thirty respondents claimed that they are black (3.3 percent), while only five students said that they are Native American (0.5 percent). Similarly, 15.8 percent, 35.1 percent, and 7.5 percent of respondents claimed to be Hispanics, Asian and Pacific Islanders (Asian hereafter), and others, respectively.[16]

The next two columns (fifth and sixth columns) show the total count of ancestral race and the percentage of each racial ancestry identified by survey respondents. For instance, of 911 total respondents, 447 respondents said that they have white ancestors (49.0 percent). While there were only five self-identified Native Americans in the sample, 135 respondents said that they have Native American as part of their ancestry (14.8 percent). The total number of ancestral designations (1,293) also exceeded the sample size, that is, the total number of subjects in the study (911), indicating that on an average, every individual makes claim to approximately 1.4 mixed ancestry in their backgrounds.

Of 1,293 total ancestral backgrounds, the category white only accounted for 34.6 percent of all ancestors, along with 5.1 percent black, 10.4 percent Native American, 14.9 percent Hispanic, and 28.0 percent Asian.

The breakdown of self-identified race by ancestral race is shown in the next five columns (seventh through eleventh). For example, 96.5 percent of self-identified white respondents indicated that they had white ancestry, suggesting that 3.5 percent of self-identified whites did not have white ancestors, but nevertheless identified themselves as white. Similarly, 5.5 percent of self-identified whites also indicated that they had black ancestry, while almost one of four self-identified whites said that they had a Native American ancestor (19.8 percent). Two other nonwhite races—Hispanic (4.7 percent) and Asian (3.8 percent)—also make up part of ancestral race for self-identified whites.

For self-identified black respondents, exactly one half of them said that they had white ancestors, while they all indicated that they shared black ancestry. Two of every three self-identified blacks also had Native American ancestors (66.7 percent). Hispanics (13.3 percent) and Asians (10.0 percent) are also part of the ancestral race claimed by self-identified blacks.

Among those who self-identified themselves as Native American, 80 percent of them had white ancestors, along with 20 percent for blacks, Hispanics, and Asians. Yet, there were only five self-identified Native Americans in the sample of 911 respondents, while 135 respondents indicated that they had Native American ancestors. For Hispanic respondents, more than one of four reported white ancestors (26.9 percent), while 5.5 percent of self-identified Hispanics also shared black ancestry. Interestingly, for Hispanic respondents, the degree of mixed ancestry with blacks (5.5 percent), Native Americans (18.6 percent), Asians (2.1 percent), and other races (9.9 percent) is similar to that of self-identified whites (5.5 percent, 19.8 percent, 3.8 percent, and 9.7 percent for blacks, Native Americans, Asians, and others).

Another similarity between whites and Hispanics is the percentage of self-identified whites and Hispanics who failed to have any ancestry of their chosen race. Thus, 3.5 percent of self-identified whites did not have white ancestors, and 3.4 percent of self-identified Hispanics did not share Hispanic ancestry. For self-identified Asians, the largest mixed race is found with whites (7.8 percent), followed by Hispanics (4.3 percent), and others (2.8 percent). Only 0.3 percent of self-identified Asians respectively had black and Native American ancestors.

The extent of racial mixture for each of the five distinct racial groups can be measured and evaluated by summing the percentages of respective ancestral races (see the bottom total in table 2.3 for each racial group). Using this approach, both self-identified blacks (246.7 percent) and Native Americans (260.0 percent) had the highest level of racially mixed ancestry, suggesting that as an average, every black and Native American individual shares two distinct racial ancestries outside their self-identified race. For Blacks, the two largest mixed ancestries come from white (50.0 percent) and Native American (66.7 percent), while the largest mixed ancestry for Native Americans comes from white (80.0 percent). The extent of racially mixed ancestry is the lowest for self-identified Asians (114.3 percent).

The breakdown of ancestral backgrounds by racial self-identity is shown in the last five columns (twelfth through sixteenth). For example, 74.4 percent of those who shared white ancestry identified as white, suggesting that almost one of every four individuals with white ancestors identified as nonwhite (3.4 percent for black, 0.9 percent for Native Americans, 8.7 percent for Hispanics, and 5.6 percent for Asian). For those who shared black ancestors, only 45.5 percent of them became self-identified black. That is, the majority of those who shared black ancestry failed to identify as black, negating the widely held belief of the persuasiveness of the one-drop rule. More than one of four individuals with black ancestry chose white as their component and self-identified race (28.8 percent), followed respectively by 12.1 percent for Hispanics, 1.5 percent for Asians and Native Americans. As far as present racial identity based on the black descent is concerned, the direction of racial "emigration," or exodus, from being "black" to "white" is the greatest, perhaps reflecting social emphasis on whiteness as a valued trait and privilege.

Among those who shared Native American ancestry, the majority of them identified as white (50.4 percent), followed by Hispanic (20.0 percent) and black (14.8 percent). Only 3.7 percent of them identified as Native American. For those who shared Hispanic ancestry, only 72.5 percent identified as Hispanic. Among other major racial groups, 27.5 percent of Hispanic descendants identified as white (8.3 percent), Asian (7.3 percent), black (2.1 percent), and Native American (0.5 percent). Among individuals who had Asian ancestors, 87.4 percent said they are also Asian. For other major racial groups, whites (3.6 percent) are the largest self-identified racial category, followed by blacks (0.8 percent), Hispanics (0.8 percent), and Native Americans (0.3 percent).

Similar to the breakdown of racial identity by racial ancestry, almost three out of four individuals who shared white and Hispanic ancestors chose their component race as white and Hispanic, respectively (74.4 percent and 72.5 percent for whites and Hispanics). Among individuals with black ancestry, the component and self-identified race remained black (45.5 percent of them identified themselves as black). Nevertheless, the percentage is the smallest among all racial groups, except Native Americans (only 3.7 percent of Native American "descendants" identified as Native American—96.3 percent of them self-identified as members of other racial groups), again negating the pervasiveness of the belief that bloodline determines racial identity, as well as supporting the notion that whiteness is perceived to possess a social privilege and valued trait in American life.

Among the four major racial categories, the largest preferred racial identity is found to be white. Even among black descendants, more than one of every four individuals with black ancestry (28.8 percent) self-identified as white, not black, suggesting that the large proportion of black descendants may be passing as a member of the racial majority—once again negating the widely shared belief of the hypodescent rule.

The gender difference on racial identity and racial ancestry is examined in table 2.4. Of the 911 respondents, 356 are male and 555 female. Racial breakdowns are somewhat similar for both genders—35.1 percent are white males and 39.5 percent white females; 3.7 percent are black males and 3.1 percent black females.

Notable gender differences are found for the relation between self-identified race and ancestral race. Except for Whites and Native Americans, the proportion of females who failed to share self-identified racial ancestry always appeared to be higher than for males. For example, 97.6 percent of self-identified white males indicated that they had white ancestors, compared with 95.5 percent for self-identified white females, suggesting that 4.5 percent of self-identified white females did not have white ancestry (2.4 percent for white males). The figures are also higher for females among Hispanics (4.0 percent) and Asians (1.6 percent). The figures also reveal that the degree of reported mixed ancestry is generally higher for females than males. The highest level of mixed ancestry is found among black females (288.2 percent). The lowest level of mixed ancestry is found among Asian males (112.4 percent).

For males, 71.8 percent of white descendants identified themselves as white, while the figure is higher for females (75.8 percent). Some 30 percent of black male descendants identified themselves as white (30.0 percent). The figure is lower for females (27.8 percent). The majority of female Native American descendants (52.8 percent) said they are white, while 45.7 percent of males identified as white. Another notable gender difference is found for Hispanics. While only 1.7 percent of male Hispanic descendants said that they are Asian, the figure is much higher for females (9.7 percent).

Self-Identified Race, Racial Ancestry, and Affirmative Action

Tables 2.3 and 2.4 provide interesting links between self-identified race and racial ancestry using the current government's racial designations and categorizations. One significant finding involves the emergence of distinctly different groupings among each of the four major racial groups. For example, the different clusters of "whites" involves the emergence of the following four groups: (1) the self-identified white; (2) the white "descendant," consisting of those who share white ancestry regardless of self-identified race; (3) the "pure" white who self-identifies white and reports white ancestry as sole ancestral race; and (4) the racially mixed white who in fact shares nonwhite ancestry. The same classifications of the four different groupings can also be applied for other racial groups.

How these various groups respond to social and civic issues also differ, indicating distinct group self-interests as social divisions and political demarcations. Table 2.5 shows the relationship between the four racial groupings for

TABLE 2.3
Racial Identity and Ancestral Backgrounds[1]

Race	Self-Identification		Ancestral Backgrounds			Self-Identification (%)					Ancestral Backgrounds (%)				
	N.	%	N.	% Responses	% Cases	Whites	Blacks	Nat/Am.	Hisp.	Asians[2]	Whites	Blacks	Nat/Am.	Hisp.	Asians
Race:															
1. Whites	344	37.8	447	34.6	49.0	96.5	50.0	80.0	26.9	7.8	74.4	28.8	50.4	8.3	3.6
2. Blacks	30	3.3	66	5.1	7.5	5.5	100.0	20.0	5.5	.3	3.4	45.5	14.8	2.1	.8
3. Native Americans	5	.5	135	10.4	14.8	19.8	66.7	100.0	18.6	.3	.9	1.5	3.7	.5	.3
4. Hispanics	144	15.8	192	14.9	21.1	4.7	13.3	20.0	96.6	4.3	8.7	12.1	20.0	72.5	.8
5. Asians/Pac. Is.	320	35.1	363	28.0	39.8	3.8	10.0	20.0	2.1	98.8	5.6	1.5	.7	7.3	87.4
6. Others	68	7.5	91	7.0	9.9	9.9	6.7	20.0	9.7	2.8	7.2	10.6	10.4	9.3	7.1
Total	911	100.0	1,293	100.0	141.9	140.2	246.7	260.0	159.4	114.3	100.1	100.0	100.0	100.0	100.0

Notes:
1. Multi-response programs in SPSS/X are used for empirical analyses.
2. Asians also include Pacific Islanders.

TABLE 2.4
Racial Identity and Ancestral Backgrounds by Gender[1]

Race	Self/Identification		Ancestral Backgrounds			Self/Identification (%)					Ancestral Backgrounds (%)				
	N.	%	N.	% Responses	% Cases	Whites	Blacks	Nat/Am.	Hisp.	Asians[2]	Whites	Blacks	Nat/Am.	Hisp.	Asians
Male															
1. Whites	125	35.1	170	34.3	47.8	97.6	38.5	50.0	31.1	8.8	71.8	30.0	45.7	10.3	4.4
2. Blacks	13	3.7	30	6.0	8.4	7.2	100.0	50.0	6.7	.0	2.9	43.3	15.2	.0	.0
3. Native Americans	2	.6	46	9.3	12.9	16.8	53.8	100.0	17.8	.7	.6	3.3	4.3	.0	.6
4. Hispanics	45	12.6	58	11.7	16.3	4.8	.0	.0	97.8	.7	8.2	10.0	17.4	75.9	1.3
5. Asians/Pac. Is.	137	38.5	160	32.3	44.9	5.6	.0	50.0	4.4	99.3	7.1	.0	2.2	1.7	85.0
6. Others	34	9.6	32	6.4	9.0	7.2	.0	.0	8.9	2.9	9.4	13.3	15.2	12.1	8.8
Total	356	100.0	496	100.0	139.3	139.2	192.3	250.0	166.7	112.4	100.0	100.0	100.0	100.0	100.1
Female															
1. Whites	219	39.5	277	34.8	49.9	95.9	58.8	100.0	25.3	7.1	75.8	27.8	52.8	7.5	3.0
2. Blacks	17	3.1	36	4.5	6.5	4.6	100.0	.0	5.1	.5	3.6	47.2	14.6	3.0	1.5
3. Native Americans	3	.5	89	11.2	16.0	21.5	76.5	100.0	19.2	.0	1.1	.0	3.4	.7	.0
4. Hispanics	99	17.8	134	16.8	24.1	4.6	23.5	33.3	96.0	7.1	9.0	13.9	21.3	70.9	.5
5. Asians/Pac. Is.	183	33.3	202	25.3	36.4	2.7	17.6	.0	1.0	98.4	4.7	2.8	.0	9.7	89.1
6. Others	34	6.1	59	7.4	10.6	11.4	11.8	33.3	10.1	2.7	5.8	8.3	7.9	8.2	5.9
Total	555	100.0	797	100.0	143.5	140.7	288.2	266.6	156.7	115.8	100.0	100.0	100.0	100.0	100.0

Notes:
1: Multi-response programs in SPSS/X are used for empirical analyses.
2: Asians also include Pacific Islanders.

each race and their economic backgrounds and sociopolitical views on affirmative action and racially controversial sociopolitical issues. The first column of the table shows the four different racial groups based on self-identified race and ancestral race. The first five rows show self-identified races, their differing views on affirmative action, their socioeconomic backgrounds, and their political opinions. For example, while the majority of self-identified whites support affirmative action in jury selection, education, employment, and business contracting (60.5 percent, 54.7 percent, 51.0 percent, and 46.4 percent, respectively), the support for affirmative action is lowest among all self-identified races.

The next five rows (sixth through tenth) show survey findings based on ancestral race of the respondents. The racial grouping, "white," based on ancestral race includes all respondents who indicated that they shared white ancestry, regardless of their racial identity. The majority of these white descendants supported race-conscious affirmative action in four areas (62.2 percent, 58.6 percent, 56.6 percent, and 48.6 percent respectively for jury selection, education, employment, and contracting), although their support is again the lowest among all ancestral races, except Asian's support for education (56.5 percent) and black support for jury selection (60.4 percent).

The next five rows (eleventh through fifteenth) indicate the opinions of "pure" race individuals—those without racially mixed ancestry. For example, the racial grouping, called "white," represents individuals who reported only white ancestry. Their support for race-based affirmative action is the lowest among all racial groups, while their socioeconomic status is the highest of all groups (6.53 for parental income in a nine-point ordinal scale that measures from (1) for less than $5,000 to (9) for $100,000 or more; and 5.95 for father's education in a eight-point ordinal scale that measures from (1) for grade or elementary education to (8) post college degrees).

The next twelve rows (sixteenth through twenty-seventh) show findings for the following three groups: (1) self-identified whites with four "nonwhite" ancestors; (2) self-identified blacks with four "non-black" ancestors (white, Native American, Hispanic, and Asian); and (3) self-identified Hispanics with four non-Hispanic ancestors (white, black, Native American, and Asian). For example, 38.5 percent of racially mixed whites with black ancestors supported affirmative action in jury selection, while 71.4 percent of racially mixed whites with Hispanic ancestors supported race-conscious remedies in jury proceedings.

There are several notable findings from table 2.5. First, the gap of support for affirmative action is greater within self-identified races than among ancestral races. For example, the difference between self-identified whites and self-identified blacks in their support for affirmative action is respectively 9.0 percent, 38.8 percent, 32.9 percent, and 37.5 percent in regard to jury selection, education, employment, and contract, compared respectively to—1.8 percent, 18.7 percent, 13.1 percent, and 16.4 percent between the overall white and black descendants. Racial differences impacted by socioeconomic backgrounds, measured by parents' annual income and fathers' educational attainment, are greater within self-identified races than among ancestral races. While the annual parental income for self-identified Hispanics was 4.97 (i.e., below $25,000 to $34,999), all respondents with Hispanic ancestral race show 5.35 (i.e., below $35,000 to $49,999). In other words, self-identified races seem to show higher socioeconomic stratification than among ancestral races, suggesting that racial identity shows greater variation for differences in political attitudes and social class positions than for racial ancestral backgrounds.

Second, though ancestral race alone may seem to lose its predictive power in explaining racial differences, both self-identified whites and those with white ancestry still have the highest socioeconomic status (6.63 and 6.53 for parents' annual income for self-identified whites and for those with white ancestors; 6.16 and 5.95 for father's educational achievement for the same groups, respectively). This finding seems to suggest that whites have been and remain the most entrenched and privileged racial group in our society, supporting the notion of whiteness as a trait offering social and economic advantage.

Third, self-identified whites with black ancestors hold the most negative views concerning race-based affirmative action policies (38.5 percent, 42.1 percent, 36.8 percent, and 31.6 percent respectively for jury selection, education, employment, and contracting), showing that no affirmative action policies had their majority support. Compared with the response of self-identified blacks who shared white ancestry, the differences are startling (75 percent, 93.3 percent, 80.0 percent, and 86.7 percent respectively for supporting each of the four affirmative action programs). While both groups share the identical racially mixed combinations, their social economic status differs markedly (6.67 and 5.57 for parents' income and father's education for whites with black ancestry and 5.28 and 4.28 for blacks with white ancestry, respectively). The differences in their political attitudes also remain large: 42.8 percent and 28.5 percent of whites with black ancestry supported two racially controversial propositions, "184" (so-called Three Strikes Law) and "187" (so-called Illegal Immigrant Legislation) compared to 27.2 percent and 22.2 percent for blacks with white ancestry.

Fourth, self-identified Asians are more likely than any other nonwhite group to share similar political opinions and social class positions with self-identified whites. Despite their similarities, however, there exist sharp differences between whites with Asian ancestors and Asians with white ancestors. While socioeconomic backgrounds are very similar for groups that share Asian ancestry—self-identified Asians and self-identified whites with Asian ancestry (6.48 and 5.45 for income and education among self-identified Asians and 6.61 and 5.38 for whites with Asian ancestry)—self-identified whites with Asian ancestry are less likely than self-identified Asians to support most affirmative action policies (except in education). Thus, respectively 50.0 percent, 61.5 percent, 30.8 percent, and 38.5 percent of whites with Asian ancestry support affirmative action in jury selection, education, employment, and contracting,

TABLE 2.5
Racial Identity, Ancestral Backgrounds, Affirmative Action, Socioeconomic Backgrounds, and Political Views

Race	Affirmative Action (%)				Socioeconomic Backgrounds		Political Views (%)		
	Jury Selection	Education	Employment	Business Contract	Parents'[1] Income	Father's[2] Education	Prop[3] 184	Prop[4] 187	Death[5] Penalty
Self-Identified Race									
1. Whites	60.5%	54.7%	51.0%	46.4%	6.63	6.16	48.6%	28.5%	57.3%
2. Blacks	69.5	93.5	83.9	83.9	5.04	4.72	21.0	11.1	59.2
3. Native Americans	80.0	80.0	80.0	80.0	6.40	5.00	50.0	50.0	40.0
4. Hispanics	80.0	85.5	82.1	66.1	4.97	3.47	49.0	6.6	56.0
5. Asians/Pac. Is.	66.9	54.5	66.4	49.5	6.48	5.45	62.0	30.2	69.6
Ancestral Race:									
1. Whites	62.2	58.6	56.6	48.6	6.53	5.95	48.1	26.9	58.6
2. Blacks	60.4	77.3	69.7	65.2	5.22	4.88	27.6	17.0	61.2
3. Native Americans	69.3	75.5	70.2	58.2	5.82	5.22	39.8	17.3	55.1
4. Hispanics	77.5	79.3	77.3	61.1	5.35	4.19	48.1	11.8	57.3
5. Asians/Pac. Is.	65.9	56.5	65.2	49.5	6.52	5.50	59.0	28.9	67.8
Self-Identified Group with Ancestors of Their Own Race:									
1. Whites	59.4	50.0	48.3	43.1	6.67	6.29	49.1	29.6	59.2
2. Blacks	75.0	100.0[6]	100.0	100.0	5.50	4.75	50.0	0.0	0.0
3. Native Americans	—[7]		—		—		—		—
4. Hispanics	82.8	85.0	80.0	66.3	4.67	3.10	58.8	7.0	50.7
5. Asians/Pac. Is.	65.4	55.0	66.5	51.1	6.51	5.39	60.9	30.2	69.0
Self-Identified Whites with Following Ancestors:									
1. Blacks	38.5	42.1	36.8	31.6	6.26	5.57	42.8	28.5	68.4
2. Native Americans	62.5	61.8	57.4	51.5	6.42	5.89	44.4	20.4	55.5
3. Hispanics	71.4	56.3	50.0	43.8	6.25	5.46	40.0	20.0	50.0
4. Asians/Pac. Is.	50.0	61.5	30.8	38.5	6.61	5.38	28.5	14.2	46.1

TABLE 2.5 (Continued)
Racial Identity, Ancestral Backgrounds, Affirmative Action, Socioeconomic Backgrounds, and Political Views

Race	Affirmative Action (%)				Socioeconomic Backgrounds		Political Views (%)		
	Jury Selection	Education	Employment	Business Contract	Parents'[1] Income	Father's[2] Education	Prop[3] 184	Prop[4] 187	Death[5] Penalty
Self-Identified Blacks with Following Ancestors:									
1. Whites	75.0	93.3	80.0	86.7	5.28	4.28	27.2	22.2	69.2
2. Native Americans	85.8	95.0	85.0	80.0	4.70	4.72	16.6	16.6	55.5
3. Hispanics	100.0	75.0	75.0	75.0	5.75	5.50	0.0	50.0	100.0
4. Asians/Pac. Is.	100.0	66.7	66.7	66.7	6.00	5.33	—	—	66.7
Self-Identified Hispanics with Following Ancestors:									
1. Whites	76.0	87.2	87.2	64.1	5.97	4.76	46.4	11.1	58.8
2. Blacks	80.0	100.0	87.5	75.0	3.42	3.62	12.5	0.0	42.8
3. Native Americans	76.4	88.9	85.2	59.3	4.49	3.36	37.6	0.0	60.0
4. Asians/Pac. Is.	50.0	100.0	100.0	66.7	4.00	5.00	33.3	0.0	100.0

Notes:

1. Parents' annual income is measured in the following scale: (1) less than $5,000; (2) $5,000 to $9,999; (3) $10,000 to $14,999; (4) $15,000 to $24,999; (5) $25,000 to $34,999; (6) $35,000 to $49,999; (7) $50,000 to $74,999; (8) $75,000 to $99,999; and (9) $100,000 or more.

2. The highest level of school for respondents' father's education is measured in the following scale: (1) grade or elementary; (2) some high school; (3) high school diploma; (4) trade, technical, or vocational school; (5) some college; (6) college degree; (7) post college work; and (8) post college-degree.

3. The question is phrased in the following: "Do you favor Proposition 184 (so-called Three strikes legislation)?"

4. The question is phrased in the following: "Do you favor Proposition 187 (so-called Illegal Immigrants legislation)?"

5. The question is phrased in the following: "Do you oppose capital punishment?" The percentage shows those who support capital punishment.

6. Of 30 self-identified blacks, merely 4 indicated that they only have black ancestors.

7. There was no Native American respondents who had only Native American ancestors.

compared with 66.9 percent, 54.5 percent, 66.4 percent, and 49.5 percent for self-identified Asians.

Such conservative views on affirmative action are not reflected in their opinions on racially sensitive legislative bills. For instance, whites with Asian ancestors are most likely to oppose the "three strike" legislation (28.5 percent) and "illegal immigrant" legislation (14.2 percent) than self-identified Asians in general (62.0 percent and 30.2 percent, respectively). The finding shows varied results, in that racially mixed whites with Asian ancestry are more likely to exhibit conservative attitudes towards affirmative action than self-identified Asians, while they are also more likely than self-identified Asians to be liberal on their views on racially sensitive policies, legislative issues, and the death penalty. Compared with negative views held by racially mixed whites with black ancestry on both affirmative action and racially sensitive legislative and legal issues, racially mixed whites with Asian ancestry seem to reveal complex and divergent political and sociolegal opinions, indicating great variations of such opinions and political perceptions even within the group of self-identified whites.

Finally, among all mixed race respondents, Hispanics with black ancestry show the lowest socioeconomic status among all races and racially mixed groups (3.42 and 3.62 for parents' income and father's education). While Hispanics with Native American ancestors exhibit lower educational achievement among their fathers (3.36), their parental annual income is substantially higher than that of Hispanics with black ancestors (4.49). Similarly, with respect to the controversial "illegal immigration" legislation (Proposition 187), whites with Hispanic ancestors and Hispanics with white ancestors showed the lowest support (7.0 percent and 11.1 percent, respectively). However, blacks with Hispanic ancestors show the greatest support for the controversial immigration legislation (50.0 percent). It seems certain that self-identified blacks and nonwhites who share black ancestry remain at the bottom of the social, economic, and political order, and that they are the primary supporters of affirmative action programs including jury selection.

DECONSTRUCTING RACE AND THE IMPORTANCE OF AFFIRMATIVE ACTION PROGRAMS

In deconstructing the government's various conceptions of race and racial classification based on self-identified race and reported ancestral race, empirical analyses shed some critical light into the complex relationship between racially mixed ancestry and self-identified race. And because one's racial identity is closely related with the views on entitlements for social opportunities and legal protections, we need to analyze the relation between racial identity, ancestral race, and individuals' perceptions of the importance of affirmative action policies and programs in education, hiring, contracting, and, for this study, jury selection.

Our empirical analysis has so far produced a number of important and disturbing findings that warrant careful examination and discussion. First, we have shown that the level of people's mixed racial heritage is quite high for all races, suggesting that the past government strategy of utilizing a set of mono-racial census categories may be both problematic and misleading, as a substantial proportion of individuals have more than one ancestral race. While the 2000 census has allowed racially mixed persons to choose more than one race, the extent to which race chosen reflects their true racial heritage, culture, ethnicity, religion, or social customs remains unknown. Race is still a malleable concept in other words and may be subject to intentional manipulation and incidental alteration. This depends on one's knowledge of ancestral race and background, the actual extent of the level of mixed racial heritage, the ability to pass as members of other racial groups, and the desirability to be members of chosen races based on societal preferences, social privileges, and the opportunity to acquire wealth and property for certain racial groups in given situations and circumstances.[17]

As an example of the arbitrariness of the construct of racial identity, a substantial proportion of individuals are "passing" as members of the dominant racial group. While the term, passing, may contain negative connotations and meanings, including deceptions, cheating, dishonesty, or deviousness, we do not imply that individuals who engage in passing are committing such unethical and dishonest acts. Rather, passing or "racial passing," a distinct form of racial transformation and personification (similar to gender or sexuality considerations), may be the expression and embodiment of individuals' constant struggles, hardship, and desperate attempts to gain their rights by establishing their own racial identity in our inequitable social setting. Racial passing is also the manifestation of racial disengagement from the rule of hypodescent—an individual's implosive attempt to assert identity with a preexisting set of government- and society-imposed racial categories. By using the term, passing, then, we do not place unethical blame on individuals who engage in passing in order to transform their racial identity.

Our analysis suggests that passing may take on the following two distinct forms that require reclassification of their status. First, a large proportion of individuals who share black and other minority ancestral races now identify themselves as white. Though the one-drop rule might require that those with black and other minority ancestral races be classified as members of their respective minority race, a large proportion of individuals with nonwhite ancestry have openly chosen white as their racial identity. Indeed, 5.5 percent of self-identified whites had black ancestry, and they selected white, not black, as their racial identity (see table 2.5). Similarly, though approximately one of five white respondents (19.8 percent) indicated that they had Native American ancestry, they did not identify as Native American.

The arbitrariness of the one-drop rule finds the majority of individuals who share black ancestry refusing to identify as black (only 45.5 percent became self-identified blacks), with 28.8 percent of them in fact declaring themselves as white and 12.1 percent identifying as Hispanic. Those findings indicate the very limited predictive powers of the one-drop logic in determining and identifying individuals' race on the basis of multiracial heritage. With respect to mixed racial heritage and racial identity, racial "emigration" or exodus is the greatest among Native American descendants, of which almost all of them refuse to identify as Native American (merely 3.7 percent of those with Native American ancestry identify as Native American). Native Americans are closely followed by black descendants, of which 54.5 percent did not identity as black, changed their racial identity, and became "non-black."

The second type of the passing takes place when individuals identify as white without white ancestry. In other words, self-identified race does not necessarily reflect or predict one's actual ancestral race, suggesting that racial identity does not always reflect the racial ancestry of his or her chosen race. Blacks seem to be the only "error free" race in which all self-identified blacks indicated their black ancestral roots.

The discrepancy of racial ancestry and racial identity may show the extent to which individuals are given certain degrees of freedom to transform their old racial identity and "inhabit" a newly acquired race. Racial mobility and the fluid nature of racial definitions may be responsible for differing patterns of racial identity among groups with different ancestries; and such racial self-description may take place at both individual and structural levels. At an individual level, for instance, individuals may exhibit the racial identity of their choice with or without full knowledge of their ancestral history. At a structural level, government and legal bodies continue to juggle various definitions of race and racial groups, and try to clarify the boundaries within which individuals can choose and determine their own identity among different racial options. Further, since there is no provision for verification of one's race and ancestral backgrounds, many people are in fact "passing" as members of the dominant racial group for social, legal, and economic reasons, supporting the notion that race is a social fabrication and political construction.

Our analysis substantiates the impact of one's racial identity and identity of ancestral race on federal affirmative action programs, racially sensitive legislative measures, and the administration of justice.[18] As the following opinions nonetheless show, there are sharply differing views on affirmative action by the two distinct groups of "passers," or those who inhabit a newly acquired race: (1) self-identified whites with actual black ancestry, and (2) self-identified whites without white ancestry.

The most negative views and opposing opinions against race-conscious affirmative action are frequently expressed by self-identified whites who, in fact, had black ancestral roots. One self-identified white female student with black ancestry explained that:

Affirmative action is still preferential treatment, although the original intentions for the program were noble. However, American society is becoming more and more segregated. Racial resentment could be toned down if every race, Black, White, Red, Yellow, Brown, if every person could know in the heart that their achievements were a result of hard work, merit, and perseverance. As far as it [preferential treatment] being payback for the past wrongs, that's B.S. . . . I agree with early outreach programs to recruit and encourage minorities (diversity *is* a good thing!). But when it comes to the actual admissions, hiring, etc., race and sex shouldn't be a factor. The only message being sent is very bad and very wrong: that minorities and women can't succeed without people bending over backwards for them.[19]

Another male student with black ancestry also said that "[m]inorities are given an unfair and undeserved advantage that whites are generally denied. The American idea of 'Equal Opportunity' is destroyed." Still another male student expressed negative views on affirmative action: "I feel no one benefits from affirmative action, but all, whether blatantly or not, suffer from its side effects. There need to be changes if it is going to work. If no changes are made, then affirmative action should be dissolved." One female student also pointed out affirmative action's negative effects: "I am against it [affirmative action] because race has nothing to do with potential. Affirmative action is not working anymore. It's only hurting people," a view that was echoed by another female student who stated: "I am against it [affirmative action] because I don't think it really helps many people. It causes more discrimination."

Despite the strong disapproval of affirmative action programs by the white respondents with black ancestry, another white male expressed an ambivalent view on the use of race in affirmative action programs, suggesting:

I am not for or against affirmative action. I feel that all aspects of the individual needs to be considered in picking people for a job or [for] admission to a college campus, regardless of race, gender, or religion. If a black is more qualified than a white, hire the black person, and vice versa.[20]

Another white male person with the black ancestry, however, suggested a different view on affirmative action, stating:

I am for affirmative action because it is the only thing of its kind. In every dispute there must be a loser. White people have been on top for far too long and need to take a step down to the loser. I who appear white and am accepted as white feel that I am obligated to step down. I am perfectly willing to be the loser.[21]

On the other hand, self-identified whites, without white ancestors, are more likely than racially mixed whites with black ancestry to support and endorse race-conscious affirmative action programs. Among all respondents in our study, one eighteen-year-old white student who identified as white, but indicated that her ancestry included only Native Americans and Hispanics also showed the strongest support for affirmative action programs. Not only did she support affirmative action in jury selection, education, hiring, and contracting based on racial considerations, but she also ascertained her strong support of affirmative policies based on class, gender, and disability considerations.[22] Another eighteen-year-old female student, who identified as white, but indicated exclusive Asian and Pacific Islanders and other race as her ancestry, said:

> I am for affirmative action because those who want a chance for opportunities can use any help they can. One good step can lead to greater achievements for minorities, they just need to get one foot through the door. The positive effect it gives a minority [person] can lead to positive change for the future.[23]

Still another self-identified white student, whose ancestry included Native American and other race, supported race-based affirmative mechanisms to eliminate racial inequality:

> I am in favor of affirmative action because I believe that measures need to be taken in order to offer somewhat equal opportunity to those that lack it. I say "somewhat" because I believe affirmative action is not the only answer to the lack of diversity within universities, workplaces, etc. I am not sure if any legislative measures can change or alter the racism that our country is built upon. But it is a step in the right direction.[24]

Student responses suggest that self-identified whites without white ancestry are more likely to endorse race-conscious affirmative action in jury selection, education, employment, and business. On the other hand, self-identified whites with black ancestry are more likely to be critical of preferential treatment given to racial minorities and remain skeptical of the consequences of positive outcomes of such racially unfair policies and programs. While race-conscious affirmative action is designed to challenge and undermine the social, legal, and racial privilege of whiteness, whites with black ancestry are more likely than whites without white ancestry to express negative views towards race-based remedies and policies.

Despite the strong belief in the pervasiveness of the one-drop rule in the United States, our findings show that the rule of hypodescent fails to neatly classify racial minorities, especially those with black and Native American ancestry. Currently the federal government shows strong interests in classifying as few persons as Native Americans as possible, largely due to the controversy of entitlements for mixed-race individuals of Native American descent. The Bureau of Indian Affairs only recognizes individuals as Native American if they can demonstrate one-quarter or more Native American ancestry, as well as a tribal membership and affiliation (Joe 1991, 149–151).[25] Many peoples considered to be Native Americans by their tribes are thus classified as white by the federal government (Zack 1995, fn31, xv, xvi).[26] Corroborating this view of classification, a very small number of individuals with Native American ancestry actually identified themselves as Native American (3.7 percent), the majority identifying as white (50.4 percent).

The arbitrariness of racial identity is also found among racially mixed Asians. In fact, Asian Americans are more likely than other racial groups to seek assimilation into mainstream white society, identifying with and pursuing acceptance by whites, even if whites as a group may not identify with or accept them. The higher rate of interracial marriages between Asians and whites than between other races may suggest this trend (Crispell 1993). Our research also substantiates that among all racial groups, the largest proportion of racially mixed Asians have white ancestors (7.8 percent). When interracial couples were asked to identify the race of their children, Asian and white couples were much more likely than other interracial parents to declare their children as white rather than as the other race (Saito 1993, 65). According to the national census, only 35 percent of Asian and white children were listed as Asian, 56 percent of Native American and white children were listed as Native American, and 66 percent of children with one African American and one white parent were listed as African American.[27]

As indicated previously, the assumption that the rule of hypodescent can or will adequately reclassify mixed-race individuals is suspect. For people of mixed race, moreover, there is no scientific test to determine their racial identity based on either the racial makeup of particular blood samples or the percentage of a particular kind of "racialized blood" that a person has in his or her veins. In fact, blood has the same color regardless of one's race. Racial identity, then, quickly reveals itself to be a metaphor, essentialized through the sign and the notion of ancestry and historical backgrounds—most likely resorting to anecdotal, ancestral testimony as an objective test and verifications of one's component race.

With respect to white identity and the legal and social terminology of white as a racial group, white as a racial identity is as much a social construct and racial fabrication as that of any other minority race. Currently, the governmental definition of white includes individuals of European origin, as well as Middle Eastern and North African origins—though a person of the latter two origins were not initially considered as part of the "white" race and were excluded from the legal definition of white in earlier governmental statistics. It was not until 1909 that the Supreme Court first declared Armenians as members of the white race, demonstrating the sociohistorical foundation of racial membership and the fluid nature of racial definitions (*In reHalladjian et al.* 17 F. 834, 1090). Since then, other Middle Easterners and Northern Africans have been added and subsumed under membership of the white race, including Syrians and other "Arabians" such as Iraqis, Iranians, Israelis, Egyptians, and Moroccans (see generally Haney-Lopez, 1996).

The singular usage of the term, "white" or "a white person" may thus be problematic, because the term obscures the significance of the social and historical derivations of race and racial classification. Similarly, the term represents an ill-defined social, cultural, and historical group because, undoubtedly, it will be subject to further fabrication, expansion, and manipulation in the future. Clearly, white identity is not a product of biology or genetic science, but of social history, reified and justified through legal declarations, adjustments, and reclassifications.

Thematically, Mexican was once considered as a racial group in the 1930 census, but the following 1940 census included Mexicans as part of the category white (see table 2.1). While Mexicans generally are of mixed racial heritage such as Spanish and indigenous Americans, the United States national census gave legal "passing" to Mexicans, claiming or taking "advantages" of their Spanish or Hispanic heritage. The 1960's social revolution and the era of racial upheavals in the United States led Mexican Americans to self-realization as a distinct racial identity, giving birth to strong race consciousness among a large number of Mexican Americans who began to declare themselves Chicanos and Chicanas. It then became their new self-attributed racial and social identity (Fuenfrios 1993). It is ironic, however, that the national census has continuously failed to recognize Chicanos/Chicanas, and to give this self-description the legal status of a distinct racial group—warranting governmental recognition in the census category of race. In fact, the 2000 census only uses the term, "Latino," besides Hispanic, which would be semantically and culturally the closest identity to the Chicano/Chicana category. Yet, the national census still treated the description "Latino" as an ethnic, not a racial, group (see table 2.1 and the last column).

In order to understand how racial identity is formed and constructed in America, one legal scholar suggests that social race and its identity depends on the following three key components: (1) "chance," which refers to morphology and ancestry or other factors that are not subject to human will or determined effort; (2) "context" of a contemporary social setting, including racially skewed social services, economic inequality, and maldistributed resources; and (3) "choice," referring to the quotidian decisions of life in which choice becomes a crucial ingredient in the designated fabrication of races in the context of racial passing, suggesting that the ability of individuals to change race exemplifies the chosen nature of race (Haney-Lopes 1994, 39–50).

While the construction of racial identity may be contingent on chance, context, and choice, the phrenological appearance of race still remains visually powerful, physically obvious, and socially explicit. Even when we are in the ideal setting of a classroom, teachers and students are consistently and unconsciously searching for some racially coded characteristics or unique physical features and attributes that may provide some clues to their race and background.

While we are not intentionally trying to sort out or discriminate against one another on the basis of race and racial backgrounds, our responses nevertheless may take on racial meanings. Thus, the absence of any biological or genetic basis to race does not always lead to the conclusion that race is wholly a hallucination, a phantasm, or the product of simple imagination. Racial designation has its social and historical roots and continuously perpetuates and reproduces its strengths in the realms of social beliefs. While various physiological characteristics and biological appearances occur by chance, determining the allocation of resources by socially designated racial categories is a social invention and the brainchild of humankind.

Another source of confusion about race is illustrated by the treatment of Hispanics and how race as a governmental definition is created and defined. As noted earlier, race can be defined in terms of a number of different criteria, such as the one-drop rule, skin colors, wealth, status, national origins, and culture. The Scots are considered as a distinct race different from the English because of national origin. Similarly, the Hispanic classification in the United States census was devised on the basis of national origin in which individuals with Spanish heritage are classified as Hispanic regardless of race. A major problem of the scheme of racial classification arises when the majority of Hispanics identify as white, while Hispanics as a racial group are considered and legally treated as a racial minority. Furthermore, although racial categories include Hispanic along with other governmentally defined racial groups such as whites, blacks, Native American, and Asian, self-identified whites with Hispanic backgrounds can still claim to be Hispanic, because racial categories continue to fail to differentiate national origin from the definition of race based on physical characteristics or cultural notions.

The deconstruction of race and racial identity suggests that race, no matter how the government has tried to classify and label individuals based on a limited set of racial categories, is still a social construction and political fabrication and is subject to intentional manipulation.[28] For such racial categories generate social privileges and legally empower some, continuously determining the allocation of social resources and legal protections. The designation of race, then, represents an important means of awarding social securities and legal empowerment in generating and perpetuating social inequality and institutional or personal discrimination. The programmatic operation of affirmative action, that specifically challenges the continuing empowerment of race and racial privilege, may be one of a few effective social policies and legal programs that directly question and undermine the valued trait of whiteness and the privileged proprieties accompanying membership in the white race. For this reason alone, progressive court action and legislative initiatives in proposing and implementation of race-specific affirmative action in jury selection must not be postponed.

CONCLUSIONS

Race and racial identities may superficially appear to reflect and represent differences among people on the basis of outward appearances, supposed traits, traditions, habits, and beliefs, effectively dividing populations into arbitrary, yet historically evolved and governmentally imposed, racial categories. By focusing a critical lens on these categories—by examining social norms, assumptions, and customs about thinking and reasoning about race—this chapter has attempted to break down and deconstruct the notion of races as immutable categories.

Government-constructed racial categories offered an obvious target of our critical inquiry, and we have substantiated the frail reliability and insubstantial validity of the racial classification scheme and racial categories specified in Directive No. 15 and its revision. Another critical lens was focused on the belief that blood mixtures determine one's race. For regardless of the drops of racial blood running through the human vein, it is the social construction of race that determines access to the cornucopia of society's resources, civil freedom, and legal rights. The hypodescent rule is, then, a social categorization of race—not a biological or genetic one.

How one challenges the existing allocation of society's resources and civil and legal rights begins with social customs that have secured certain groups, classes, castes, and racial members at the expense of others. Once these violations of equity have been unearthed, it is possible to invest ourselves with the racial identities of choice, in order to make changes in the social domain.

This is the focal point for empirically deconstructing social race by examining government-constructed racial categories, self-identified race, and self-reported ancestry, analyzing how racially mixed ancestry affects one's self-identified race. We have argued that the measurements of race as empirical standards and instruments suffer from lack of internal consistency, the failure to classify people of mixed race, the lack of any known empirical method to verify one's self-reported racial identity, and the failure to detect the "passer." Though we do not present a moral assessment or social judgment on individuals who "pass" as members of other races, we suggest that the arbitrary classification of mixed-race persons may be problematic because the reclassification methods used by governmental agencies were adopted as administratively expedient, without examining the appropriateness of classifying mixed raced individuals in mono-racial categories based on the assumed given criteria.

While the revision to Directive No. 15 allows one to claim mixed racial heritage and multiple racial ancestry, identified racial heritage does not necessarily reflect one's knowledge of true ancestral backgrounds or even the desired racial group to which one wishes to be classified. As we have demonstrated, the reclassifying scheme does not necessarily reassign mixed race individuals into the most appropriate mono-racial category.

Thus, our analysis leads to a single conclusion regarding race, racial classification, and racial definitions: Race is not an empirically reliable or valid concept and is subject to intentional manipulations and individual fabrications. Current race and racial classifications victimize those who are "immobile" or "trapped" in assigned non-white racial categories due to their supposed traits, physical appearance, bodily characteristics, or specific cultural backgrounds, factors that especially impact racial minority groups. Racially mixed individuals who appear to be white, and may be treated and accepted as white socially and politically, are able at will to change their racial identity and "pass" as members of the racial majority. The majority of Hispanics are also given "statutory passing" rights; and approximately half of Hispanics, according to the 1990 and 2000 censuses, identified as white. But those who, because of assorted traits or characteristics, are unable to transform their racial "status" from racial minority to racial majority, are victimized and kept from attaining proportional access to social opportunities and legal privileges.

If our society is genuinely committed to correct and eliminate past and present discrimination, we must also be willing to accept the role that race and racial classification play in establishing, maintaining, and perpetuating individual racism and institutionalized racial inequality. As race dominates personal lives and impacts social and economic prospects, all racial groups must be prepared to critically examine their own racial self-image and identity. For it is not only minority groups who find their identities mediated and empowered by race. White identity is just as much a racial construction and social fabrication as the identity of racial minorities.

Given the importance of one's racial identity and ancestral race in the social designation and construction of race, the historical background and the potential application of affirmative juries are critically examined in the next chapter. As we will see, there are three sets of race-conscious affirmative action programs affecting the legal realm, allowing us to judge how to facilitate and secure racially mixed juries and eliminate racial inequality in jury selection.

Chapter 3

RACIALLY MIXED JURIES
AND AFFIRMATIVE ACTION

During the 1990s and early 2000s, some of the most serious and most controversial social assumptions and suppositions revolved around the constitutional and civil status of "races" and affirmative action programs. In the course of the ongoing battle, at least three major lines of thought emerged.

First were disagreements over the propriety of some forms of race-conscious remedies and the need for affirmative action programs in certain social and political settings. Controversial narratives emerged from a heated debate about effective policy making on the foundation of past racial discrimination, thus embracing a spirit of favoring equality for minorities based on the equal protection clause of the U.S. Constitution. The 1991 appointment of Clarence Thomas to the Supreme Court was said to illustrate that he was nominated solely because of his race to replace Justice Thurgood Marshall, the first African American judge on the Court who had been an effective civil rights attorney. Though Justice Thomas has held a political posture that conflicts with Marshall's and has remained a strong opponent of affirmative action, President George H. W. Bush openly acknowledged the symbolic value and political benefit of specifically selecting an African-American candidate for the highest court (Ryoko 1991).

President Clinton also followed a similar political scenario—that his Attorney General would be a woman, appointing Janet Reno after an exclusive panel of four female candidates was reviewed for the position (Berke 1993; Lauter 1993; Lewis 1993).[1] The political appointments of Thomas and Reno then led to decisions that influenced affirmative action policies, going both for and against the currents of conservative courts in many state and federal districts that have often ruled against many forms of race-conscious affirmative action programs. Public acceptance of some forms of affirmative action was also only sometimes reaffirmed by the political action of the executive branch of government, contrary to the judicial pronouncement by the Supreme Court, which more or less denounced the merit of affirmative action programs.[2]

Second, there was strong general consensus that the vision of individual equal opportunity—which may be considered by some to be hostile to the spirit of affirmative action—is deeply embedded in the American ethos. To explain the differences between opportunity and the merit, we need to look to the underlying concept of affirmative action that is embraced by the provision of the equal protection clause in the Fourteenth Amendment, which states: "No state shall . . . deny to any person within its jurisdiction the equal protection of the laws." When the Fourteenth Amendment was drafted and passed by the Reconstruction Congress in 1868, the primary intention of the doctrine was to prohibit the enforcement of the "Black Codes," laws that denied freed slaves and other African Americans the same rights granted to the white majority. It was not designed to provide the modern conception of special affirmative assistance to African Americans or other minority members to offset or remedy various measures of past discrimination (Brest 1987, 282; Klarman 1991, 228). However, the wording of the constitutional amendment was color-blind; and the intention of the Congress drafting the amendment was not based on specific race-conscious principles. This allowed the Reconstruction era Supreme Court to interpret the Constitution, incorporating the dramatic changes in the post-Civil War social settings, with its altered race relations and institutional arrangements.

Third, the debate on affirmative action and preferential treatment of racial minorities has so far been limited to non-juridical areas such as employment, contracting, and college admission. Although affirmative action in jury selection and efforts to attain racially diverse juries are as important as affirmative action policies in other fields, the possibility for the adoption of affirmative juries creating racially mixed tribunals have so far escaped public attention.

In this chapter, we argue that mandatory affirmative juries hold historical precedent and were once used extensively in both England and the United States, suggesting that the Supreme Court's recent emphasis on the color-blind principle is a relatively new phenomenon. The first section that follows examines the historical background of affirmative action in jury selection, offering some critical comparisons for the possible mandatory application of affirmative action in criminal jury proceedings. Here we examine three different types of racially mixed juries—the jury "de medietate linguae," the Hennepin jury model, and the social science jury model.

The next and final sections of this chapter examine the question of whether an affirmative, racialized mechanism to secure racially mixed juries creates the appearance of justice and fairness in criminal jury proceedings, legitimizing its use. Thus, focus is placed on the analysis of the public's perception and evaluation of the three types of mixed jury models, examining how various segments of the general public view the applicability and feasibility of race-conscious affirmative action in jury selection. Critical analysis is also placed on whether or not the mandatory affirmative mechanism to secure racially representative juries is essential to both the appearance and substance of fairness in criminal jury proceedings. And the final question we address is whether or not efforts to secure maximum public confidence in selecting a racially balanced jury are a compelling social, legal, and governmental interest.

AFFIRMATIVE ACTION IN JURY SELECTION

In August 1992, in Ramsey County, Minnesota, Judge Lawrence Cohen held that a Hispanic defendant could not be tried from a jury pool of 113 potential jurors that included only one Hispanic.[3] As only 2.2 percent of county residents were Hispanic according to the 1990 census, in an effort to increase the chance for a racially mixed jury to try the Hispanic defendant, Judge Cohen and the attorneys agreed to supplement the jury pool with the names of two more Hispanic jurors, who were already scheduled to appear at the courthouse the following week.

In another case, in Erie County, Pennsylvania, African American church leaders were requested to submit the names and addresses of their adult congregation for the local court's master list of potential jurors. The submission of names added 251 African American parishioners, though only seventy-three of them were registered voters and originally included in the master list. The additional list of parishioners thus substantially enhanced African American participation in jury panels (Domitrovich 1994, 99).

In Pennsylvania, the issue of minority underrepresentation on juries has also been addressed by the state legislature and community action groups. The state general assembly proposed legislation to require minimum minority compositions of jury pools when a defendant comes from a minority race.[4] Citizens Against Racism, a non-profit community organization, is also searching for solutions to rectify African American underrepresentation on criminal juries in the region (McKinnery 1993).

A solution has yet to be implemented on a broad geographic scale. While many courts have begun to experiment with race-conscious jury selection methods to increase minority participation, the Supreme Court's recent jury selection decisions suggest that the law currently does not provide any affirmative mechanism for ensuring that racial minorities are included as jury members, even in those cases that involve unmistakable elements of racism. In highly publicized trials such as the Rodney King and Reginald Denny beating cases in Los Angeles, and the Lorenzo case in Miami, there were no procedural mechanisms to guarantee racially mixed juries or ensure the inclusion of racial minorities in criminal juries. As noted earlier, a number of legal and extra-legal factors, such as discriminatory jury selection procedures, socioeconomic barriers and judicial discrimination, create racially disproportionate and unrepresentative juries. Most jury venires simply do not fairly reflect the percentage of minority populations in the local community, thereby exacerbating problems of underrepresentation by minority jurors (Fukurai, Butler, and Krooth 1993; King 1993a, 719).

Recognition of the importance of racially mixed juries did not begin with the Rodney King beating case, or even with the civil rights revolution of the 1960s. The emergence of heterogeneous juries even predates the American experience of the jury trial. As early as the twelfth century, English law recognized the use of the jury of the split tongue, called the "jury de medietate linguae," in both civil and criminal cases involving minority members, including Jews, Italians, Germans, and other foreigners engaged in commerce and finance. This practice of mixed juries, with half English natives and half aliens, was essential because of the danger that inhered in allowing members of essential minority communities to be tried entirely by English jurors. This jury form endured throughout almost seven hundred years until it was finally repealed in 1870 (Ramirez 1994). During this entire period, the mandated mixed jury remained half for natives and half for Jews or alien minorities, suggesting that the United States Supreme Court's "color-blindness" in the area of jury selection and jury trials is a relatively recent concept.

Another example of affirmative action as a jury selection measure has been proposed and implemented in Hennepin County, Minnesota, where the jury's racial representativeness is designed to reflect the respective proportions of both majority and minority groups in the general population. Similar affirmative action measures are also currently under consideration or have already been established in other jurisdictions. In DeKalb County, Georgia, eligible jurors are divided into thirty-six classified groups, and jury commissioners rely on computer selection to obtain proportional representation of various demographic groups for composing jury venires. The Arizona Bar Committee has proposed juror classifications by race to obtain proportional jury representation. Such race-conscious selection procedures are only used to ensure proportional jury representation at jury panel or venire stages of jury selection, however, not in the actual jury box selected or assembled. But the Hennepin model of racial quotas remains unique, as it sets proportional racial representation in the composition of the jury itself.

Still another jury quota system has been suggested by social scientists. Their jury research indicates that, without a minority of at least three jurors, group pressures by the majority may be too overwhelming for the minority to maintain the independence of their opinion and judgment. These experts argue that the affirmative mechanism that ensures both a racially heterogeneous jury and viable and meaningful jury deliberation requires at least three minority jurors to be included in the twelve-member jury. The absolute number of at least three minority jurors in the jury room environment, they argue, ensures that there will be ample opportunities for both articulation and discussion of the independent judgment by minority jurors during the jury deliberation process.

It is important to reiterate that in the United States, both the conception and racial components of the jury structure are the sociopolitical and legal expression of wider, underlying conflicts by class, race, and gender. The jury as a potential democratic forum within the frame of this larger political and social demographic system is clearly on the cutting edge in the pursuit of essential fairness, equity, and racial justice. Seeming narrow debates on jury composition thus reflect the wider social and racial struggle to dominate or emancipate, for inequality or equitability, the ongoing conflict leading to alternative ways to structure a body of peers in our time, especially by racial makeup. Towards such ends, the following elaboration of three jury models incorporates affirmative jury selection mechanisms to increase jury participation by racial minorities: (1) the jury de medietate linguae (or so-called party or split jury), in which half of the jurors come from the majority population and the other half from minority groups; (2) the Hennepin jury model, in which the extent of juries' racial representativeness reflects the respective proportion of both majority and minority groups in the general population; and (3) the social science model of jury representation, in which the jury must have at least three minority jurors to successfully resist the group pressure of the majority in the jury decision-making process.

THE JURY "DE MEDIETATE LINGUAE" MODEL

The concept of "peers" has changed over the last eight hundred years. The ancient jury de medietate linguae made its historical appearance as a narrowly defined conception of equity, with the judging group composed of representatives of an accused's peers. For the jury de medietate linguae, the peers are in most cases defined in terms of the defendant's own social, racial, and national identity.

The concept of the jury de medietate linguae originated in the treatment of Jews in twelfth-century England (Constable 1994). The term literally means jury of the "half tongue" as the jury selection method applied to people who were considered alien or foreign and spoke different languages. The English viewed the Jews as aliens in race, religion, and culture; and considerable animosity existed against the Jews because they were known as the anti-Christ and "Christ-killers" (Quinley and Glock 1972, 94–109), and because "they were darker-skinned and spoke a mysterious and foreign language" (Ramirez 1994, 783).

In 1090, Emperor Henry IV had given the Jews a charter to settle in Worms. But six years later, in 1096, the First Crusade spread to the Rhineland, leading to the forced conversion and massacre of Jews throughout the area and the expropriation of their wealth and positions (Johnson 1987, 205, 207–08). Nonetheless, William the Conqueror initially followed a different tact—importing Jews to England from Rouen, France, where they had been compelled to act as financial agents for the crown. Once arrived in England, the Jews then took up residence in the larger towns that were also centers of royal administration. Two hundred years later in thirteenth-century England, in an attempt to convert Jews to Christianity, the Crown then required Jews to reside in the *Domus conservarum,* assigning them the role of tax collectors as part of the government's strategies to integrate Jews into Christian society (Stacey 1992). Repeatedly accused of apostasy, they continued to live in England only by virtue of the king's efforts to secure them from religious accusers, who claimed the Jews killed Christian children and drank their blood.[5]

The Jews were considered a form of property, too. In his reign, Henry III had pawned the English Jews for a loan of five thousand silver marks to his brother, Richard of Cornwall. Richard, in turn, had secured his chattel interest by intervening to save seventy-one Jews after others had been executed on the vague suspicion of complicity in a ritual murder of an eight-year-old Christian child in 1255. The Jews were accused of having fattened-up the "little saint" on "milk and other childish nourishment" before crucifying him and gorging on his blood. Christian holidays, especially Easter, were thus times for Jews to hide from pogroms often triggered by the Easter sermon vilifying Jews as Christ-killers (Davis 1993, 121).

Here and elsewhere, a deeper logic prevailed, for the emergence of the already unpopular Jews as moneylenders in the twelfth and early thirteenth century only added to animosity towards them. As Christian debtors could not or would not repay their debts, they seized upon the unpopularity of the Jews as a convenient means of extricating themselves from their predicament. A riot or massacre might fortuitously destroy the records of the transaction, thereby canceling the debtors' obligation and precluding the King, as owner of the Jews, from claiming retribution (McCall 1979, 281).

Caught between scheming debtors and the King, the Jews relied on the Crown for protection. And in the throes of mass riots and violence in 1190 directed against wealthy and influential Jews who were clearly the King's property, King Richard I enacted a charter on April 10, 1201, giving Jews the right to the jury de medietate linguae—a half-Jewish jury (Wishman 1986, p.31).[6] Thereby was the jury de medietate linguae granted to Jews to protect the Crown's property interest in Jews and their effects (Massaro 1986, 550, n238).[7] Though England subsequently banished all Jews in 1290, foreign merchants from Italy and Germany soon became the King's financial agents replacing the Jews; and the newcomers were given the privilege of a trial de medietate linguae—a trial by a jury composed of half of their own countrymen and the other half with Englishmen qualified to serve as jurors.[8]

While the extension of trial by juries de medietate linguae to Jews and later alien merchants served to prevent diminution of the King's resources, the jury provided substantive fairness and protection against unfair verdicts derived from prejudice against ethnic minorities in England. Even after the expulsion of the Jews, the mixed jury privilege provided foreign merchants a perception of substantial fairness and equity in disputes involving aliens. The international composition of the jury was intended to insure foreign merchants a fair trial without the possibility of local prejudice. These courts applied law as they perceived it, almost regardless to the source of law, in order to achieve transnational commercial benefits and fairness.

> [T]he [Court's Royal] Chancellor in 1475 said: This suit is brought by an alien merchant who has come to conduct his case here; and he ought not to be held to sue according to the law of the land, to await trial by twelve men and other solemnities of the law of the land, but ought to sue here, and it ought to be

determined according to the law of nature in the chancery, and he ought to be able to sue there from hour to hour and day to day for the speed of merchants. . . . And he said besides the merchants, etc., [they] shall not be bound by our statutes where statutes introduce new law, unless they are declaratory of ancient law, that is to say nature, etc. . . . but that will be according to the law of nature which is called by some the law merchant, which is universal law throughout the world (Potter 1958, 188).

The jury de medietate linguae was not limited to the royal courts, Parliament articulating the principle of the jury de medietate linguae in a 1354 enactment:

And that in all Manner of Inquests and Proofs which be to be taken or made amongst Aliens and Denizens, be they Merchants or other, as well before the Mayor of the Staple as before any other Justices or Ministers, although the King be Party, the one half of the Inquest or Proof shall be Denizens, and other half of Aliens, if so many Aliens be in the Town or Place where such Inquest or Proof is to be taken (Statute of 28 Edw. 3, ch. 13 [1354]).

An inquest to the staple court "was to consist wholly of aliens when both parties to the suit were aliens; wholly of denizens when both parties are denizens; and half of aliens and half of denizens when one party was an alien and the other a denizen" (Gross 1908, xxvii).

The de medietate concept had wider applications, too. When, for instance, an English university scholar was indicted for treason, felony, or mayhem, the vice-chancellor of the university could claim jurisdiction, and the resulting trial was before the high steward and a jury formed de medietate—half from a panel of eighteen freeholders returned by the sheriff and half from a panel of eighteen matriculated laymen returned by the beadles of the university (Oldham 1983). Similarly under a *writ of jure patronatus* concerning church patronage, the dispute could be tried by the bishop or by a specially appointed commission, before a jury of six clergymen and six laymen of the neighborhood (Oldham 1983, 168–169).

The right of juries de medietate linguae in England endured until 1870, when Parliament passed the Naturalization Act, which permitted aliens to serve on juries and to acquire, hold, and dispose of property in the same manner as an England-born citizen, eliminating the need for the mixed jury privilege (Ramirez 1994).

Drawing on English tradition, the American colonies and courts also experimented with the use of juries de medietate linguae after English settlers developed their sense of equity, justice, and laws. At various times between 1671 and 1911, a number of states including Kentucky, Maryland, Massachusetts, Pennsylvania, New York, Virginia, and South Carolina each provided for juries de medietate linguae. As early as 1674, the courts in the Plymouth colony used mixed juries composed of half Native Americans and half colonists.[9] In 1675, when the Plymouth court tried three Native Indians allied with King Philip and accused of murdering an Indian named John Sassamon, the jury of Englishmen and six Indians jointly adjudicated the case, sentencing the defendants to death (Kawashima 1986, 131; Ramirez 1994). The mixed jury was used in the early colonies as a way to ensure substantive fairness, enhance the legitimacy of jury verdicts, and prevent native upheaval. "[The mixed jury] was important to the colonists as the natives' perception of unfairness may have triggered bloody unrest or, at least, social tension," one jury study notes (Ramirez 1994, 790).

Since independence and the passage of the Bill of Rights in 1789, the United States Supreme Court has discussed the right to a jury de medietate linguae only once, in *United States v. Wood* (1936), in dictum and without analyses, declaring that:

> the ancient rule under which an alien might have a trial by jury de medietate linguae, 'one half denizens and the other aliens'—in order to insure impartiality—no longer obtains.[10]

At the state court level, possible applications of juries de medietate linguae have also been reviewed and discussed. The Massachusetts Supreme Court in 1986 examined the applicability of the jury de medietate linguae, having to compare the denizen with the noncitizen alien.[11] Article 12 of the Massachusetts Declaration of Rights drawn from the Magna Charta, c. 39, entitles denizen defendants to explicit rights, namely, "no freeman shall be taken or imprisoned, or be *disseized* of his freehold, or liberties, or free customs, or be outlawed or exiled, or other wise destroyed; nor will we not pass upon him, nor condemn him, but by lawful judgment of his peers, or by the law of the land." The defendants in this case argued that Article 12 calling for "lawful judgment of peers" afforded them the right to a trial by jury de medietate linguae, contending that the statutory requirements of a jury composed by citizenship and command of English were unconstitutional.[12]

The court, however, held that the right to the jury de medietate linguae was not of constitutional magnitude in this case, and that the requirement that jurors speak and understand English and be United States citizens withstood constitutional challenges raised under the Sixth Amendment and the Constitution's equal protection clause.[13]

Yet, neither the United States Supreme Court nor the Massachusetts court fully explored the roots of the jury de medietate linguae in English common law or statutory history; nor did they discuss the wisdom or practicality of the mixed jury as a jury of peers. Thus, the debate on the jury de medietate linguae ceased, and the mandatory mixed jury disappeared from application under American law.

It is important to note that the use of the split jury was not only found in northeastern America, but it was also extensively used in other British colonies as well. When the criminal case involved European or American defendants, the Barbados court, for instance, allowed a racially mixed tribunal that included up to six European or American jurors in the twelve-member jury. The Nigerian courts also relied on the trial de medietate in criminal cases with non-native defendants. The racially mixed jury in the Gold Coast and North Borneo similarly permitted the majority participation of non-native jurors in criminal cases involving non-native defendants (Ramirez 1994). As recent as the early 1970s, petit and grand juries in Okinawa were also made up of both Americans and Japanese-Okinawans to adjudicate both civil and criminal matters. Racially mixed juries were considered to be an important element of increased public awareness and respect in the administration of justice in Okinawa (JFBA 1992).

In our time, the equitability of a mandatory balanced jury must not be ignored. The essential feature of the de medietate linguae model is that, regardless of the composition of aliens or minority groups in the general population, the composition of the mixed jury is considered to be fixed: Half of the jury should come from the majority and the other half from the minority group. Similarly, the fixed measure of the jury's composition is derived from an acknowledgment that prejudice has historically existed against the minority group, and an ordinary jury composition using the traditional method of selection would not necessarily produce a fair result (Constable 1994). Thus, the fixed allocation of jury seats is viewed as an essential feature of the jury's composition to ensure both the appearance and substance of fairness and equity in jury verdicts. Though the concept and application of the mixed jury principle may have originally developed out of the economic concerns of England during the medieval period, its wisdom and practice in both England and the United States held broader implications concerning the fundamental notion of fairness in jury proceedings and legitimacy of jury verdicts.

THE HENNEPIN COUNTY MODEL

Another model for racially mixed juries is found in the courts of Hennepin County, Minnesota, where, according to the 1990 United States Census, approximately 9 percent of the adult population was minority (4.59 percent African Americans, 2.22 percent Asian-Pacific Islanders, 1.10 percent Native Americans, and 1.12 percent Hispanics). While the Hennepin County model focuses on the grand jury, this affirmative action principle can easily be extended to the petit jury.

The Hennepin model is different from the juries de medietate linguae model in that the allocation of jury seats for the minority is derived on the basis of the proportional minority composition of the general population. The racial compositional distribution of the Hennepin model is not fixed, but remains changeable, depending on the gyrating racial composition in the jurisdiction.

In Hennepin County, the grand jury consists of twenty-three members; thus, 9 percent of the twenty-three grand jurors is specifically reserved for minority groups, requiring that at least two minority grand jurors sit on every twenty-three member grand jury. The allocation process works as follows:

[if] after randomly selecting the first 21 grand jurors either only one or no minority persons appear on the panel, selection [shall] continue down the list of 55 randomly selected and qualified persons until there are at least two minority persons out of 23 on the grand jury. If no minorities appear in the list of 55 potential grand jurors, another 55 qualified persons should be selected until the goal of at least two minority jurors is obtained. If random selection of the first 21 grand jurors yields two or more minority persons, the selection should simply proceed to the next two persons on the list (*Office of the Hennepin County Attorney*, 1992, 45).

Besides setting up the proportional allocation of the jury to racial minorities, the task force proposal for the Hennepin model also recommended additional race-neutral reforms to increase the representativeness of grand juries, including: (1) integrating lists from the Immigration and Naturalization Service of recently naturalized citizens and from tribal membership rolls into source lists; (2) raising the jury fee to $30 per day; and (3) establishing a day-care center for jurors' children (Smith 1993, 55–58). Following the Hennepin County model, though it is impossible to estimate how widespread are such racially proportionate juries, five states including California do not require that grand juror names be drawn randomly from the grand jury venire and instead allow judges or jury commissioners the discretion to select who will actually serve as final jurors (Fukurai 1994, 2000).[14]

Though the de medietate linguae model requires the equal distribution of jury seats for both majority and minority groups, the Hennepin model assumes that the mixed jury is created to reflect the minority composition within the general population, thus requiring that varying numbers of minority jurors be selected for the jury box.

THE SOCIAL SCIENCE MODEL

Besides the two types of mixed juries and racial quotas in the Anglo-Saxon tradition of law, social science research offers a different version of racially mixed juries. For the previous two jury models, the central issue is the number of jurors who are similar in race, national origin, social status, or occupation to the defendant and to which a defendant should be entitled in equity for a fair-minded verdict. The classical jury de medietate linguae thus entitles the defendant to six jurors of twelve, or half of the total number of jurors in jurisdictions using smaller juries. But the possible disadvantage of the de medietate model is that six jurors of the defendant's race might be difficult to obtain in some areas. A split jury system may also offer an incentive for the state to elect the use of smaller size juries, a change generally deemed undesirable (Kaye 1980, 1004) And the nativist response of denizens to practical difficulties in picking a jury is to limit the defendant's right to one juror similar to the defendant's race. Yet, jury research demonstrates that a single dissenting juror rarely succeeds in either "hanging" a jury, blocking a verdict, or reversing its predisposition (Kalven and Zeisel 1966, 463).

Recent psychological studies show that without a minimum of three minority jurors, they may not be able to withstand the group pressure of the majority, suggesting that one or two dissenting jurors eventually accede to the majority's opinion (Saks 1977; Kerr and MacCoun 1985; See also *Ballew v. Georgia*, 435 U.S. 223, 231–39, 1978).[15] Behavioral studies also suggest that a reasonable compromise between the jury de medietate linguae and the Hennepin model, especially applied in a jurisdiction with small minority populations, is to secure three minority jurors in order to preserve not only the appearance of fairness, but also the legitimate viability of jury deliberations and verdicts. A minimum of three members of racial minority jurors are thus viewed as necessary to offset the group pressures of the dominant white jurors during jury deliberation (Johnson 1985, 1698). Thus, one or even two jurors are unlikely to maintain their own judgment of the proper and fair verdict in the face of opposition by the remaining jurors, much less change the other jurors' opinions— contrary to the Hollywood version of a single juror who was able to convince his fellow jurors to reverse their original guilty verdicts, as Henry Fonda did in *Twelve Angry Men*. Sidney Lumet, the film's director, recently revealed that he "always felt *Twelve Angry Men* was romantic, and in a sense, unrealistic. I had no illusions even then. It's hard enough to find a jury with even a single unprejudiced person."[16]

Would the inclusion of a racial minority in a traditionally white-dominated jury increase the incidence of hung juries in those cases where an all-white jury would have acquitted a white defendant? Based on social scientific studies on group dynamics in jury deliberation, the jury may require at least ten racially similar jurors to make acquittal a predictable jury verdict. In such a case, a unanimous verdict would require both majority and minority members of the jury to work out their differences, possibly preventing wrongful convictions. As happens in most cases involving white defendants, as well as in many criminal cases involving minority defendants, the strength or weakness of the evidence will usually result in a unanimous verdict. It is only in cases where there is marginal evidence that the mixed jury might be more expected to argue with sharply divergent opinions than under the current color-blind system.

If representativeness is the key to impartiality, a race neutral verdict may be expected when at least three minority jurors are selected to judge a criminal or civil case that involves the rights of a defendant with the same minority racial characteristics and backgrounds. Professor Sheri Lynn Johnson (1985) argues that the Court could create for defendants accused of interracial capital crimes, a right to a jury that includes jurors of the defendant's race. If at least three jurors were of the same race as the defendant, one of this group alone could "hang" a jury otherwise prone to imposing a racially motivated death sentence. As a member of a minority race historically suffering from discrimination, this approach allows the defendant to have a juror-advocate and fight against the majority's group pressure. Proponents of this remedy argue that such guaranteed racial quotas would (1) appease society's dissatisfaction with racially discriminatory peremptory challenges; (2) lead to fairer decisions, on the assumption that minority jurors are more able to correctly judge the character of a defendant with similar racial heritage and experiences; and (3) increase society's faith in the fairness of the jury system (Johnson 1985, 1706–07).

The equitably balanced jury thus provides the indispensable condition for rendering a just verdict that holds legitimacy in the eyes of both minority communities and the public at large. The numbers game of how many jurors will come from racial minority groups is closely related to Pennsylvania's "jury peer representation" bill, that has been proposed to mandate minimum representation of minorities in order to prevent racial discrimination in jury deliberations (H.B. 1182, 177th Gen. Assem., 1993 Reg. Sess., 1993). The bill provides that, if a defendant or victim is a member of a racially classified group representing 25 percent or more of a judicial district, and there is no juror from the same racial group, then three jurors of the victim's or defendant's race must be secured in the jury (H.B. 1182 Sec. 1 [a][1]). The problem with this bill is that the required racial representation is imposed on the jury panel or venire level, and not on the composition of the final trial jury. Nonetheless, three minority members in the jury box do appear to constitute the minimum number of minority jurors needed to maintain the fairness of jury deliberations and to increase potential acceptance of jury verdicts by the general community.[17]

PUBLIC PERCEPTIONS OF RACIALLY BALANCED JURIES

Does an affirmative and mandatory jury selection mechanism to secure racially mixed juries create the appearance of fairness in criminal jury proceedings? To answer this question, focus is placed on the three types of mixed jury models, emphasizing how the general public and its various segments in the community view the applicability of race-conscious affirmative action policies in jury proceedings and trials, possibly providing an important clue to increased legitimation of jury deliberation and future verdicts.

In order to examine the above inquiry, in the spring of 1997, a community survey was conducted to examine the public's perception of the criminal justice system and criminal jury proceedings. The research site was Santa Cruz County, California (see appendix A for detailed descriptions of the community survey).[18]

The following three statements were used to solicit respondents' reactions to mixed juries and jury verdict's fairness and legitimacy: (1) "the racial makeup of the jury should reflect the racial makeup of the community"; (2) "if racially mixed juries are called for, they should have half majority and half minority jurors"; and (3) "Some research says that without at least three minority jurors, group pressure may be simply too overwhelming. Thus, if racially mixed juries are called for, juries should have at least three minority members." The first question was designed to examine the applicability of the Hennepin model (the proportional jury) and the public's perception of racially representative juries and statistically engineered racial heterogeneity based on population compositions in the community. The second question focused on the jury de medietate linguae (the split jury) and the equal racial distribution of jury seats with or without regards to racial compositional balances in a given jurisdiction. The third question measured respondents' perceptions of jury structures based on social science studies, requiring that at least 25 percent of jury seats be reserved for racial minorities (the quarter-jury).

A number of questions also examine individual perceptions on affirmative action mechanisms in jury selection, their judicial effectiveness and usefulness in different types of trials, and the legitimacy of jury verdicts: (1) "racial quotas to create racially mixed juries are discriminatory"; (2) "racial quotas should be mandated to increase minority participation on juries"; (3) "decisions reached by racially diverse juries are more *fair* than decisions reached by single race juries"; and (4) "affirmative action is reverse discrimination." These questions examined the public's perception on the use of racialized jury allocations, the legitimacy of racially mixed juries, as well as whether racially heterogeneous juries are able to render fairer and more legitimate verdicts than racially homogeneous juries.

With respect to the use of mixed juries in racially sensitive trials, the following two statements were designed to elicit respondents' perceptions on the utility of racially heterogeneous juries: (1) "trials should include African American jurors when the defendant is African American"; and (2) "the jury should have the power to ignore the law when they feel the law is inappropriate." Given the controversial verdict by the O. J. Simpson jury and other criminal juries in racially sensitive trials, those two propositions provided additional reference points concerning how respondents view the legitimacy of the jury trial and the fairness of jury verdicts, and the possibility of jury nullification in highly controversial trials. All answers by the respondents were measured on a five-point likert scale with the following attributes: (1) "strongly agree," (2) "somewhat agree," (3) "uncertain," (4) "somewhat disagree," and (5) "strongly disagree." The respondents' perceptions and opinions on the different jury structures, the use of race-specific affirmative jury selection, and the fairness of racially diverse juries were then examined in relation to respondents' race, gender, and social class backgrounds.

RESULTS

Three Structures of Jury Models

Table 3.1 shows respondents' views on three structures of affirmative juries and the legitimacy of jury verdicts reached by racially mixed juries. With respect to the three different jury models, a large proportion of respondents favor the Hennepin

(89.0 percent) and social science models (70.2 percent). The jury de medietate linguae (48.6 percent) received the least support among the three jury structures.

Empirical analyses also suggest considerable variations of respondents' perceptions on racially mixed juries by race, gender, and social class. Among self-identified races, Asians (60.0 percent) are less likely than whites (90.2 percent), African Americans (85.7 percent), or Hispanics (87.5 percent) to favor Hennepin jury models. The respondents who shared Asian ancestry also showed the least support to all three jury models among three ancestral races (81.3 percent, 33.3 percent, and 57.1 percent for Hennepin, de medietate, and social science jury structures, respectively). Another notable finding is that, while previous analyses suggested the varying patterns of attitudes among self-identified whites with different ancestral races, attitudes towards the three affirmative jury structures remain almost identical between self-identified whites and those who share white ancestry regardless of racial identity.

The analysis also revealed significant differences in support for the jury de medietate linguae based on race, gender, and parental earnings, with whites (44.5 percent and 47.5 percent for self-identity and ancestral race), males (39.4 percent), and those with postgraduate education (30.7 percent) being less likely to favor the equal allocation of jury seats for both majority and minority jurors than Hispanics (75.0 percent and 67.4 percent for self-identity and ancestral race), females (57.0 percent), and those with some college education (60.0 percent). With respect to the social science jury model, self-identified Hispanics (86.9 percent) are most likely to favor the jury model of the three minority seats in jury trials among all self-identified races (69.4 percent, 80.0 percent, and 75.0 percent, for white, black, and Asian, respectively)

Race-Conscious Affirmative Action and Its Applications

Respondents were asked about their views on affirmative action in jury selection and the distribution of jury seats in criminal trials. The survey revealed that, when respondents' racial and gender backgrounds were incorporated into the analysis, whites (49.3 percent), Asians (70.5 percent), and males (57.6 percent) were more likely to feel that racialized quotas to create racially mixed juries were discriminatory than did African Americans (0.0 percent), Hispanics (33.3 percent), or females (37.8 percent). Differences in support for racial quotas based on social class were also revealed, with those with postgraduate education (59.2 percent) being more likely to oppose the use of racial quotas than those with less education (39.1 percent for those with high school education or less, 45.9 percent for those with some college, and 44.0 percent for college graduates).

Differences emerged based on respondents' backgrounds supporting the mandated use of racial quotas to increase minority jury participation. Hispanics (80.0 percent), blacks (60.0 percent), and women (51.8 percent) were most likely to favor the use of mandated racial quotas to create racially mixed juries,

TABLE 3.1
Measures of Variables and Descriptive Statistics[1]

Race	Total Population	Self-identified Race				Ancestral Race				Sex		Education			
		Whites	Blacks	His-panics	Asians[2]	Whites	Blacks	His-panics	Asians[2]	Male	Female	<= H.S.	Some Coll.	Coll.	Post-Gr.
JURY STRUCTURES															
(1) Hennepin Models	89.0	90.2	85.7	87.5	60.0	89.7	88.2	94.3	81.3	85.8	90.1	84.4	86.4	88.8	93.1
(2) Juries de Medietate Linguae	48.6	44.5	85.8	75.0	20.0	47.5	77.2	67.4	33.3	39.4	57.0	58.3	60.0	37.3	30.7
(3) Social Science Models	70.2	69.3	80.0	86.9	75.0	70.3	85.7	75.6	57.1	60.3	79.1	70.7	75.5	71.9	58.9
AFFIRMATIVE ACTION MECHANISMS															
(1) Racial quotas are discriminatory[3]	47.1	49.3	0.0	33.3	70.5	47.4	25.1	42.3	62.5	57.6	37.8	39.1	45.9	44.0	59.2
(2) Racial quotas should be mandated[4]	44.6	41.5	60.0	80.0	33.3	44.6	56.3	58.8	31.3	36.8	51.4	50.0	48.5	47.8	28.3
(3) Racially mixed juries' decisions are fairer[5]	68.2	68.3	50.0	82.6	83.3	68.7	58.8	75.0	68.8	63.5	72.4	65.8	71.3	69.0	63.3
(4) Affirmative action is discriminatory[6]	45.2	49.0	14.3	20.0	40.0	46.4	33.4	34.6	56.3	51.2	39.8	54.3	38.9	47.7	46.5
TRIAL TYPES AND AFFIRMATIVE ACTION															
(1) Mixed juries for African American defendant[7]	70.7	72.3	67.2	84.0	50.0	71.7	50.0	76.0	43.8	63.1	77.3	59.2	69.0	77.6	74.8
(2) Jury should have the power to ignore law[8]	34.5	30.8	33.3	60.8	0.0	33.4	47.0	39.6	37.5	2.5	28.3	52.2	35.3	31.9	22.3

Notes:

1. Figures show % of respondents who either "strongly" or "somewhat" agreed with individual statements.
2. Asians also include Pacific Islanders.
3. "Racial quotas to create racially mixed juries are discriminatory."
4. "Racial quotas should be mandated to increase minority participation on juries."
5. "Decisions reached by racially diverse juries are more *fair* than decisions reached by single race juries."
6. "Affirmative action is reverse discrimination."
7. "Trials should include African-American jurors when the defendant is African-American."
8. "The jury should have the power to ignore the law when they feel the law is inappropriate."

while men (36.8 percent) and those with postgraduate education (28.3 percent) were least likely to favor this. With respect to the effect of ancestral race, self-identified racial groups exhibited greater support for the racialized allocation of jury seats to create racially diverse juries than those with same ancestral races, except that self-identified Whites (41.5 percent) showed less support to affirmative action in jury selection than those with white ancestry (44.6 percent).

Respondents were also polled on the issue of the fairness of jury verdicts based on juries' racial compositions. Overall, 68.2 percent said they felt that decisions reached by racially diverse juries are fairer than decisions reached by single race juries, with Hispanics (82.6 percent), Asians (83.3 percent), and females (72.4 percent) being more likely to agree with the statement than whites (68.3 percent), blacks (50.0 percent) or men (63.5 percent). Similarly those with postgraduate education were least likely to agree with the statement (63.3 percent).

With respect to their views on affirmative action, differences were also found across race and gender, with whites (49.0 percent), Asians (40.0 percent), and men (51.2 percent) more likely to feel that affirmative action is discriminatory than African Americans (14.3 percent), Hispanics (20.0 percent) or women (39.8 percent). The respondents with Asian ancestry exhibited the most negative opinions on affirmative action (56.3 percent), even more so than the self-identified Asian (40 percent). While past research suggested that Asians have exhibited the most negative attitudes towards gender- and race-specific affirmative action (Takagi 1992; Fukurai and Davies 1997), our analysis also found that individuals with Asian ancestry, regardless of self-identified race, showed even stronger negative perceptions on affirmative action policies.

Trial Types and Affirmative Action in Jury Selection

The survey examined respondents' opinions regarding whether the jury should include African Americans in a criminal case where the defendant is African American. The overwhelming majority of respondents (70.7%) agree that trials should include African American jurors when criminal defendants are African American. However, Asians (50.0%) are less likely than whites (72.3%), blacks (67.2%), or Hispanics (84.0%) to agree with a race matching equation in criminal trials. The same pattern of negative supports to race-matching schemes between the jurors and defendants is shown by those with Asian ancestry (43.8%). Those with high school education or less (52.2%) are most likely to support the inclusion of African-American jurors in trials involving African American defendants than those with higher education.

With respect to the question on jury nullification, only 34.5% of the respondents felt that the jury should have the power to ignore the law when they feel the law is inappropriate. However, the majority of the following groups supported the jury's power for nullification: Hispanics (60.8%) and those with high school education or less (52.2%).

Three Jury Structures and Views on Affirmative Action in Jury Selection

Table 3.2 reports respondents' opinions on the relationship among three structures of jury models, different racial distributions of jury seats, views on affirmative action, and socio-demographic variables. The first column shows the jury models and the questions on affirmative mechanisms and racial quotas. The second through fifth columns suggest the analyses of views on Hennepin jury models cross-referenced by the opinions on affirmative action mechanisms in jury selection. The sixth through ninth columns show the analysis for the jury de medietate linguae. The last four columns then reveal an empirical examination of the social science model. Those columns show the means, standard deviations, and two indices indicating the shape of a frequency distribution—skewness and kurtosis. The former measure shows the shape and the latter indicates the length of the response distribution.

There are some important findings from the analysis. Please note that the variables are measured with a five-point likert scale, that is, one for strong agreement and five for strong disagreement. Those who feel that racial quotas are discriminatory are more likely to support the Hennepin model (1.80 for an average score) than the de medietate linguae (3.32) or the social science model (2.84). Similarly, those who support the use of racial quotas for creating racially heterogeneous juries tend to offer more support to both the Hennepin model (1.66) and social science models (1.89) than the jury de medietate linguae model (2.49). Moreover, those who support racially diverse juries because of perceived verdict fairness are more likely than others to support the Hennepin model (1.65) than the de medietate linguae or social science jury models (2.91 and 2.18, respectively).

The findings suggest the clear divergence of jury preference between the Hennepin model and other two jury structures, and that the Hennepin model represents the most preferred structure of affirmative action in jury selection. However, there are also large variations in their support for affirmative juries. Those who favor the use of racial quotas tend to support both the Hennepin and social science models which guarantee either the proportional distribution or 25 percent of jury seats allocated to racial minorities. On the other hand, those who share negative views on the use of racial quotas are least likely to favor the de medietate model (3.77) which guarantees 50 percent of jury seats to racial minorities.

Three Jury Models, Trial Types, and Affirmative Action

What conclusions can we draw from the survey findings? The survey discloses that those who support African American's jury participation in trials involving African American defendants are more likely than others to support both Hennepin and social science models of jury structures (1.67 and 2.25, respectively). With respect to the jury de medietate linguae, there are not significant differences between those who favor or oppose the inclusion of African American jurors in trials involving defendants of the same race (3.01 and 3.02, respectively).

Jury Structures and Jury Preferences

Comparisons of jury structures with individual preferences suggest a number of notable findings. For instance, though the differences are small, those who do not favor the Hennepin model are more likely to support the de medietate linguae jury (3.06) than individuals who favor the Hennepin model (3.16). Similarly, those who support the split-half de medietate model are more likely to favor the social science model (1.94) than those who oppose the de medietate linguae (3.16). While both groups still hold similar favoritism on the social science model (i.e., scores less than 3.0), the degree of their support for jury models with mandated fixed racial quotas is stronger for individuals who favor the jury de medietate linguae. As the social science model sets the basic goals of selecting the minimum of three minority jurors with possibilities for even greater minority participation, the finding suggests that those who support the social science model may also be willing to accept six minority jury participants (2.72).

The finding also shows that those who support the social science model (1.53) also support the de medietate linguae to a greater degree than those who oppose the social science model (4.14). As a negative kurtosis index indicates (−1.31), the frequency distribution is shorter than a normal distribution, suggesting that their opinions on the de medietate jury are more likely to cluster around individual means and thus their opinions on the split-half juries are more coherent and unified. The finding also suggests that individuals who are willing to accept mathematically formulated numerical goals are more likely to support both the split-half jury (the de medietate) as well as the one-fourth minority jury (social science models) as an important, race-conscious jury selection to increase minority jury participation.

The present analysis also used ordinary least square regression (OLS) to further examine public perceptions on the relationship between three types of race-conscious affirmative jury selection procedures and various attitudinal and socio-demographic measures. The regression analysis is a useful method to identify statistical significant variables while it simultaneously allows the analysis to control the effects of other variables in the equation. For example, some individuals may endorse the fact that the makeup of the jury should reflect the racial makeup of the community without favoring race-conscious affirmative methods suggested by the Hennepin model. Similarly, it is probable that the supporters of color-blind random selection may also favor racially representative juries and endorse jury decisions reached by racially mixed juries. Thus, the regression analysis allows the examination of people's perceptions on race-conscious or race-neutral preferences by simultaneously incorporating other relevant questions and opinions on the three jury structures, verdict fairness, the use of racial quotas, and socio-demographic characteristics.

Table 3.3 shows ordinary least regression analyses of the public's perceptions on racially mixed juries, racially representative juries, and mandated racial quotas. The first column shows exogenous and criterion variables to explain the

TABLE 3.2
Perceptions on Three Different Structures of Racially Mixed Juries[1]

Variable	Hennepin Models				De Medietate Linguae				Social Science Models			
	Mean	SD[5]	Kurtosis	Skewness	Mean	SD	Kurtosis	Skewness	Mean	SD	Kurtosis	Skewness
Total Population	1.80	1.13	1.43	1.51	3.11	1.46	-1.42	-0.02	2.55	1.40	-0.92	0.59
AFFIRMATIVE ACTION MECHANISMS:												
Racial Quotas[2]												
Discriminatory	1.80	1.21	1.89	1.70	3.32	1.47	-1.51	-0.15	2.84	1.50	-1.38	0.26
Non-Discriminatory	1.80	1.11	0.80	1.35	2.95	1.44	-1.36	0.09	2.28	1.32	-0.20	0.96
Racial Quotas[3]												
Mandated	1.66	1.03	2.66	1.80	2.49	1.33	-1.02	0.48	1.89	1.07	1.67	1.40
Not Mandated	1.85	1.22	1.22	1.51	3.77	1.37	-0.94	-0.70	3.09	1.49	-1.47	0.06
Racially Mixed Juries' Decisions[4]												
Fair	1.65	0.99	3.33	1.88	2.91	1.24	-1.36	0.18	2.18	1.29	0.06	1.06
Unfair	2.04	1.30	-0.19	1.05	3.53	1.47	-1.34	-0.44	3.18	1.45	-1.47	-0.06
Affirmative Action[5]												
Discriminatory	1.75	1.06	2.10	1.61	3.47	1.45	-1.26	-0.42	2.92	1.48	-1.40	0.26
Non-Discriminatory	1.74	1.15	1.77	1.65	2.89	1.42	-1.29	0.23	2.18	1.22	0.08	0.97
TRIAL TYPES:												
Racially Mixed Juries For African American Defendants[6]												
Yes	1.67	1.00	2.59	1.74	2.94	1.40	-1.30	0.13	2.25	1.31	-0.19	0.95
No	2.01	1.33	1.77	1.65	3.51	1.60	-1.48	-0.45	3.21	1.49	-1.40	-0.10
Jury with the Power to Ignore the Law[7]												
Yes	1.76	1.25	1.14	1.56	3.01	1.52	-1.52	0.10	2.57	1.45	-0.97	0.64
No	2.34	1.27	0.69	-0.55	3.02	1.10	0.07	-1.01	2.54	1.42	-1.00	0.58

(continued on next page)

TABLE 3.2 (Continued)
Perceptions on Three Different Structures of Racially Mixed Juries[1]

Variable	Hennepin Models				De Medietate Linguae				Social Science Models			
	Mean	SD[5]	Kurtosis	Skewness	Mean	SD	Kurtosis	Skewness	Mean	SD	Kurtosis	Skewness
AFFIRMATIVE ACTION JURY MODELS:												
Hennepin Models												
Yes	1.33	0.47	-1.50	0.72	3.16	1.43	-1.40	-0.05	2.45	1.36	-0.67	0.73
No	4.47	0.51	-2.11	0.12	3.06	1.69	-1.76	0.10	3.24	1.63	-1.61	-0.23
De Medietate Linguae												
Yes	1.82	1.20	1.00	1.44	1.59	0.49	-1.90	-0.36	1.94	1.13	1.00	1.27
No	1.78	1.10	2.07	1.65	4.60	0.49	-1.85	-0.42	3.16	1.47	-1.53	0.07
Social Science Models												
Yes	1.61	0.98	3.68	1.98	2.72	1.41	-1.25	0.34	1.53	0.50	-2.01	-0.10
No	2.04	1.40	-0.35	1.07	4.14	1.30	0.34	-1.31	4.66	0.48	-1.58	-0.68
SOCIO-DEMOGRAPHIC BACKGROUNDS												
Sex												
Male	1.82	1.24	1.25	1.55	3.39	1.49	-1.39	-0.32	2.89	1.48	-1.35	0.32
Female	1.78	1.04	1.49	1.44	2.89	1.41	-1.27	0.21	2.29	1.28	-0.33	0.82
Self-Identified Race[8]												
Whites	1.71	1.07	2.44	1.75	3.22	1.45	-1.39	-0.13	2.55	1.43	-1.01	0.59
African Americans	1.71	1.11	3.23	1.78	1.56	1.07	-2.71	1.52	2.42	0.98	0.04	0.28
Hispanics	1.78	1.15	1.23	1.44	2.30	1.46	-0.60	0.87	2.04	1.19	1.06	1.25
Asians/Pacific Islanders	3.14	1.35	-1.28	0.80					2.57	0.98	0.04	-0.28

(continued)

TABLE 3.2 (*Continued*)
Perceptions on Three Different Structures of Racially Mixed Juries[1]

Variable	Hennepin Models				De Medietate Linguae				Social Science Models			
	Mean	SD[5]	Kurtosis	Skewness	Mean	SD	Kurtosis	Skewness	Mean	SD	Kurtosis	Skewness
Ancestral Race[9]												
Whites	1.73	1.07	2.12	1.67	3.16	1.45	-1.42	-0.05	2.54	1.41	-0.94	0.61
African Americans	1.72	1.02	1.02	1.39	2.56	1.50	-0.80	0.87	2.28	1.07	1.14	0.98
Hispanics	1.68	0.09	3.03	1.64	2.61	1.45	-1.07	0.51	2.41	1.33	-0.53	1.73
Asians/Pacific Islanders	2.44	1.29	0.63	1.24	3.50	1.43	-1.09	-0.48	2.78	1.22	-1.03	0.04
Education												
HS or Less	1.96	1.27	0.44	1.22	2.85	1.53	-1.48	0.27	2.54	1.35	-0.79	0.56
Some College	1.88	1.12	1.10	1.33	2.80	1.43	-1.28	0.30	2.42	1.31	-0.53	0.72
College Degree	1.69	1.12	2.72	1.87	3.42	1.43	1.26	-0.33	1.41	1.41	-0.82	0.71
Post Graduate Work	1.59	1.04	3.88	2.06	3.57	1.36	-1.02	-0.51	2.83	1.60	-1.54	0.27
Jury Service[10]												
Eligible	1.79	1.14	1.56	1.56	3.11	1.48	-1.45	-0.02	2.54	1.42	-0.94	0.60
Not Eligible	2.08	1.00	-2.25	-0.19	3.25	0.87	0.23	0.44	2.75	0.87	0.23	-0.44

Notes:

1. All variables are measured in a five-item likert scale: (1) strongly agree; (2) somewhat agree; (3) uncertain, (4) somewhat disagree; (5) strongly disagree.
2. "Racial quotas to create racially mixed juries are discriminatory."
3. "Racial quotas should be mandated to increase minority participation on juries."
4. "Decisions reached by racially diverse juries are more *fair* than decisions reached by single race juries."
5. "Affirmative action is reverse discrimination."
6. "Trials should include African-American jurors when the defendant is African American."
7. "The jury should have the power to ignore the law when they feel the law is inappropriate."
8. Race refers to self-identified race.
9. Race refers to reported ancestral race.
10. "Jury eligibles" include the owners of automobiles or those who are registered voters or have California ID cards.

public's attitudes towards affirmative action mechanisms in jury selection. The second column shows both unstandardized and standardized ordinary least square regression coefficients for criterion variables in explaining whether or not individual respondents favor the Hennepin model of affirmative juries. The third and fourth columns also show regression coefficients for the de medietate linguae and social science models.

Empirical findings suggest that among three models of affirmative juries, the negative regression coefficients involve both Hennepin and de medietate linguae models (regression coefficients in the first three rows), suggesting that individuals who support the Hennepin model are more likely to oppose the split-half jury model of the jury de medietate linguae and vice versa. The Hennepin model and the de medietate linguae then represent opposite ends of the spectrum of views on the affirmative action juries. The analysis also demonstrates that when the three models of affirmative juries are simultaneously considered, the social science model is more likely to draw support from individuals who favor both Hennepin and de medietate linguae models (.123 and .293, p<.001 unstandardized regression coefficients for Hennepin and de medietate models, respectively). This finding also suggests that individuals tend to view the social science model as a middle ground as well as a reasonable compromise between the jury de medietate linguae and the Hennepin model.

Regression analyses also show that, in keeping respondents' social and ideological backgrounds constant and neutral, both whites and racial minorities (self-identified blacks and Hispanics) strongly support the ideal of proportional jury representation of the Hennepin model (−.598 and −.824, respectively). The relationship is statistically significant (p <.05 for both groups), suggesting that the Hennepin model is more likely to gain strong support across various racial groups. Black and Hispanic respondents closely followed by whites are more likely to support the proportional jury representation than other racial groups, namely, Asians—a reference group in the analysis. The finding is consistent with the previous analysis that self-identified Asians displayed the most negative views on the Hennepin model. The OLS finding is significant because Asian's negative views are consistent, even after age, gender, education, and other attitudinal variables are controlled and held constant, suggesting that regardless of socio-ideological traits, self-identified Asians held statistically significant negative views on the application of the proportional jury representation. Another notable finding is that the younger respondents and individuals with higher education are the greatest supporters of the proportional jury representative model (both coefficients are statistically significant at .05 and .10, respectively). Unlike the de medietate linguae, the Hennepin model does not rely on the same universally applied racial quotas across all jurisdictions.

Empirical findings also suggest that when race, sex, and other socioeconomic or sociopolitical backgrounds are held constant, individuals who favor the social science models and endorse mandated racial quotas to increase minority participation are more likely to support the de medietate linguae model (.315 and .358 with p<.001). Similarly, those who endorse the presence of African American jurors when the defendant is African American are more likely to support the split affirmative jury (.162 with p.<.05).

Another important finding is that self-identified minorities (blacks and Hispanics, especially) are strong supporters of the split-jury model, while individuals with white ancestral race are strong opponents of the de medietate model (−.618 and .487 with p.<.05, respectively), suggesting that regardless of self-identified race of individuals, those who share white ancestry are less likely to support the split-jury model. The finding may reflect the strong opposition of white descendants against racial minorities aspiring to gain their right to representation in jury trials. While the general population is least likely to support the de medietate linguae model among three affirmative juries (48.6 percent, see table 3.1), the finding suggests that for racial minorities and those who favor the mandated use of racial quotas and support the inclusion of black jurors for the trial of black defendants, the de medietate linguae jury represents the most ideal type of the affirmative jury structure.

While racial quotas for the Hennepin model may vary depending upon the jurisdiction, all three models of affirmative juries require the racialized jury distribution to create racially integrated juries. The ordinary least square regression analysis demonstrates that the de medietate linguae is likely to gain greater support from advocates of affirmative action policies in jury selection and individuals who favor the use of racial quotas by guaranteeing the fixed percentage of jury seats to racial and ethnic minorities. On the other hand, the Hennepin model is more likely to gain support from individuals who even oppose affirmative action mechanisms because the Hennepin model does not rely on the same, universally applied racial quotas across all jurisdictions. The irony of the proportional jury representation, however, is that, in communities with small minority populations, the Hennepin model can be effectively used to exclude racial minorities from serving on juries.

RACIALLY DIVERSE JURIES, RACIAL QUOTAS, AND PEREMPTORY CHALLENGES

The analyses of the three structures of jury representation show that, overall, the general population is more likely to support both the Hennepin and social science models than the de medietate linguae model. There are, however, considerable variations in selection among those models by race, gender, and social class. Women are more likely than men to approve all three types of jury structures. The majority of Hispanics, blacks, and those with nonwhite ancestral race largely support the de medietate linguae model of jury representation. Generally, those from higher social class backgrounds (as measured by the level of education) are least likely to support the fixed and rigid use of mandated racial quotas in the de medietate or social science models.

TABLE 3.3
Ordinary Least Square Regression Analyses of the Hennepin Model, the Jury de Medietate Linguae, and the Social Science Model[1]

Variables	Hennepin Models		De Medietate Linguae		Social Science Models	
JURY STRUCTURES[2]						
Hennepin Models	—	—	-.145	(–.106)	.123	(.093)
Juries De Medietate Linguae	–.125	(–.171)	—	—	.293	(.303)****
Social Science Models	.114	(.151)	.315	(.305)****	—	—
AFFIRMATIVE ACTION MECHANISMS						
Racial quotas are discriminatory[3]	–.067	(–.094)	.102	(.105)	–.065	(.068)
Racial quotas should be mandated[4]	.006	(.009)	.358	(.351)****	.157	(.159)*
Racially mixed juries' decisions are fairer[5]	.049	(.062)	.049	(.045)	.104	(.098)
Affirmative action is discriminatory[6]	.089	(.123)	.005	(.005)	–.213	(.223)***
TRIAL TYPES AND AFFIRMATIVE ACTION						
Mixed juries for African American defendant[7]	–.070	(–.092)	.162	(.156)**	.130	(.129)*
Jury has the power to ignore the law[8]	.059	(.081)	–.110	(–.110)	–.138	(–.142)*
SOCIO-ECONOMIC BACKGROUNDS						
Self-Identified Race						
Whites (White=1; Nonwhite=0)[9]	–.598	(–.290)**	–.092	(–.032)	.185	(.068)
Minority (Black/Hispanic=1; Others=0)[10]	–.824	(–.309)**	–.618	(–.169)**	.701	(.199)**
Ancestral Race						
Whites (White=1; Nonwhite=0)[11]	.010	(.004)	.487	(.150)**	–.051	(–.016)
Minority (Any Miniroty race=1; Others=0)[12]	–.121	(–.071)	.071	(.031)	–.056	(–.025)
Other Socio-Demographic Variables						
Sex (1=Male; 2=Female)	–.083	(–.050)	.111	(.049)	–.257	(–.118)
Age	.009	(.179)**	.000	(.006)	.006	(.090)
Education[13]	–.088	(–.164)*	.034	(.046)	.024	(.034)
Driver's License (1=Yes; 2=No)	–.297	(–.081)	.232	(.046)	.059	(.011)

(continued)

TABLE 3.3 *(Continued)*
Ordinary Least Square Regression Analyses of the Hennepin Model, the Jury de Medietate Linguae, and the Social Science Model[1]

Variables	Hennepin Models		De Medietate Linguae		Social Science Models	
Other Socio-Demographic Variables (continued)						
Registered Voters						
(1=Yes; 2=No)	–.265	(–.102)	–.734	(–.208)***	.089	(.026)
Intercept	2.940		0.780		1.138	
R^2	.149		.473		.476	

* p<.10   ** p<.05   *** p<.01   **** p<.001

Notes:
1. Figures in parenthesis show standardized regression coefficients.
2. The questions are measured in a five-point likert scale (1: "strongly agree" 2: "somewhat agree" 3: "uncertain" 4: "somewhat disagree" 5: "strongly disagree").
3. "Racial quotas to create racially mixed juries are discriminatory."
4. "Racial quotas should be mandated to increase minority participation on juries."
5. "Decisions reached by racially diverse juries are more *fair* than decisions reached by single race juries."
6. "Affirmative action is reverse discrimination."
7. "Trials should include African-American jurors when the defendant is African-American."
8. "The jury should have the power to ignore the law when they feel the law is inappropriate."
9. Whites include respondents who self-identified as white.
10. Minorities include respondents who self-identified as either black or Hispanic.
11. Ancestral Whites include individuals who had white ancestors regardless of self-identified race.
12. Minorities include individuals who had one or more of the non-white ancestral race.
13. Education is measured in a following scale: (1) grade or elementary; (2) some high school; (3) high school diploma; (4) trade, technical, or vocational school; (5) some college; (6) college degree; (7) post graduate work; (8) post college degree.

With respect to the possible use of racial quotas, whites, males, and those from the upper social class are most likely to feel that mandated racial quotas are discriminatory. However, it is equally ironic to find that a large proportion of whites (44.1 percent) also feel that racial quotas should be mandated to increase minority jury participation. Support of the mandated racial quota by whites is even greater than that of Asians (33.3 percent). Their differing views on racial quotas may suggest that, for whites, the greater benefits of racial quotas in enhancing minority jury participation can be seen as canceling out the negative, discriminatory effects of mandatory uses of racial quotas in jury selection. Similarly, Asians are more likely than other racial groups to feel that racially diverse juries produce trial fairness and verdict legitimacy. At the same time, they are least likely to approve the race-conscious selection of blacks in trials involving only black defendants, suggesting that Asians may feel that jury selection should not rely necessarily on the race of defendants as an important factor to create racially diverse juries. The race-matching equation, according to Asians, may not constitute the most important element of creating racially integrated juries.

With respect to racially differing views on affirmative juries, racial minorities' support for Hennepin and de medietate jury structures (especially among blacks and Hispanics) are found to be strong and statistically significant. The irony, however, is that, in keeping the socio-demographic and socio-ideological backgrounds constant and neutral, racial minorities are less likely to support the social science model (.701 and p.<.05). The impact of one's racial ancestry on support for the affirmative juries is minimal, except for the de medietate model, in which individuals with white ancestry are least likely to support the split-jury model. The effect of ancestral race, however, is not found to be statistically significant for the proportional jury model or the social science model. Nevertheless, keeping socioeconomic and socio-ideological backgrounds of individuals constant, those who share white ancestry are found to be the strongest opponents of the most radical application of mandated racial quotas in jury selection.

The extent of support for the use of racial quotas is also found to vary significantly, depending upon respondents' views on different affirmative jury models. Those who oppose the use of racial quotas are less likely to support the de medietate linguae or social science models, in which jury structures respectively require 50 percent and 25 percent of jury seats for racial minorities. While the Hennepin model also relies on the use of racial quotas, its quotas are considered variable and changeable, depending upon the racial makeup of given jurisdictions. Thus, the Hennepin model may be a viable option for those who opposed the use of universally applied racial quotas across all jurisdictions.

The problem of the Hennepin model, as we noted earlier, is that it is possible to have a racially exclusive jury, with absolutely no jury seats awarded to racial minority groups in communities with small racial minority populations. While those who support the Hennepin model also indicate that jury decisions reached by racially mixed juries are fairer than the verdicts rendered by single-race juries, again the Hennepin model has the potential to deny minority jury participation and may not lead to a racially diverse jury. In order to overcome the shortcoming of the proportional jury model, some jurisdictions may propose a minimum number of minority jurors in an effort to ensure racially mixed juries, just like the ones proposed by social science models.

All these race-based selection reforms are designed to counter the discriminatory use of peremptory challenges and overcome racially discriminatory procedural mechanisms in jury selection. Before the Hennepin model was instituted in early 1990s, Harold McDougall (1970), one of the earlier proponents of race-conscious affirmative jury selection, proposed in 1970 that trial juries should be proportionately representative of the jurisdiction (548). Derrick Bell (1980) also advocated legislation that, in a criminal case involving a racial minority defendant, at least 50 percent of the jury pool should be comprised of members of the defendant's race, the affirmative model equivalent to the de medietate jury (273–274). M. Shanara Gilbert (1993) also advocated the passage of race-conscious, change-of-venue statutes as another method of proscribing racial discrimination in jury selection, arguing that the court must consider the racial characteristics of the proposed venue, because the decision on the venue change and the final venue destination may result in racial discrimination against potential minority jurors.

While a number of proposals have examined the possibility of creating racially more inclusive juries, many of those suggestions and proposals tend to focus on the racially diverse pools at jury venire stages of jury selection, not the final jury itself. For example, the last two proposals involve race-conscious methods prior to the empanelment of the final jury, that is, a venue decision and a jury panel stage of jury selection. Because of discriminatory uses of peremptory challenges and purposeful exclusions of racial and ethnic minority jurors before reaching the jury box, those proposals would not guarantee the presence of minority jurors for the final criminal trial (Melilli 1996).

This is no small concern. The racially integrated jury can become an important mechanism to prevent vengeful conviction of innocent minority defendants. Recent studies on jury nullification show that nullification can take either of two forms: merciful acquittal or vengeful conviction (Finkel 1995, 30–31; see also Abramson 1994). While many studies on nullification have focused on merciful acquittal, it has also been used in an indisputably unjust manner, such as the well-documented history of all-white southern juries nullifying the law in cases of violent crimes by whites against blacks. The specter of juries maliciously convicting innocent defendants is so haunting that even the Supreme Court has cited the possibility of such convictions as one reason to avoid explicitly informing federal juries of their de facto power to nullify the law (*Sparf and Hansen v. United States,* 156 U.S. 51, 101–102, 1895). In addition, a landmark two-year study of capital punishment in the United States identifies "conviction demanded by community outrage" as a "main" cause of wrongful convictions (Bedau and Radelet 1987, 56–57). Such victimization often emerges when issues of race and ethnicity are implicated, suggesting that white racism coupled with white control of legal agencies may lead to convictions and death sentences of innocent black defendants (Bedau and Radelet 1987, 63).

Rather than relying on color-blind jury selection and all-white juries to determine the trial outcome, the racially diverse jury then becomes an important judicial vehicle to enhance a viable deliberation process by placing greater burdens on both majority and minority groups to work out differences. The racially integrated jury is also more likely to increase the opportunity of members of minority groups to participate in jury trials and to allow the race at risk to fight against the majority's group pressure in the deliberation process. While the relationship between racially diverse juries and the jury nullification is discussed and analyzed in chapter 8, it is sufficient to note that racially diverse juries can prevent the wrongful conviction that has routinely taken place in the South involving black defendants and alleged white victims.

In evaluating the application of affirmative action programs, it is important to emphasize that the term "quota" has stirred deep negative emotions among many individuals, leading to their rejection of affirmative action in jury selection and other general programs (Barnes 1995). While fixed percentages are reserved for racial minorities, such as 50 percent in the de medietate linguae and 25 percent in social science models, race-conscious allocations of jury membership based on mathematical calculations may remain an important alternative to redress jury discrimination (Barnes 1995, 865).[19] The present analyses show that both Hennepin and social science models are overwhelmingly supported by respondents as the ideal types of racially mixed juries. While the endorsement for the jury de medietate linguae was less than the other two jury models, our finding suggests that equal jury participation by both majority and minority members has support of those who favor the social science model and its use of mandated racial quotas, as well as by those who believe that racially mixed juries' decisions are fairer than the verdicts rendered by single-race juries.

With respect to racial quotas and their usage, the Supreme Court has expressed mixed opinions on their utility and constitutionality. On one hand, the Court in *City of Richmond v. J. A. Croson Co* (488 U.S. 469, 1989) held that race-conscious remedies, including goals for achieving racial balance to redress past discrimination, are acceptable; and the Court's plurality opinion by Justice Elizabeth Day O'Connor reaffirmed the use of quotas, though it declared the city of Richmond's particular use of the quota to be unconstitutional (*City of Richmond v. J. A. Croson Co.*, 488 U.S. 469 486–87 491–92, 1989).

On the other hand, the problem with the use of quotas as part of remedial plans to rectify past discrimination in jury selection and criminal trials is that the mathematically derived goals may be seen as the setting of a minimum as a maximum. Hypothetically, for instance, if the number of minority jurors selected reaches the fixed quota, it should not prevent the courts from further selecting minority jurors because the quota is a fixed mathematical goal in setting the minimum for racial minorities, rather than the maximum number of minority jurors that may be included on the jury venire or final jury. Since the fixed maximum number of minority jurors are established on the de medietate linguae model, and even the Hennepin model once the jurisdiction's racial makeup is established, the social science model may be the only viable option in creating the minimum floor goals of three minority jurors and thus providing even greater participatory opportunities for minority jurors.

CONCLUSIONS

Racial and ethnic minorities continue to be substantially underrepresented on the juries empaneled in vast majority of both state and federal courts. The social impact of unrepresentative juries has prompted both lawmakers and the courts to consider race-conscious measures to ensure minority representation; and a growing number of courts are beginning to experiment with the use of race-conscious methods to select jurors.

One problem with race-conscious jury selection methods is that there are no clearly defined formulas to determine the extent of minority participation. Little information is available about public reactions to this race-conscious affirmative measure. Past jury research has failed to show whether potential jurors would react negatively to racial quota methods in obtaining racial representation, or if potential negative reactions to racial quotas would cancel out the positive reactions that racially mixed juries might generate. Similarly, little research has been done to examine whether mathematically formulated quotas are perceived by the public as imposing a ceiling for minority applicants by setting a minimum, or for the racial majority by setting a maximum.

After reviewing the history of Anglo-Saxon legal traditions as well as social science research on jury representativeness, we empirically examined and analyzed the three different structures of affirmative juries and the use of racial quotas to create racially heterogeneous juries. The public was overwhelmingly in favor of the Hennepin model, which requires that the jury's racial makeup reflects that of community, and the social science model that requires at least three minority jurors to form racially mixed juries.

While the de medietate linguae model was not viewed as favorably as the other two affirmative juries, those who favored the social science model also supported de medietate's 50 percent guaranteed minority jury seats. Our findings also revealed that whites and those from the upper social classes are most likely to feel that mandated racial quotas are discriminatory. At the same time, the analysis suggested that a large proportion of whites also feel that racial quotas should be mandated to increase minority jury participation. Such mixed views on racial quotas suggest that, for whites, the greater benefits of mandated uses of racial quotas for increasing minority jury participation may be seen as canceling out the negative, discriminatory effects that racial quotas produce in creating racially mixed juries.

Given the strong endorsement for the Hennepin and social science models of affirmative juries, both legislative and court-initiated actions may be needed to energize the public debate concerning the importance of racially representative juries, the size of mandated racial quotas, and the sociopolitical implications of affirmative action in jury proceedings. Moreover, affirmative action policies and the benefits or drawbacks of racially mixed juries should be carefully considered and debated in order to increase minority jury participation and improve the public's respect and confidence in the jury system and jury verdicts.

Chapter 4

EUGENE "BEAR" LINCOLN AND THE NATIVE AMERICAN JURY

Affirmative Action in Jury Selection and Peremptory Inclusion

From the early sixteenth century to the beginning of the twentieth century, the jury de mediate linguae had been both recognized and tried in northeastern America. Over these more than three centuries, one consistent feature of the trial de mediate was that most of the criminal trials involved racial minority defendants; and perceived fairness of the jury verdicts was considered to be an important element for maintaining peace in the local community. Not surprisingly, a large number of the trial demediate involved Native American defendants, strong animosity, fear, and racial hostility against the American Indians remaining a powerful force within the white community.

After the war for Independence, in 1788, Thomas Jefferson also recognized the need to maintain peace with Native Indians and gave the strong support to the practice of racially mixed juries, stating in a letter to James Madison, that "[i]n disputes between a foreigner and a native, a trial by jury may be improper. But if this exception cannot be agreed to, the remedy will be to model the jury, by giving the mediate linguae, in civil as well as criminal cases" (Koch and Peden 1944). In theory, then, Jefferson advocated the use of the trial de mediate in both civil and criminal cases, and earlier American courts relied on the racially mixed jury to adjudicate criminal cases involving Native American defendants. Such jury trials adhered to features similar to today's use of race-conscious affirmative action in jury selection, as well as those trials securing half of the jury seats for the members of racial minorities.

In our moment, strong resentment and hostility against Native Americans still exist. Racial discrimination against the Indian population is found in employment, housing, and business, as well as institutionally through law enforcement and the judicial system. When a trial involves a Native American defendant accused of killing a white person and the minority defendant is tried by an all-white jury, the minority community often questions the legitimacy of the jury composition, deliberations, and their verdicts. Even if the jury includes minority members, who share the same racial background with the defendant, the central question remains: Do optimum conditions for respect and integrity of the jury's composition, deliberations, and verdict exist? And if an all-white or racially mixed jury renders the same verdict, would the public's reaction to the verdict be identical?

These questions are the focus of this chapter, concerning perceived legitimacy and integrity of the jury composition, deliberations, and verdict in a racially explosive case. We begin our analysis by examining three specific features of affirmative jury structures that have been discussed in greater detail in the previous chapter—the jury demedietate linguae, the proportional Hennepin model, and the social science model.

This chapter also introduces another innovative, affirmative selection strategy called "affirmative peremptory inclusion." This method is different from other three types of affirmative jury structures, as it is based on an affirmative voir dire strategy to achieve the ideal goals of affirmative jury structures. It is specifically designed to neutralize the biases affecting race-based peremptory challenges, so that the final jury is chosen by affirmatively selecting from the eligible pool those jurors who share the same racial, sociocultural, and other cognizable background characteristics as that of the defendants. Thus, the three types of affirmative jury structures may be seen as the formative configuration of the racialized jury box, while peremptory inclusion is a procedural strategy taken in the courtroom to attain the ideal racial balance in the jury box.

In order to illustrate the importance of the affirmative mechanism for creating the racially mixed jury and to evaluate a strategy to ensure a diverse jury in a racially sensitive trial, this chapter specifically focuses on *People of the State of California v. Eugene "Bear" Lincoln* (no. c12632), a recent criminal trial which received extensive national attention and international media coverage. Accused of murdering a white police officer on an Indian reservation in Mendocino County, California, Bear Lincoln's trial touched on both tangible and unmistakable elements of racism. The case was racially charged from its beginning—the minority defendant arguing that he was ambushed by two white deputies, while the police maintained that one of the officers was shot by the defendant when trying to escape. The different perception of community residents about the course of events led to a split verdict along racial lines, the overwhelming majority of prospective white jurors believing the defendant guilty, while the same proportion of Native Americans felt that the defendant was either probably or definitely "not guilty." During jury selection, the prosecution's peremptory challenges eliminated all Native Americans in the jury pool, so the defendant was tried by an all-white jury, and the white jury's verdicts of part acquittal and part deadlock angered both white and American Indian residents in the community.

The backdrop for this case helps explain how this case originated, looking at the historical evolution of interracial hostility between the white and American

Indian communities. In the second section, we cover the trial itself, reviewing and examining defense counsel's pretrial strategies to increase the likelihood that Native American jurors would be present on both the master lists and the jury panel. As we will see, the court refused to consider the merit of affirmative action methods, and defense strategies clearly faced logistical problems as well as the limitations of traditional jury selection procedures in creating a racially diverse jury.

The third section of the chapter explores the specific application of two kinds of affirmative action strategies: (1) the three types of affirmative jury structures we have already covered, and (2) affirmative peremptory inclusion during voir dire, an attempt to secure the presence of racial minorities in the final jury. The chapter's final section discusses the potentialities for such peremptory inclusion to bring forth diverse juries based on race and socioeconomic factors as specific selection criteria. As we will see, this strategy demonstrates the greater flexibility of an inclusive voir dire approach, using less time and efforts than traditional and exclusive jury selection using peremptory challenges.

Our conclusion is straightforward: the Eugene "Bear" Lincoln case shows that the use of such affirmative strategies can create racially diverse juries. This case illustrates that affirmative action in jury selection—using an affirmative jury structure and peremptory inclusion of peers—may be the most effective and equitable method to decrease the public's mistrust of jury verdicts rendered by single race juries. It may also increase the perceived legitimacy by various communities of the inherent, conflictual nature of jury trials, deliberations, and verdicts.

PEOPLE V. EUGENE "BEAR" LINCOLN

Trial Background

The Eugene "Bear" Lincoln case is a bitter reminder that racial hatred and discrimination still haunt the landscape of race relations in the United States. The case calls attention to the police state that prevails on Indian reservations and the quest for justice by Native Americans.

Eugene Allon "Bear" Lincoln, a Wailaki Indian from the Round Valley Indian Reservation in Mendocino County, California, was accused of killing Deputy Sheriff Bob Davis in April 1995. What actually took place on the desolate road of the Round Valley Indian reservation on the night of April 14, 1995 may never be known for certain. What is known, however, is that a series of three fatal shootings left two Native Americans and a white deputy sheriff dead, resulting in an intensive manhunt for the alleged "cop" killer, as well as charges of a police cover-up and civil rights violations against the residents of the Round Valley Indian Reservation—one of ten federally recognized Native American reservations in Mendocino County. To fully understand the impact of this incident on the Indian community and its relationship to reservation law enforcement, it is necessary to put local reservation life in historical perspective.

Shaped by differing levels of ties and associations with the outside white community, two main factional groups exist within the Indian community in Mendocino: traditionalists and assimilationists. Traditionalists, many of them educated and returned to live in the community, are more interested in striving to preserve and restore traditional cultures, assert tribal sovereignty and political self-determination, and seek economic and social independence from outside white communities. As leaders in the traditionalist movement on the reservation, Bear Lincoln, his wife Edna, and his cousin Pat Lincoln were instrumental in working to revive traditional culture and religious practices. On the other side were assimilationists well connected to the Christian church and integrated into the local non-Indian, white community. Local police had more frequent and friendlier contacts with the assimilationists; and traditionalists felt that the white community throughout the county favored assimilated Indians much more than themselves as Native Americans continuously seeking political and economic self-determination for the reservation.

Differential treatment by local law enforcement officials was evident in the handling of family members of Richard Allen Davis, whose name later became known nationally and internationally as the abductor and killer of Polly Klaas. Davis had previously been staying with his sister and her family in a home rented from a tribal member on the Coyote Valley Reservation in Mendocino County. After alleged drug dealings and other misbehavior by Davis and his sister on the reservation, traditionalist members living on the reservation tried vainly for two years to stop the drug-related activity. Numerous times reporting to both local and federal police, they tried to evict Davis, his sister, and her family from the reservation. But the local police never responded to the calls or ever attempted to question or investigate them. It was only after the arrest of Richard Allen Davis that the FBI removed his sister and her family from their home for questioning, so that an investigation of drug activities and a search for illegal substances could take place (Goldberg-Ambrose 1997, 1430).

This was only one small aspect of what was to come. When teenage boys of the traditionalist Lincoln and Peters families had had a fight with teenage boys of the assimilationist Britton family in 1995, the first incidence of homicide between them left a backwash of hostilities. A month before the killing, sixteen-year old Byron Peters had been severely beaten by several members of the Britton family. In retaliation, Byron Peters had shot at a truck driven by twenty-year old Justin Britton, which later resulted in Byron Peters' arrest ("100 year old clan feud is behind 3 Mendocino County killings" 1995). Complaints also continued against members of the Britton family and their traditionalist allies, leading to several incidents in which shots were allegedly fired outside the Peters' family home. But the sheriff's department made no arrests for such infractions, only asking the Britton family to stop the harassment against the traditionalist Peters and Lincoln families.

On April 14, 1995, the day of the killing, Byron's father, traditionalist Leonard "Acorn" Peters, got into a fight with young Neil Britton, later leaving the scene with another traditionalist friend, Eugene "Bear" Lincoln. In retaliation, Leonard Peters' brother Arylis Peters then went hunting for Neil Britton, but instead encountered Neil's father, Eugene Britton in the high school parking lot. After a heated confrontation, Britton climbed into his car, and Arylis Peters shot him through the car's back window. Witnesses saw and named Arylis Peters as the gunman. The Mendocino County sheriff's department was notified and the next morning Peters was arrested.

Three hours after the first shooting, while still searching for Arylis Peters on a remote road, two white sheriff's deputies Bob Davis and Dennis Miller shot and killed Arylis Peters' brother Leonard "Acorn" Peters, forty-four, who bore little physical resemblance to Arylis. Deputy Miller said that he and Bob Davis shot Peters after he refused orders to put down a gun and began shooting at them.

Moments after Peters was shot, according to Deputy Miller, another shot was fired by an unseen assailant from nearby bushes, and Deputy Davis died in the ensuing shoot-out. That same night, a massive police manhunt was launched for Davis' unknown assailant. Over twenty-four hours later, investigators announced that they suspected Eugene "Bear" Lincoln who lived nearby. Nobody had seen Lincoln at the shooting scene, but the police reported that they had found his hat at the shooting scene.

Mendocino County police immediately began a zealous manhunt, searching for Bear Lincoln both on and off the reservation; many Native Americans on the reservation accused law enforcement of warrantless searches involving police brutality and civil rights violations. Comparisons were made between the Lincoln case at Round Valley and the 1975 police behavior on the Pine Ridge Reservation—which ended with Native American Leonard Peltier being convicted of killing FBI agents. Similar to the Pine Ridge incident, police were again accused of warrantless searches, excessive uses of force, brutality against elders, pointing guns at children, and false arrests.

The Lincoln family defended, releasing the following statement to the press on April 20, 1995, specifying numerous incidents of police abuse and misconduct:

1. Pulling the Lincoln family including a five-year-old child, a three-year-old, and two infants from a pickup truck and placing guns at their heads;

2. Throwing Bear Lincoln's sixty-five-year-old physically disabled mother to the ground, verbally and physically abusing her, leaving her severely bruised;

3. Knocking out the windows of Bear Lincoln's mother's home, discharging weapons in her home, hitting the cradleboard of one of her infant grandchildren;

4. Entering at least fifty homes without warrants or consent, searching each room with guns cocked;

5. Pointing a machine gun at a ninety-nine-year-old elder as the police searched her house and her young grandchildren watched in horror;

6. Pulling a ninety-five-year-old man out of his truck at gunpoint and roughing him up for no reason;

7. Stopping countless vehicles at gunpoint;

8. Interrogating minors in their homes while their parents were away at a press conference;

9. Searching homes while only minors were present, with guns pointed at the minor children;

10. Taking minors into custody without their parents' knowledge or consent;

11. Throwing a mentally disabled man to the ground and harassing him (Goldberg-Ambrose 1997, 28–29).

Acting less than twenty-four hours after receiving a request from Mendocino County Sheriff Jim Tuso, California Governor Pete Wilson, a soon-to-be Republican candidate for president, posted the maximum reward allowed under the state penal code for cases involving the killing of a law enforcement officer. Bear Lincoln went on the run after it was allegedly reported that a shoot-to-kill order was issued by Mendocino County Sheriff. Despite a massive manhunt and a $100,000 reward from Pete Wilson, Lincoln eluded capture for four months.

On August 16, 1995, Eugene "Bear" Lincoln finally gave himself over to the custody of the San Francisco Police Department at the office of criminal defense attorney J. Tony Serra. Serra had previously won a new trial and acquittal for Patric "Hooty" Croy, another Indian man who had been sent to death row for killing a deputy in Shasta County, California; and on retrial, the jury found that Croy acted in self-defense (Talbot, 1990). At Lincoln's surrender—over fifty members of the press and an equal number of his family and supporters on hand as witnesses—Serra and his paralegal led a unique ceremony, which opened with a prayer and the American Indian Movement (AIM) anthem—"Wesley Bad Heard Bull's Song"—accompanying the beating of a drum. Addressing the gathering, Serra declared that Lincoln

> is not surrendering: he's challenging. He's submitting to the legal jurisdiction because he will be vindicated. Our perspective of the case is that [Leonard] Acorn [Peters] was murdered[;] and with Bear, there was an attempted murder. So we are not here submitting or surrendering. We're here challenging. We believe that we have a very strong case. We believe that when all the facts are

out, he will be vindicated. He will be found not guilty. This will be a historical symbol and we invite the litigation (Heimann 1995).

Bear Lincoln's cousin Pat Lincoln spoke on behalf of Lincoln's family and his community: "[T]here are many things which have happened since April 14th. We have been persecuted by the police. There have been warrantless searches. Guns have been pulled on children. Our elders have been abused. We have cried out to the world: 'Somebody help us.' . . . Our brother Acorn was murdered. Who killed him? Why did they do it? On our own reservation, he was subjected to this. We are angry. It is just like it was in the 1800s" (Heimann 1995).

Two weeks after his surrender, on August 30, Lincoln pleaded not guilty to two counts of murder stemming from an exchange of gunshots with Mendocino County deputy sheriffs on the Round Valley Indian Reservation; and he was arraigned in Mendocino County Municipal Court in Ukiah, facing six felony charges and special circumstance allegations. Charged for the murder of the deputy, Lincoln was also charged under the unique legal theory of vicarious liability in the death of his friend, Leonard Peters, who had been killed by deputies during the alleged shoot-out. Although Lincoln clearly did not kill Peters, Lincoln was considered to be responsible for Peters' death because he allegedly initiated the gunbattle (Snyder 1995).

The grand jury had already indicted Lincoln after his surrender. In November, a Mendocino County judge had dismissed the grand jury indictment because the prosecution failed to tell the grand jury about earlier "inconsistent statements" made by a key witness, Deputy Sheriff Dennis Miller. Miller had initially told investigators that he and Davis saw a lone figure on a reservation road, while searching for a suspect in the earlier murder of Eugene Britton. Subsequently, however, Miller told the grand jury that he saw two figures on the road before the shooting, and the District Attorney erred in failing to provide the grand jury with Miller's initial contradictory statement. The District Attorney then promptly refiled charges against Lincoln who remained in jail on a no-bail hold.

Meanwhile, on April 9, 1996, alleging that law enforcement agents violated their civil rights during the manhunt at the Round Valley Indian Reservation, approximately fifty traditionalist members including the Lincoln and Peters families filed $10 million class action lawsuits in federal court.[1] The defendants named in the suits were officers from the FBI, the Bureau of Indian Affairs, the California Highway Patrol, and various local police jurisdictions, all whom allegedly broke into homes without warrants, held adults, children, and infants at gunpoint, and committed other violations (Snyder 1996). Believing that Leonard Peters was ambushed in the dark by the white deputies when they mistook him for his brother, Arylis Peters—and that law enforcement personnel were engaging in a cover-up of their mistake—Leonard Peters' family filed a wrongful death claim against Mendocino County, maintaining that deputies shot an innocent man during their search for Arylis Peters (Wilson 1995a). Peters' widow said that she believed that he was unarmed and he was night blind as a result of diabetes, stating that there was no way for him to be threatening officers with a gun in the dark.

On June 18, the defense filed a brief summary of the case with the court, asserting that:

> (1) Mr. Lincoln did not provoke this incident in any manner, (2) the prosecution will not be able to prove beyond a reasonable doubt that any shot fired by Mr. Lincoln was responsible for killing deputy Davis, (3) every action taken by Mr. Lincoln was done in self-defense, (4) that a cover-up ensued, which included the making of false statements and reports by deputy Miller regarding the incident, and the negligent and/or intentional failure of investigating officers to preserve evidence at the scene, and (5) law enforcement personnel failed to follow proper police procedures beginning with the Britton homicide investigation and continuing throughout the Davis/Peters homicide investigation, which included acts of misconduct, unlawful searches, and excessive force, fueled by a bias and prejudice against Indian people ("Native man framed for police murder" 1997).

The defense was weakened somewhat, as material and forensic evidence was limited when Deputy Davis' body was cremated and the ashes were sprayed over the ocean. But as the defense got underway, pretrial motions covered a number of important issues, including: a request for a venue change to obtain fairer and more impartial jurors and to reduce the likelihood of an all-white jury; a jury compositional challenge to establish a prima facie case of discrimination against Native American jurors; a request to use Indian tribal lists to improve Native Americans' jury representation; and a request for an extended voir dire session so that, during a sequestered voir dire session, the defense could examine individual jurors' possible biases and prejudice against the defendant and prejudgment about his participation in the alleged crime.

As witnesses presented testimony about the history of racial discrimination and periodic genocide of Native Americans in Mendocino County, Indian attorney and tribal Judge Lester Marston recounted that Native Americans have great skepticism about the fairness of any government-related agencies, including criminal justice and judicial systems; and he requested that the court and the jury commissioner make a more concerted effort to reach out for Native Americans to serve on the jury. Marston also testified that more than 90 percent of northern California tribes died within a short time after white colonists began arriving in large numbers in the 1840s and 1850s, and that many Indians today living in Mendocino County have relatives, who were alive only a few decades ago when public policy (lasting until 1910) to exterminate them meant that they were hunted down and killed.

For almost one hundred fifty years, the Round Valley, the largest Indian Reservation in California, has been witness to racism, murder, and the unspeakable horrors of genocide. More of a concentration camp than resettlement area, Native Americans were driven to the reservation from throughout the Redwood Empire of northern California. As white settlers poured into the valley in 1850s, the genocide of Indians continued, Marston recounted. As there were few white women in the region, many young Native American women were raped; and two years after the reservation was established in the Round Valley, 20 percent of the people were found to have venereal disease. Also common was kidnapping of their children, who were highly esteemed as house servants, regularly fetching $50 for a child who could cook, and up to $100 dollars for a "likely young girl," suggesting that the reservation provided white slave traders with a ready supply of sexual merchandise (Elliott 1995).

Marston's testimony echoed and reflected the studies of historical genocide and racial discrimination against Native Americans in northern California, Columbia University student Amelia Susman visiting the Round Valley in 1937, reporting that the valley was as segregated as the Deep South and that whites made no secret of their claims to superiority and only spoke well of Indians when they were servants (Susman 1976; see generally Heiser 1974).

This was the backdrop for jury selection, that finally began on April 15, 1997, lasting three months, with the summoning of over 3,800 potential jurors. Based on their answers to a written questionnaire, or due to requests to be excused on the basis of hardship, the overwhelming majority of the jury candidates were actually excused. After the first five weeks, only 383 juror candidates remained for individual questioning by the judge and the attorneys for both sides. During the voir dire stage of jury selection, however, the systematic use of the prosecution's peremptory challenges eliminated all three potential Native American jurors, as well as two other racial minority jurors who had survived from the original panel. These race-based peremptory challenges left an all-white jury of five males and seven females. And all five alternate jurors were white as well.

In order to control media publicity of the case, the court issued a gag order, prohibiting both prosecutors and defense attorneys from making any public statements about the case. Yet, from the moment the Mendocino grand jury indicted Bear Lincoln, his supporters maintained a continuous vigil outside the courthouse, fearing that, given the anti-Indian sentiments in law enforcement and white communities, vengeful conviction would be the likely outcome of the trial. Many long-scheduled, Lincoln support rallies were held right in front of the courthouse in order to increase public awareness of the case and win public support for the defendant.

Two days before the trial near Covelo, Mendocino, defense attorney J. Tony Serra held a rally, telling the large crowd that, in response to the gag order imposed by the court, "We are angry! We, on the legal team, are angry and frustrated that we have been forced by the system to give up one constitutional right, the First Amendment, in order to secure another constitutional right: Our right to a fair trial. . . . What we ask that you do is, you speak on our behalf. You take the facts, take the evidence, you take what occurs in court, and you disseminate it. You be our voice. You be, ultimately, Bear Lincoln's voice" (Wilson 1997a).

A day before the opening day of the trial, two hundred fifty people participated in another public gathering, featuring speeches by nationally known American Indian Movement (AIM) field director Dennis Banks, former Congressman Dan Hamburg, and Round Valley Indians for Justice Leader Cora Lee Simmons. "America is going to be watching what happens here in Ukiah," Banks proclaimed, "AIM will commit all its resources to this trial. We will commit people to come here to monitor the trial. Ukiah is going to be America. We're going to watch you, Ukiah" (Wilson 1997a).

The trial began on July 29, 1997, covering a wide array of racially sensitive and explosive issues—long-standing tensions and racial conflicts between law enforcement and Native Americans on the reservation, police misconduct including physical abuses of the defendant's family, neighbors, and residents on the reservation.

Jury tampering was placed in evidence, that, in the courtroom hallway, a white court bailiff had falsely disclosed to one of the male jurors that Lincoln had confessed to the killing. The juror immediately reported the incident to the judge, later testifying, "we are having a conversation. It seems to come almost out of the blue, . . . after he said that, it was like everything else in my brain stopped. . . . Then he said that I shouldn't say he said it because it wasn't a good idea" (Wilson 1997e).

The defense also accused a white bailiff of taking advantage of crowded conditions in the courtroom, as he tried to eavesdrop on the conversations at the defense table and spy on notes passing between Lincoln and his attorneys. The defense requested the court to hold the bailiff in contempt and that the matter be investigated by the district attorney or the California Attorney General's office for felony prosecution (Snyder 1997a). Defense attorney Serra stated in an interview: "Does it take a rocket scientist to know that you cannot communicate with a juror, one, in any respect, and two, to tell them that someone has confessed, and three, to tell them falsely that someone has confessed! What an outrage! If I had done that, if any member of our legal team had done that, if any Indian had done that, they would be arrested, they would be jailed, they would be prosecuted to the full extent of the law" (Willson 1997a).[2]

The prosecution meanwhile tried to eliminate a juror who showed signs of empathy towards one of the defense witnesses. Using evidence of a sworn declaration by Sheriff's Correctional Transportation Officer Nalini Gupta, the prosecutor filed a motion accusing one of the jurors of being "teary eyed" during part of the defense opening statement, and showing other signs of empathy during Bear Lincoln's mother's testimony that she was told by officers the night of the killing—"Turn your fucking lights off; get your fucking hands up or we'll blow your fucking heads off," detailing further profanity and rough treatment at the hands of officers who told her to walk faster. When she protested that she was crippled, a CHP officer said, "Fuck the cripple," and shoved her to the wet ground and handcuffed her (Wilson 1997b). "My own sense of fair play is offended by this motion, this procedure, even the fact that this motion was made in this way," Defense attorney DeJong stated, "we picked the jury; we did it fair and square [though they are all white]. The prosecutor is trying to exercise yet another peremptory challenge under the guise of this motion" (Wilson 1997c).

The evidence against Bear Lincoln was both weak and uncorroborated. Many regular trial observers agreed that a murder conviction was unlikely, as the prosecution had not come even close to proving the charges beyond a reasonable doubt. California Department of Justice criminalist Joyce Pardo presented DNA evidence, linking slain Deputy Bob Davis to a trail of blood spots, suggesting that after the shootout, Davis traveled from the shooting scene almost to Lincoln's gate and back again, which was not explained in the scenario told by surviving deputy Dennis Miller, who maintained that Davis was killed at the initial shoot-out. There was no evidence that any bullet fired by Lincoln struck or killed Deputy Bob Davis, and the prosecution was not able to rule out that Davis was in fact killed accidentally by his partner's own bullet. The prosecution's case was circumstantial at best: Lincoln was there and fired a bullet; and Davis was struck and killed by a bullet.

The defense argued that Lincoln fired only in self-defense after he was shot at and had seen his best friend killed without warning by unseen assailants. Davis, the defense said, was killed by a bullet after the defendant returned fire with a single shot, while being fired on a second time by Deputy Dennis Miller with a fully automatic M-16. Miller fell down; but just before, he felt the impact of falling rocks struck by the defendant's single shot. And since the defendant fired only one shot and it struck rock, it could be ruled out as the shot that killed Deputy Davis. Rather, the deadly bullet might have to come from Miller's spray of automatic fire as he fell down, unless there was another unknown person at the scene firing another gun. But no other shell casings were found. Davis' blood was also found at the scene of the shoot-out, leading to the gate of Lincoln's house, suggesting that Davis was still alive and had tried to capture the defendant long after the initial exchange of gunfire. It seemed likely that there would be acquittal on all charges, including all felony counts.

Jury Verdicts and the Aftermath

Throughout the trial, Lincoln supporters had held daily demonstrations outside the downtown Ukiah courthouse, pounding drums and waving placards. Inside the courtroom, Lincoln continued to wear a traditional Indian "ribbon shirt" with colorful embroidery and multicolored ribbon ornamentation, displaying his adherence to Indians beliefs in cultural and political independence, responding to his loyal supporters outside the courtroom. Meanwhile, before the verdict was to be read, the District Attorney called for the SWAT team to surround the courthouse, allegedly to prepare for potential racial riots and community disturbances. After deliberating for three days, on September 24, 1997, jury foreperson Eileen Urich declared Lincoln innocent of separate murder charges stemming from the April 14, 1995 shoot-outs that left two men dead. But the jury deadlocked on allegations of manslaughter; and Aaron Williams, the chief prosecutor of the case, quickly announced that the prosecution would seek a retrial (Geniella 1997d).

Immediately after the verdict, approximately one hundred people, including Lincoln, his dozen-member defense team, family members, and political and social activists gathered outside the courthouse for a petition drive calling on District Attorney Susan Massini to drop further prosecution plans. Yet, retrial was granted by the judge, set for February 6, 1998.

Postverdict interviews revealed that two white jurors would not budge from their belief that Lincoln should in some way be held responsible for the deaths of Davis and Peters, with their split vote resulting in the deadlock on manslaughter charges. Shellie Vanoven of Willits, who voted for the complete acquittal of all charges admitted, "we were very frustrated and disappointed that we had to give up [on a deadlock]" (Geniella 1997c).[3] Five members of the Lincoln jury also held a press conference at the Ukiah courthouse. But as only five of the twelve-member jury were willing to be interviewed after the verdict, no records exist as to the actual breakdown of split votes on the manslaughter charges.

White residents were meanwhile enraged, hostility emanating throughout the community. Official harassment began right after the verdict was announced, as Lincoln and his supporters were on their way to waiting cars, and Sheriff's detective Alvin Tripp, who is white, climbed from his parked car, confronted Lincoln, and shouted, "You lie with a forked tongue. You know what I mean" (Callahan 1997). In the verdict aftermath, a crank call to a ratio station threatened that the Ku Klux Klan would mete out vigilante justice (Elliott 1997). Phyllis Davis, wife of Bob Davis, denounced the verdict as a "major miscarriage of justice" (Geniella 1997a). Declaring that Bob Davis had won military medals and decorations during three tours of duty in Vietnam and subsequent assignments to Lebanon and Grenada, she added, "it's hard for me to believe we were sitting in the same courtroom" (Geniella 1997a). She responded to the acquittal and the role of the defense team; "this case wasn't about race . . . they [Lincoln's lawyers and his supporters] have used it to further their own careers and promote their political causes" (Geniella 1997b).

Chief Prosecutor Aaron Williams fulminated, "people getting away with murder is a cliché, but in this case that man got away with it. . . . It sickens me" (Geniella 1997b). Williams could not accepted the not guilty verdict of first degree murder based on the jury's assessment of reasonable doubts, adding "when the not [guilty] verdicts for the second degree murder were read, I was floored" (Geniella 1997a). The Native American community was also dissatisfied with the hung jury on the manslaughter charges, as well as the jury's failure to issue a complete acquittal. Lincoln supporters remained apprehensive, fearing that his acquittal might lead to his lynching. Cora Lee Simmons, a spokeswoman for Round Valley Indians for Justice (RVIJ), said that she expected Lincoln to go into seclusion, insisting that "[white] people have to get used to the idea [of his release]" (Callahan 1997).

DEFENSE STRATEGIES TO INCREASE
THE LIKELIHOOD OF A RACIALLY DIVERSE JURY

Given the nature of the case's racial sensitivity and divisive community hostility, the defense initially devised a number of pretrial strategies to increase the likelihood of placing Native American jurors in the jury box. Though their efforts failed to secure a racially mixed jury by the close of jury selection, it is of great importance to review the defense strategies and analyze their failure in order to understand how it might be possible to design an affirmative jury selection procedure to ensure a racially diverse jury for a racially sensitive trial.

Defense efforts in the Lincoln trial may well reflect future pretrial strategies to be employed by defense attorneys in criminal cases beset by heightened racial overtones. The most notable defense strategies included the following:

1. Arguing for the use of supplemental lists to be included in the source lists in order to increase the number of Native Americans to be summoned and appear at the courthouse, to improve the likelihood of placing Native Americans in the final jury;

2. Longitudinally examining the racial composition of venired jurors who actually appeared at the courthouse and were assigned for jury trials at the superior courthouse. This suggests that Native Americans' underrepresentation in the master list also led to their underrepresentation in the jury pool and the diminishing likelihood of their presence in the final jury under the existing method of jury selection;

3. Arguing for a change of venue to a more racially diverse community in order to decrease the probability of empaneling an all-white jury; and

4. Presenting to the court different options for race-based affirmative action in jury selection, including the de medietate jury, the social science model, and the Hennepin model, so that the court might consider the merit of such affirmative action strategies to create a racially mixed jury.

To educate the judge about the racially sensitive nature of the case and to evaluate the racially demarcated perception of the potential trial outcome, it was important to suggest these affirmative action strategies, in hopes that the court would rule favorably in a number of race related pretrial motions, increasing the likelihood of Native Americans' presence in both jury pools and the final jury.

Tribal Lists as Supplements for Source Lists

The defense's initial strategy to increase the likelihood of Native American jury representation was to ask the court to consider the use of supplemental tribal lists as part of the master list. Though the master list of potential jurors is compiled from DMV (Department of Motor Vehicle) and ROV (Registrar of Voters) lists in California, the defense argued that Native Americans are less likely to be identified by those two lists, because those who are registered on Indian reservations no longer need to possess state-issued drivers' licenses to drive in and out of their reservation. The tribal-issued license is legally sufficient for the driving privilege in the state. Similarly, because their own tribal elections are considered far more important than municipal or state elections, and indigenous voting is more likely to influence their tribal politics and reservation lives, tribal Indians are less likely to register to vote for general public elections. Consequently, their names are less likely to be included in the master list, leading to a significant deficit in their representation in jury pools or venires.

Significant underrepresentation of Native American jurors in the master list was statistically documented. Table 4.1 shows the number of Native American residents living on eight federally recognized reservations, as well as the number of residents whose names were not included in the master list. The tribal lists identified a total of 5,577 Indian residents on the reservation, but only 1,291 residents had a county address and were thus considered to be eligible jury candidates. The 1996 master list for jury service, moreover, failed to identity 693 (53.7 percent) of those eligible Indian residents on the reservation, suggesting that the majority of reservation residents in eight federally recognized tribes were not included in the master list for jury service. The extent of Native Americans' underrepresentation could have been even much greater than 54 percent, if the analysis had covered the tribal lists of two additional Indian reservations that absolutely refused to provide the tribal membership information, because of their deep distrust of any government-related agencies, including criminal justice and other judicial bodies. Despite overwhelming evidence of Native Americans' significant exclusion from the master list, the court nonetheless denied the defense request that the tribal lists be used as a supplemental roll for jury service.

TABLE 4.1
Indian Service Populations and Jury Representation in the Master List

Reservation	Population[1]	Total Eligible[2]	No. Included	No. Excluded
Coyote Valley	302	48	27	21
Guidiville	125	—	—	—
Hopland	353	338	64	274
Laytonville	504	87	48	39
Manchester/Point Valley	253	188	107	81
Pinoleville	259	93	48	45
Potter Valley	341	—	—	—
Redwood Valley	135	44	29	15
Round Valley	3,013	368	215	153
Sherwood Valley	292	125	60	65
Total	5,577	1,291	598	693 (53.7%)

Note: Some tribes, such as Hopland, provided lists in 1989 for the Whitlock case *(People v. Whitlock)*, but would not provide lists to the defense at this time, fearing county involvement in their business. Hopland, for example, would only give us their list with names only. Both were provided. Similarly, the Guidiville and Potter Valley refused to provide any information on their tribal enrollments in any governmental matter including the Lincoln case.

1. The tribal populations were supplied by Ray Frei at Bureau of Indian Affairs office in Sacramento on December 27, 1996. The information shows the population figure (latest available, 1995) by reservation of federally recognized tribes in Mendocino County. Two other reservations, Noyo River and Yokayo, are not federally recognized and thus eliminated from the analysis.

2. Because a large number of tribal members live around the county boundary, total eligible jurors were identified by only tribal members whose residential addresses are within the boundary of Mendocino County.

Jury Panels and a Lack of Native American Jurors in the Jury Pool

The defense then moved to establish a prima facie case of discrimination against Native American jurors, showing that the jury selection system itself was racially biased, asking the court's permission to distribute a jury survey questionnaire at the courthouse in order to examine racial compositions of jury panels. After the court granted the motion, the questionnaire was distributed to potential jurors who actually appeared at the courthouse between April and December of 1996.

The jury questionnaires were used to reveal the jurors' self-identification of race and thus the degree of racial exclusion and inclusion on the jury panel. Table 4.2 shows the twenty-seven jury panels during the eight month survey period, as well as Native Americans' jury representation at the courthouse. The survey findings show that, of 2,042 potential jurors who appeared at the courthouse, fifty jurors identified themselves as Native American (the third and fourth columns), indicating that 2.44 percent of the jury pool was comprised of Native American jurors (the fifth column).

In order to establish statistical disparity for Native American's representation at the jury panel, the defense decided to rely on the 1990 U.S. census figure of 3.61 percent as the base figure for the Native American's percentage in the jurisdiction. While a more accurate estimate of Native Americans populations in the jurisdiction was higher than the census figure of 3.61 percent (the sixth column), the defense relied on the census figure to compute disparity figures, arguing that the statistical disparity essentially indicates the most conservative estimate of Native Americans' underrepresentation on the jury panel. The use of more accurate figures for Native American populations in the jurisdiction would obviously lead to an even greater disparity of their representativeness on the jury pool.

In examining the degree of Native American representation on jury panels, statistical analyses show the absolute disparity of negative 1.16 percent (the seventh column) and the comparative disparity of negative 32.17 percent (the eighth column), indicating that approximately one out of every three Native Americans in the community was excluded from jury service at the jury panel stage of the selection process. The Z score (the last column) also reveals that the underrepresentation of Native Americans was statistically significant, showing that the likelihood of their underrepresentative disparity taking place by pure chance was less than two in one thousand. All statistical tests indicated that Native Americans were significantly and systematically underrepresented in the jury panel at the Mendocino Superior courthouse.

The 1996 finding of the significant underrepresentation of Native American jurors was not an anomaly, however. A previous 1991 jury compositional challenge case in Mendocino County showed that, between July 1989 and February 1990, a total of 1,200 potential jurors appeared at the courthouse, though only twenty-eight of them were Native American—a mere 2.33 percent of the jury pool. During the same period, 1,146 (95.5 percent) of the jurors in the pool were white.[4] The 1989–90 figure of Native American's representation was almost identical to that of the 1996 representation (2.44 percent), suggesting that Native Americans have been consistently underrepresented in the jury pool at the Mendocino Superior Court. As the overwhelming majority of potential jurors in the pool have been white, this is both statistical and legally compelling proof that, given the very small percentage of Native Americans in the jury pool, the chance for a racially diverse Lincoln jury was exceedingly slim. It may also suggest that judges in Mendocino County should be required to take legal notice of the use of statistical methods in designing the procedures for securing a representatively balanced jury pool. The court, however, ruled that the defense failed to establish a prima facie case of discrimination, declaring that the existing jury selection method did not lead to the systematic exclusion of Native American residents in Mendocino County from serving on the jury.

TABLE 4.2

Mendocino County Petit Jury Compositions of Native Americans:
April 30 to December 16, 1996[1]

	Date	Total Jurors[2]	Native American Jurors	%	Native American Adults (%)[3]	Disparities Absolute	Comparative	Z Score
1	4-30-96	62	0	0.00%	3.61%	−3.61%	−100.00%	−1.523
2	5-21-96	53	1	1.88	3.61	−1.72	−47.73	−0.672
3	5-28-96	99	2	2.02	3.61	−1.58	−44.03	−0.847
4	6-18-96	64	3	4.68	3.61	1.07	29.84	0.462
5	7-8-96	40	1	2.50	3.61	−1.11	−30.74	−0.376
6	7-9-96	48	1	2.08	3.61	−1.52	−42.29	−0.567
7	7-22-96	52	3	5.76	3.61	2.15	59.81	0.834
8	7-29-96	80	3	3.75	3.61	0.14	3.87	0.067
9	8-12-96	85	1	1.17	3.61	−2.43	−67.41	−1.202
10	8-14-96	45	1	2.22	3.61	−1.38	−38.44	−0.499
11	8-26-96	70	1	1.42	3.61	−2.18	−60.42	−0.978
12	9-9-96	55	1	1.81	3.61	−1.79	−49.63	−0.712
13	9-16-96	46	2	4.34	3.61	0.73	20.43	0.268
14	9-23-96	47	1	2.12	3.61	−1.48	−41.06	−0.544
15	9-30-96	243	7	2.88	3.61	−0.72	−20.20	−0.609
16	10-2-96	249	8	3.21	3.61	−0.39	−11.00	−0.335
17	10-7-96	105	2	1.90	3.61	−1.70	−47.23	−0.936
18	10-8-96	79	4	5.06	3.61	1.45	40.25	0.692
19	10-15-96	107	2	1.86	3.61	−1.74	−48.22	−0.965
20	10-21-96	62	0	0.00	3.61	−3.61	−100.00	−1.523
21	10-28-96	44	2	4.54	3.61	0.93	25.91	0.332
22	11-12-96	38	0	0.00	3.61	−3.61	−100.00	−1.192
23	11-13-96	38	0	0.00	3.61	−3.61	−100.00	−1.192
24	11-18-96	51	1	1.96	3.61	−1.64	−45.68	−0.631
25	11-19-96	68	0	0.00	3.61	−3.61	−100.00	−1.595
26	12-9-96	67	1	1.49	3.61	−2.11	−58.65	−0.929
27	12-16-96	45	2	4.44	3.61	0.83	23.11	0.300
Total		2042	50	2.44	3.61	−1.16	−32.17	−2.813*

Source: Mendocino Superior Court. 1996. The Jury Panel Survey at the Superior Courthouse. Ukiah, Mendocino County, CA.

Notes:

1. Figures are based on the 1990 U.S. Bureau Census.

2. Prospective jurors who refused to identify race and/or who identified more than one categories were excluded from analyses.

3. Percent-Native American adults were computed for individuals who are 18 or over in Mendocino County.

* Statistically significant at 0.002 probability level (i.e., the likelihood exhibited disparity would occur by chance was two in one thousand, i.e., one in five hundred).

A Change of Venue Motion

As the survey finding indicated the paucity of Native Americans in the jury panel, the defense feared that any remaining Native Americans on the jury venire would be subsequently eliminated by the prosecution's race-based peremptory challenges. Given the long history of racial discrimination against Native Americans in Mendocino County, defense council filed a change of venue motion, arguing that the Native American defendant was unlikely to receive a fair trial, unlikely to be tried by a group of impartial jurors, and likely to face an all-white jury. From a preliminary report by a jury expert, it was clear that pretrial publicity was "extremely high" and prejudicial, with some 142 newspaper articles appearing in just the first ninety days following the shootings on April 14, 1995. The defense showed that a community survey indicated that 92.7 percent of a representative sample of eligible jurors already recognized the case.

Table 4.3 shows the 1996 Mendocino community survey results, revealing the extent of the public's awareness and knowledge of the case and the defendant. The survey found that 81.6 percent of the representative sample of the county residents were aware that the defendant was at large for four months before turning himself into the legal authorities. Bear Lincoln's background was widely publicized, including an earlier charge of murdering a two-year-old girl. Though the defendant was never convicted, 13.2 percent of eligible jurors believed that Lincoln had been previously convicted of murder. More than one of five county residents (21.8 percent) had also watched *America's Most Wanted*, in which the defendant was portrayed as a dangerous "cop-killer" who was on the run. Almost three of four eligible jurors who made a prejudgment on the trial outcome believed that the defendant was either probably or definitely guilty (21.1 percent for definitely guilty and 53.3 percent for probably guilty). The survey results reflected the conservative nature of Mendocino's eligible jurors, with the majority of residents agreeing that a defendant had to prove his or her innocence, though, under the law, the prosecution or the state must shoulder the burden of proof of guilt (43.3 percent for strongly agree and 12.1 percent for somewhat agree).

Based on statistical findings, the defense now argued that the potential jurors' prejudgment on the trial outcome differed significantly in terms of their identified race and whether or not they had access to prejudicial information (see table 4.4). Approximately 80 percent of prospective white jurors felt that the defendant was either probably or definitely guilty (23.0 percent and 56.4 percent, respectively), while almost the same percentage of eligible Native American jurors believed that the defendant was probably or definitely not guilty (50.0 percent and 27.8 percent, respectively). With regard to gender, however, the potential jurors' prejudgment of the trial outcome did not differ significantly, though males were slightly more likely than females to feel that the defendant was guilty (76.2 percent and 72.4 percent for male and female, respectively).

TABLE 4.3

Mendocino County Community Survey on the Bear Lincoln Case

Likely Trial Outcomes and Criminal Justice Attitudes

Questions	Responses	N	Percentage	Valid Percentage
HAVE YOU READ, SEEN, OR HEARD[1]				
1. The defendant, Bear Lincoln, was at large for four months before turning himself in to the authorities?[2]	Yes	315	78.9	81.6
	No	71	17.8	18.4
	Don't Know	13	3.3	—
2. Bear Lincoln had previously been convicted of murdering a two-year-old girl?	Yes	52	12.9	13.2
	No	341	84.6	86.8
	Don't Know	10	2.5	—
3. The victim, Deputy Bob Davis, was a Vietnam war hero?	Yes	173	42.9	44.6
	No	215	53.3	55.4
	Don't Know	15	3.7	—
4. There was a television story about this case on a program called *America's Most Wanted*. Did you see that broadcast?	Yes	87	21.5	21.8
	No	312	77.2	78.2
	Don't Know	5	1.2	—
5. Do you believe there is a history of tension between Indians and non-Indians in Mendocino County?	Yes	333	75.9	84.7
	No	60	13.7	15.3
	Don't Know	46	10.5	—
6. Do you believe there is some prejudice against Indians in Mendocino County?	Yes	302	68.6	77.6
	No	87	19.8	22.4
	Don't Know	51	11.6	—

(continued on next page)

TABLE 4.3 (Continued)
Mendocino County Community Survey on the Bear Lincoln Case
Likely Trial Outcomes and Criminal Justice Attitudes

Questions	Responses	N	Percentage	Valid Percentage
7. Based on what you have read, heard, or seen about the case, do you believe that the man accused, Bear Lincoln, is definitely guilty, probably guilty, probably not guilty or definitely not guilty of the first degree murder of Deputy Davis.	Definitely Guilty	51	13.0	21.1
	Probably Guilty	129	32.8	53.3
	Probably not Guilty	44	11.2	18.2
	Definitely not Guilty	18	4.6	7.4
	Don't Know	51	38.4	—
CRIMINAL JUSTICE ATTITUDE QUESTIONS				
8. Even the worst criminal should be considered for mercy.	Agree Strongly	66	15.1	16.2
	Agree Somewhat	104	23.8	25.6
	Disagree Somewhat	64	14.6	15.7
	Disagree Strongly	173	39.6	42.5
	Don't Know	30	6.9	—
9. Regardless of what the law says, a defendant in a criminal trial should be required to prove his or her innocence.	Agree Strongly	179	40.9	43.3
	Agree Somewhat	50	11.4	12.1
	Disagree Somewhat	44	10.0	10.7
	Disagree Strongly	140	32.0	33.9
	Don't Know	25	17.3	—

(continued)

TABLE 4.3 *(Continued)*
Mendocino County Community Survey on the Bear Lincoln Case
Likely Trial Outcomes and Criminal Justice Attitudes

Questions	Responses	N	Percentage	Valid Percentage
10. It is better for society to let some guilty people go free than to risk convicting an innocent person.	Agree Strongly	99	22.8	27.6
	Agree Somewhat	97	22.4	27.0
	Disagree Somewhat	62	14.3	17.3
	Disagree Strongly	101	23.3	28.1
	Don't Know	75	17.3	—
11. The plea of insanity is a loophole allowing too many guilty people to go free.	Agree Strongly	260	59.6	62.4
	Agree Somewhat	64	14.7	15.3
	Disagree Somewhat	49	11.2	11.8
	Disagree Strongly	44	10.1	10.6
	Don't Know	19	4.4	—

Note: 1996 Mendocino County Community Survey.

1. Respondents who refused to provide answers were excluded from the analysis.
2. Analysis of questions, 1 through 4 and 7 only included respondents who recognized the case.

Pretrial publicity and strong beliefs on race relations between Indian and non-Indian communities also held the potential to exert significant influences on their prejudgments. Almost 30 percent of the representative sample of eligible jurors with prejudicial knowledge of Lincoln's previous murder accusation believed that the defendant was definitely guilty (29.7 percent). Similarly, 34.4 percent of those who watched the above mentioned TV program supported the "definitely guilty" verdict for the defendant.

A large proportion of eligible jurors who said that they did not believe the presence of historical racial tensions between Indian and non-Indian communities, or who held no prejudice against Indians, believed that defendant was definitely guilty (41.2 percent and 43.9 percent, respectively). On the contrary, county residents who were aware of historical conflicts and racial prejudice felt that defendant was not guilty (26.3 percent and 33.6 percent, respectively). Prejudicial pretrial publicity and perceived racial tension and prejudice in the community thus had a significant impact on county residents' prejudgment of the case. From the standpoint of race and its relation to prejudgment, the racial identification of eligible jurors alone seemed to nearly determine the trial outcome.

By presenting empirical evidence of significant underrepresentation of Native Americans on the jury panel, the defense argued that the racially demarcated trial outcome might require the use of a race-based, affirmative jury selection method in order to ensure the presence of Native American jurors as the defendant's peers, thereby increasing the public's respect for and the legitimacy of the jury's deliberation and the verdict. Yet, due to the small Native American population in the jurisdiction, a statistical probability alone would not guarantee even one single Native American juror in the jury box, suggesting that at least 8 percent of the population would be necessary to ensure at least one Native American juror representative in the twelve-member jury. Thus, the defense argued that, given the scarcity of Native Americans in the jury summons and panel stages of jury selection, almost all available jury candidates for the Lincoln jury would be white. But the court was adamant, denying the merit of considering the potential use of affirmative action in jury selection. Ultimately as the defense feared, the prosecutors' race-based, peremptory challenges eliminated all Native American jurors from the venire pool, creating an all-white jury to try this Native American defendant.

AFFIRMATIVE JURY STRUCTURES AND PEREMPTORY INCLUSION

The attempts to increase the likelihood of placing Native American candidates in the Lincoln jury reflect typical pretrial strategies employed by defense attorneys in racially sensitive trials and in interracial criminal cases. Courts, however, routinely deny the overwhelming majority of such defense strategies. Other than legally mandated ROV and DMV files, no California's court has ever allowed the use of supplemental lists, such as welfare rolls, telephone registration lists,

TABLE 4.4
Mendocino County Community Survey on the Bear Lincoln Case
Community Perceptions on the Likely Trial Outcome

| | Race | | Gender | | Pre-Trial Publicity | | | | | | | | Race Relations | | | |
| | | | | | Hiding[1] | | Girl[2] | | Vietnam[3] | | TV[4] | | Tension[5] | | Prejudice[6] | |
Outcomes	White	Indian	Male	Female	Yes	No	Yes	No	Yes	No	Yes	No	Yes	No	Yes	No
THE MAN ACCUSED, BEAR LINCOLN, IS:[7]																
Guilty Definitely[8]	23.0%	5.6%	23.0%	19.0%	18.8%	34.6%	29.7%	18.8%	25.2%	16.2%	34.4%	15.8%	17.9%	41.2%	13.8%	43.9%
Guilty Somewhat	56.4	16.7	53.2	53.4	53.6	50.0	56.8	52.3	52.3	56.4	45.9	56.5	55.8	38.2	52.7	49.0
Not Guilty Somewhat	15.7	50.0	16.7	19.8	19.3	11.5	8.1	20.8	14.4	20.5	13.1	20.3	17.9	20.6	22.8	7.0
Not Guilty Definitely	4.9	27.8	7.1	7.8	8.2	3.8	5.4	8.1	8.1	6.8	6.6	7.3	8.4	0.0	10.8	0.0

Notes: 1996 Mendocino County Community Survey.

1. "Have you read, seen, or heard if the defendant, Bear Lincoln, was at large for four months before turning himself in to the authorities?"
2. "Have you read, seen, or heard if Bear Lincoln had previously been convicted of murdering a two-year-old girl?"
3. "Have you read, seen, or heard if the victim, Deputy Bob Davis, was a Viet Nam war hero?"
4. "There was a television story about this case on a program called *America's Most Wanted*. Did you see that program?"
5. "Do you believe there is a history of tension between Indians and non-Indians in Mendocino County?"
6. "Do you believe there is some prejudice against Indians in Mendocino County?"
7. "The authorities have charged a man named Eugene 'Bear' Lincoln with the murder of Sheriff's Deputy Bob Davis. Based on what you have read, heard, or seen about the case, do you believe that Bear Lincoln is definitely guilty, probably guilty, probably not guilty, or definitely not guilty of the first degree murder of Deputy Davis?"
8. Respondents who said "don't know" or refused to answer the question were excluded from the analysis.

Native American tribal lists, or utility rolls, to increase jury representation of racial minorities. Jury studies show that such supplemental lists have elsewhere increased significant numbers of blacks, Hispanics, Native Americans, the poor, the youth, and the elderly for inclusion in the master list (see generally Fukurai, Butler, and Krooth 1993).

The United States Supreme Court has yet to extend cognizable status to Native Americans to be protected against discrimination in jury selection. Although the Court has given cognizable and protective status to Blacks (*Strauder v. West Virginia*, 100 U.S. 306, 1880), Hispanics (*Hernandez v. Texas*, 347 U.S. 475, 1954), and women (*Taylor v. Louisiana*, 419 U.S. 522, 1975), as well as upheld their cross-sectional representation at the jury panel stage of jury selection, the Court has failed to recognize Native Americans as a distinct group in the community that needs legal protections against discriminatory jury selection procedures. The Court also has recognized blacks, Hispanics, and women as minority groups that need protection against discriminatory uses of peremptory challenges in voir dire (Fukurai, Butler, and Krooth 1993; Fukurai, 2000). But Native Americans have not yet been given the same cognizable protective status against the abuses of peremptory exclusion in voir dire.

The defense strategies in the Lincoln trial failed to increase the likelihood of empaneling racial minority jurors in the jury panel or the final jury. Given the conservative court's approach and response to the defense's attempt to increase the likelihood of including these minority jurors—and even in other cases in which the court has granted defense motions such as a jury compositional challenge or a change of venue motion—defense strategies have routinely failed to secure a racially diverse jury.

For these reasons, we believe, as previously indicated, that the following two affirmative action approaches may provide important guidelines for future litigation as effective defense strategies to ensure a racially mixed jury in criminal trials: (1) affirmative jury structures, with the use of mandated racial quotas to allocate jury seats to racial minorities; and (2) peremptory inclusion during voir dire, in which participating attorneys are allowed to affirmatively identify and select potential jurors for the final jury. Clearly, the affirmative jury selection method is a conceptual departure from the current system of jury selection methods, in which the final jury is the by-product of a continuous elimination process, as attorneys routinely identify and peremptorily challenge "undesirable jurors" from jury service.

In the following sections, we elaborate these approaches. The first section examines the theoretical applicability of the three affirmative jury structures in the Lincoln case in order to illustrate possible implementations of mandated racial quotas in trial. The second section then presents the practical application of affirmative peremptory inclusion and shows how the inclusionary approach can be used to ensure the selection of the "targeted" minority jurors for the final jury.

Affirmative Jury Structures

As we have examined in the previous chapter, three distinct structures of affirmative juries are possible: (1) the jury de medietate linguae, (2) the Hennepin jury, and (3) the social science model. Given the scarcity of Native American jurors in Mendocino County, however, the Hennepin model in itself would be unable to secure the presence of Native Americans in the final Lincoln jury. This is because their respective proportion among eligible jury populations in the community did not reach 8 percent (the minimum statistical probability to place at least one juror among a twelve-member jury). Thus, the use of proportional affirmative jury selection would effectively eliminate any chance of Native American jurors from the Lincoln jury.

The jury de medietate linguae also poses problems, as only three Native Americans survived from the initial jury panel after screened for excuses, qualifications, and challenges for cause. In fact, the final qualified jury pool only included five nonwhite jury members, making it impossible to empanel the minimum of six minority jurors required for the de medietate linguae.

The Lincoln case also illustrated the logistical difficulty and procedural deficiencies of the current jury selection system, especially when the logistical problems are compounded with an extremely small proportion of racial minorities in the jurisdiction. Given the scarcity of available Native Americans for the trial, the social science model appears to be the only possible jury structure in the Lincoln case to ensure the presence of three Native American jurors, as well as viable jury deliberation to secure a fair and equitable verdict.

In order to understand how people perceive the idealized composition of racially diverse juries, the following college student survey analysis may provide some critical insights into the ideal racial balance for hypothetical trials involving racial minority defendants and victims (see appendix A for detailed information on the survey and data collection methodologies). Assuming that racially diverse juries are legally granted for a given trial, the perceived ideal composition for an affirmative jury structure is shown in table 4.5. Each respondent was asked how many of the twelve-member jury should be the same as the race of a defendant, or a victim, in a trial which was permitted to empanel a racially mixed jury. The first five rows show the ideal jury composition when the defendant's race was asked to be given a special consideration in jury selection. The last five rows show the analysis in terms of the race of a victim. The first through fourth columns indicate views on the three types of affirmative jury structures, and the fifth and sixth columns show respondents' perceptions on affirmative action policies. The last seven columns show respondents' gender and racial backgrounds vis-à-vis their conception of the ideal jury structure.

This results show that, when respondents are asked that the race of the defendant be considered in empaneling the ideal twelve-member jury, those who support affirmative jury structures indicate the strongest support for six of similar race jurors (29.8 percent, 47.5 percent and 34.3 percent for Hennepin, de medietate linguae, and social science models, respectively). Similar results are also found in considering the race of a victim (31.7 percent, 48.4 percent, and 34.9 percent, respectively), suggesting that the split jury appears to gain the strongest support as the most ideal jury compositional structure among pro-affirmative action respondents. Approval for the split jury is the strongest even among those who support the Hennepin or social science models.

With regard to the views on affirmative action in jury selection, those who do not perceive affirmative action as reverse discrimination support the split jury as the ideal jury structure as well (32.4 percent and 33.6 percent for the race of a defendant and a victim, respectively). Similarly, the split jury is found to gain the strongest support from women (31.5 percent for both a defendant and a victim). With respect to racial breakdown, both blacks and Hispanics give the strongest support for the split jury as the ideal jury compositional structure in considering the race of a defendant (62.5 percent and 50.0 percent for blacks and Hispanics, respectively) and a victim (62.5 percent and 51.7 percent, respectively). Whites, on the other hand, tend to consider smaller numbers of minority jurors as ideal balances of racially diverse juries in trials with minority defendants (22.9 percent for three or less jurors). Asians also support the social science model of the jury structure (31.8 percent) much more so than the de medietate jury (22.7 percent). Overall, racial minorities' support for the fixed forms of ideal structures for a racially mixed jury is much stronger than among white respondents. In considering the race of both victims and defendants in jury selection, the de medietate jury also received the strongest support from blacks, Hispanics, women, and those who support affirmative action in jury selection.

The recommendation for the selection of six jurors shows that the split jury—for which racial makeup reflects that of defendants and victims—provides the strongest element of perceived fairness and legitimacy in the structure of racially mixed juries. Further, the analysis supports historical evidence of the public's strong preference for the use of the ancient jury de medietate linguae under the Anglo-Saxon legal tradition in both England and the United States. While the research result is based on the assumption that a racially diverse jury is granted at a trial, the split jury model received the largest approval from racial minorities, reiterating the strong perception of verdict legitimacy and trial fairness in the ancient practice of the de medietate linguae jury. It is no wonder that the demedietate jury had been widely utilized in England and America's northeastern states until quite recently.

Affirmative Peremptory Inclusion

Now we will slightly switch our perspective. Empaneling racial minorities in the final jury, through the race-based exercise of peremptory challenges by the prosecution, poses unique methodological problems for the defense. After screening

TABLE 4.5
Ideal Jury Compositions, Affirmative Juries, and Socio-demographic Characteristics

| Defendant/Victim | Total | Affirmative Juries | | | Reverse Discm[1] | | Gender | | Racial Self-Identification | | | | |
		Hennepn	De Med. L.	Soc. Sci.	Yes	No	Male	Female	White	Black	Hisp	Asian	Others
RACE OF THE DEFENDANT[2]													
a. 2 or less	7.1%	6.7%	4.9%	8.3%	3.3%	8.1%	5.4%	7.6%	4.9%	0.0%	10.0%	13.6%	8.7%
b. 3 jurors	17.3	20.2	24.6	21.3	30.0	15.3	14.3	20.7	18.0	37.5	13.3	31.8	8.7
c. 4 or 5 jurors	25.6	25.0	19.7	28.7	20.0	27.0	30.4	22.8	29.5	0.0	16.7	22.7	39.1
d. 6 jurors	30.8	29.8	47.5	34.3	26.7	32.4	28.6	31.5	21.3	62.5	50.0	22.7	21.7
e. 7 or more	19.2	18.3	3.3	7.4	20.0	17.1	21.4	17.4	26.2	0.0	10.0	9.1	21.7
RACE OF THE VICTIM[3]													
a. 2 or less	7.0	5.8	4.8	9.2	0.0	9.1	5.3	7.6	4.8	0.0	13.8	9.1	8.7
b. 3 jurors	16.6	20.2	22.6	20.2	29.0	14.5	14.0	19.6	17.4	37.5	13.8	31.8	4.3
c. 4 or 5 jurors	26.1	25.0	19.4	28.4	19.4	28.2	26.3	26.1	27.0	0.0	17.2	22.7	47.8
d. 6 jurors	32.5	31.7	48.4	34.9	32.3	33.6	33.3	31.5	23.8	62.5	51.7	27.3	21.7
e. 7 or more	17.8	17.3	4.8	7.3	19.4	14.5	21.1	15.2	27.0	0.0	3.4	9.1	17.4

Note: 1997 UC Santa Cruz Survey (n=205).

1. The question is phrased as: "Affirmative action is reverse discrimination."
2. The question asks:"For a jury of 12, how many should be the same as the race of the defendant?"
3. The question asks:"For a jury of 12, how many should be the same as the race of the victim?"

for qualification, eligibility, excuses, and challenges for cause, if peremptory challenges are still procedurally allowed—as they have been under the current jury selection system—Native American and other minority jurors would likely be eliminated from serving on the final jury. In other words, the formation of affirmative jury structures would require either some restrictive usage, if not the complete abolition, of peremptory challenges so as not to impair the jury representation of racial minorities in the final jury.

Initially proposed by Tracey L. Altman (1986) as an alternative to peremptory challenges to empanel the final jury, this innovative strategy of peremptory choice or inclusion requires that both sides may exercise their challenges for cause to enlist twelve jurors in order of preference. The judge then initially selects any juror whose name appears on both parties' lists, regardless of how the juror was ranked. Alternating between both lists, the judge proceeds to take the highest-rated juror from each list until a complete panel of twelve is assembled.

Many legal commentators and jury studies advocate the elimination of the peremptory challenge system, suggesting that, if the courts truly mean to eliminate racial discrimination in the jury selection process, the elimination of peremptory challenges is the only effective remedy (King 1993a; Ramirez 1994; Hoffman 1997). Once eliminating the discriminatory effects of peremptory challenges on minorities' jury representation, affirmative peremptory inclusion is considered to be an important strategic alternative to peremptory challenges.

Our proposal for affirmative action in jury selection is a strategic departure from previous debates, which called for either the complete elimination of peremptory challenges or Altman's peremptory inclusive strategy in favor of an alternative jury selection approach, such as affirmative peremptory inclusion. Rather, we suggest allowing both peremptory challenges and peremptory inclusion to coexist during voir dire. After screening for qualifications, excuses, exemptions, and cause challenges, our proposed method requires that both sides select a fixed number of jurors from the qualified jury pool. The specific number of these peremptory inclusions may depend on the availability of targeted potential jurors in the qualified jury pool. For example, in a jurisdiction where the targeted racial minority population in the community is very small like Mendocino County, the availability of Native Americans in the qualified jury pool would be significantly limited. In the Lincoln trial, there were only three Native American jurors who survived from the initial jury panel, indicating that the minimally required six jurors for the de medietate linguae jury were not available.

As we have already argued, in a jurisdiction with a small number of minority jurors, the number of minority jurors should be at least three in order to ensure viable jury deliberations as proposed by the social science model. From a practical standpoint, the selection procedure requires that in jury selection during voir dire, both sides prepare a separate preferential list of three potential jurors in the pool, making up a total of six peremptorily chosen and identified jurors by both parties. The jury seats for the six remaining jurors and alternatives would then be filled by randomly selecting the jurors from the qualified jury pool. If both sides identified the same jurors in their preferential list, seven or more jurors would be randomly selected from the qualified jury pool. In a trial which may last a month or more, a large pool of alternative jurors might be necessary and those jurors would also be selected randomly from the qualified jury pool. For the final jury, peremptory challenges can still be exercised in the selection of those remaining jurors as normally done under the current jury selection procedure.

We also propose the affirmative selection of three jurors as the minimum number of required jury seats to be filled for each side. Thus, the number of peremptory inclusions should range from three to six in order to assure the minimum condition for viable jury deliberations. As the social science model proposes, the inclusion of at least three jurors would ensure a race neutral verdict to "judge a criminal or civil case that involves the rights" of a minority defendant (Colbert 1990, 124). This suggests that jury representation of three minority persons in the twelve-member jury is the compromise between the harm of having one or no racially similar jurors, and the impracticability of obtaining a jury evenly balanced along racial lines (Bell 1980, 273-274).

It is our conclusion that the affirmative peremptory choice can protect those impacted by race or whatever interest the parties deem important in given trials. If political representation is important to the party, then the attorney can make the selection based on potential jurors' political beliefs or affiliations. While race plays an important role in the public's perception of the legitimacy and integrity of jury trials and verdicts impacting many race-sensitive and publicized trials, each side should be allowed to consider race as one of many possible criteria in forming a jury, suggesting that whatever were considered to be significant cognizable characteristics in a given case may become the basis of peremptory choices. Each side can generate its own criteria, with the combination of important cognizable factors such as racial identity, ancestral race, gender, sexuality, and any other socio-ideological factors, including education, social class, religion, and political affiliation.

Peremptory choices in the Lincoln jury might have concentrated on the criteria of race and the degree of Native American's assimilation into the white community, for example. Although those parameters may not necessarily reflect the jurors' views and attitudes towards the guilt or acquittal of the minority defendant, peremptory inclusion can nevertheless allow both parties to engage in critical evaluation of jurors' potential biases and prejudice.

Peremptory inclusion does not always create the tendency towards polarized jury deliberations, leading to hung juries. Still, speculative concerns exist that affirmative inclusive selection may possibly increase the instances of hung juries. This suggests that the minimum for a cohesive unit in forming strong opinions may be at least fulfilled by seating three affirmatively chosen jurors, though the selection criteria may have been based on both parties' predisposition towards selecting prospective jurors based on race or other cognizable characteristics and considerations. We believe, however, the problem of hung juries may be overexaggerated. For example, we need to question whether or not peremptory inclusion creates the possibilities for a hung jury, presents a significant problem in jury deliberations, and builds up an unreconcilable barrier for reaching an unified judgment in a given trial. Attorneys' peremptory inclusion is inevitably exercised on imperfect knowledge of jurors' probable behavior or performance in the deliberation process, so the assessment of an increase in the number of hung juries is undoubtedly overstated. Furthermore, challenges for cause presumably will have removed demonstrably biased and prejudiced individuals prior to the system of peremptory inclusion, thereby reducing the likelihood of split jury decisions.

The debate on the problematic nature of hung juries is also distorted because it reveals the judicial system's long-standing bias in favor of more homogeneous, all-white juries. While such single-race juries may reach unified judgments on a consistent basis and in a shorter period, there is no reason to assume that these outcomes are genuinely fair, lawful, or free of racial prejudice or other biases. Jury research has shown that the small six-member jury is less likely to render hung jury verdicts than the twelve-member jury, because small sized juries are more likely to be homogeneous in race, opinions, and attitudes than the twelve-member jury (Cocke 1979; Kaye 1980; Roper 1980). In case of conflict resolution, a hung jury is an expression of substantive or emotive disagreements over the evidence, the testimony, and the nature of the case—not necessarily a negative result. Rather, after jurors reach differing conclusions as they evaluate the same evidence and testimony, a hung jury may provide a positive result, suggesting that there is not consensus among the community that the defendant is guilty.

The system of peremptory inclusion also provides the positive effect of preventing miscarriages of justice in cases with weak evidence, especially involving members of racial minority defendants. Tanya E. Coke (1994) suggests that the prosecution normally makes racialized, calculated decisions and risk assessments about which cases to bring to trial—based in part on their knowledge that most jury panels are predominantly white and pro-prosecution. The system of peremptory inclusion and racially diverse tribunals will force the prosecution to assess the merit of the case and the credibility of their criminal charges, or to make efforts to strengthen the state's evidence and testimony, as the government rightfully bears the burden of proving guilt beyond a reasonable doubt (385–386).

Peremptory inclusion will likely bring about a small "revolution" in equity, allowing the defendant to attempt to achieve representation of his or her peers on the final jury. These peers might look like the accused, perhaps better understand the defendant's circumstances, and respond to the state of mind and conditions of the defendant. The peremptory inclusionary approach also enhances the public's perceived legitimacy of the jury composition, its deliberations and verdicts by balancing the defendant's personal rights to a fair trial with the minority community's interests. Due to the straightforward process of peremptory inclusion, less time would be spent for voir dire jury selection, so that the inclusionary approach would allow more rapid processing and disposition capability of jury trials than by following traditional jury selection procedures.

Affirmative Peremptory Inclusion and Fill-it-up Quota Methods

Affirmative peremptory inclusion, as we propose, is conceptually and methodologically different from the so-called backloading selection methods used by the court for the Hennepin's racially diverse jury. The Hennepin model asks for proportional jury representation by filling in the jury boxes as individual minority jurors become qualified and are brought into the courtroom from the jury pool, suggesting that no priority or preference is given among minority jury candidates in the qualified jury pool for occupying the required number of jury seats. As long as the court assigns the required number of jury seats to the member of racial minorities in the exact order as they were brought into the courtroom, then the Hennepin selection method for the final jury is complete.

Yet, the Hennepin model of jury selection has some significant procedural problems and logistical deficiencies. First, the agents of conducting affirmative inclusive jury selection would best be both the defense and the prosecution, not the court. The active participation by both parties in jury selection is essential as America's courts are based on an adversarial system, and allowing peremptory inclusion by opposing parties would help maintain the logic that the final verdict will be determined after opposing views are fully articulated and carefully debated by affirmatively chosen jurors. By contrast, a judge's decisions or views are not necessarily race- or gender-neutral, as the judge is also a person with individual biases and proclivities based on his or her racial identity, ancestral race, gender, social class, and other socio-demographic characteristics (Meyer and Jesilow 1997).

The advantage of affirmative peremptory inclusion allows both sides to determine the variability and characteristics of jurors for the required number of jury seats. While race continues to exert a disproportionate impact on public perceptions and jury selection in racially sensitive trials, the critical task of ascertaining one's racial identity is not a straightforward, but a very complex, task, suggesting that both objective or subjective evaluations of one's race do not necessarily correspond to the person's self-determined racial identity or presumed racialized opinions. As demonstrated earlier, one's racial self-identity does not always reflect or correspond to one's racial ancestral history, suggesting that jurors with the same racial identity may often fail to share similar life experiences, social values, ideologies, customs, or traditions. And yet those with similarly circumscribed, racialized experiences are important in accurately imputing the defendant's motives and interpreting racially sensitive issues and circumstances in criminal trials.

As evidenced in the pretrial public poll in the Lincoln case, survey analyses revealed that approximately 20 percent of Native Americans felt that the defendant was either probably or definitely guilty (22.3 percent for guilty verdicts), suggesting that even the same racial identity does not always lead to the same, stereotypical opinions or attitudes towards a defendant. Although race may remain an important determinant of how the public critically evaluates trial fairness and verdict legitimacy, peremptory inclusion allows the defense and prosecution to identify and determine the most relevant and important cognizable characteristics for the selection of final jurors in criminal trials.

Unlike the backloading selection method used in Hennepin, peremptory inclusion is frontloaded, allowing both parties to engage in examining and identifying significant and crucial factor in the given case. Under the social science model, for example, if the defense wishes to ensure the inclusion of at least three Native American jurors, the defense can affirmatively choose them, while the prosecution may also affirmatively select an equal number of white jurors from the pool, suggesting that affirmative peremptory inclusion insures viable and active jury deliberations because—regardless of other six remaining jurors to be chosen from the panel under the traditional jury selection procedure—each side has at least three jurors to make sure that their views are considered and fully articulated in the deliberation process. Another advantageous aspect of the affirmative selection method is that selecting three jurors by both sides ensures a greater degree of group autonomy and self-determination, without being overwhelmed by the majority group's pressure during the jury deliberation.

THE NEED FOR PROGRESSIVE LEGISLATIVE AND COURT ACTION

Given the many benefits of racially mixed juries, legislative action to ensure racially heterogeneous juries is needed to rectify jury underrepresentation by racial minorities. In assessing the readiness and effectiveness of legislative and court-initiated legal actions, legislative actions, including the 1968 Jury Selection and Service Act, may be more effective and less problematic than judicially designed, race-conscious remedies.

Since legislative actions reflect public concerns, the job of fashioning a remedy is more properly reserved for legislators. In the current conservative climate of anticrime and proprosecutorial legislative policies, however, such legislative reforms seem unlikely. Especially in California, since the mid-1990s, social and political narratives of a number of controversial events and conservative measures have made it almost impossible to implement race-conscious remedies. These political agendas and legislative measures include the passage of four propositions, numbered: 184 (three-strikes), 187 (anti-immigration), 209 (California Civil Rights Initiative eliminating affirmative action), 21 (anti-gang), and the University of California Board of Regents' decision against affirmative action.

Passed overwhelmingly by voters in November 1994, Proposition 184 allows twenty-five-years-to-life sentences for anyone convicted of three felonies; and a large proportion of "three-strikers" have been racial minorities (Johnson 1995). Proposition 187 bars public education and non-emergency health and social services to illegal immigrants, with Mexicans and/or Hispanics making up most of such immigrants (Holding 1995). In July 1995, the University of California Board of Regents voted to end affirmative action in college admissions on the basis of race and gender. Governor Pete Wilson also filed suit in Sacramento in August 1995 against his own administration and other constitutional officers to prohibit them from carrying out affirmative action and "racially preferential programs," calling the issue a "matter of urgent statewide concern" (Gunnison 1995). In November 1996, Californians also approved Proposition 209, a measure to prohibit state and local governments from using race- and gender-based programs in hiring, education, and contracting in California (Lempinen and Burdman 1996). And in March 2000, the public overwhelmingly approved Proposition 21, which was designed to punish juvenile and gang-affiliated youths who are most likely to be members of racial and ethnic minorities (Drizin and Harper 2000).

The passage of these propositions held wider social ramification and judicial consequences, too. Then San Francisco Supervisor Terence Hallinan, who later became San Francisco District Attorney, argued that the three-strikes law worked a tremendous hardship on both the courts and those accused, noting that 70 percent of persons receiving "three strikes" were African-American and 75 percent of these were nonviolent offenses (Johnson 1995). Dramatic increases of criminal jury trials were expected in near future, as few defendants were willing to enter guilty pleas, even including nonviolent offenses. As remediation and reform, given the procedural simplicity and conceptual clarity of the affirmative jury structures and peremptory inclusion, the legislature and the courts thus need to consider progressive actions on the affirmative mechanism to ensure racially mixed juries as a protective shield for minority defendants in general and for advancing the interest of society at large.

While positive legislative action would be more direct and inclusive than judicial case-by-case decisions, nonetheless such legislation remained highly unlikely in the conservative political climates of late 1990s or early 2000s. Although such remedies have been historically left to the legislature, today's courts may have to devise their own remedies in the area of criminal procedure and the jury selection system in criminal cases. While the proposed remedy of imposing affirmative mechanisms to ensure racially mixed juries does not foreclose legislative debates or initiatives, judiciary-imposed remedies may be essential to protect the rights of minority defendants and advance the public interest of marginalized segments of the community. Such race-conscious remedies may be of even greater significance in highly publicized criminal cases that involve sensitive issues of race and racism. As the seriousness of the consequences at stake argues more strongly for intervention by the courts than does any program in other areas, the courts need to carefully consider the merit and consequences of race-conscious, affirmative action measures to prevent discrimination in jury selection, thereby restoring the public's confidence in the jury system, improving the fairness of trial proceedings, and enhancing the public's acceptance of jury verdicts.

CONCLUSIONS

We have shown that the final verdict by the all-white jury failed to satisfy Native American communities in the case of Bear Lincoln. His supporters felt that Lincoln was the one who invited litigation and created the opportunity to call on the court to critically assess local law enforcement's discriminatory practices against Native Americans in the community. The mixed verdicts of acquittals and hung decisions, however, failed to reflect the sentiments shared by the Native American population. Even the white community refused to show the support for the verdicts of an all-white jury, as the overwhelming majority of whites felt that the defendant was guilty and criticized the jury's failure to secure the conviction of the alleged "cop killer."

Using the Lincoln case as a classic example, emphasizing the perceived legitimacy and integrity of jury deliberations and verdicts in a racially explosive case, this chapter looked to the potential applications of affirmative action in jury selection—affirmative jury structures and peremptory inclusion—as well as the importance of systemic defense strategies in trying to place minority members on jury panels and the final juries, neutralizing the biasing effects of race-based peremptory challenges.

We conclude that affirmative jury structures can effectively form racially mixed juries. Peremptory inclusion is an affirmative, voir dire strategy to ensure the presence of minority jurors, so that the final jury is chosen by affirmatively selecting from the eligible pool jurors who share a similar racial and socio-ideological background as the accused. The chapter also discussed the unique feature of affirmative jury selection methods and examined how peremptory inclusion differs from the conventional voir dire procedure, as well as a kind of the "any-minority-will-do" type of jury selection in the Hennepin model.

Critical analysis of the Lincoln case and affirmative strategies for creating racially diverse juries illustrate that affirmative action in jury selection may be the only viable option to overcome the discriminatory use of peremptory challenges, while eliminating the public's mistrusts of single race jury's verdicts in racially sensitive trials. Progressive court action may be necessary to provide the necessary means to achieve racially diverse juries and to enhance the community's perceived legitimacy of jury deliberations and verdicts.

Before we turn to the next chapter's consideration of constitutional questions with respect to the merit and the applicability of the racially mixed jury, we leave the readers with an excerpt by defense attorney J. Tony Serra on his views on the prospect for a new trial on the deadlock charges in the Bear Lincoln case. His views on those issues reflect his trial experience in this racially explosive case and illustrate the extent of hardship and difficulties faced by the defense team in trying to ensure and secure a fair and just trial for his client.

In the postverdict interview, Serra declared his faith in the community's sense of fairness and equality:

> [T]his case should not be retried. This is the time to reunify. This is the time to come back together. This is the time to build bridges, not to destroy bridges. And if the District Attorney seeks to go forward, she will do nothing but create hostility and acrimony in this county. So if she intends to go forward, she should be denounced. All of you in many forms should make your voices heard. You should communicate with her and with other public officers. You should denounce any prospect of a retrial. Let us go forward; let us go forward in peace, as Bear has said (Wilson 1997e).

On April 23, 1999, newly elected district attorney announced that his office had decided not to pursue the deadlock charge against Eugene "Bear" Lincoln; and Mendocino County Superior Court Judge John Golden dismissed the matter—ending Lincoln's four-year ordeal over being charged with the capital murder of a white deputy sheriff (Wilson 1999).

Chapter 5

THE SIXTH AMENDMENT
AND THE RACIALLY MIXED JURY

Affirmative action in jury selection is unlike previous efforts that deliberately limited opportunities for blacks, women, and other racial and ethnic minorities for jury service. Today's courts are attempting to establish racial and gender ratios, to set varying equilibriums, in composing juries—to explicitly increase minority representation in jury pools, on panels and venires, and even in jury boxes that approximates or sometimes surpasses their proportion in the local community.

Racially diverse and balanced juries nonetheless have a checkered history. Despite their slowly growing recognition today, the nation's founding fathers did not share a similar vision concerning racial diversity or an equitable balance of jurors by race, though they did consider the guarantee of an independent and impartial jury to be a fundamental right (Meyer 1994, 256). In the drafting of the Constitution in 1787, for instance, these legislators provided for the guarantee of trial by jury for all crimes, except impeachment (Van Dyke 1977, 7). Today this guarantee is extended by the Sixth Amendment of the Bill of Rights which provides:

> In all criminal prosecutions, the accused shall enjoy the right to a speedy and public trial, by an impartial jury of the state and district wherein the crime shall have been committed, which district shall have been previously ascertained by law, and to be informed of the nature and cause of the accusation; to be confronted with the witnesses against him; to have compulsory process for obtaining witnesses in his favor, and to have the assistance of counsel for his defense.

The Sixth Amendment ideally envisions the jury as a microcosm of the community, providing the accused the guarantee of trial by an unbiased jury. This ideal of an impartial decision-making body to make legally binding decisions is nonetheless the reference point against which inequitable methods for selecting jurors have been rationalized and legitimized. Yet, in order to fully understand the significance of the Sixth Amendment, its effects on the possibility for the creation of a racially mixed jury, and the legality and practicality of applying affirmative action in jury selection, the following concepts need to be clearly defined and examined: (1) impartiality; (2) a jury of one's peers; and (3) a fair cross section of the community.

These three concepts overlap in many respects and are closely entwined with one another. At the same time, they are categorically and diametrically opposed to each other (Massaro 1986, 542). For a "jury of one's peers" may neither necessarily represent a fair cross section of the local community nor be impartial. Similarly, an impartial jury may not include "peers," or may not be representative of the general populace in the jurisdiction. As a jury in highly sensitive and publicized trials is often exposed to some prejudicial materials, though such a jury could represent a fair cross section of the community, the members may not be "impartial," and the defendant may thus be deprived of receiving a fair trial (Abramson 1994, 17–18).

Though all three terms represent important concepts in understanding the value and importance of the Sixth Amendment for the impanelment of criminal juries and the administration of a criminal jury trial, few studies have examined the implications of these constitutional concepts and the feasibility of applying affirmative action in jury selection. Past studies have also failed to critically evaluate the legality and applicability of affirmative mechanisms for creating racially diverse juries. And little research has assessed whether or not such race-conscious, affirmative methods may do violence to the constitutional ideals of a fair trial and an impartial jury in ensuring a racially heterogeneous jury.

To fill in the missing spaces of the literature, we examine these three constitutional concepts derived from the Sixth Amendment, assessing how these concepts are closely entwined with affirmative requirements to ensure a racially diverse jury. In doing so, this chapter explores the essential balancing of these concepts in composing a racially mixed jury and conducting a fair trial.

IMPARTIALITY

The Sixth Amendment explicitly guarantees the right to an "impartial jury" in criminal cases. One legal scholar contends that the guarantee of trial "by an impartial jury" may be the most important constitutional standard governing a fair trial (Van Dyke 1977, 45–46). While close attention was given to the right to a jury trial at the time the Constitution was drafted, there is little evidence of original understanding of the requirement that the jury must also be impartial (Van Dyke 1977, 46–47). The first United States Supreme Court pronouncement on the question concerning an impartial jury did not appear until the case of *U.S. v. Wood* (299 U.S. 123, 1936), which declared that the Constitution mandates specific qualifications for jury service or for any particular mode of selecting jurors (299 U.S. 123, 145, 1936).[1] Yet, the Court defined impartiality as follows:

> Impartiality is not a technical conception. It is a state of mind. For ascertainment of this mental attitude of appropriate indifference the Constitution lays

down no particular test and procedure is not chained to any ancient and artificial formula. (299 U.S. 123, 145, 146, 1936)[2]

The Court thus acknowledged that impartiality involves the cerebral quality of an individual's relative, unbiased mental state, not capable of explicit definition or clarification. Legal scholar Toni M. Massaro also argues that "[a]n impartial juror is not a completely neutral person, but is one who evidences no extreme bias for or against the accused" (1986, 543).

Other studies examining the historical concept of impartiality reveal that the term entailed three original purposes. First, the Sixth Amendment guarantee of an "impartial jury" was intended to insure the impartiality of the individual jurors in criminal trials (Massaro 1986, 542). Second, impartiality also referred to the fairness of the jury selection process in an effort to conduct a fair trial (Van Dyke 1977, 47). And the third still emerging concept of impartiality turns on the assessment of fairness, or the impartiality of the composite jury as a collective whole, rather than the impartiality of each individual juror.

The Supreme Court has argued that, in order to assess the impartiality of individual jurors, each juror may be questioned for biases and abilities to impartially consider evidence, the Court noting that:

> the function of the [peremptory] challenge is not only to eliminate extremes of partiality on both sides, but to assure the parties that the jurors before whom they try the case will decide on the basis of the evidence placed before them, and not otherwise (*Swain v. Missouri,* 380 U.S. 207 219, 1965).

Voir dire is the traditional means by which judges and attorneys attempt to uncover whether individual jurors are impartial by the use of peremptory challenges (for which no cause or reason needs to be stated) and/or challenges for cause. These devices help assure that potential jurors with extreme biases or prejudice against the defendant, or others linked to criminal trials, can be assessed by the parties and eliminated from serving on the jury. The difficulty implicit in this methodological approach for securing "impartial" jurors, however, is that it assumes that an impartial jury can be picked, not by selecting jurors with impartial minds, but by identifying and eliminating jurors who are considered incapable of impartially evaluating evidence. That is, a juror might be biased, yet able to impartially consider the evidence. But the defense and the prosecution, holding different perspectives of the trial outcome, are also likely to develop different definitions of which individuals are impartial potential jurors and thus strategies for eliminating partial jurors (Massaro 1986, 544). Attorneys are thus likely to exercise their peremptory challenges in a way that they do not seek to empanel impartial jurors, but instead try to eliminate partial jurors who may side with the posturings of the opposition, regardless of whether or not they are capable of impartially considering evidence presented at the trial.

Impartiality as a Group and Composite Construct

Besides the notion of impartiality of each individual juror and his or her ability to assess evidence without extreme prejudice, impartiality is also considered a group concept. Assuming that no individual person is truly impartial, the gathering of twelve persons with their own personal views and opinions can produce a "diffused impartiality" from the heterogeneous mix of jurors' different expectations and life experiences (Massaro 1986, 511; Meyer 1994). The broad, representative character of the jury thus leads to the assurance of impartiality in conducting a fair trial, shifting the analytical focus from the impartiality of an individual juror to the composite and group assurance of impartiality. Since race is closely correlated with group affiliation and identity, distinct life styles, life experiences, and social attitudes, minority jurors are likely to bring to the courtroom divergent opinions and assumptions about the defendant, the prosecution, and the criminal justice and court systems (see generally Fukurai, Butler, and Krooth 1993). Thus, the fairness or impartiality of the jury as a group concept may be a far more important issue than whether the individual jurors who comprise the jury are impartial.

Diffused impartiality by racially diverse juries may be also an important element in increasing the public's acceptance of jury verdicts and enhancing the perceived fairness of jury deliberations. One need only look at public reaction to controversial verdicts rendered by single-race juries to find support for the conceptual importance of racial diversity on the jury. The jury of a single race is seen to reflect a particular, nonneutral viewpoint, uninformed of different perspectives and diverse opinions, suggesting that an impartial jury is not simply a group of individuals acting in good faith, but depends upon perspectives and unconscious assumptions that to some degree are affected by and predicated upon social class, group affiliations, racial experiences, cultural identity, and the different social and racial backgrounds and customs of jury participants.

Impartiality as a group and composite concept may be more likely to find its expression in racially mixed juries than in single race juries. And such a view of impartiality culminating in the racially mixed jury is also more likely to be shared and accepted by both the public and the community. Support by greater public acceptance can be gleaned from table 5.1's examination of public perceptions of the fairness of jury verdicts by racially diverse juries as compared with decisions by single-race juries. The overwhelming majority of the public apparently feels that jury decisions reached by racially diverse juries are fairer than decisions reached by single-race juries (67.9 percent for those who "somewhat" and "strongly" agreed—the last column), suggesting that the fairness of verdicts and impartiality of jury decision-making processes are significantly related to the diversified racial profiles of the members of the criminal jury.

The support for racially diverse jury verdicts is consistent across gender, racial groups, and socioeconomic backgrounds. Though the majority of all these cognizable groups agree that unified expressions of verdicts by racially diverse juries are fairer than the verdicts by single-race juries, there are some variations in the level of their agreement with respect to verdicts as a group concept and a racially diverse expression of impartiality. For example, the following groups are more likely than other groups to agree that decisions reached by racially diverse juries are fairer than decisions reached by single race juries: (1) blacks (78.7 percent), (2) Hispanics (79.1 percent), (3) women (72.6 percent), (4) those with some college education (68.8 percent), and (5) the retired (69.5 percent).

On the other hand, Asians are least likely to perceive the verdict fairness by racially diverse juries (22.2 percent and 33.3 percent for "strongly" and "somewhat" agreeing with the statement). It is interesting to note that non-Asians, who nonetheless share Asian ancestry, demonstrate stronger agreement with the benefit of racially mixed tribunals (31.3 percent and 37.5 percent, respectively).

On another level, the issue of a fair and impartial trial also involves the concepts of the jurors' fair cross-sectional representation and as peers. The need for group and diffused impartiality stems from the realization that in a heterogeneous society, no persons is truly impartial, unbiased, or unprejudiced. Thus, a jury's fact-finding function can best be optimized, not by one person, but by jurors' cross-sectional participation in the decision making process, suggesting that jury impartiality necessarily may be premised upon the diversity and heterogeneity of juror backgrounds. The Supreme Court has held that an impartial jury must be representative, explaining that:

> It is part of the established tradition in the use of juries as instruments of public justice that the jury be a body truly representative of the community. For racial discrimination to result in the exclusion from jury service of otherwise qualified groups not only violates our Constitution and laws enacted under it, but is at war with our basic concepts of democratic society and a representative government (*Smith v. Texas,* 311 US 128 130, 1940).

In order to challenge the discriminatory nature of jury selection procedures, racial minorities must show that, without their inclusion, the jury will not be representative. The Supreme Court has ruled that blacks, Hispanics, and women are cognizable groups for the purposes of representativeness and they need special protection against discrimination in jury selection (*Strauder v. West Virginia,* 100 U.S. 306, 1880; *Hernandez v. Texas,* 347 U.S. 475, 1954; *Taylor v. Louisiana,* 419 U.S. 522, 1975).

Impartiality of jurors, however, is explicitly the privilege and the right of the defendant only in criminal trials. The Seventh Amendment, which extends the constitutional right of the jury to civil cases, does not explicitly require impartiality, though the Courts have held that the Due Process Clause requires an impartial trial (*Withrow v. Larkin,* 421 US 35 46, 1975).[3]

TABLE 5.1
Fairness of Jury Verdicts by Racially Mixed Juries Over Single Race Juries[1]

Response	Racial Identity (Racial Ancestry)[2]					Gender		Education				Employment Status[3]			
	White	Black	Hispanic	Asian & Pac. Is.	Others	Male	Female	<= H.S.	Some Coll.	College Grad.	Post Grad.	Full	Part	Retired	Total
Strongly Agree	31.0% (33.2)[2]	27.6% (29.4)	41.9% (33.3)	22.2% (31.3)	35.7% (21.6)	27.2%	35.9%	28.1%	33.0%	32.6%	30.5%	27.6%	43.6%	41.7%	32.0%
Agree Somewhat	35.9 (35.5)	50.0 (29.4)	37.2 (41.7)	33.3 (37.5)	42.9 (51.0)	34.9	36.7	40.6	35.8	34.7	29.3	38.1	25.6	27.8	35.9
Disagree Somewhat	18.0 (15.6)	5.6 (11.8)	9.3 (14.6)	11.1 (12.5)	7.1 (13.7)	17.4	15.1	12.5	17.3	16.8	18.3	17.2	10.3	16.7	16.1
Strongly Disagree	15.1 (15.6)	16.7 (29.4)	11.6 (10.4)	33.3 (18.8)	14.3 (13.7)	20.5	12.2	18.8	13.9	15.8	22.0	17.2	20.5	13.9	15.9
Total	100.0	99.9[3]	100.0	99.9[3]	100.0	100.0	99.9[3]	100.0	100.0	99.9[3]	100.1[3]	100.1[3]	100.0	100.1[3]	99.9[3]

Notes:
1. Subjects responded to the following question, "Decisions reached by racially diverse juries are more *fair* than decisions reached by single race juries."
2. The figure in parentheses shows the percentage of respondents with different ancestral races. For example, 33.2% indicates that almost one third of survey respondents with white ancestry agreed strongly with the statement.
3. Due to rounding errors.

THE FAIR CROSS-SECTION REQUIREMENT

The second concept, a "fair cross section of the community," represents society's interests in broad community participation in the jury system. This is rooted in the conception of local justice that is enhanced when the jury is drawn from a fair cross section of the local community, representative of the community population, and thus more democratically balanced. Under this assumption, a jury drawn from a fair cross section is also better suited to fulfill the jury's function of serving as a democratic check on government personnel directing the criminal justice system, including judges, prosecutors, and the police. The Supreme Court has stated that the fair cross sectional doctrine "guard[s] against the exercise of arbitrary power" and "make[s] available the commonsense judgment of the community as a hedge against the overzealous or mistaken prosecutor" (*Taylor v. Louisiana,* 419 US 522, 530–31, 1975 (quoted in *Lockhart v. McCree,* 476 U.S. 162, 174–75, 1986)), as well as "the professional or perhaps overconditioned or biased response of a judge" (*Taylor v. Louisiana,* 419 U.S. 522, 531, 1975). The judgment of the community and its representative segments is thus less likely to share the prejudices of either prosecutors or judges (Massaro 1986, 508–510)

The term, "cross section" first appeared in the case of *Akins v. Texas* (325 U.S. 398, 1945), Justice Murphy's dissenting opinion noting:

> If a jury is to be fairly chosen from a *cross section* of the community, it must be done without limiting the number of persons of a particular color, racial background or faith—all of which are irrelevant factors in setting qualifications for jury service (325 U.S. 398 409, 1945). [emphasis added][4]

Speaking in terms of "representative" groups, the Court first defined the cross-sectional requirements in *Glasser v. United States* (315 U.S. 60, 1942), arguing that a fair cross-sectional jury is drawn from a jury pool in which no distinctive group is underrepresented due to systematic exclusion. As in the Akins case, Justice Murphy held that any jury selection method that failed to include representative groups of the local community is detrimental to the effectiveness of a fair trial:

> Tendencies, no matter how slight, toward the selection of jurors by any method other than a process which will insure a trial by a representative group are undermining processes weakening the institution of jury trial, and should be sturdily resisted. That the motives influencing such tendencies may be of the best must not blind us to the dangers of allowing any encroachment whatsoever on this essential right. Steps innocently taken may one by one lead to the irretrievable impairment of substantial liberties (315 US 86, 1942).

Four years later in *Thiel v. Southern Pacific Co* (328 U.S. 217, 1946), Justice Murphy also offered another definition of a fair cross section of the community in which jurors must be selected by court administrators "without systematic and intentional exclusion of any . . . group" (328 U.S. 217 220, 1946). The case then extended the fair cross section requirement and gave the cognizable group status to the class of daily wage earners who needed special protection against discrimination in jury selection.

However, the expectation that the representative principle would lead to broader jury participation based on wider cross sectional representation of the community was considerably restricted by the Court's decision in *Swain v. Alabama* (380 U.S. 202, 1965). The Court held that a defendant was not entitled to jury pools or venires that are "a perfect mirror of the community or accurately reflect the proportionate strength of every identifiable group" (380 U.S. 202 208, 1965).

Yet some progress appeared a decade later in the case of *Taylor v. Louisiana* (419 U.S. 522, 1975). The Court held that the fair cross section requirement was violated by a state provision that excluded women from jury service unless they individually requested to serve in writing. Since the provision effectively eliminated 53 percent of potentially eligible jurors from jury service, the Court ruled that women's systematic exclusion from jury service violated the Sixth Amendment mandate that the jury be the representative body of the community, reiterating that a fair cross-sectional representation was an important component of the Sixth Amendment's guarantee for the jury trial (419 U.S. 522 531, 1975). Justice White, writing for the majority, stated that this "Court has unambiguously declared that the American concept of the jury trial contemplates a jury drawn from a fair cross section of the community" (491 U.S. 522 525, 1975).

The Court extended this analysis and formulated a test for a Sixth Amendment cross section violation in *Duren vs. Missouri* (439 U.S. 357, 1979). Under the Duren test, a defendant must demonstrate that: (1) the people excluded are members of a distinct, also known as a cognizable, group within the community; (2) the representation of this cognizable group in the jury venire or panel was not fair and reasonable in relation to its population in the community; and (3) the underrepresentation of the group was due to a process that systematically excluded the group (439 U.S. 357 364, 1979). Once a defendant makes this showing, the burden then shifts to the state to explain the jury pool composition and that disproportionate representation was designed for the primary purpose of advancing a significant state interest (439 U.S. 357 366–138, 1979). Despite the Court's emphasis on the jury as a truly representative body of the local community, however, the Court held that such a fair cross-sectional requirement only extends to jury selection stages up to the jury panels or venire pools, not the criminal jury itself.

The prospect that the representative requirement might become an important vehicle for promoting greater diversity and heterogeneity of the chosen jury was restricted by the Court decision in *Holland v. Illinois* (493 U.S. 474, 1990), in which the defendant appealed his conviction on the ground that the state's peremptory challenges of black venire members violated the Sixth Amendment right to be tried by a representative cross section of the local community (493 U.S. 474 477–478, 1990).[5] The Court reiterated that the requirement for the fair cross-sectional representation applies only to the jury pool or venire, not the final jury itself (493 U.S. 474 478–484, 1990). The ruling also argued that the fair cross-sectional requirement failed to impose any limitations on the exercise of arbitrary peremptory challenges. The jury selection procedure the Court thereby approved continued to diminish the representativeness of the criminal jury (see generally Fukurai, Butler, and Krooth 1993).

Social Functions of Cross-Sectional Representation

From a broader democratic perspective, however, the requirement of cross-sectional jury participation serves three important, racial, public, and social interests. If a broader range of community groups is represented in the jury selection process, the jury's ultimate verdict is more likely to be perceived as a legitimate expression of popular conscience and collective sentiments shared throughout the local community (King 1993b). The community's interest in the fair cross-sectional requirement is also likely to satisfy the community's desire to maintain some control over the criminal justice system. Since the provincial jury interjects community sentiments into the jury deliberation process, broad community participation tends to enhance the community's willingness to accept trial deliberation and jury verdicts. When distinct racial segments of the community are excluded from jury service, however, jury findings may not be perceived as the legitimate expressions of the community as a whole. After systematically excluding racial minority jurors from jury service, the verdicts of all-white juries have been explosive, the capstone of numerous urban rebellions and disturbances venting community anger and rage.

Fair cross-sectional participation also serves governmental interests. For broad community jury participation is likely to bring every distinct class of citizens to experience the process and implications of jury decisions, educating citizens in the mechanics of criminal justice and court systems, as well as demonstrating civic participation and individual responsibility in maintaining the quality of government (Massaro 1986, 151). To the extent that representative experiences by distinct social, political, and racial segments of the local community enhance democratic participation, increasing public respect for criminal justice and jury systems, such public confidence also preserves just government power and authority—as legitimacy of the government in the eyes of both enfranchised and marginalized members of the community is critical to the continued authority of government itself (Tocqueville 1994, 128).

The fair cross-sectional requirement also serves the interest of the defendant. The court can best protect criminal defendants by expanding and providing jury opportunities to traditionally underrepresented classes of citizens such as women, racial minorities, and the poor. The heterogeneous jury drawn across racial, gender, and class lines is also likely to include potential jurors with similar life experiences and history as the defendant's, and the community and parties may be less likely to complain that a verdict is unfair when it is rendered by a balanced, representative jury (Smith 1993).

The critical question, however, still remains: how will various segments of the general public view the importance of the jury's cross-sectional representation? Unless the general community shares a similar view on the cross-sectionality of jury representation, the American jury may not maintain its authority and legitimacy in the eyes of community members. For race remains an important social and political emblem in the evaluation of representative fairness and equality, shaping the public's perception of the requirement of a fair cross-sectional representation involving the jury's racial makeup. Table 5.2 helps to define the framework, under the assumption of the random selection method, in which every qualified juror in the jurisdiction has the same probability of being selected for jury service. The resulting representativeness of the jury should then ideally reflect the racial diversity and the proportional strength of minority groups in the community.

When respondents were asked whether they agree or disagree to the statement, "the racial makeup of juries should be reflective of the community," the overwhelming majority of all racial groups, except Asians, agreed that the racial makeup of the juries should reflect the racial makeup of the community (82.9 percent whites, 79.0 percent blacks, 84.8 percent Hispanics, and 37.5 percent Asians). Both genders (82.9 percent and 85.5 percent respectively for male and female), the employed, and the highly educated are more likely to support the jury's cross-sectional representation (89.6 percent and 87.7 percent respectively for the full-time employed and postgraduates). While there are some variations with respect to racial identity, gender, and social class, the requirement and the practical measures to achieve proportional racial representation in the final jury—such as the Hennepin jury structure—are more likely to receive a positive response and strong support from the general population in the community.

A contradiction remains. For the impact of cross-sectional requirements protecting the defendant's interests is that—due to the practical and methodological problems of the Hennepin model—the fair cross section requirement offers few benefits or, in certain circumstances, may even harm the defendant's rights to a fair trial. This is because the requirement for a statistically based, cross-sectional model leads to systematic exclusion of traditionally underrepresentated groups, including racial minorities and the poor. Since white jurors from upper- and middle-social classes are found to show far greater representation in the vast majority of both state and federal jurisdictions, the representative jury, even if it mirrors the cognizable characteristics of the community composition, may be dominated by the racial majority, whose interests and values may not reflect those of a minority race and other marginalized segments of the larger community.

TABLE 5.2
The Requirement of a Fair Cross-Sectional Representation[1]

Response	Racial Identity (Racial Ancestry)[2]					Gender		Education				Employment Status[3]			
	White	Black	Hispanic	Asian & Pac. Is.	Others	Male	Female	<= H.S.	Some Coll.	College Grad.	Post Grad.	Full	Part	Retired	Total
Strongly Agree	53.3% (59.7)[2]	47.4% (58.0)	58.7% (55.8)	0.0% (18.8)	38.9% (57.4)	53.5%	56.9%	59.5%	51.3%	52.5%	62.2%	60.4%	61.7%	53.5%	55.4%
Agree Somewhat	29.6 (30.0)	31.6 (29.4)	26.1 (38.5)	37.5 (62.5)	27.8 (29.5)	29.4	28.6	17.6	34.0	32.2	25.5	29.2	23.4	32.6	29.0
Disagree Somewhat	7.4 (5.8)	5.3 (11.8)	6.5 (3.8)	12.5 (0.0)	22.2 (9.8)	7.5	7.8	12.2	6.8	7.6	6.1	4.5	14.9	4.7	7.6
Strongly Disagree	6.7 (4.5)	15.8 (0.0)	8.7 (1.9)	50.0 (18.8)	11.1 (3.3)	9.6	6.7	10.8	7.9	7.6	7.1	5.8	0.0	9.3	8.0
Total	100.0	100.1[4]	100.0	100.0	100.0	100.0	100.0	100.1[4]	100.0	99.9[4]	99.9[4]	99.9[4]	100.0	100.1[4]	100.0

Notes:

1. Subjects responded to the following question, "The racial makeup of the juries should be reflective of the communities."
2. The figure in parentheses shows the percentage of respondents with different ancestral races. For example, 33.2% indicates that almost one third of survey respondents with white ancestry agreed strongly with the statement.
3. The analysis of the employment status response came from the 1997 community survey.
4. Due to rounding errors.

Take a black defendant tried at the Santa Cruz Superior Court in California, for instance. Today he or she continues to face predominantly, if not, all-white criminal juries, because black adults constitute less than 1 percent of the eligible adult population in the jurisdiction (Fukurai 1994).[6] The proportionally representative jury thus systematically and procedurally fails to include black jurors in criminal trials. Mere statistical chance alone will not guarantee that even one black will be included in the jury of twelve. Though the fair cross-sectional requirement may be an important ingredient of the democratic ideals expressed in the Sixth Amendment, the statistically based, fair cross-sectionality of racial segments in the community may not always translate into a fair jury composition for minority defendants or guarantee the presence of racial minorities in final juries. Thus, those jurisdictions may need to turn to affirmative action in jury selection in order to ensure the placement of minority jurors in criminal proceedings.

Peremptory Challenges and Racial Representation

Peremptory challenges pose still another significant threat to cross-sectional jury representation. Once jurors are summoned for jury duty in the venire, lawyers for both parties seat six to twelve individual jurors by alternatively excluding jurors they deem unsuitable. The lawyers may exclude undesirable potential jurors for legally recognized reasons known as challenges for cause, or for intuitive, instinctive, and often subjectively imputed reasons known as peremptory challenges. In an attempt to include minority jurors in the final jury, defense attorneys have had relatively little success pressing complaints of unrepresentative juries under the Equal Protection Clause of the Fourteenth Amendment, because courts have defined Equal Protection by holding that the Fourteenth Amendment only requires that nondiscriminatory procedures be used in jury selection, not in composing a final jury of any particular racial balance.[7] Discriminatory uses of peremptory challenges have thus continued to eliminate a large number of racial minorities from serving on juries—thereby deploying procedural strategies blocking representative juries (see generally Fukurai, Butler, and Krooth 1993).

If the peremptory challenge emerged historically as a violent and notorious tool of racial discrimination, why did the Supreme Court fail to abolish it altogether when it had the opportunity in the 1965 Swain case? Not until 1986 did the Court move to critically examine and curb the racially discriminatory practice of peremptory challenges. The Court in the landmark decision of *Batson v. Kentucky* (476 U.S. 79, 1986) required state prosecutors to justify, with a race-neutral explanation, the peremptory strikes of black jurors (476 U.S. 79, 97). The Court also required that trial judges assess and determine whether the explanation was genuine or a mere pretext for racial discrimination (at 98).

In a landmark study of post-Batson peremptory challenges on jury representativeness, Kenneth J. Melilli (1996) reviewed virtually all relevant reported decisions of every federal and state court applying Batson between April 30, 1986 (the date of the Batson decision) and December 31, 1993, concluding that many of the currently accepted bases for peremptory challenges such as economic and geographic criteria, as well as attorneys' subjective judgments, continued to exert a disproportionate negative impact on choosing black and Hispanic jurors (Melilli 1996, 501). The study revealed that among 1,156 Batson complaints, 95 percent of them were logged against criminal prosecutors' uses of peremptory challenges and that blacks and Hispanics constituted 87.3 percent and 6.7 percent of targeted groups of such peremptory challenges.[8]

Examining the abuse and misuse of peremptory challenges, Melilli pointed to their racialized roots and the social consequences: "the exclusion from jury service because of group stereotyping brands the excluded group members as inferior, insults individuals by reducing their worth as jurors to cosmetic or trivial characteristics, makes underrepresented groups less accepting of the court system and its results, and injures society as a whole by frustrating the ideal of equal citizen participation in the jury process" (501). The study found that the vast majority of black and Hispanic jurors had been removed by peremptory challenges because of group stereotyping such as prior criminal activities (31.6 percent) and unemployed (19.3 percent) (496–498). Melilli concluded his study by arguing that "Batson has provided us with the first opportunity to examine the reasons lawyers use peremptory challenges, and what has emerged is the legal version of the emperor's new clothes. . . . It has also been revealed to be the refuge for some of the silliest, and sometimes nastiest, stereotypes our society has been able to invent" (503).

State and federal appellate courts have ruled that leaving one or two African Americans on the jury precludes any inference of purposeful racial discrimination on the part of the prosecutor, and that striking only one or two jurors of the defendant's race does not constitute a "pattern" of strikes.[9] Trial and appellate courts have been willing to accept virtually any explanation offered by the prosecutor to rebut the defendant's inference of purposeful discrimination. Because Batson and its progeny of cases have failed to eradicate unlawful discrimination in jury selection, many scholars and commentators have advocated the elimination of peremptory challenges altogether (Alschuler 1989, 209; Cammack 1995, 486; Fahringer 1995, 299; Ward 1995, 1362).

The Batson progenies have thus failed to eradicate the entrenched abuses of peremptory challenges directed against jurors of color from deliberating in criminal cases (Melilli 1996). Given the ineffectiveness of the Batson doctrine in virtually all state courts, affirmative action in jury selection may be the only promising alternative. Thus, it is of great significance that individual attorneys and/or progressive and innovative trial judges take important initiatives by moving towards, or granting, affirmative jury selection approaches in individual trials, especially in cases that touch the sensitive terrain of racism and in jurisdictions with small minority populations.

JURY OF ONE'S PEERS

The previous two concepts—impartiality and a fair cross section—have been examined and refined by the Supreme Court and legal scholars. Yet, the most controversial and debated concept ensuring a fair trial—a jury of one's peers— has escaped critical legal scrutiny. This is partially due to the fact that the term is not directly included in the Sixth Amendment right to a jury trial. The term nonetheless represents a significant component of conducting a fair trial, as well as expands on a historical understanding of the notion of a jury trial—thereby requiring extensive and careful investigation of its origin and its potential inter- section and overlap with racially diverse juries.

There is a link between the implicit Sixth Amendment assumption that the jury be composed of one's peers and establishing the criteria for the status and definition of who peers are comprised of and who they actually represent. A critical examination of the Supreme Court's views on the definition of peers is necessary, as the criteria for the evaluation of peers and their racial components may provide an important foundation for creating racially mixed juries. For if the concept of peers has no logic in making up a jury with racial diversity or racial components, such an interpretation negates the need for explicit race- conscious jury selection in creating racially diverse juries.

In explaining the concept of a jury of peers and the depth of its origins, the First Continental Congress in 1774 stated that the colonists had the right to be "tried by their peers," itself being an idea lifted from the Magna Carta, which provided that "No freeman shall be taken, or imprisoned, or disseized or outlawed, or exiled, or in any way harmed—nor will we go upon or send upon him—save by the lawful judgment of his peers or by peers or by the law of the land" (Magna Carta, section 39). When the Magna Carta was written in 1215, peers meant "equal," implying that a knight's peer was a knight or a baron's peer; and a Jew's peer was a Jew (Barber 1994, 1229).[10] The ancient English jury system, the jury de medietate linguae, then assumed that, when a Jewish person was accused of a crime, the jury had to include half Englishmen and the other half Jewish members to try the Jewish defendant (Ramirez 1994). The implicit assumption of the de medietate linguae jury was to impanel fellow community members: "de medietate peers" refer to individuals belonging to the same community, so the shared law of a community linked alien parties as jurors.

In the United States, the Supreme Court first defined peers in *Strauder v. West Virginia* (100 U.S. 303, 1880), noting:

> the very idea of a jury is a body of men composed of the peers or equals of
> the person whose rights it is selected or summoned to determine; that is, of his

neighbors, fellows, associates, persons having the same legal status in society as that which he holds (100 U.S. 303 308, 1880).

The definition of a "jury of peers" holding the "same legal status in society" is thus vague, no more transparent than jury impartiality or the fair cross section requirement. In the Strauder case, a black man was accused of trespassing and convicted by an all-white jury. Although the Court did not define the right to a "jury of one's peers" to be the right to a criminal jury composed in whole or part of persons of the defendant's own race, many of its subsequent decisions suggest a more inclusionary imperative for the criminal jury (*Batson v. Kentucky*, 476 U.S. 79, 85, 1986).[11]

Over the centuries, the definition and the concept of a jury of peers have also been developed and elaborated. Until the mid-twentieth century, white male property owners were the favored persons permitted to sit on juries in the U.S. (DiPerna 1984, 80). Later, racial minorities such as blacks and Hispanics, women, and the poor, including daily wage earners, were allowed to sit on the jury. Nevertheless, in the latter half of the twentieth century, in examining the ways in which one's peers are defined and evaluated, we believe that the following two different types of groups have emerged as the contemporary concept of one's peers: (1) broadly defined peers, and (2) narrowly defined peers. Those two types of peers comprise racial and social segments of the community, constituting important elements for conducting a fair trial.

"Broadly" Defined Peers

The jury composed of broadly defined equals or peers included potential jurors considered to be relatively independent of government-related, political influence (Massaro 1986, 548). The idea of nongovernment affiliated persons as broadly defined peers stems from the fact that the American jury historically showed a strong antipathy to the British government's control over the colonies' judiciary and criminal court proceedings (Clark 1975). Broadly defined peers thus excluded professional judges, prosecutors, public defenders, police officers, public administrators, and other agents employed by the government. The common sense judgment by the jury of broadly defined peers was perceived to protect the defendant from an abuse of power by government officials, as well as the political interest of governmental organizations, including the judiciary and law enforcement. By 1968, for instance, the Supreme Court had held that such a jury provides a "safeguard against the corrupt or overzealous prosecutor and against the compliant, biased, or eccentric judge" (*Duncan v. Louisiana*, 319 U.S. 145 156, 1968).[12]

How does the public today view the participation of judges and other governmental employees in trial proceedings and in other judicial decision-making processes? There are three basic levels within the judicial system that involve different assessments of the role of judges and jurors in criminal courts. The first level is the bench trial system in which the judge is the sole decision maker concerning fact-finding and legal applications. The second is the jury system that relies on the lay person's participation and precludes the judge from acting as a fact-finder. The jury system assumes that the judge is not considered one of the jurors, thus not one among the accused's defined peers in jury trials. The third level is the mixed tribunal or court found in Europe, such as in France, Germany, and Italy. The mixed tribunal allows the participation of both professional and lay judges in both fact-finding and legal decision-making procedures, suggesting that the defined peers under the mixed court system include both the judge and lay persons from the community.

Table 5.3 examines the public's perception on the three different types of judicial decision-making systems: (1) the jury system exclusively utilized in England, the United States, and other former British colonies, including Australia and Hong Kong, where the broadly defined peers generally exclude professional judges from the jury's decision-making process; (2) the bench trial system found in the majority of the countries in the world, where only judges are empowered to render decisions; and (3) mixed tribunals in European countries, including Germany, France, and Italy, where the broadly defined equals include lay persons who are to collaborate with professional judges to reach final verdicts.

The jury trial is still overwhelmingly accepted as the preferred model of a judicial decision-making system, despite recent controversial jury decisions in the Rodney King assault case, the O. J. Simpson trial, and Amadou Diallo case, suggesting that professional judges are not perceived as members of the jury's broadly defined equals in the trial. United States survey findings cutting across all racial groups show overwhelmingly strong support for the jury trial over the bench trial system or mixed courts (68.0 percent whites, 50.0 percent blacks, 70.7 percent Hispanic, and 85.7 percent Asians). No racial group, gender, or educational background indicates majority support for the bench trial system, where judges are main decision makers concerning both law and facts. While blacks showed the highest support for the bench trial system among racial groups (38.5 percent), controversial jury verdicts may have been the factor that led to the decrease in their respect for the legitimacy of jury verdicts. This is especially true for those with black ancestry (i.e., including non-black individuals who share black ancestry) who show very little support for the bench trial (18.8 percent). Among four major racial groups, the majority of whites (52.3 percent percent) and Asians (66.6 percent) also strongly support the mixed tribunal system. However, their preference did not exceed that of the jury trial.

"Narrowly" Defined Peers

The second definition of the peers—narrowly defined peers or equals—emphasizes the importance of the defendant's race, gender, and his or her socioeco-

TABLE 5.3
Racial Identity, Racial Ancestry, Socioeconomic Variables, Jury Trials, Bench Trials, and Mixed Tribunals

Response	Racial Identity (Racial Ancestry)[1]					Gender		Education				Employment Status			
	White	Black	Hispanic	Asian & Pac. Is.	Others	Male	Female	<= H.S.	Some Coll.	College Grad.	Post Grad.	Full	Part	Retired	Total
Jury Trials[2]	68.0%(70.6)	50.0%(50.1)	70.7%(68.6)	85.7%(73.3)	71.5%(70.5)	70.9%	64.7%	65.2%	71.5%	59.8%	70.5%	71.7%	66.7%	75.0%	67.5%
Bench Trials[3]	19.5 (16.5)	38.5 (18.8)	24.4 (21.6)	33.3 (35.3)	21.4 (24.2)	20.2	23.7	27.1	21.9	19.8	15.8	12.5	25.6	26.2	22.0
Mixed Tribunals[4]	52.3 (55.0)	25.0 (36.4)	44.4 (45.5)	66.6 (50.0)	57.2 (56.1)	48.3	54.5	30.6	53.5	58.2	60.6	56.6	30.4	38.4	51.6

Notes:

1. The figure in parentheses shows the percentage of respondents with different ancestral races. For example, 70.6% indicates that almost 71% of survey respondents with white ancestry agreed with the statement.

2. The question is phrased as" The jury is one of the most democratic institutions."

3. The question is phrased as" The bench trial where a single judge makes a decision is better than the jury trial."

4. The question is phrased as" Some European models that rely on both lay persons and professional judges to reach a verdict are better than the American jury system which only relies on lay persons as jurors." The figures came from the 1997 Santa Cruz Community Survey.

nomic background. In other words, the profile of the defendant, such as his or her social outlook, racial identity, ancestral history, societal affiliation, and group membership is likely to dictate how peers are defined in a criminal trial. Narrowly defined peers emphasize jurors' assurance of empathy for the accused and their ability to evaluate facts and evidence from the critical perspective of the defendant.[13] The jurors' ability to accurately assess evidence and determine guilt or innocence of the accused depends largely on their life experiences, individual personalities, social knowledge, and racial understandings. The capacity to empathize is important because jurors make decisions on the credibility and viability of witnesses, as well as the circumstantial weight of evidence. The jury that includes narrowly defined peers may be able to empathize and identify with the defendant and his/her experience, viewing the prosecutor's presentation of evidence differently than would a jury of broadly defined peers, who could well be "impartial" but might be incapable of correctly imputing the defendant's motives.

The following case offers a clue about jurors' empathetic capacities. Delbert Tibbs, a black divinity student, gave his personal account of who the narrowly and broadly defined peers were in his trial. After being convicted by an all-white jury in 1974 for a rape and related murder, he found himself with death row prisoners in Florida, spending three years in prison before appellate reversal. He gave this account of who the "peers" consisted of in his trial:

> PEER: one of equal rank; one among equals. I knew the definition of that word, and there was nothing remotely akin to this meaning existing between me and these seven hard-eyed White Men and five cold-eyed White Women who made up this jury of my "peers." I knew that any peerage that they comprised, as indeed they did comprise such a thing, totally excluded me, at least, in their eyes. . . . Peers, indeed. I'm sure that in the eyes of that jury I was not just another human being. Oh, no. I was dangerous, because, darker. I didn't belong (Abu-Jamal 1991, 1000).

Narrowly defined peers can be generally reclassified into two different groups: (1) the jurors whose racial identification and socioeconomic backgrounds are reflective of the condition of the criminal defendant; and (2) the equals whose socio-demographic profiles are reflective of, or copacetic with, those of the victim's. Examples of the first group of narrowly defined peers include the predominantly white jury in the Rodney King beating trial that acquitted the criminally charged four white police officers in Simi Valley where approximately half of LAPD officers lived (Fukurai, Butler, and Krooth 1994). Similarly, the first two Miami trials, that led to two large scale, civil disturbances, are represented by the first types of the narrowly defined equals, whose racial and social backgrounds reflected those of the white defendants. For black defendants, on the other hand, the predominantly black juries that tried Washington D.C. Mayor Marion Barry for the charge of drug possession in 1990, and Lemrick Nelson for the murder of a Jewish student in New York in 1992, represent examples of narrowly defined peers whose racial profiles reflected those of the criminal defendants (Gottlieb 1992; Ortner 1993).

"Narrowly" Defined Peers and Jury Nullification

Recent public concerns over possible instances of "jury nullification" in urban courts—where a large number of minority defendants have been acquitted by predominantly minority juries—also illustrate that jurors are more likely to share the racial and socio-demographic profiles of the defendants, not the victims. The jury in racially charged trials that have received broad public scrutiny—and verdicts that raised public skepticism of the fairness and legitimacy of jury verdicts—were more likely to be represented by the first type of the narrowly defined peers.

Yet, the second type of jury peers or equals in interracial crimes have also failed to escape public scorn or criticism. An example of this type of narrowly defined peers or equals, leading to public concerns and generating public skepticism of the legitimacy of jury verdicts, include the Scottsboro or other rape-related trials, where all-white juries convicted black defendants accused of raping white victims. The civil, not criminal, jury in the second O. J. Simpson trial in Santa Monica, California, also exemplifies the narrowly defined group of jury peers, whose racial profile and social backgrounds reflected those of the two white victims, not the defendant. The civil jury which found Simpson liable for the deaths of Ronald Goldman and Nicole Brown Simpson did not include any black jurors in its twelve-member panel (Chiang 1997).

The analysis of narrowly defined peers or equals illustrates the danger of exclusive reliance on either one of the two groups of classified peers in trial, especially when the crime involves a highly sensitive racial element. In interracial crimes, in particular, the mixture and balancing of these two different types of the narrowly defined equals may provide the ideal type of the jury structure. For the racially diverse jury would then include potential jurors that reflect the race and socio-demographic profiles of both the defendants and victims.

The disturbing image of black defendants tried, convicted, and sentenced by all-white juries in capital cases reiterates the fact that a minority's view may not be correctly reflected upon or understood by white jurors. In racially sensitive trials, the mixture of the two types of narrowly defined peers are more likely than broadly defined peers to provide greater legitimacy to the jury verdict in the eyes of the defendants, as well as increase public acceptance of the jury's decisions.

The important question concerning narrowly defined peers is elementary: given the effect of racially discriminatory jury selection procedures and the lack of minorities' jury participation in trials, would it still be possible to include racial minority jurors in trials in which racial minorities are criminal defendants? Specifically, what would be the public's general perception of the fairness of the trial and legitimacy of jury verdicts, when the trial for black defendants ensures the presence of black jurors as the narrowly defined peers of the defendants? Moreover, given the two distinct classifications of narrowly defined peers based on the racial profile of defendants and victims, would the public believe that the race of defendants or victims dictates the potential trial outcome? If they would, would they also support the affirmative use of racially mixed juries in interracial criminal trials?

To help answer those questions, table 5.4 examines the public's perception of the jury of one's peers and the fairness of the jury's verdicts. With respect to the inquiry if "trials should include black jurors when the defendant is black," the majority of the groups supported the institution of a race matching equation between the jury and the defendants, suggesting that the narrowly defined peers for black defendants are indeed black jurors (73.3 percent white, 57.2 percent blacks, 84.0 percent Hispanic, 50 percent Asian). As one rationale for matching the race of jurors with that of defendants, the public was also asked whether or not "trial outcomes are strongly influenced by the race of defendants or victims." The overwhelming majority of all racial groups agreed that race is the most significant determinant of trial outcomes (81.1 percent for the total). Similarly, when the public was asked whether racially mixed juries should only be used in a racially sensitive trials like the Rodney King beating trial, the overwhelming majority of all racial groups said that racially integrated juries should not be limited to the jury trials that involve highly sensitive issues of racism, but should also be used in all criminal trials (83.5 percent of the total respondents disagreed with the selective and exclusive use of racially integrated juries solely in racially sensitive trials).[14]

Once the community-held concepts of physical appearances and cultural differences defining race, along with the beliefs of each racial group, are accepted, one's race is likely to dictate the trajectory and breadth of one's experience in ways that may be relevant to criminal cases—raising race-specific issues involving rape, murder, drug addiction, or spousal abuse.

Race and ethnicity are often easily recognizable and visual, enhancing the importance of public perception about what experiences, and thus what group affiliations, are important in a given case, as well as which target group should be identified as the one from which to draw narrowly defined empathetic jurors. The importance of perceived group identifications derives from the fact that both the public and trial participants can easily recognize the widely shared beliefs in the traits and characteristics of race or gender, and impute whether or not those group identifications will affect the nature of jury deliberations and verdicts. Since the popular notion of racial fairness determines what seems just, the appearance of racial justice is just as critical and important for legitimacy as the substance of justice. Similarly, the racially mixed jury, which includes narrowly defined peers of both defendants and victims, may help overcome racial bias, improve the appearance of justice, and enhance public respect and acceptance of

TABLE 5.4
Racial Identity, Jury of One's Peers, and Jury Verdicts

Response	White	Black	Hispanic	Asian & Pac. Is.	Others	Total	
1: Black Jurors for Black Defendants[1]							
Strongly Agree	41.0%	42.9%	52.0%	16.7%	40.0%	155	(40.8%)
Agree	32.3	14.3	32.0	33.3	10.0	86	(30.5)
Disagree	10.9	28.6	8.0	16.7	30.0	36	(12.8)
Strongly Disagree	15.7	14.3	8.0	33.3	20.0	45	(16.0)
2: Verdicts Influenced by Race of Defendants/Victims[2]							
Strongly Agree	32.7%	51.9%	36.3%	28.0%	41.3%	269	(33.0%)
Agree	47.7	33.3	46.0	53.4	39.7	392	(48.1)
Disagree	13.7	14.8	12.9	13.9	12.7	110	(13.5)
Strongly Disagree	6.0	0.0	4.8	4.7	6.3	44	(5.4)
3: Racially Mixed Juries Only in Racially Sensitive Trials[3]							
Strongly Agree	3.0%	11.1%	9.7%	8.7%	7.9%	58	(6.7%)
Agree	6.3	11.1	11.2	13.6	6.3	85	(9.8)
Disagree	19.9	11.1	13.4	24.9	19.0	177	(20.3)
Strongly Disagree	70.8	66.7	65.7	52.8	66.7	550	(63.2)

Notes:
1. The results came from the 1997 Community Survey in Santa Cruz, California. The question is pharased as: "Trials should include African-American jurors when the defendant is African-American."
2. The results came from the 1995–1997 UC-Wide survey. The question is phrased as: "Trial outcomes are strongly influenced by the race of defendants or victims."
3. The results came from the 1995–1997 UC-Wide survey. The question is phrased as: "Racially mixed juries are necessary only in racially sensitive trials like the Rodney King beating trial."

jury verdicts (King, 1994).[15] Then the structure of racially diverse juries along with the use of peremptory inclusion will possibly allow these two types of narrowly defined peers to merge and overlap, forming an important element for the composition of the final jury.

Such a jury may be critical to the legitimacy of the court system. As noted previously, the general apprehension that the jury has failed to treat the defendant fairly becomes palpable when an all-white jury tries a black defendant for the rape of a white woman or the murder of white victims (Baldus, Woodworth and Pulaski 1990). Equally, the same apprehension is generated when predominantly black juries have tried and acquitted black defendants in interracial crimes (Butler, 1995b). Given the popular perceptions about the unfairness of white juries toward black defendants, the public generally understands that white jurors are not a black person's peer, especially in the context of cross-racial crimes. Such trials also reflect public perceptions that peers are essential to a fair proceeding; and the affirmative mechanism to ensure a racially mixed jury thus becomes an important community, public and governmental lever for enhancing the legitimacy of jury trials and the perceived fairness of jury verdicts.

CONCLUSIONS

In elaborating the democratic ideal of the legitimacy of government through judicial participation by an emergent, diverse population, Alexis de Tocqueville once described the American jury in *Democracy in America* in 1848: "Trial by jury, which is one of the forms of the sovereignty of the people, ought to be compared with the other laws which establish that sovereignty—Composition of the jury in the United States—Effect of trial by jury upon the national character—It educates people—How it tends to establish the influence of the magistrates and to extend the legal spirit among the people" (Tocqueville 1994, 280). Legal scholar Akhil Reed Amar points to the democratic thread of Tocqueville's views woven into the American jury, emphasizing that it was the Sixth Amendment that specifically awarded structural and political powers to the citizenry through the jury trial, securing a valued right of persons accused of crime, that they would and must be tried by the members of their own community (Amar 1991, 1183–1185).

Such fundamental precepts inherent in the contemporary discussion of the Sixth Amendment and its constitutional ideals have revolved around three key concepts ensuring that a defendant be tried by a fair jury that is: (1) impartial, (2) represents a cross section of the community, and (3) comprises a jury of peers. These concepts represent distinct and sometimes contradictory values that the Supreme Court often has failed to reconcile or fully recognize, leaving the field open for further examination and elaboration.

This chapter's analysis suggests that the contemporary notion of impartiality is recognized more as a group and diffused concept, than the individualized conception of the impartial state of mind of each trial juror. That is to say, the concept of impartiality rests on the premise of the jury's diversity. This dovetails with the public view that the fairness and the integrity of jury verdicts are much enhanced if they are rendered by racially diverse juries, rather than single race juries, suggesting that a jury is more likely to fit the contemporary notions of neutrality and impartiality if it is made up of various racial segments and groups of a particular community. Thus, the public views the jury's racial diversity and the jury verdict's impartiality as closely entwined.

Similarly, the contemporary requirement that the jury represent a fair cross section of the community is based on the concept of impartiality linked to the jury's compositional diversity. The Supreme Court once said that the jury may not be able to exercise impartial judgment "if the jury pool is made up of only special segments of the populace or if large, distinct groups are excluded from the pool" (*Taylor v. Louisiana*, 419 U.S. 522, 530, 1975). In practice, the greater is the diversity of juror backgrounds, the more likely it is to reflect the diversity and heterogeneity of racial groups, social settings, historical experiences, and the racially impacted opinions of various segments in the community. The present study's community survey also corroborates that the public believes that the makeup of juries should be racially diverse, supporting the ideal of the fair, cross-sectional, racial representation in the final jury.

Our analysis of a jury of peers also shows that there are two distinct classifications of peers or equals: (1) broadly defined peers, and (2) narrowly defined peers. The former group of peers excludes government-affiliated employees or officials from the potential pool of eligible jurors, thus excluding professional judges, prosecutors, law enforcement officers, and other public officials. The analysis of public perception of the professional judges' participation as potential jury members shows that the public is more likely to show their strong preference for a jury system where the judges remain neutral and play the role of nondecision makers, as compared to other judicial systems such as the bench trial or mixed tribunals, in which professional judges are empowered, with or without the participation of lay judges, to render verdicts. The segments of the general population which prefer the jury system over alternative judicial systems are also strong supporters of democratic ideals and equities when trials by jury guarantee the jury's racially proportionate representation, reflecting the racial makeup in the community.

As for the definition of the narrowly defined peers, this study's survey reveals that white jurors are not considered the peers of black defendants, especially in the context of interracial crimes. One important reason for white jurors' failure to be considered as peers for blacks is that jury verdicts are believed to be reflective of, and influenced by, the race of defendants and/or victims. Since the public strongly believes that race of victims and defendants influences the potential trial outcome, affirmative action in jury selection should allow the participation of narrowly defined peers of both victims and defendants in the final jury. As social policy, this procedural reform should thus be viewed as an important legal mechanism designed to create racially heterogeneous juries, thus increasing public acceptance of trial proceedings and jury verdicts.

Turning to a preview of the next chapter, we focus on the practical aspects of jury selection, arguing that—despite the constitutional ideals of a fair trial, requirements for cross-sectional representation, impartially, and a jury of one's peers—the current jury selection process is beset by a variety of procedural deficiencies, logistical difficulties, and socioeconomic inequalities, helping to eliminate a large number of racial minorities and the poor from serving on juries. Thus, the analysis of legal and extra-legal factors and racially discriminatory jury selection practices sets the critical stage for redesigning and implementing race-conscious, affirmative mechanisms as social and legal policies to

Chapter 6

SHORTCOMINGS OF PROCEDURALLY BASED REMEDIES

Jury Representation from the Beginning to the End of the Jury Selection Process

"As a result of my own trial experience and what I have learned from jury research, I believe I would be ineffective as a lawyer if I did not make both race-conscious and gender-conscious strategic decisions on behalf of criminal defendants. This includes decisions relating to jury selection."
—Abbe Smith, a criminal defense lawyer

Current laws guiding jury selection offer no affirmative mechanisms or procedural remedies to ensure the presence of members of diverse racial and social groups in the final jury. This chapter thus attempts to demonstrate that affirmative action strategies are the only viable alternative for securing such diversity in the trial jury.

By focusing our lens on all stages of the jury selection process, we hope to illustrate that the traditional, non-affirmative jury selection system handed down from the past fails to produce a heterogeneous final jury. To do this, we will show that current procedural remedies, as well as non-affirmative reforms designed to improve representative imbalances—all the way up to the jury panel stage of jury selection—neither lead to fair cross-sectional jury representation nor guarantee the diversity of the final jury on the basis of race, gender, social class, or other cognizable characteristics. As an alternative, we argue that peremptory inclusion at the voir dire stage of jury selection not only aims to create racially and socially diverse juries, but is the only viable alternative and unfailing strategy to ensure the placement of members of diverse groups in the trial jury.

The purpose of this chapter, then, is twofold: (1) to provide systematic and critical analyses of jury participation and representation at each of the distinct jury selection stages, encompassing a general population, jury qualified pools, jury eligibles, jury panels, and actual trial jurors; and (2) to assess the composition and representation of the jury by examining prospective jurors' sociodemographic backgrounds and ideological profiles, illustrating that such jury profiles and backgrounds do not reflect a balanced representation of the composition of the community population at the various and composite stages of the jury selection process.

As we demonstrate in the examples that follow, trial participants in final juries not only fail to reflect a fair representation of the general population, but by and large they represent particular racial and social segments of the community population—namely, white, male, married or retired, well-educated, middle-aged, middle-to-high income earners, employees in large firms, and individuals with supervisory responsibilities (Fukurai, Butler, and Krooth 1993). Even if the non-affirmative jury selection system produces a fair cross-sectional representation in final juries, it might also fail to produce a racially and socially diverse jury. This is because the proportion of racial minorities in most jurisdictions is so small that they may be procedurally and legally excluded from the final twelve-member jury. As the large proportion of criminal defendants are racial minorities, this lack of minority jurors' participation in the final jury often fails to produce not only the chance for equitable findings, but also the perception of racial justice and racial fairness of judicial decision-making in the eyes of minority populations. All this leads to a simple conclusion: Affirmative action in jury selection is the unfailing strategy to ensure minority participation in final juries. And this is what we aim to illustrate in this chapter.

We begin with a brief overview of constitutional law mandating the empanelment of juries, addressing the fair cross-section doctrine that is the focus of contemporary jury selection procedures. We then address the many ways that patent, race-neutral procedures that are used to compile jury master lists and draw names from them, actually fail to secure representative or racially diverse jury pools. By examining jury representation of various groups from a general population, as well as those brought together in qualified jury pools, jury panels, and final juries, we attempt to critically analyze the cumulative effects of screening mechanisms from the beginning to the end of the jury selection system. As we will see, such methods and their impact at different stages of jury selection are the controlling factors that shape jury composition and its fair cross-sectional representation of demographic and socioeconomic segments of the community.

THE GOAL OF RANDOM SELECTION AND THE FAIR CROSS-SECTION DOCTRINE

There are major problems associated with achieving the two goals of constructing representative juror master lists—inclusion of every eligible citizen, and representation of all segments of the community. These matters appear at the very beginning of the juror identification process, when court jurisdictions compile master lists of residents to serve as jurors (Fukurai, Butler, and Krooth 1993, 41).

In compiling and updating a master list of all eligible residents in a community, disparities arise from both policy choices and logistical or mechanical difficulties, for governments have traditionally turned to two sources that presumably approximate such a list: voter registration rolls (ROV) and, less often, driver registration records (DMV). Both are probably the most comprehensive, single-source lists available in most jurisdictions. Yet each list faces the difficulty of enlisting actual residents of any community, due to significant deficiencies of representativeness and exclusiveness that cannot be easily corrected.

Why does the use of voter rolls contribute to under-inclusive and unrepresentative jury panels? The underrepresentation of poor citizens and people of color on voter registration rolls had become so entrenched (Piven and Cloward, 1988) that it prompted a series of Supreme Court decisions to do away with restrictions on the franchise, as well as restrictions under the Voting Rights Act (*Kramer v. Union Free Sch. Dist.*, 395 U.S. 621, 1969; *Harper v. Virginia Bd. of Elections,* 383 U.S. 663, 1966; *Raynolds v. Sims,* 377 U.S. 533, 1964; see also Voting Rights Act of 1965, Pub.L. No. 89–110, 79 Stat. 445, codified as amended at 42 U.S.C. ss 1971, 1973 to 1973bb–1, 1988).

Several decades after these reforms, Congress still recognized a need to improve voter registration rates under the National Voter Registration Act of 1993 (42 U.S.C.A.s, 1973gg, West Supp. Sept. 1993—effective May 20, 1993). Until the Voter Registration Act, however, few serious efforts had been made to ensure that voter registration lists were fully inclusive of the eligible population. Still, some states refused to implement the Act, impacting not only voter qualifications, but also those of prospective jurors as well. The ROV lists are estimated to exclude up to one-third of the adult population from jury service, skewing the jury pool to overrepresent the elderly and relatively affluent, and to underrepresent racial minorities (Fukurai, Butler, and Krooth 1993, 17–20). The decision to draw names from a source so well known—and in some cases so deliberately manipulated and so unrepresentative—might be seen as a disingenuous effort to compile a "representative" jury wheel (Fukurai 1996).

The hope for a balanced, representative jury drawn from a cross section of the community must be contrasted to earlier views of jury selection that rested on the assumption that the best jurors are active, upstanding citizens of good moral character, and, in that respect, making up an elite subgroup of the community. This vision of the community does not mesh with the contemporary notion of impartiality that depends upon a representative cross section of citizens. What, however, is the foundation for this latest standard? Some people undoubtedly decline to register to vote, not simply out of laziness, but often as an affirmative demonstration of their disaffection with the political process and public institutions (Dustin 1986; King 1994). Their nonregistration is an individualized demonstration of a social perspective that, nonetheless, needs to be represented as one element of a community's diverse viewpoints, particularly since part of the role and task of many juries is to assess the credibility and legitimacy of public officials, as well as police departments and their investigative links to city and district attorney's offices (Fukurai, Butler, and Krooth 1993). If the community includes disaffected populations that do not register to vote, then, they will not appear in the jury pool.

A minority of state jurisdictions have recently made efforts to improve the representativeness of the jury pool by supplementing ROV with other sources of names. A common list is a driver registration record (DMV lists). However, the DMV source lists—although they document all drivers including low-income citizens and racial minorities in numbers closer to their actual proportions in the population—still underrepresents the elderly and women, both of whom drive less than their younger, or male counterparts (Fukurai, Butler, and Krooth 1993 43–45). Other source lists such as public welfare records, property tax records, and annual local census data are available. However, they are not in widespread use and are likely to have comparable problems of under-inclusiveness.

Other logistical problems hinder the gathering of comprehensive jury pool information (Fukurai, Butler, and Krooth 1993). Combining two or more source lists creates obvious problems of name duplication that are surprisingly intractable; some jurisdictions have conceded that their computer programs simply cannot eliminate all duplicate names. Colorado once reported that, even after scanning for duplicate names, 10 percent of residents' names appeared more than once on jury wheels (Fukurai, Butler, and Krooth 1993, 50). Minority residents' names, moreover, are less likely to appear twice on a multiple-source list, which means that in a random selection of jurors from the combined list, they have a reduced chance opportunity of being called. Atlantic City County, New Jersey, at one point had 180,000 names on its jury master list, when only 130,000 adults lived in the county (Fukurai, Butler, and Krooth 1993, 44–47). As minority jurors are underrepresented on both ROV and DMV records, though to a lesser extent on the latter, one list does not necessarily include most of the names missing from the other. The representativeness of jury wheels is thus unintentionally, but distinctly, undermined by these logistical difficulties.

How frequent jury master lists are updated from source lists also affects jurors' representativeness. Federal law requires updating jury wheels once every four years. Relying on ROV, such an interval between updates means that residents who are seventeen at the time of an update will not be added to the jury wheel until they are twenty-one, if they register to vote in that interval. Jury studies have shown that infrequent updates of jury wheels further undermine the representation of minority residents found in voter rolls (Fukurai 1994; Fukurai and Butler 1994).

Finally, another practical difficulty that limits minority residents' participation in jury pools is the relation between residential mobility and juror participation. African-Americans, as well as other minority groups such as Asians and Hispanics, have higher rates of residential mobility than do whites. Studies suggest that this situation is a reflection of relative income and job status: minorities are more likely to be employed in low wage, seasonal, or otherwise unstable sectors of the labor market, which correlates with more frequent residential changes (Fukurai, Butler, and Krooth 1993; St. John, Edwards, and Wenk 1995). Residential mobility may affect whether citizens are ever added to any jury master lists; but, even more directly, once on the master list, it affects the citizen's chance opportunity to be summoned. If a master list underrepresents African Americans to begin with, then the inability to track down even those few on the list with summons by mail means that they will be underrepresented as a group. Worse, it is argued, jury commissioners often make little effort to track down "undeliverables," "unreacheables," and other "non-respondents," and simply purge them from master lists (Fukurai, Butler, and Krooth 1993, 21–26).

Numerous legal and nonlegal variables impact selectivity in jury participation; and the nonrandom nature of jury selection procedures and nonrepresentative jury participation have not been systematically documented. Past studies have largely concentrated on the composition of jury panels and trial jurors gauged by general population characteristics. But these studies have often failed to identify nonrandom factors and procedural deficiencies built into the different stages of jury selection. Jury research, for instance, has failed to critically examine the extent and the scope of the jury composition of various subpopulations during the entire process of jury selection—that involves screening from the general population to qualified jurors, to jury pools, and finally to actual jurors.

EMPIRICAL CHECKPOINTS IN JURY SELECTION

Before examining jury representativeness of various groups, it is important to reiterate that there are eight distinct stages of jury selection (see figure 1.1 in chap. 1). In order to examine the extent of jury participation and representation at the different stages of jury selection, seven key checkpoints in the jury selection process are identified. Those are: (1) a general population living in the trial site and the original jurisdiction (stage 1); (2) a ROV pool (stage 2); (3) prospective jurors identified by multiple source master lists (or wheels) (stage 3); (4) qualified jurors (stage 4); (5) jury eligibles (stage 5); (6) jury panels (stage 6); and (7) trial jurors who sit in jury boxes (stage 8 and the final stage of jury selection).

These key passage points allow us to examine representative disparities of jury composition between the different stages of jury selection. The difference between the first (the general population) and second (ROV) checkpoints indicates, for example, the degree of exclusionary impact that voter registration has upon jury representation. Similarly, the difference between the sixth (jury panels) and the seventh (final juries) indicates the effect of voir dire on the representation of the final trial jury.

In the present analyses, the general population refers to the composition of potential jurors in the trial site of the original jurisdiction. A ROV pool refers to registered voters who reside within the jurisdiction. A pool of prospective jurors based on multiple source lists also includes community populations who are identified by DMV and ROV, such as registered voters and/or those who have automobile licenses or identification cards issued by the DMV.

A pool of qualified jurors includes prospective jurors identified by the source lists and who have passed mandatory qualification criteria. Qualification requirements include such factors as: jurors must be United States citizens, eighteen-years-old or more, a resident of the county or jurisdiction, possessed of a sufficient degree of knowledge of the English language, "in possession of natural faculties or of at least ordinary intelligence," with no conviction of "a felony, malfeasance in office or other high crime," and not currently "serving as a grand juror in a court" of jurisdiction.[1] The question on the citizenship status is asked again at the last stage of jury selection, as prospective jurors identified by multiple-source lists may include permanent resident aliens or other noncitizens, and the DMV list does not screen for citizenship status.

Qualified jurors are further screened for their eligibility to serve on juries. Automatic exemptions are given to certain occupations such as police officers, attorneys, and judges, for which there may be an overlap of interests, biases, or responsibilities. While there may be some variations among different jurisdictions, excuses are also granted and include such factors as "physical or mental incapacity or disability that would entail undue risk of harm" to jurors' health; personal obligations "to provide actual and necessary care to another and it is not feasible to make alternative arrangements for that care"; "economic injury or extreme financial burden"; "extremely difficult transportation or travel conditions"; previous juror service "during the immediately preceding twelve months"; and other excuse requests that the court may grant.[2]

Jury panels include prospective jurors who have actually appeared at the courthouse after receiving jury summonses. A large proportion of qualified and eligible jurors, however, do not necessarily respond to jury summonses sent by the jury commissioner's office. As a stark example, 44 percent of prospective jurors in Los Angeles were classified as nonrespondents—including "undeliverables" (15 percent) that post offices failed to locate, and "recalcitrants" (29 percent) who refused to respond to jury calls (Fukurai, Butler, and Krooth 1993, 122).

Not all jurors who appear at the courthouse end up in jury boxes, either. A large proportion of potential jurors on panels are excluded by peremptory challenges and/or challenges for cause during voir dire. Judges also screen prospective jurors for possible excuses and exemptions. Similar screening questions are asked of qualified jurors at earlier stages of jury selection. However, the effect of voir dire on jury participation by certain subpopulations is considered to be even more significant, especially because a large proportion of the same groups are already excluded before reaching the courthouse (Fukurai, Butler, and Kooth 1993).

These seven distinct, empirical checkpoints provide the basic framework for screening prospective jurors from a general population to their status as final trial jurors who sit as participants in the jury box. In tracing jury participation from the first to the last stage of jury selection, a variety of legal and extra-legal variables and exclusionary procedural practices can be identified and analyzed.

As well, a critical examination of jury representativeness between different stages of jury selection also provides important insights into the effect of discriminatory factors that exclude from jury service both racial minorities and other social subgroups that have been historically underrepresented in both jury pools and jury boxes.

JURY REPRESENTATION FROM THE BEGINNING
TO THE END OF JURY SELECTION

In order to examine and assess jury representation at various stages of jury selection, a community-wide survey was conducted in 1986–87 in Orange County, California, one of the major metropolitan areas in southern California. The 1986–87 county-wide survey was sponsored by the Superior Court in Santa Ana, Orange County. According to the 1990 census, Orange County had a population of 2.4 million and the majority of the residents were white (64.5 percent), followed by Hispanic (23.4 percent) and Asian or Pacific Islander (10.0 percent). Black residents comprised only 1.6 percent of the county population.

The method used by the survey was straightforward. Potential respondents were randomly selected from the California County Master Key List; and a total of 1,275 community residents were contacted to gather information on their race/ethnic backgrounds, social class, prior jury service, and eligibility to serve on juries (see Appendix A for detailed descriptions of the survey).

Once the selection was made and the information was compiled, three statistical measures were used to examine representative disparity of jury participation by various population subgroups: (1) an absolute disparity, (2) a comparative disparity, and (3) z scores. An absolute disparity measures the simple, absolute difference between the percentage of people in the community who are in a designated cognizable group and the percentage of that group as represented in the different jury pools. Using data from table 6.1, for example, 8.88 percent of the general county population earned less than $10,000 annual income (see the second column in table 6.1 under income), whereas 6.78 percent of individuals identified by ROV had the same annual income (the third column in table 6.1 under income). The difference between these two numbers (8.88 minus 6.78) produces an absolute disparity of 2.1 percentage points. The figure shows that people with less than $10,000 annual income are *underrepresented* in the ROV list.

Is 2.1 percentage points big enough to indicate a skewed violation of a fair cross section of the community? An absolute disparity may not provide that answer. Let us suppose, for example, that a group represented 60 percent of the community, but only 57.9 percent were represented in the ROV list. This would still yield a 2.1 percentage point absolute disparity, but it is doubtful that the figure indicates the violation of a fair cross-sectionality, because the group in question still represented a clear majority of people in the ROV. On the other hand, consider the situation in which the community percentage of a cognizable group was 2.1 percent, but none of those individuals showed up in the ROV list. This would also be 2.1 percentage point absolute disparity, but one which would raise considerable concern, because the group in question is being completely excluded from the ROV list.

The clearest way to show how important or substantive an absolute disparity might be is to relate the absolute disparity to the cognizable group's percentage in the entire community. This produces a measure known as a comparative disparity. Comparative disparity is so called because it relates the size of the absolute disparity to the size of the community percentage of the cognizable group. An absolute disparity of 2.1 percentage points, in relation to the expected community percentage of those with income less than $10,000 of 8.88 percent, produces a ratio equal to 2.1 divided by 8.88=0.236, which we multiply by one hundred to get a measure of percentage of underrepresentation. Thus, the figure indicates that approximately 24 percent of those with annual income less than $10,000 are underrepresented in the ROV list (see table 6.2 under income).

Tests of statistical significance provide a mathematically derived tool for indicating whether or not a particular difference (a disparity) is large enough that it is unlikely to have occurred just by chance alone as a result, for example, of sampling error. Statistical significance provides us with a means to assess the reliability or stability of the observed disparity. When differences are based on large numbers (for example, one thousand people or more), the results tend to be quite stable, suggesting that the disparity is "real," not just a statistical artifact. Thus, a small disparity based on a large number of people may well turn out to be statistically significant and thus demand greater scrutiny and further analysis. For example, what is the probability that a random sample of 1,275 adult residents could have been drawn from the community in Orange County and by chance alone have generated an absolute disparity as large as 2.1 percentage points and a comparative disparity of twenty-four percentage points?

Table 6.3 of Z scores gives the answer in terms of the standard deviation units away from the mean in normal distribution. If absolute z values exceed more than 1.96, it means that there are less than five chances in one hundred that the observed disparity could have been generated by chance alone (from sampling error). This is based on a two-tailed test of the significance between two populations. The conclusion, then, is that this is, indeed, a statistically significant difference with respect to those with income less than $10,000 (−2.312), suggesting that the ROV list underrepresented the low-income residents in the county at a statistically significant level.

ANALYSES AND FINDINGS

The following three tables (tables 6.1 through 6.3) detail the statistical information discussed above. The first column in table 6.1 shows jurors' different backgrounds—demographic, socioeconomic, and attitudinal dimensions. The second through eight columns show seven different checkpoints in the jury selection process: (1) a general population, (2) ROV pools, (3) multiple-source pools (ROV and DMV), (4) jury qualified pools, (5) jury eligible pools, (6) jury panels, and (7) jury boxes. The figures in parentheses show the percentage of excluded jurors for respective groups. The cumulative effect of jury selection processes is also shown in the table that, for example, 43.83 percent of trial jurors are males while 45.45 percent of males in jury panels failed to serve on juries (a figure shown in a parenthesis at the last column for males). The figures also suggest that 56.17 percent (100 percent-43.83 percent) of trial jurors were female and voir dire excluded 54.54 percent of female jurors from serving on juries. That is, while the majority of trial jurors were female, voir dire also eliminated more female jurors than male counterparts from serving on actual trials.

Table 6.2 shows comparative disparity figures for different jury pools. The second through seventh columns show the comparative disparity of individual jury pools from a general population. A positive sign shows the *overrepresentation* of a group and a negative sign for the *underrepresentation*. The last five columns indicate representative disparities of different jury pools from immediately preceding jury selection stages. The first of the last five columns in table 6.2, for instance, shows comparative disparities pools between ROV and multiple-source lists (ROV and DMV). The supplemental use of DMV lists leads to a 26.69 percent increase for Hispanic jurors' representation over ROV alone.

Table 6.3 shows z scores, suggesting the statistical significance of under- or over-representation of groups as indicated in table 6.2. For example, a z score of 4.213 for white (the second column) suggests that whites are overrepresented at a statistically significant level in the jury pool which is solely created by ROV source.[3] This also shows that if ROV is the only source for creating a jury pool, it almost always leads to significant overrepresentation of white prospective jurors.

Demographic Backgrounds

The tables also show a number of important findings in jurors' demographic representation on different jury pools. First, the use of ROV list alone does not lead to a fair cross-sectional representation of various demographic subgroups of the population. Rather, it leads to significant overrepresentation of the following groups, as their percentages of ROV representation are higher than those who are excluded (as shown in parentheses). Those overrepresented groups include: (1) males, (2) whites, (3) those forty-years old or over, (4) the married, and (5) the widowed. Similarly, the use of ROV alone leads to significant underrepresentation for blacks, Hispanics, other racial groups, those less than forty-years-old, the single or never married, and the separated. The DMV supplemental list, however, recovers some of the losses, raising percentages of the same disenfranchised groups to the same or even greater levels than their respective proportions in the general population. The only exception is prospective jurors of seventy-years-old or more. The finding coincides with previous research, as the elderly are less likely to retain automobiles and thus DMV identification (Van Dyke 1977; Hans and Vidmar 1986; Fukurai, Butler, and Krooth 1993). While many state and federal courts still rely on ROV alone to create a jury pool, the findings show that the use of ROV does not lead to representative jury pools, and thus support the use of multiple-source lists to create a fair cross-sectional representation of community populations in jury pools.

The proportional demographic representation changes, however, once the qualification requirements are introduced into the selection process. Jury qualification requirements tend to skew the jury representation towards (1) males, (2) whites, (3) forty to sixty-nine-year-olds, (4) the married, and (5) the widowed, showing similar effects to the ROV list upon jury participation. The only exception is that less than twenty-years-old jurors are overrepresented on the qualified jury pool. However, citizenship status, language requirements, prior criminal records, and subjective selection criteria such as possessions of "natural faculties" and "ordinary intelligence" tend to disenfranchise racial minorities, the single, the separated, and those between twenty and thirty-nine-years of age.

After screening for both exemptions and excuses, a mixed pattern of jury participation begins to emerge. For instance, both exemptions and excuses make racial representation of jury eligible pools very similar to that of a general population. However, significant departures from the general population are observed for two groups, males and those between forty and sixty-nine years of age. After being screened for exemption and excuses, for instance, 57.30 percent of jurors are between forty and sixty-nine years of age, and their proportion in eligible pools is even greater than in jury qualified pools (53.59 percent).

Among those who respond to jury summonses and appear at the courthouse, the jury panel composition shows mixed results. Males, whites, those between forty and 69 years of age, the married and widowed are overrepresented on jury panels, results that are similar to the jury pool selected by only ROV lists. Jury box composition becomes even more skewed, showing greater representation of the same groups and the retired, except males. The significantly underrepresented groups include blacks and those less than twenty-years-old. In fact, the findings showed no one younger than twenty-years-old ever served on the juries.

Socioeconomic Backgrounds:

Similar to demographic jury profiles of prospective jurors, the use of ROV lists alone leads to skewed jury representation, overidentifying the following groups: (1) those with college or postgraduate education, (2) higher incomes (over $30,000), (3) business owners, (4) those with supervisory responsibilities, (5) prospective jurors with salary compensation, and (6) the retired. The additional use of supplemental lists (DMV) also show similar attenuating effects found in

TABLE 6.1
Demographic, Socioeconomic, Attitudinal Backgrounds of Jury Population at Seven Key Checkpoints of Jury Selection

Variable	(1) General Population	(2) ROV	(3) ROV & DMV	(4) Jury Qualifiers	(5) Jury Eligibles	(6) Jury Panels	(7) Jury Boxes
Sex Male	44.16%	44.85% (43.40%)	44.89% (35.64%)[1]	44.52% (42.80%)[2]	48.71% (42.93%)[3]	44.35% (44.68%)[4]	43.83% (45.45%)[5]
DEMOGRAPHIC BACKGROUND:							
Race							
White	85.69	90.42 (64.25)	86.33 (73.33)	90.89 (65.04)	85.55 (86.19)	90.54 (90.26)	92.52 (87.61)
Black	0.74	0.62 (1.45)	0.60 (3.33)	0.41 (2.03)	0.73 (0.75)	0.92 (0.40)	0.31 (1.83)
Hispanic	7.69	5.77 (14.98)	7.31 (15.00)	5.22 (17.48)	7.43 (8.58)	5.38 (5.37)	4.67 (6.42)
Others	5.89	3.19 (19.33)	5.76 (8.34)	3.48 (15.45)	6.28 (4.48)	3.15 (3.97)	2.49 (4.13)
Age							
Less than 20	0.99	0.83 (1.99)	1.04 (0.00)	1.23 (0.00)	1.12 (0.96)	0.19 (2.19)	0.00 (0.46)
20–39	38.36	32.99 (67.16)	38.42 (37.04)	34.50 (54.51)	34.08 (39.57)	29.72 (41.63)	22.71 (39.91)
40–69	49.79	55.53 (26.87)	51.08 (22.22)	53.59 (33.91)	57.30 (47.66)	62.06 (43.23)	67.51 (54.13)
70 or More	10.85	10.65 (3.98)	9.45 (40.74)	10.68 (11.59)	7.49 (11.81)	8.04 (12.95)	9.78 (5.50)
Marital Status[6]							
Never Married	16.94	14.58 (31.13)	17.38 (11.88)	15.34 (22.88)	16.61 (17.03)	13.79 (17.87)	9.57 (20.20)
Married	64.31	69.93 (53.77)	67.21 (30.69)	66.93 (54.61)	63.35 (67.90)	71.51 (61.03)	73.15 (69.09)
Separated	8.47	8.56 (10.38)	8.94 (2.97)	7.38 (8.76)	8.07 (9.96)	7.34 (10.84)	8.33 (5.91)
Widowed	5.65	6.12 (2.36)	5.71 (4.95)	5.98 (4.43)	5.98 (4.43)	6.43 (5.32)	8.02 (4.09)

(continued)

TABLE 6.1 (*Continued*)

Demographic, Socioeconomic, Attitudinal Backgrounds of Jury Population at Seven Key Checkpoints of Jury Selection

	(1) General Population	(2) ROV		(3) ROV & DMV		(4) Jury Qualifiers		(5) Jury Eligibles		(6) Jury Panels		(7) Jury Boxes	
						Jury Selection Checkpoints (1) Through (7)							
Variable													
SOCIOECONOMIC BACKGROUND:													
Education													
Less Than High School	10.17	8.53	(18.13)	9.78	(34.15)	8.10	(21.56)	7.63	(11.52)	6.87	(9.41)	6.71	(7.11)
High School	31.03	30.06	(35.75)	31.03	(29.27)	31.45	(28.90)	30.15	(31.21)	29.96	(32.85)	32.59	(26.07)
Some College	27.85	27.83	(27.98)	28.34	(14.63)	28.89	(23.39)	28.63	(27.63)	27.67	(29.92)	26.84	(28.91)
College	16.80	18.34	(9.33)	16.86	(9.76)	18.12	(10.09)	18.70	(16.00)	20.99	(14.23)	18.85	(24.17)
Post Graduate	14.15	15.25	(8.81)	13.99	(12.20)	13.43	(16.06)	14.89	(13.65)	14.50	(13.60)	15.02	(13.74)
Income													
Less than $10,000	8.88	6.78	(16.58)	8.10	(30.77)	7.54	(14.35)	4.31	(10.19)	4.47	(10.56)	5.25	(3.35)
$10,000–$29,999	34.45	32.60	(42.21)	34.21	(41.03)	33.33	(39.01)	32.94	(34.88)	32.10	(34.91)	33.11	(30.62)
$30,000–$49,999	28.47	29.10	(26.63)	29.94	(15.38)	28.85	(26.91)	30.20	(27.97)	27.63	(30.39)	24.26	(32.54)
$50,000–$74,999	17.31	19.26	(9.55)	17.83	(2.56)	18.91	(10.76)	17.65	(17.21)	22.57	(14.87)	24.26	(20.10)
$75,000 or More	10.90	12.25	(5.03)	10.92	(10.26)	11.37	(8.97)	14.90	(9.74)	13.23	(9.27)	13.11	(13.40)
Organization													
Business Owner	13.16	13.72	(10.29)	13.39	(7.14)	14.03	(9.61)	14.89	(6.84)	9.68	(17.99)	10.00	(9.22)
Supervisor	47.85	50.08	(38.22)	47.59	(56.52)	49.32	(41.67)	48.86	(44.72)	49.34	(50.47)	45.41	(54.60)
Salary Compensation	50.20	53.21	(39.58)	50.81	(28.57)	50.00	(51.15)	43.33	(71.51)	72.73	(24.75)	75.35	(69.18)

(*continued*)

TABLE 6.1 (Continued)
Demographic, Socioeconomic, Attitudinal Backgrounds of Jury Population at Seven Key Checkpoints of Jury Selection

			Jury Selection Checkpoints (1) Through (7)				
Variable	(1) General Population	(2) ROV	(3) ROV & DMV	(4) Jury Qualifiers	(5) Jury Eligibles	(6) Jury Panels	(7) Jury Boxes
Employment Status							
Full-Time	59.25	57.92 (67.20)	59.56 (50.00)	59.18 (59.52)	57.81 (63.92)	63.17 (56.02)	59.67 (68.29)
Part-Time	12.97	12.65 (13.76)	12.94 (13.89)	12.88 (13.33)	13.22 (12.15)	9.50 (15.74)	9.00 (10.24)
Retired	18.12	19.95 (7.41)	17.89 (25.00)	18.47 (16.67)	18.39 (17.25)	18.61 (18.06)	21.67 (14.15)
ATTITUDINAL BACKGROUND:							
Criminal Justice Biases							
(1) Defendant Required to Prove Innocence	41.46	37.21 (67.05)	44.77 (71.43)	38.20 (55.65)	36.00 (42.86)	34.23 (42.92)	30.57 (40.95)
(2) Person is Guilty if Brought to Trial	25.49	25.09 (22.62)	25.59 (21.43)	25.85 (23.89)	25.00 (25.62)	22.92 (29.54)	19.49 (29.25)
(3) Person with a Criminal Record is Guilty	26.96	26.39 (30.58)	27.05 (23.08)	26.20 (30.36)	20.31 (28.72)	24.50 (42.92)	19.59 (33.65)

Note: The attitudinal questions are phrased as: (1) If the prosecution goes to the troubles of bringing someone to trial, the person is probably guilty; (2) Regardless of what the law says, a defendant in a criminal trial should be required to prove his or her innocence; (3) A person who has a criminal record and is accused of a very serious crime is probably guilty:

1. a figure shows a percentage of males who were not included in ROV (Registrar of Voters) or DMV (Department of Motor Vehicle) lists.
2. a figure shows a percentage of jurors who failed to qualify for jury service.
3. a figure shows a percentage of jurors who were unqualified or asked for exemptions or excuses.
4. a figure shows a percentage of qualified jurors who failed to appear at a courthouse.
5. a figure shows a percentage of qualified jurors in jury panels who failed to sit on jury boxes.
6. Other living arrangements including cohabitation or currently divorced are not included in the analyses.

TABLE 6.2

Comparative Disparities for a Fair Cross-Sectional Representation of Demographic, Socioeconomic, Attitudinal Backgrounds of Jury Population

	Disparities from a General Population						Disparities from a Previous Selection Stage:				
Variable	*(2) ROV*	*(3) ROV & DMV*	*(4) Jury Qualifiers*	*(5) Jury Eligibles*	*(6) Jury Panels*	*(7) Jury Boxes*	*(2)–(3)*	*(3)–(4)*	*(4)–(5)*	*(5)–(6)*	*(6)–(7)*
DEMOGRAPHIC BACKGROUND:											
Sex Male	1.56%	1.65%	0.82%	10.30%	0.43%	−0.75%	0.09%	−0.82%	9.41%	−8.95%	−1.17%
Race											
White	5.52	0.75	6.07	−0.16	5.66	7.97	−4.52	5.28	−5.88	5.83	2.19
Black	−16.22	−18.92	−44.59	−1.35	24.32	−58.11	−3.23	−31.67	78.05	26.03	−66.30
Hispanic	−24.97	−4.94	−32.12	−3.38	−30.04	−39.27	26.69	−28.59	42.34	−27.59	−13.20
Others	−45.84	−2.21	−40.92	6.62	−46.52	−57.72	80.56	−39.58	80.46	−49.84	−20.95
Age											
Less than 20	−16.16	5.05	24.24	13.13	−80.81	−100.00	25.30	18.27	−8.94	−83.04	−100.00
20–39	−14.00	0.16	−10.06	−11.16	−22.52	−40.80	16.46	−10.20	−1.22	−12.79	−23.59
40–69	11.53	2.59	7.63	15.08	24.64	35.59	−8.01	4.91	6.92	8.31	8.78
70 or More	−1.84	−12.90	−1.57	−30.97	−25.90	−9.86	−11.27	13.02	−29.87	7.34	21.64
Marital Status											
Never Married	−13.93	2.60	−9.45	−1.95	−18.60	−43.51	19.20	−11.74	8.28	−16.98	−30.60
Married	8.74	4.51	4.07	−1.49	11.20	13.75	−3.89	−0.42	−5.35	12.88	2.29
Separated	1.06	5.55	−12.87	−4.72	−13.34	−1.65	4.44	−17.45	9.35	−9.05	13.49
Widowed	8.32	1.06	5.84	5.84	13.81	41.95	−6.70	4.73	0.00	7.53	24.73
SOCIO–ECONOMIC BACKGROUND:											
Education											
Less than High School	−16.13	−3.83	−20.35	−24.98	−32.45	−34.02	14.65	−17.18	−5.80	−9.96	−2.33
High School	−3.13	0.00	1.35	−2.84	−3.45	5.03	3.23	1.35	−4.13	−0.63	8.78
Some College	−0.07	1.76	3.73	2.80	−0.65	−3.63	1.83	1.94	−0.90	−3.35	−3.00
College	9.17	0.36	7.86	11.31	24.94	12.20	−8.07	7.47	3.20	12.25	−10.20
Post Graduate	7.77	−1.13	−5.09	5.23	2.47	6.15	−8.26	−4.00	10.87	−2.62	3.59

(continued)

TABLE 6.2 (Continued)
Comparative Disparities for a Fair Cross-Sectional Representation of Demographic, Socioeconomic, Attitudinal Backgrounds of Jury Population

Variable	Disparities from a General Population						Disparities from a Previous Selection Stage:				
	(2) ROV	(3) ROV & DMV	(4) Jury Qualifiers	(5) Jury Eligibles	(6) Jury Panels	(7) Jury Boxes	(2)–(3)	(3)–(4)	(4)–(5)	(5)–(6)	(6)–(7)
Income											
Less than $10,000	-23.65	-8.78	-15.09	-51.46	-49.66	-40.88	19.47	-6.91	-42.84	3.71	17.45
$10,000–$29,999	-5.37	-0.70	-3.25	-4.38	-6.82	-3.89	4.94	-2.57	-1.17	-2.55	3.15
$30,000–$49,999	2.21	5.16	1.33	6.08	-2.95	-14.79	2.89	-3.64	4.68	-8.51	-12.20
$50,000–$74,999	11.27	3.00	9.24	1.96	30.39	40.15	-7.42	6.06	-6.66	27.88	7.49
$75,000 or More	12.39	0.18	4.31	36.70	21.38	20.28	-10.86	4.12	31.05	-11.21	-0.91
Organization											
Business Owner	4.26	1.75	6.61	13.15	-26.44	-24.01	-2.41	4.78	6.13	-34.99	3.31
Supervisor	4.66	-0.54	3.07	2.11	3.11	-5.10	-4.97	3.64	-0.93	0.98	-7.97
Salary Compensation	6.00	1.22	-0.40	-13.69	44.88	50.10	-4.51	-1.59	-13.34	67.85	3.60
Employment Status											
Full–Time	-2.24	0.52	-0.12	-2.43	6.62	0.71	2.83	-0.64	-2.31	9.27	-5.54
Part–Time	-2.47	-0.23	-0.69	1.93	-26.75	-30.61	2.29	-0.46	2.64	-28.14	-5.26
Retired	10.10	-1.27	1.93	1.49	2.70	19.59	-10.33	3.24	-0.43	1.20	16.44
ATITTUDINAL BACKGROUND:											
Criminal Justice Bias											
(1) Defendant Required to Prove Innocence	-10.25	7.98	-7.86	-13.17	-17.44	-26.27	20.32	-14.68	-5.76	-4.92	-10.69
(2) Person is Guilty If Brought to Trial	-1.57	0.39	1.41	-1.92	-10.08	-23.54	1.99	1.02	-3.29	-8.32	-14.97
(3) Person with a Criminal Record is Guilty	-2.11	0.33	-2.82	-24.67	-9.12	-27.34	2.50	-3.14	-22.48	20.63	-20.04

Note: The attitudinal questions are phrased as: (1) If the prosecution goes to the troubles of bringing someone to trial, the person is probably guilty; (2) Regardless of what the law says, a defendant in a criminal trial should be required to prove his or her innocence; (3) A person who has a criminal record and is accused of a very serious crime is probably guilty.

TABLE 6.3
Z Scores for a Fair Cross-Sectional Representation of Demographic, Socioeconomic, Attitudinal Backgrounds of Jury Populations

| Variable | Disparities from a General Population | | | | | | Disparities from a Previous Selection Stage: | | | | |
	(2) ROV	(3) ROV & DMV	(4) Jury Qualifiers	(5) Jury Eligibles	(6) Jury Panels	(7) Jury Boxes	(2)-(3)	(3)-(4)	(4)-(5)	(5)-(6)	(6)-(7)
DEMOGRAPHIC BACKGROUND:											
Sex Male	0.435	0.504	0.230	1.508	0.089	-0.120	0.028	-0.236	1.388	-2.035	-0.188
Race											
White	4.231	0.626	4.705	-0.066	3.230	3.511	-4.761	4.206	-3.055	3.310	1.218
Black	-0.439	-0.560	-1.220	-0.019	0.490	-0.903	-0.087	-0.780	0.824	0.521	-1.150
Hispanic	-2.257	-0.489	-2.937	-0.161	-2.022	-2.040	2.263	-2.544	1.636	-1.823	-0.566
Others	-3.592	-0.189	-3.243	0.273	-2.714	-2.599	5.011	-3.101	2.515	-3.009	-0.680
Age											
Less than 20	-0.506	0.173	0.768	0.216	-1.885	-1.800	0.793	0.593	-0.164	-2.061	-0.785
20–39	-3.459	0.042	-2.515	-1.449	-4.144	-5.793	3.957	-2.554	-0.145	-2.145	-2.761
40–69	3.596	0.884	2.408	2.473	5.724	6.379	-3.068	1.591	1.225	2.244	2.022
70 or More	-0.201	-1.542	-0.173	-1.778	-2.107	-0.619	-1.333	1.332	-1.700	0.487	1.152
Marital Status											
Never Married	-1.971	0.402	-1.352	-0.145	-1.959	-3.537	2.719	-1.706	0.580	-1.767	-2.203
Married	3.674	2.074	1.733	-0.330	3.505	3.321	-2.032	-0.189	-1.253	3.950	0.654
Separated	0.101	0.578	-1.240	-0.236	-0.947	-0.091	0.465	-1.732	0.434	-0.625	0.683
Widowed	0.638	0.089	0.453	0.235	0.788	1.848	-0.586	0.369	0.000	0.443	1.167
SOCIO-ECONOMIC BACKGROUNDS:											
Education											
Less than High School	-1.699	-0.442	-2.170	-1.383	-2.546	-2.061	1.533	-1.792	-0.284	-0.668	-0.114
High School	-0.657	0.000	0.288	-0.313	-0.539	0.607	0.725	0.288	-0.461	-0.097	1.033
Some College	-0.014	0.375	0.735	0.286	-0.094	-0.406	0.390	0.387	-0.094	-0.495	-0.334
College	1.290	0.055	1.119	0.837	2.614	0.987	-1.310	1.066	0.248	1.370	-0.946
Post Graduate	0.989	-0.157	-0.655	0.350	0.234	0.449	-1.201	-0.512	0.705	-0.256	0.266

(continued)

TABLE 6.3 (Continued)
Z Scores for a Fair Cross-Sectional Representation of Demographic, Socioeconomic, Attitudinal Backgrounds of Jury Populations

Variable	Disparities from a General Population						Disparities from a Previous Selection Stage:				
	(2) ROV	(3) ROV & DMV	(4) Jury Qualifiers	(5) Jury Eligibles	(6) Jury Panels	(7) Jury Boxes	(2)–(3)	(3)–(4)	(4)–(5)	(5)–(6)	(6)–(7)
Income											
Less than $10,000	-2.312	-0.940	-1.493	-2.645	-3.616	-2.297	1.799	-0.650	-2.014	0.184	0.679
$10,000-$29,999	-1.219	-0.173	-0.747	-0.523	-1.153	-0.508	1.177	-0.588	-0.136	-0.417	0.389
$30,000-$49,999	0.437	1.116	0.267	0.631	-0.434	-1.679	0.634	-0.754	0.491	-1.306	-1.357
$50,000-$74,999	1.614	0.471	1.340	0.148	3.243	3.307	-1.243	0.894	-0.530	3.010	0.728
$75,000 or More	1.357	0.022	0.478	2.113	1.744	1.276	-1.390	0.457	1.831	-1.094	-0.064
Organization											
Business Owner	0.519	0.233	0.815	0.842	-2.401	-1.683	-0.329	0.595	0.408	-3.413	0.195
Supervisor	1.398	-0.178	0.932	0.333	0.696	-0.879	-1.706	1.098	-0.151	0.224	-1.415
Salary Compensation	1.886	0.418	-0.127	-2.262	10.510	9.054	-1.648	-0.513	-2.196	13.838	1.059
Employment Status											
Full–Time	-0.848	0.216	-0.045	-0.482	1.861	0.154	1.138	-0.245	-0.459	2.531	-1.306
Part–Time	-0.298	-0.031	-0.085	0.122	-2.409	-2.127	0.299	-0.057	0.167	-2.562	-0.307
Retired	1.488	-0.205	0.288	0.115	0.297	1.659	-1.766	0.480	-0.034	0.132	1.415
ATTITUDINAL BACKGROUNDS:											
Criminal Justice Biases											
(1) Defendant Required to Prove Innocence	-2.702	2.302	-2.097	-1.824	-3.423	-3.979	5.359	-4.187	-0.745	-0.860	-1.388
(2) Person is Guilty if Brought to Trial	-0.287	0.079	0.262	-0.185	-1.375	-2.478	0.395	0.189	-0.320	-1.120	-1.469
(3) Person with a Criminal Record is Guilty	-0.402	0.069	-0.543	-2.467	-1.293	-2.990	0.513	-0.606	-2.205	2.429	-2.055

Note: The attitudinal questions are phrased as: (1) If the prosecution goes to the troubles of bringing someone to trial, the person is probably guilty; (2) Regardless of what the law says, a defendant in a criminal trial should be required to prove his or her innocence; (3) A person who has a criminal record and is accused of a very serious crime is probably guilty.

demographic representation by correcting the skewed jury representation caused by the ROV back to that of the general population, further supporting that the multiple source lists are more likely to represent the socio-economic cross section of community populations.

Jury qualification requirements, however, tend to skew jury compositions to those with higher education (some college or more), higher income ($30,000 or more), business owners, supervisors, and the retired. Exemption and excuse clauses further skew the profile of jury eligibles within the same socioeconomic groups. The greatest increase is observed for those with annual incomes of more than $75,000 (10.92 percent of jury pools based on multiple-source lists and 14.89 percent of jury eligibles).

The analyses of jury composition in jury panels show mixed results. While jurors with higher education and greater annual income are overrepresented, the greatest increase is observed for those with salary compensation programs. Prospective jurors from organizations with salary continuation policies make up approximately half of a general population (50.20 precent) as opposed to 72.73 percent of jurors in the jury panel. Table 6.3 shows that, in comparing with the general population of the community, the overrepresentation of salary-compensated jurors is statistically significant ($z = 10.510$ and 9.054 for jury panels and boxes, respectively), suggesting that if jury selection is truly random, such overrepresentation of jurors whose salaries are to be continued during jury service would only occur less than one in one million trials, suggesting that all jury selection stages prior to the jury panel are most likely to disenfranchise individual jurors who lack organizational resources and benefits of employers' salary continuation policies. Moreover, their disproportionate representation becomes even greater when they are assessed for actual jury service (75.35 percent), showing that more than three out of four trial jurors who sit on jury boxes are compensated by employers or other outside sources for jury duties. The trial jurors are also even more skewed to represent those with higher incomes ($50,000 or more) and the retired population.

Ideological Backgrounds and Jury Biases

Similar to demographic and socioeconomic backgrounds of community members, attitudinal profiles of individual jurors also show significant fluctuations throughout the entire phase of jury selection procedures. Empirical analysis shows that the general population is most likely to assume guilt when the criminal defendant is brought to trial (25.49 percent). Similarly the general population is most likely to assume that the offender has to prove his or her innocence (41.46 percent); and that if a person has a prior criminal record, he or she is assumed guilty (26.96 percent).

The eligible jury population is more likely to show less bias about the assumption of guilt (25.00 percent), the burden of proof (36.00 percent), and negative perceptions due to prior criminal records than the general population

(20.31 percent). The perceptive biases of criminal justice concepts are less for those in jury panels or final juries than the general population and the jury eligibles. The one exception, however, is that those in jury panels are more likely than the jury eligibles to assume that the offenders with criminal records are guilty (24.50 percent).

Trial jurors showed the least bias with respect to the presumption of innocence, prior criminal records, and burden of proof. The analysis shows the statistically significant difference between trial jurors and the general population ($z = -3.979, -2.475,$ and -2.990 for the burden of proof, presumed innocence, and guilt due to criminal records, respectively), suggesting that actual trial experiences perform important educational functions in teaching jurors about criminal justice concepts and assumptions.

PARTIAL REMEDIES AND THEIR IMPACTS ON JURY SELECTION

We now shift our focus to the impact of various reforms on jury selection and representation. The evolution of the requirement that an impartial jury must necessarily be drawn from a cross section of the community represented a historical shift from several earlier views about the nature of juries, collective impartiality, and human judgment. For the representative jury replaced the notion of the elite "blue ribbon" jury composed of handpicked jurors of "exemplary moderation and wisdom" (Kotler 2000, 92)—a necessarily unrepresentative group from which some members of the community were deliberately excluded (Amar 1984). The contemporary requirement that the jury represent a fair cross section of society premises the concept of impartiality exhibited by a diverse jury. Yet, we have attempted to show that the ROV list tends to skew jury representativeness more towards whites, males, those with higher incomes, those forty years of age or older, the married, and the widowed. A similar effect is observed for jury qualification requirements, especially after screened for jurors' citizenship status, residency requirements, sufficient knowledge of the English language, previous felony convictions, and other subjective factors, including possessions of so-called ordinary intelligence, sound judgment, and a fair character.

The supplemental use of DMV lists and jury exemptions and excuses tend to correct the representative imbalances caused by ROV and jury qualification requirements. For the use of DMV lists leads to greater inclusion of racial minorities such as African Americans and Hispanics, those less than forty years of age, and never married groups, as well as those with less than a high school education and those who earn less than $30,000 annually.

Similarly, the general population does not seem to possess correct factual knowledge about the burden of proof (41.46 percent). After the DMV is introduced as a supplemental list to ROV, however, jurors' bias towards criminal processes, particularly knowledge about the burden of proof, is increased. While it is incongruous to argue that the level of "biases" is recovered by the introduction of DMV sources, such biases and prejudice are in fact represented in jury pools as one element of the community's diverse perspectives.

Excuses and exemptions also help correct the skewed imbalance of the jury, returning it to a more diverse reflection of the overall population. The authorities may screen out those with physical and mental disabilities and capacities. But self-screening is also at work, as some prospective jurors claim excuses due to personal obligations, economic hardship, transportation difficulties, and prior jury service. Those remaining are often previously underrepresented groups such as racial minorities, never married and separated jurors, and part-time employees—all more likely to be included in jury pools. The exceptions are that, after qualified jurors are screened for their exemption status and excuse items, those potential jurors with annual earnings exceeding $75,000, those with college or postgraduate degrees, and jurors between forty and sixty-nine are overrepresented to an even greater degree.

The jury panel stage of jury selection tends to further accentuate underrepresentation of the same groups that ROV excluded from jury service, such as Hispanics, those less than forty years of age, jurors who separated or never married, those with high school education or less, those with less than $10,000 annual income, and part-time employees. Since jury panels consist of prospective jurors who have come to the courthouse after responding to jury summonses, and a large proportion of qualified and eligible jurors do not necessarily respond to jury summonses, effective follow-up enforcement seems necessary for those who fail to respond to jury summonses.

Not all jurors who show up at the courthouse end up in the final jury box, either. Once jurors report to the courthouse, judges often screen prospective jurors for possible excuses and exemptions. As noted earlier, while similar screening questions are asked of qualified jurors at earlier stages of jury selection, the exclusionary effect on jury participation at this stage is considered to be even more significant, as a large proportion of jury candidates have already been excluded before reaching the courthouse. As our findings show, the results are significant overrepresentation of the following groups in the final jury: whites, forty years of age or older, the married, the widowed, high school graduates and those with postgraduate education, those yearly earning between $50,000 and $74,999, business owners, jurors with salary continuation plans, and the retired.

These findings thus suggest that taken together, ROV and jury qualification requirements tend to distort what otherwise would be an ideal representative jury drawn from the general population. Short of an ideal jury, to reestablish the original demographic and socioeconomic makeup of the general population, DMV and jury eligibility requirements are likely to correct some representative imbalances caused by ROV and qualification requirements. Without effective follow-up enforcement, however, a representative crosssection of the general population is unlikely to be secured at the courthouse. Even greater skewness is found between those in jury panels and trial jurors. This is because the voir dire screening process is more likely to increase the representative imbalance towards white and middle-class jurors—racial and social groups that already dominate the vast majority of both state and federal courts.

Employees in firms or organizations that have salary continuation plans also tend to dominate the makeup of both jury panels and trial juries. More than three out of four trial jurors do not need to worry about the loss of income because of jury service. In Orange County, like most counties in California, jurors were awarded $5 for their day's commitment to jury service. While the fee was increased to $15 per day in July 2000, it is still insufficient for many daily or hourly wage earners to report to the courthouse, let alone to carry out their civic duties by serving on the jury.

The representative cross section of the general population is not found when the list of potential jurors are picked by voter registration lists and by jury qualification standards. Similarly, when jurors are given discretion to report to the courthouse after receiving jury summonses, jury representativeness becomes even more remote from the socioeconomic and demographic makeup of the general population. And the voir dire process exerts another significant disrupting effect on the balanced representation of the trial jury.

Jurors' individual and organizational resources are also factors that determine whether jurors are able to manage to survive throughout the cumbersome jury selection process. Jurors' ability to serve on the final jury may depend on whether or not jurors are monetarily compensated for their civil service. Most jurisdictions have woefully failed to compensate jurors adequately, so jury members may not be able to cover the cost of parking, lunch, or the needed expenses for child or elder care for those who have domestic responsibilities. Recently Massachusetts, Connecticut, and Colorado have instituted similar jury compensation measures, with employers required to pay jurors their full salary for the first three days.

A problem with requiring employers to compensate juror-employees is that it may be too costly for small businesses that would be unable to maintain a competitive market posture.[4] This may feed into the imbalance of organizational resources and the lack of income needed to balance the jury pool in terms of an individual's economic survival, as well as by other socio-demographic factors like race and gender. Thus, the court granting excuses based on economic hardship may introduce a systematic exclusionary bias in jury panels and trial juries, as those being excused are excluded by class, race, and gender—not randomly distributed among the general population (Fukurai, Butler, and Krooth 1993, 120).

FINAL JURY COMPOSITION: INEQUITIES, REMEDIES, AND FUTURE REFORMS

Addressing the jury's racial representativeness, the 1986 Batson and Batson progeny cases are perhaps the most important Supreme Court pronouncements, because they explicitly forbid attorneys from using race as the criteria in the exercise of their peremptory challenges. The Court in *Kentucky v. Batson* (106

S. Ct. 1712, 1986) ruled that the Equal Protection Clause of the Bill of Rights forbids prosecutors from exercising peremptory challenges to strike prospective jurors solely on account of their race. Under Batson, the state may not exclude all members of the defendant's race from the jury box on account of race, or on the false assumption that members of his/her own race as a group are not qualified to serve as jurors (1716–1718). Although Batson initially offered hope that the goal of a representative jury was attainable, an examination of cases decided since 1986 suggests otherwise.

As shown in chapter 5, Kenneth J. Melilli (1996) reviewed virtually all relevant reported decisions of every federal and state court applying Batson between April 30, 1986 (the date of the Batson decision) and December 31, 1993. He concluded that many of the currently accepted bases for peremptory challenges, such as economic and geographic criteria and attorneys' subjective judgments, continued to exert a disproportionate negative impact on blacks and Hispanics (Melilli 1996, 501). Given Batson's ineffectiveness and the persistent racial disparity in jury selection, we propose the following possible remedies and modifications of jury qualification requirements in order to open the eligible jury pool to historically underrepresented racial and social groups.

So far the present analysis has substantiated that jury qualifications eliminate a large proportion of racial and ethnic minorities. In the name of needed reforms, then, an expanded definition of qualified jurors should include these and many other traditionally excluded subpopulations, covering "permanent resident aliens," previously convicted felons with satisfactory records of legal rehabilitation, and potential jurors lacking sufficient knowledge of some aspects of English language proficiency that do not impede comprehension of jury proceedings, yet are considered as elements for disqualification in many jurisdictions.[5]

Legal Resident Aliens on Juries

In the history of modern juries, legal resident aliens have actively participated in both grand and petit juries. As we have seen, before Okinawa reverted from United States control to Japan in 1972, general residents of Okinawa enjoyed the right to jury trials (Japan Federation of Bar Associations [JFBA] 1992, 14). Similar to the jury trial in the United States, petit jury deliberations in Okinawa required a unanimous verdict, while grand jury deliberations were based on majority vote.

Jury qualification also required that potential jurors be at least twenty-one years of age. Okinawa residency was established after living three months on the islands. Jurors needed proficiency in English, and both United States and non-United States citizens were allowed to participate together in the trial jury. The simple random selection method was used to select potential jurors from not only the residents of Okinawa Island, but also from the other surrounding Ryukyu islands. They were subject to voir dire, and might be peremptorily stricken or challenged for cause. The grand jury consisted of six to nine members, and the petit jury was made up of twelve members (JFBA 1992, 11–14).

Jury selection of the first ever trial in Okinawa took place on March 20, 1963, and the first petit jury was composed of eight Okinawans and twelve United States citizens which also included eight alternates ("Baishin seido ga sutaato" 1963; JFBA 1992, 180). The first jury selection for the grand jury occurred in March 27, 1963, including three Americans, one Philippino, and five Okinawans (JFBA 1992, 182).

Turning back the pages of history, since late twelfth-century England, another tribunal, the jury de medietate linguae, also allowed noncitizens such as French and German residents to participate in jury trials (Constable 1994). Permitting noncitizens to participate in jury trials still can have a significant impact in extending greater opportunities for underrepresented groups such as Hispanics in the United States (Bleyer, McCarty, and Wood 1995, 250; Fukurai 2001).

The statistics also indicate the potentiality for allowing legal resident aliens an opportunity to serve as jurors. The 1990 census indicates that 19.8 million living in the United States were foreign born. Nearly twelve million of those foreign born and living in the United States were legal resident aliens; over ten million resident aliens were eighteen-years-old or older. And the number of legal resident aliens have almost doubled since 1980 (5.7 million).[6]

The Urban Institute, a research organization that specializes in immigration issues, estimates the number of permanent resident aliens of Mexican nationality in the United States at between 2.3 and 3 million (Dillon 1996). The continued increase of permanent resident aliens will undoubtedly provide greater participatory opportunities for Hispanics in the future. Yet, an important direct effect of current anti-foreign sentiments is the inability of permanent resident aliens to obtain a fair trial in the United States (Raskin 1993). The jury may be influenced by xenophobic views or more subtle, anti-foreign sentiments in deciding cases involving non-citizens. The potential threat is all the more acute because legal resident aliens are also legally barred from jury service in all United States jurisdictions.

Legally Defined Felons and the Loss of Civil Rights

Today's American Bar Association (ABA) has not helped to extend the rights of jury service to legally defined felons, either. Its standards recommend that convicted felons "who have not had their civil rights restored" be excluded from jury service, because many may resent the justice system and unduly favor criminal defendants, noting also that their presence on juries would weaken respect for the judicial system (ABA 1993, 39–40). The legal exclusion of convicted felons, however, significantly impacts jury representation. While it may be a radical and certainly a controversial proposal, we would like to create a window for discussion, to consider the possibility that certain kinds of nonviolent felony defendants should have the privilege to serve on juries, once they become eligible for release from correctional institutions. Such rehabilitation certainly must follow systematic procedures and stringent standards to restore their civil rights in order to become future jury candidates. Yet, lacking such procedural mechanisms, a large proportion of racial minorities will forever be ineligible or unqualified to serve on the jury.

As of December 31, 1999, black and Hispanic inmates respectively constituted 45.7 percent and 17.9 percent of 1.4 million inmates in state and federal prisons. The absolute number of black inmates were also greater than that of whites, though black males constitute only 6 percent of the United States population (U.S. Department of Justice 2000, 432). Almost 10 percent of black males in their late twenties were in prison in 1999 (9.4 percent). The majority of the total inmates (52 percent), however, were convicted for nonviolent crimes, including offenses involving property (21 percent), drugs (21 percent), and public order (10 percent). Public-order infractions included weapon possession, drunk driving, court offenses, commercial vice, liquor law violations, and other offenses (see generally, U.S. Dept. of Justice 2000).

Other new laws and regulations have also produced a large number of felons who are nonviolent. The three strikes law in California, for example, allows the elevation of the crime of petty theft into a felony if the defendant has had a prior record of felonies, even including juvenile felony convictions. Though many such individuals may have had their civil rights restored after serving out their sentences and penalties, the three strikes law continues to allow those defendants convicted of petty theft or other nonviolent offenses to be criminally prosecuted for either a second or third felony strike (see generally Marion 1999). Such laws exert racially disproportionate inequalities on convicted felons, and so far have sent more than fifty thousand to prisons. As of December 31, 1999, black and Hispanic three strike offenders constituted 44.1 percent and 25.9 percent of the total third strike cases. Nonviolent crimes constituted the majority of their convictions—31.0 percent for property, 19.0 percent for drug-related, 8.9 percent for other nonviolent offenses (FACTS 2000). While the three strikes law in California has been harshly criticized because of its inability to discern violent and habitual offenders from nonviolent criminals, the law nonetheless has had racially disproportionate consequences in sentencing a large number of racial minorities to prison (Zimring, Kamin, and Hawkins 1999).

As evidence that the person is restored to his or her civil rights, the majority of states provide a certificate of discharge or an order of discharge to the convicted person. But some states still automatically disqualify persons ever convicted of a felony from jury service. Missouri, for instance, permanently disqualifies individuals with prior felony convictions from jury service, imposing legal disabilities on all convicted felons (Mo. Rev. Stat. s 561.026 [3], 1989). New Jersey requires that, in order to qualify for jury service, one "shall not have been convicted of a crime" (N.J. Stat. Ann. s 2A:69–1 (West 1976), see also *United States v. Breckenridge,* 899 F.2d 540 541, n.2 [6th Cir. 1990]).

Individuals with prior felony convictions obviously face great difficulties in serving as jurors. So the issue of qualification for jury service makes it incumbent on legislatures to establish procedures for the restoration of civil rights to convicted felons. Similarly, voir dire procedures such as peremptory challenges, challenges for cause, and court discretion that prevent summoning ex-felons need to be eliminated from jury selection procedures (Komives and Blotner 1991; King 1993a). For clearly, otherwise, a large proportion of African-Americans and other racial and ethnic minorities will continue to be excluded from jury service.

Language Proficiency and Jury Qualification

Language proficiency as another criterion for jury qualification further eliminates a large proportion of eligible Hispanics, recent immigrants, and their communities. Cynthia L. Brown (1994) has argued that a juror qualification provision that bars non-English speaking citizens from jury service violates not only the Sixth Amendment, but also the Equal Protection Clauses of the Fourteenth Amendment. She further suggests that a statute such as the New York Judiciary Law, with its English language requirement, fails to meet the fundamental right for citizens to participate in jury service because: (1) the state fails to treat similarly situated individuals alike with respect to the legislature's objectives in enacting the law; (2) the legislature has acted for an impermissible purpose; and (3) the state is denying Hispanic citizens a fundamental right by assuming that their lack of knowledge of the English language makes them incapable of performing jury service (Brown 1994, 479).

Most state laws nonetheless require jurors to read, write, and speak the English language with a degree of proficiency, though such requirements have a racially discriminatory impact on jury representation, especially given the fact that Hispanics are the largest growing segment of the United States population. According to the 2000 census, Hispanics accounted for 12.5 percent of the United States population and 32.4 percent of the population in California. In some jurisdictions, the proportion of potential Hispanic jurors, who speak Spanish as their primary language, has also increased dramatically for the last several decades. Many states continue to exclude non-English speakers from serving on juries, however, denying equal access to this fundamental right based on language alone (Perea 1992; Brown 1994, 479–490). Though, in Canada, a resident alien is entitled to a jury composed of at-least-half of whose members speak her language, in the United States, jury service still requires English language proficiency, thereby eliminating a large proportion of Hispanic and other non-English speaking populations (Potash 1973, 92).

Besides the disparate effect of jury qualifications on racial representation, traditional, non-affirmative jury selection system continues to create racially and socially unbalanced juries. Our analysis, however, has its limits, relying on the effectiveness of voir dire, including peremptory challenges and challenges for cause. The true extent of voir dire's impact on disproportionate jury representation is not entirely clear. There is a skewed distribution by race and socioeconomic categories throughout the jury selection process. While our recommendations for the extended opportunities for qualified jurors may increase the chance opportunity of previously disenfranchised groups for jury service, they do not guarantee the inclusion of individuals from the same group or members of other underrepresented communities in the final trial jury. Affirmative action strategies are the only viable alternative and unfailing practical remedies to empanel racially and socially diverse tribunals.

CONCLUSIONS

It is clear that current jury selection methods fail to provide specific affirmative mechanisms to guarantee both the cross-sectional representation and the presence of racial minorities on the final jury itself. Although the Sixth Amendment's fair cross section requirement forbids systematic discrimination in the creation of the jury venire and panel itself, it does not guarantee a racially and socially diverse tribunal. This chapter has examined jurors' representativeness through the entire stage of the jury selection process, from the general population in the jurisdiction, to jury qualified pools, jury eligibles, jury venires or panels, and trial jurors.

Our analyses of jury representativeness have identified a number of legal and extra-legal factors that impact jury participation. The critical examination of jury representativeness between different stages of jury selection has also revealed many exclusionary factors and practices. The supplemental use of DMV lists and jury exemptions and excuses tend to correct the representative imbalances caused by ROV and jury qualification requirements. But the lack of systematic follow-up, the voir dire process, and jury qualification standards tend to disrupt jury representation after jurors have appeared at the courthouse. Jurors employed in firms or organizations that provide their employees salary continuation programs are positioned to significantly dominate the composition of jury panels and final juries, so much so that more than three out of four trial jurors do not need to worry about losing income while serving on the jury.

In order to increase jury participation for those racial and social communities that have historically been disenfranchised, we have proposed a number of deep seated reforms and procedural remedies to improve jury representation in source lists, qualified pools, and jury panels. Such procedural-based proposals and recommendations included changes and modifications in jury qualification requirements, use of multiple-source lists, systematic follow-up procedures, and potential monetary compensation to neutralize differences in jurors' organizational resources.

Nonetheless, such remedies and proposals may only have a significant impact up to the jury panel stage of jury selection, not to the final jury. Voir dire would still lead to racial imbalances in the composition of the final jury. Only the affirmative peremptory inclusion of those now disenfranchised during voir dire will lead to a restructuring of the racial and social composition of the final jury. Otherwise, the historically underrepresented and disenfranchised minority communities and their members will continue to be underrepresented on the trial jury.

Chapter 7

JURY NULLIFICATION AND THE MINORITY-DOMINANT CRIMINAL JURY

The O. J. Simpson Verdict and Acquittal by Race

I n America's racial milieu, a single criminal trial often raises deep social questions, signifying moral and ethical feelings, as well as disparate perceptions of the legitimacy of the criminal justice system. Such was the O. J. Simpson trial and the verdict of "not guilty" that held the momentary attention of the nation and the world as one more proof that race and ethnicity are paramount matters, impacting the concepts of justice and equity in the legal system (Rich 1995; Wilgroren 1995). Clearly, not everyone did or could agree with the jury verdict, the portrayal of the facts, or the application of the criminal code. Yet, as the debate raged over the verdict and the future of America's criminal justice system, legal observers and courtroom commentators saw the O. J. Simpson trial as a metaphor of the deep racial rifts that cleave America's race-conscious society and contaminate the integrity of its criminal justice system and court proceedings (Carlsen and Wildermuth 1995).

For some, the Simpson verdict elevated the strategic place of "jury nullification," as a predominantly African American jury rejected overwhelming evidence of guilt in favor of their own conception of justice ("O. J. Simpson case: A legal aberration" 1995). One legal analyst even declared that African American "defense lawyer Johnnie Cochran had urged the jurors [towards] . . . 'jury nullification,' the basic idea being that jurors have the right to refuse to enforce unjust laws or laws that have been unjustly enforced" (Abramson 1995). Among defense members of the so-called Dream Team, intense disagreement also raged over the propriety of making the racial issue—the "race card"—an integral part of the defense strategy, thus increasing the possibility for racially based nullification by a jury that included nine African Americans, one Hispanic, and two whites (Hubert 1995).

The criminal jury is legally empowered to completely disregard the application of the law (Sauer 1995, 1253–1254). Indeed, jury nullification refers to the jury's unfettered ability to sidestep substantive legal requirements by using its discretionary power, meaning that a jury may acquit a defendant contrary to evidentiary facts and/or the law. Black's Law Dictionary notes that "[j]ury nullification refers to the power of the jury to acquit the defendant, regardless of the strength of the evidence" (6th ed. 1990). A legal scholar defines jury nullification as the "power to ignore a strict interpretation of the law when mitigating circumstances justify a more lenient approach" (Van Dyke 1983, 939–40) In other words, a jury holds the power to ignore both the facts and the law in its verdict.

Given African Americans' widespread perceptions of law enforcement agencies harassing and discriminating against them, a jury of their number might well play the political function of acquitting a black defendant by reasoning that a conviction might violate their sense of personal public morality and that, applying the law to the defendant, would lead to a grave social injustice (Van Dyke 1970, 225). On a broader plane, the Supreme Court has characterized the jury's fundamental role in criminal cases as a defense against arbitrary enforcement, stating in *Duncan and Louisiana* (391 U.S. 145, 1968):

> A right to jury trial is granted to criminal defendants in order to prevent oppression by the Government. Those who wrote our constitution knew from history and experience that it was necessary to protect against unfounded criminal charges brought to eliminate enemies and against judges too responsive to the voice of higher authority. . . . Providing an accused with the right to be tried by a jury of his peers gave him an inestimable safeguard against the corrupt or overzealous prosecutor and against the compliant, biased or eccentric judge (391 U.S. 145, 155).

Given African Americans' experience with harsh and unequal law enforcement agencies in urban centers like New York, Los Angeles, and Washington, D.C., government investigators' public disclosure of purported evidence and prosecutors' misuse of facts and evidence hold little or no place in believability in black communities, often losing any persuasive power among minority jurors. Racial nullification of both law and fact—racially based jury nullification—has today emerged as a powerful check on the exercise of abusive governmental power, serving as a judicial shield protecting broad minority interests. The report of racial nullification has frequently appeared today in criminal cases involving racial minority defendants, with acquittal verdicts made by predominantly racial minority juries.

The open question, however, is whether or not particular criminal offenses are linked to broadly defined social crimes against public order, and whether or not such order is based on laws securing an unjust racial and social system. For there is a difference between broad racial and social inequality enforced by structural government discrimination against racial minorities on one side, and on the other the specifics of a particular case involving a defendant of color charged with a particular crime. Some legal scholars argue that in a criminal trial involving "racially charged" accusations and African American defendants, a predominantly African-American jury should have the moral obligation to acquit the defendants by disregarding the evidence, however powerful, as a protest against racial injustice and discrimination in the criminal justice system. George Washington University Law Professor Paul Butler thus openly urges African Americans to acquit African American defendants who may be "technically guilty" of nonviolent, *malum prohibitum,* offenses such as drug possession, as well as to consider jury nullification for African American defendants charged with nonviolent, *malum in se,* crimes such as theft or perjury (Butler 1995a). Butler specifically argues that: "Considering the costs of law enforcement to the black community and the failure of white lawmakers to devise significant nonincarcerative responses to black antisocial conduct, it is the moral responsibility of black jurors to emancipate some guilty black outlaws" (1995a, 679).[1]

Such racial acquittals express the "anti-democratic" nature of jury nullification, because they provide racial minorities the power to determine justice in a way that majority rule does not (Weinstein 1993). Thus has endorsement of the power of a predominantly African American jury to engage in race-based jury nullification become an explosive and racially sensitive issue in the criminal court system (Butler 1995b). Despite the significance of racially based acquittals and their effects on the integrity of the criminal justice and court systems, little research has been done to determine whether or not "apparent" jury nullification cases provide an example or outcome of minority jurors' decisions to negate and ignore the application of law (Simon 1992). The lack of empirical research on racial nullification has led the contemporary media to represent racial minority juries as lawless, because their race-based acquittals signify their failure to follow the strict application of law by transgressing the social and legal role assigned to them by the court and by dominant culture and society (Weinstein 1995).

But what if the acquittals by predominantly minority juries reflect their adherence to the strict application of the law and legal concepts in evaluating testimony and evidence—such as a presumption of innocence, the burden of proof, and reasonable doubt? In highly publicized criminal trials involving unmistakable elements of racism and racial discrimination, past jury research has failed to reveal the dynamics of this contextual scenario of jury nullification. Little doubt, given racial minorities' experience with racially discriminatory law enforcement and criminal court processes, they have developed a strong sense of skepticism, mistrust, and suspicion about the credibility and validity of criminal charges, the veracity of witnesses against them and evidence presented in court. In other words, rather than widely accepted images and media representations of lawless and "untamed" racial minority juries negating and nullifying the application of law, acquittal verdicts may in fact reflect the higher, evaluative standards of racial minority juries in assessing testimony and evidence presented in court, as well as their unanimous or split consensus that the government failed to meet the legal standard of proving the defendant's guilt beyond a reasonable doubt.

Jury nullification also has important relevance to our discussion of an affirmative strategy to empanel racially diverse juries. One harsh criticism against selecting a race-specific jury is that racially diverse tribunals may lead to higher instances of hung juries, reflecting the perceived difficulty of racially mixed tribunals to reach a unanimous verdict. Similarly, skepticism and cynicism exist that minority jurors may harbor deep racial anger, igniting a determination and propensity to disregard compelling evidence and testimony in trials of minority defendants, thereby increasing the chance of jury nullification.

What precisely the jurors actually debate and decide may be unknown or only partially revealed. Prior assumptions of jurors and their power to nullify the law show that the jury can impact public policy by acquitting criminal defendants when they feel a conviction may violate public morality, suggesting that the jury is empowered to act as judges of both fact and law (Scheflin 1972, 181–89; Scott 1989, 419–23). This contrasts with traditional standards that view jury deliberations as limited to judging facts, not law. According to this traditional view of the jury's role in criminal cases, acquittal verdicts may be considered to reflect the jury's genuine determination that the state failed to prove a defendant's guilt beyond a reasonable doubt, suggesting that the jury followed the strict and rational applications of the legal principles delineated and described in the judge's instructions about finding the facts, rather than nullifying the law and finding a defendant not guilty.

This is the subject of this chapter, its main thrust attempting to examine the deliberative performance of racially diverse tribunals in racially sensitive criminal trials. We attempt to critically examine the capabilities of such juries to evaluate the facts and evidence by adhering to fundamental criminal justice concepts. Part I presents a brief background on legal concepts of the criminal process during the guilt determining phase of the jury trial—involving the presumption of innocence, the burden of proof, and reasonable doubt. It also examines past research findings on jurors' comprehension of these legal principles in criminal trials.

Part II then presents empirical analyses of these three basic legal concepts, and reviews the extent of their application by the O. J. Simpson jury in examining evidence and rendering a verdict. This section specifically examines whether or not—in a highly publicized, racially charged criminal trial—racial minorities as members of racially diverse tribunals exhibit a greater or lesser propensity to follow the strict application of criminal justice principles in evaluating the validity and reliability of the evidence. Finally, Part III discusses the role and deliberative performance of the racially diverse jury in racially charged criminal trials that involve racial discrimination by law enforcement authorities, as well as the pervasiveness of public scrutiny of racism in the criminal justice system.

PRESUMPTION OF INNOCENCE, THE BURDEN
OF PROOF, AND REASONABLE DOUBT

In criminal proceedings, three critical legal standards form an important foundation in reaching a just verdict: the presumption of innocence of the accused, the presence or absence of reasonable doubt, and the government's burden of proof. The presumption of innocence squarely places on the government the burden of proving a defendant's guilt beyond a reasonable doubt. In the following sections, each of these legal concepts is carefully examined, elaborated, and held up to the standard of equity.

Presumption of Innocence

The right of an accused to a presumption of innocence is basic to the United States system of justice, carrying with it the concomitant right to take reasonable steps to ensure that, no matter what crime has allegedly been committed and how strong evidence may appear to be, the accused is presumed innocent until he/she is adjudicated guilty of the crime in a court of law. The presumption of innocence is, then, a rule of evidence that shifts the burden of proof to the prosecutor or the government and serves as a foundation for the procedural requirement of proof beyond a reasonable doubt (Laufer 1995, 332).

　　The U.S. Supreme Court has also made it clear that the presumption of innocence is the fundamental premise of our legal system, reflecting broad societal concerns of justice and fairness (*Estelle v. Williams,* 425 U.S. 501, 503, 1976). Justice Stewart noted in *Kentucky v. Whorton* (441 U.S. 786, 1979) that: "No principle is more firmly established in our system of criminal justice than the presumption of innocence that is accorded to the defendant in every criminal trial" (790). The presumption of innocence also provides a normative and legal direction to police and prosecuting officials as to how they are to proceed in the disposition of criminal defendants throughout the criminal proceeding (Packer 1968, 149–152). The presumption of innocence has been called a "general principle of our political morality" (Twining 1990, 208), "a cornerstone of Anglo-Saxon justice" (Thayer 1898, 553), "a touchstone of American criminal jurisprudence" (*People v. Layhew,* 548 N.E.2d 25, 27 [Ill. App. 1989]), and a "bedrock 'axiomatic and elementary' principle whose 'enforcement lies at the foundation of the administration of our criminal law'" (*Coffin v. United States,* 156 U.S. 432, 453, 1895).

　　The presumption of innocence also earns its rhetorical prominence by deriving its meaning and authority from the right to a fair trial, as well as the right to trial by an impartial jury (Laufer 1995, 338). In the landmark case of *re Winship* (397 U.S. 358, 1971), the Supreme Court ruled that the presumption of innocence guards against extra-legal suspicion and unwarranted inference

(362). In other words, the right to be judged on evidence presented at trial, and not on mere suspicion, inference, or supposition, is a fundamental element of the right to an impartial jury which is guaranteed by the Sixth Amendment and the Fourteenth Amendment's due process and equal protection clauses.[2]

A number of social science studies have examined jurors' comprehension of the concept of presumed innocence in both potential and actual trials, showing that the presumption of innocence is one of the most misunderstood concepts of the criminal justice process. The 1991 National Jury Project survey of potential jurors in various federal district courts revealed that a substantial number of eligible jurors, including 41.6 percent of those in the Dallas Division of the Northern District of Texas, believed that when the government brings someone to trial, that person is probably guilty of some crime (Bonora and Krauss 1993, 2–12, 15). Another 1991 California survey also found that nearly half of potential jurors (48 percent) did not know that a defendant is presumed innocent, and that both African American and Hispanic eligible jurors reported a lower level of knowledge about this presumption than white and Asian jurors (Ellers 1993, 2185). Similarly, a 1978 National Center study and a 1992 Massachusetts study confirmed that only 57 percent and 62 percent of respondents in California and Massachusetts respectively knew the correct answer regarding this presumption. Another study also revealed that correct factual knowledge about the presumption of innocence was more likely among past jurors than among past litigants, indicating that litigants who are the most personally involved with the courts and have the most at stake are not properly informed about the rules and the mechanics of the court process (Ellers 1993). So, too, the 1992 *National Law Journal/* Lexis poll found that 28 percent of trial jurors did not comprehend the meaning of a presumption of innocence, feeling that a criminal defendant reaching the trial stage was probably guilty ("Many jurors consider deep pockets and ignore presumption of innocence" 1993).

Two additional California surveys in 1986 and 1995 also substantiate that those who have actually served on jury trials failed to believe in a fair and just disposition of criminal defendants, suggesting that our criminal justice system has been served by those who have held that defendants were assumed guilty when brought to trial (Fukurai 1999a; Fukurai and Davies 1997). These studies have shown that even after serving as trial jurors, a substantial proportion of jurors were still unable to correctly comprehend the principle of the presumption of innocence.

Burden of Proof

The presumption of innocence places on the government the burden of proving a defendant's guilt beyond a reasonable doubt. According to the reasoning of United States courts, the fact that the government bears a greater burden of proof in criminal trials than litigants in civil cases has historically stemmed in part from the position of the state as the plaintiff in criminal actions and the government's superior position of power, authority, and advantage over the criminal defendant (*United States v. Shapleigh,* 54 F. 126, 129 [8th Cir., 1893]).

In the Simpson as well as other criminal trials, the burden of proof is thus placed on the prosecution, not on the defendant. In order for the Simpson jury to issue a verdict to convict, then, it was required to reach unanimous consensus during deliberations that the government had proved the defendant's guilt beyond a reasonable doubt.

Yet, social science studies on jurors' knowledge of the meaning of the burden of proof have revealed that, while the government bears the burden of persuasion in criminal cases, a large proportion of both potential and actual jurors have failed to understand the legal concept of the burden of proof. A 1985 Illinois study suggests that, in examining the comprehension of the judge's Illinois Pattern Instructions (IPI) and juror comprehension of which side shoulders the burden of proof in a criminal case, a large proportion of criminal jurors still failed to comprehend the fundamental principle of the burden of proof. The same study also suggested that African Americans were less likely to be familiar with the concept than white jurors (Tiersma 1995). Two California surveys similarly examined the public's understanding of the concept of the burden of proof. A 1986 Survey in Orange County showed that while 41.4 percent of the general population felt that the defendant must prove his/her innocence, 30.5 percent of those who actually served in jury trials also felt the same (see chap. 6). A 1995 California Survey in Santa Cruz County also found that 44.0 percent of eligible jurors felt that the defendant shoulders the burden of proof in a criminal case (Fukurai 1997).

Similarly the United States Supreme Court has acknowledged the public's misconception of the concept, citing a national survey that 37 percent of the public believes that it is a defendant's responsibility to prove his innocence (*Carter v. Kentucky* 450 U.S. 288, 303 n.21, 1981). Other research has also cast doubt on the public's understanding of the burden of proof, showing that over half of those participating in a nationwide random survey felt that a criminal defendant should be required to take the stand and prove his innocence (Gold 1984, 190, fn116).

Reasonable Doubt

The meaning of reasonable doubt is a central legal concept in criminal proceedings. While the standard of reasonable doubt does not appear within the actual text of the Constitution, the Supreme Court has stated that the due process guarantees of the Fifth and Fourteenth Amendments "protect the accused against conviction except upon proof beyond a reasonable doubt of every fact necessary to constitute the crime with which he is charged." In

California courts, for instance, reasonable doubt is defined by the California Jury Instruction as follows:

> It is not a mere possible doubt; because everything relating to human affairs, and depending on moral evidence, is open to some possible or imaginary doubt. It is that state of the case which, after the entire comparison and consideration of all the evidence, leaves the minds of the jurors in that condition that they cannot say they feel an abiding conviction, to a moral certainty, of the truth of the charge (see Section 2.90 in *California Jury Instructions, 1988*)

In *re Winship's* enunciation of the right to proof beyond a reasonable doubt, the Court similarly stated that: "The requirement that guilt of a criminal charge be established by proof beyond a reasonable doubt dates at least from our early years as a Nation" (In *re Winship,* 397 U.S. 358, 361, 1971). The Winship Court explained that the reasonable doubt standard "is a prime instrument for reducing the risk of convictions resting on factual error" (363). Since criminal convictions "besmirch" the defendant's good name and impose considerable hardship, courts should not allow a conviction to "befall" an innocent person. To prevent that from happening, the due process clause requires the state to surmount a high burden of proof to secure a conviction (363–64).

The Winship Court recognized two characteristics of the criminal process as supporting the high constitutional standard of reasonable doubt: first is the difficulty of defending against a charge of crime, a "disadvantage" that would amount to a denial of "fundamental fairness, if [the defendant] could be adjudicated guilty and imprisoned for years on the strength of the same evidence as would suffice in a civil case" (363).

The second aspect of the criminal process on which Winship relied is the difference between so-called Type I and Type II errors—erroneous convictions and erroneous acquittals. Justice Harlan, in a concurring opinion, emphasized the connection between the reasonable doubt standard and "a fundamental value determination of our society that it is far worse to convict an innocent man [type I error] than to let a guilty man go free [type II error]" (at 372, Harlan, J., concurring). In explaining the importance of the reasonable doubt rule, the Court declared that: "a society that values the good name and freedom of every individual should not condemn a man for commission of a crime where there is a reasonable doubt about his guilt."

On the jurors' knowledge of the proof beyond a reasonable doubt, two separate studies by the London School of Economics and the Chicago Jury Project documented that jurors take the "beyond a reasonable doubt" standard seriously only until they find out that the defendant is a criminally prone individual. Those studies concluded that the presumption of innocence only operates for defendants without prior criminal records (Kalven and Zeisel 1966). The

1995 Santa Cruz survey in California also found that 58.4 percent of potential jurors understood the basic premise of the reasonable doubt standard, agreeing that "it is better for society to let some guilty people go free than to risk convicting an innocent person" (Fukurai 1997).

In sum, past research has found that even after serving as trial jurors, a substantial proportion of them were unable to correctly understand the principles of the presumption of innocence, the burden of proof, and reasonable doubt. Even after trial, 50 percent of instructed jurors did not understand that the defendant did not have to present evidence of innocence. Average comprehension levels of trial instructions were 51 percent among one thousand serving jurors in attempted murder cases (Strawn and Buchanan 1977). Thus, prospective jurors enter the courtroom with insufficient familiarity with basic legal standards and hold potentially problematic attitudes and opinions concerning the criminal justice system and their role as jurors. Those attitudes may have significant impacts on jurors' abilities to comprehend legal concepts, evaluate evidence, and determine the outcome of criminal trials.

THE SIMPSON JURY AND A HYPOTHETICAL SCENARIO

Although studies provide ample evidence substantiating the relative lack of general knowledge of the basic legal concepts in criminal proceedings, there is little empirical research dealing with the general understanding of legal standards in criminal trials involving pervasive publicity, intense public scrutiny, and the elements of racism. So here we attempt to address the relationship between such understanding involving race on one side, and on the other, the knowledge of legal concepts in the high profile O. J. Simpson trial. The general discussion of the relationship between potential verdicts reached by different racial groups, their knowledge of legal standards, and their conception of criminal trials suggest a number of testable propositions.

First, considering the legal standards in criminal trials, evidence of racial discrimination by law enforcement authorities might be expected to have a significant effect on potential jurors' assessments of the prosecutor's evidence, as well as the potential outcome of a trial. Though past studies have shown that racial minorities are less likely to understand the fundamental principles of the criminal process, evidence of racial biases is more likely to incense them, leading to greater scrutiny of the legal concepts of the presumption of innocence, a reasonable doubt, and the burden of proof in assessing the prosecution's evidence and determining the potential outcome of the criminal trial.

As perceived racial biases of the criminal justice system may well affect criminal juries in their evaluation of both the reliability and viability of evidence presented in court, greater scrutiny of these three legal concepts may also have influenced potential jurors' perceptions in the Simpson verdict. Such jurors who perceived prejudice and discrimination in the criminal system were more likely to adhere to the precepts of a presumption of innocence, pay attention to the government's burden of proof, and apply stricter standards of reasonable doubt than those who otherwise perceived fewer inequities and discrimination in law enforcement.

In highly publicized and celebrated trials involving minority defendants and highly charged elements of race and racism, moreover, potential jurors are more likely to adhere to the legal rules impacting the criminal process than to ignore applications of legal standards in acquitting racial minority defendants. In other words, the jury's role as a fact-finder is enhanced, and the incidence of jury nullification is actually reduced, in highly publicized and "racially charged" criminal trials involving racial minority defendants.

The last proposition is thus related to the previous hypothesis: in a highly publicized criminal case involving a minority defendant, minority jurors are more likely to exhibit deeper perceptions of the social consequence of their verdict. The jury's fact-finding role may thus be accentuated by racial minority jurors, suggesting that the popular and widely accepted perception of jury nullification and racial acquittals by minority jurors may be an anomaly applied only in those criminal cases that draw high levels of media attention and public scrutiny. The high visibility of a trial, despite evidence of racism on the part of the government, may even heighten minority jurors' effort to "stick" to legal doctrine and concepts of the criminal process in their evaluation of evidence, so that the popular image of minorities' jury nullification in criminal trials becomes questionable.

A HYPOTHETICAL SCENARIO: RESULTS AND FINDINGS

In the spring of 1995, a community-wide telephone survey was conducted to examine the public's perception of the criminal justice system and criminal jury proceedings impacted by the O. J. Simpson trial. The research site was Santa Cruz County, California. The community survey included a number of questions and attitudinal measures concerning the criminal justice system, qualifications for jury participation, and the probable outcome of the Simpson trial (see appendix A for more detailed information on the survey and analytic methods).

Measurements

A total of ten measurements were analyzed to examine the relationship among criminal justice biases, three criminal justice assumptions, and the final outcome of the Simpson trial. All variables were measured in a four-point likert scale, ranging from "strongly agree" to "strongly disagree." The following three questions were then used to obtain the public's perceptions of the fairness of law enforcement agency practices. Those questions included: (1) "people living in poor neighborhoods are more likely to receive bad treatment by police officers than people living in well-off neighborhoods"; (2) "people of color are more likely to be harassed by police officers than white people"; and (3) "police officers sometimes break the law." The first question was designed to address questions on the potential bias of the law enforcement agency on the basis of social class. The second question focused on racial biases, especially selective law enforcement based on racial backgrounds of criminal suspects or defendants. The third question measured the public's perception on whether or not police officers are strict enforcers of the law, examining possible biases and discrimination by law enforcement authorities.

A total of four questions were designed to obtain information on public's perceptions on the three basic assumptions of our criminal justice process—a presumption of innocence, carrying the burden of proof, and guilt beyond a reasonable doubt. The measurements of the presumption of innocence included the following two questions: (1) "if the prosecution goes through the trouble of bringing someone to trial, the person is probably guilty," and (2) "a person who has a criminal record and is accused of a serious crime is probably guilty." The first question examined potential jurors' understanding of whether the presentation of criminal charges automatically leads to the presupposition of the defendant's guilt. The second question was designed to measure the potential effects of the accused's prior criminal records on the presumption of innocence.

The burden of proof was measured by the question: "regardless of what the law says, a defendant in a criminal trial should be required to prove his/her innocence." In our criminal justice system, the burden of proof rests on the prosecution or the state, not on the defendant. Thus, this question was designed to measure respondents' knowledge and awareness of who shoulders the burden of proof in our criminal justice proceedings.

The standard of guilt beyond a reasonable doubt was also measured by the question: "it is better for society to let some guilty people go free than to risk convicting an innocent person." In order to render a guilty verdict in a criminal trial, the jury must consider whether or not the defendant was proven guilty beyond a reasonable doubt, suggesting that a verdict of conviction is legally and intrinsically separated from jurors' belief about whether the defendant actually perpetrated the alleged crimes. In the O. J. Simpson case, the jury's belief or presupposition on whether Simpson murdered his exwife and her friend had little bearing on their legal commitment to decide whether Simpson's guilt was proven beyond a reasonable doubt. If the government or the prosecution failed to convince the jury of Simpson's guilt beyond a reasonable doubt, the jury was legally bound to issue an acquittal verdict. The last question, "O. J. Simpson is guilty of murder," then analyzed people's perceptions about the potential outcome of the Simpson trial.

Table 7.1 shows the results of our survey, and table 7.2 shows the analytical result to examine our hypotheses. The first three columns in the table show the impact of criminal justice biases on both criminal legal concepts and the Simpson verdict for three different groups: (1) a total population; (2) white potential jurors; and (3) potential racial and ethnic minority jurors (i.e., African Americans and Hispanics). The fourth through ninth columns indicate the impact of the three legal concepts on the Simpson verdict for the three different groups.

Criminal Justice Biases and Three Legal Concepts

The analyses of responses of the general population show that the belief of discriminatory criminal law enforcement leads to stricter applications of the three basic assumptions of the criminal justice process (see table 7.2 for regression coefficients of $-.143$, $-.010$, and $.319$ for a presumption of innocence, a burden of proof, and a reasonable doubt, respectively). Empirical analyses also indicate racially different patterns of adherence to criminal justice assumptions. For instance, for racial minority jurors, the perception of racial discrimination by law enforcement authorities leads to higher scrutiny of the presumption of innocence standard ($-.228$ and $-.512$ for whites and minorities), suggesting that in criminal cases involving racial biases by law enforcement authorities, racial minority jurors are less likely to assume defendants' guilt regardless of the defendants' possible prior records or the severity of charges filed against the accused.

White respondents also reveal that racial discrimination tends to elevate their scrutiny of two criminal justice standards—the presumption of innocence ($-.228$) and the concept of reasonable doubt ($.417$). While the effect of law enforcement discrimination on the presumption of innocence is not as strong as the one among racial minorities, the finding suggests that white jurors are more likely to believe that the defendant is presumed innocent in criminal proceedings and that the jury should not convict a defendant where there is a reasonable doubt about his or her guilt. Thus, based on the racial makeup of potential jurors, empirical analyses define racially different patterns of perceptions of biases in law enforcement and about the three basic assumptions about criminal justice. Specifically, perceived discriminatory law enforcement tends to raise and strengthen the belief in the presumption of innocence among racial minority jurors, while racial biases by law enforcement authorities lead white jurors to apply stricter scrutiny of the standards of presumed innocence and reasonable doubt in criminal trials.

The Simpson Verdict

With respect to the effect of discriminatory law enforcement and criminal justice assumptions on the potential outcome of the O. J. Simpson trial, the responses of white jurors and racial minorities revealed very different results. For racial minorities, given their strong negative perceptions of biases and discrimination in law enforcement, all three criminal justice assumptions indicated statistically significant effects on the assessment of the Simpson verdict ($.422$, $-.435$, and $-.422$ for the presumption of innocence, the burden of proof, and reasonable doubt, respectively).

TABLE 7.1
Measures of Variables[1] and Descriptive Statistics

Variable	Total Sample[2]				White Respondents[3]				Minority (Black/Hispanic)[4]			
	Mean	SD[5]	Skewness	Kurtosis	Mean	SD	Skewness	Kurtosis	Mean	SD	Skewness	Kurtosis
LEGAL CONCEPTS												
Presumption of Innocence												
If the prosecution goes through[6]	3.16	0.89	-0.80	-0.26	3.22	0.86	-0.89	-0.03	2.72	1.07	-0.28	-1.14
A person who has a criminal record[7]	3.14	0.83	-0.73	-0.08	3.23	0.80	-0.84	-0.16	2.88	0.91	-0.51	-0.37
Burden of Proof												
Regardless of what the law says[8]	2.72	1.20	-0.25	-1.51	2.84	1.19	-0.41	-1.40	2.02	1.13	0.69	-0.95
Reasonable Doubt												
It is better for society[9]	2.35	1.09	0.23	-1.24	2.31	1.07	0.27	-1.17	2.60	1.16	-0.11	-1.44
LAW ENFORCEMENT DISCRIMINATION												
People in poor neighborhoods[10]	1.83	0.87	0.99	0.44	1.87	0.86	0.93	0.40	1.68	0.96	1.32	0.77
People of color are more likely[11]	1.92	0.92	0.84	-0.06	1.92	0.90	0.86	0.10	1.81	0.89	0.67	-0.67
Police officers sometimes[12]	1.39	0.59	1.68	3.79	1.39	0.57	1.50	3.26	1.47	0.82	1.88	3.06
TRIAL OUTCOME												
O.J. Simpson is guilty of murder	1.99	1.13	0.76	-0.86	1.92	1.09	0.91	-0.52	2.08	1.21	0.62	-1.22

Notes:
1. All variables are measured in a four-item likert scale: (1) strongly agree; (2) somewhat agree; (3) somewhat disagree; (4) strongly disagree.
2. n=327.
3. n=263.
4. n=38.
5. Standard deviation.
6. "If the prosecution goes through the trouble of bringing someone to trial, the person is probably guilty."
7. "A person who has a criminal record and is accused of a serious crime is probably guilty."
8. "Regardless of what the law says, a defendant in a criminal trial should be required to prove his/her innocence."
9. "It is better for society to let some guilty people go free than to risk convicting an innocent person."
10. "People living in poor neighborhoods are more likely to receive bad treatment by police officers than people living in well-off neighborhoods."
11. "People of color are more likely to be harassed by police officers than white people."

TABLE 7.2
Covariance Structural Models
Exogenous Effects on Endogenous Factors

Variables	Criminal Justice Bias			Presumption of Innocence			Burden of Proof			Reasonable Doubt		
	Coeff[1]	Standard error	Critical[2] ratio	Coeff.	Standard error	Critical ratio	Coeff.	Standard error	Critical ratio	Coeff.	Standard error	Critical ratio
TOTAL POPULATION[3]												
Presumption of Innocence	-.143	.087	-1.642	—	—	—	—	—	—	—	—	—
Burden of Proof	-.010	.065	-.152	—	—	—	—	—	—	—	—	—
Reasonable Doubt	.319	.069	4.609****	—	—	—	—	—	—	—	—	—
Simpson's Guilt	.027	.072	.373	-.059	.070	-.840	-.015	.061	-.236	-.119	.062	-1.905*
WHITES[4]												
Presumption of Innocence	-.228	.118	-1.923*	—	—	—	—	—	—	—	—	—
Burden of Proof	-.031	.072	-.427	—	—	—	—	—	—	—	—	—
Reasonable Doubt	.417	.079	5.255****	—	—	—	—	—	—	—	—	—
Simpson's Guilt	-.092	.085	-1.070	.036	.082	.434	.033	.071	.460	-.048	.073	-.657
RACIAL MINORITIES[5]												
Presumption of Innocence	-.489	.201	-2.431**	—	—	—	—	—	—	—	—	—
Burden of Proof	.042	.193	.217	—	—	—	—	—	—	—	—	—
Reasonable Doubt	-.089	.190	-.467	—	—	—	—	—	—	—	—	—
Simpson's Guilt	.593	.249	2.379**	.422	.223	1.894*	-.435	.182	-2.379**	-.422	.180	-2.344**

Notes:
1. Standardized coefficients.
2. Significance levels are based on a two tailed test.
3. $\Delta = .895$, $\rho = .851$, $\chi^2 = 32.660$ for 13 degrees of freedom.
4. $\Delta = .878$, $\rho = .827$, $\chi^2 = 31.281$ for 13 degrees of freedom.
5. $\Delta = .833$, $\rho = .691$, $\chi^2 = 15.298$ for 9 degrees of freedom (4 residual corrections are freed).

* $p<.10$ ** $p<.05$ *** $p<.01$ **** $p<.001$

This finding also suggests that in criminal trials involving racial biases by law enforcement authorities, racial minority jurors were more likely to raise all three criminal process legal standards in assessing and determining the outcome of the Simpson trial.

For white jurors, on the other hand, none of the same factors indicated a statistically significant impact on the verdict, suggesting that white jurors' understandings of three criminal process standards, as well as their awareness of racial biases in the criminal justice system, fail to explain their jury verdict. It may be possible that some extraneous factors may have been left out from the proposed empirical model because white jurors' views of the Simpson verdict did not depend upon racially biased criminal prosecution and/or their understandings of the legal concepts impacting the criminal process.

For racial minority jurors, the analyses also suggested some unexpected findings. For instance, racial minority members with accurate knowledge concerning the government's burden of proof in the criminal process were more likely to feel that Simpson would be found guilty as charged (−.435). Conversely, this finding also suggests that minority jurors, who believe that individual criminal defendants have to prove their innocence in a court of law, tend to agree that Simpson would not be found guilty.

The analysis revealed that racial minorities are more likely than white jurors to feel that, under the normative criminal justice proceedings where the government shoulders the burden of proof, minority defendants are likely to be found guilty. At the same time, racial minorities also believe that if Simpson bore the burden of proving his innocence, he still may have succeeded in obtaining a "not guilty" verdict.

Empirical analyses also show that racial minorities who believe that the criminal justice system discriminates against racial minorities are more likely to feel that Simpson would be found guilty than those who assume less racial biases in the criminal justice system (.593 for a coefficient, p. <0001). This finding may suggest that racial minorities tend to feel that the government's superior position in criminal prosecution and its reliance on evidence collected by racially biased law enforcement authorities may all lead towards "proving" Simpson's archetypal guilt, and that minority jurors are thus more likely to share the perception of structural disadvantages both implicit and explicit in criminal proceedings and criminal court systems.

JURY NULLIFICATION, RACIAL IDENTITY, AND LEGAL CONCEPTS

The above analyses show that so long as the model of the Simpson verdict incorporates the jurors' perceptions about criminal biases, minority jurors who believe there is discriminatory law enforcement tend to draw a much stronger presumption of innocence than do whites. Any discriminatory and racialized element in criminal justice investigations and proceedings thus greatly affect minorities' presumption of innocence in determining the outcome of criminal trials.

While criminal biases have also sensitized white jurors to raise the matter of the defendant's presumed innocence and to require proof beyond reasonable doubt, none of the three basic precepts impacting criminal processes show a statistically significant effect on the determination of the Simpson verdict among white jurors. For racial minorities, on the other hand, all four factors—racial discrimination in law enforcement as well as the three legal concepts—show statistically significant influence on the Simpson verdict, suggesting that in a criminally sensitive, highly scrutinized trial, racial minorities are more likely than white jurors to elevate their understanding of these legal standards in determining the trial outcome.

There are some mixed and unexpected findings, however. For instance, racial minorities who believe that the government shoulders the burden of proof are more likely than whites to assume that Simpson would be found guilty. Although racial discrimination by law enforcement authorities fuels minorities' greater scrutiny of the presumption of innocence, their correct understanding of the burden of proof only points to Simpson's guilt.

Another important finding is that racial minorities who hold that there is racial bias in the criminal justice system would be more likely to believe that Simpson would be found guilty. Because of the government's superior position and prosecutorial advantages in criminal cases—and the state's reliance on evidence supplied by law enforcement authorities who may be racially biased—racial minorities who hold that racial discrimination exists in the criminal justice system are more likely to believe that Simpson would be adjudicated guilty.

Allegations of Racial Bias and Discrimination Inside the LAPD

The perception of African Americans that the criminal justice system discriminates against them is pervasive and deep (Fukurai, Butler, and Krooth 1993). Factors such as the disproportionate number of African American males on death row for murdering white victims supports this perception. Between 1977 and 1990, for instance, sixty-three African Americans have been executed for murdering white victims, while only one white person has been executed for murdering an African American (Fukurai, Butler, and Krooth 1993).

Further, the appearance of justice, which prevails when the victim is white, further exacerbates minorities' distrust and lack of faith in the criminal justice and criminal court systems. In Los Angeles where the Simpson trial took place, research substantiated that the Los Angeles Police Department (LAPD) and the District Attorney's office have been repeatedly accused of racial discrimination, including excessive use of force in arresting racial minority members, discriminatory uses of police dogs against minority suspects, and incompetence of court-appointed defense counsel (Riordan 1994, 708).[3] In the aftermath of the Rodney King assault trial, moreover, the Christopher Commission in 1991 documented evidence of brutality, racism, and mismanagement inside the LAPD (Christopher 1991).

In the period between January 1986 and December 1990, there were a total of 8,274 allegations in complaints made by the public against LAPD officers and 24.7 percent of them were allegations of LAPD officers' excessive force, which was the greatest public complaint during that time. As a result, there have been a variety of lawsuits alleging improper use of force by LAPD officers. In the review of all eighty-three cases of alleged excessive or improper force by LAPD officers, that resulted in individual settlement or judgment of more than $15,000 between 1986 and 1990, the majority of the cases appeared to involve clear and often egregious misconduct. The LAPD's investigation of these eighty-three cases, however, was flawed and the discipline against the officers involved was frequently light or nonexistent. The LAPD had never had adequate procedures in place to review or learn from the results of such litigation. Many of those complaints came from the neighborhoods with the largest concentration of racial and ethnic minorities (Christopher 1991, 55).

Thus, the lack of leadership and failure to discipline the officers appeared as a green light for many LAPD officers to continue to use excessive force to subdue criminal suspects. One of the complaints about excessive force against members of racial and ethnic minorities has been the use of police dogs. By 1991, police dogs had been used more frequently than in the past ("Sheriff Abuse Hearing 1991, 93–95, 136–137; Zinzun 1992). Besides police abuse and dogs used against racial and ethnic minorities, there also have been many reports of the presence of Ku Klux Klan activities within the LAPD (*Contemporary Social Issues in Los Angeles* 1992; Zinzun 1992). Some black officers were continuously harassed, and they were criticized by both officers and their superiors, especially when they attempted to report racial discriminatory violence to their superiors. One officer directly met Chief Daryl Gates and reported such an incident, but Chief Gates made no investigations and referred the case to the immediate superior of the officer who made the initial claim. Thus, police investigations into such allegations have been almost nonexistent, clearly showing the lack of leadership as well as procedural policies and structure to investigate such allegations within the department (Christopher 1991).

This is the basis for negative perceptions of law enforcement widely shared and accepted by the minority communities in Los Angeles and elsewhere (Chow 1992).[4] In assessing the potential outcome of the Simpson trial in Los Angeles, then, our empirical analysis found that minority jurors tended to feel that racially impacted criminal processes were likely to merge in finding the minority defendant guilty (–.435, p.<.05). Evidence of possible biases and discrimination by the law enforcement agency might also lead racial minority jurors to elevate their understanding of the standards of presumed innocence

(.422, p.<.10) and reasonable doubt in their hypothetical deliberation of the Simpson verdict (–.422, p.<.05).

Minority-Race Jurors' Greater Scrutiny of Presumed Innocence and Reasonable Doubt

Racial prejudice is not limited to jurors and law enforcement officials alone. Prosecutors, judges, and defense lawyers may have their own racial biases, which influence their attitudes towards crimes and those accused, as well as their exercise of discretion in the criminal process (Lipton 1983; Johnson 1985; "Presumed innocent" 1992; Butler 1995a; Mello 1995). In the typical criminal case, for example, racial minorities are disproportionately represented by public defenders. And a large proportion of racial minority defendants face the disadvantage by being represented by court-appointed lawyers, who often lack the knowledge, skill, resources, sensitivity and inclination to handle the case (Nunn 1995). Those lawyers may also fail to recognize and challenge discrimination against racial minorities in the composition of jury pools or the role that race plays in jury decision making processes (Klein 1986; Nunn 1995). Further, for a large proportion of racial minority defendants, the perception of a fair trial and their inferior position relative to the prosecution's is further exacerbated by the inadequacy of their counsel's preparation, the lack of counsel's competency, and the continued underfunding of the public defense system (Marcus 1994, 219–220). Rebecca Marcus (1994) argues that the underfunding of public defender offices results in representation that violates indigent racial minorities' Sixth Amendment right to counsel and their Fourteenth Amendment right to equal protection of the law (220).

The sharp distinction of the Simpson trial from other typical criminal cases is that the Simpson trial overcame the widely shared legal assumption of the government's leverage and supremacy of power in relation to that of criminal defendants. Since Simpson's wealth and fame enabled him to retain perhaps the best private, criminal defense counsel in the country, some legal commentators suggested that the balance of power was shifted from the government to the defense counsel (Deutsch 1995). Corroborating the views of racial minorities—that the criminal defendant must prove his innocence—were feeling that Simpson's defense counsel might be able to establish his innocence and Simpson would not be found guilty.

For racial minority jurors who believe there are pervasive racial biases and discrimination built into the criminal justice system, the present analysis demonstrates that Simpson's acquittal was technically attainable through the following three strategies: (1) raising the jurors' understanding of presumed innocence and need for the proof beyond a reasonable doubt; (2) mobilizing the defendant's superior resources in assembling competent and skillful defense counsel, which, regardless of the defendant's factual guilt or innocence, could best present the interest of the accused; and (3) raising the possibility for jury nullification by ignoring the law and acquitting the defendant.

One important factor that optimizes the jury's greater scrutiny of presumed innocence and reasonable doubt during the guilt determination phase of criminal trials is the showing of possible racial biases and prejudice by the law enforcement agency in its investigative capacity. The current survey was taken prior to Mark Furman's testimony in the Simpson trial. If the survey had been taken after the Furman testimony, potential jurors would likely have exerted even greater level of scrutiny of both presumed innocence and reasonable doubt in determining Simpson's acquittal. Our analyses thus demonstrated that Simpson's acquittal was not by the jury's decision to ignore the application of law. Rather, the trial outcome was a by-product of the jury's greater adherence to the rationale, and greater scrutiny, of two of the three basic precepts of the criminal process—a presumption of innocence and proof beyond a reasonable doubt.

Our findings also suggest that racism in many urban police departments, perhaps together with routine police perjury, will lead those who experience such treatment firsthand to readily develop greater understanding of the concepts of reasonable doubt and presumption of innocence. Indeed, the prosecutors in this case linked themselves publicly to two very doubtful, and in the end harmful, police witnesses, ultimately tainting the entire prosecution in the eyes of the predominantly minority jury, whose members were composed mainly of those scorned by their own police (Silvergate 1995).

Jury nullification was not the thrust controlling the jury's decision to acquit Simpson, however. Recalling that advocates for racially based jury nullification argue that racial minorities should hold the moral obligation to acquit minority defendants by disregarding evidence—and that such racial acquittals represent an important public protest against racial inequality in the criminal justice and court systems—our empirical findings suggest otherwise: that racial minorities are more likely to be aware of discriminatory structures of law enforcement and the mechanisms of criminal court injustices. Such awareness strengthens their belief in the defendants' presumed innocence, regardless of the accused's criminal record or the severity of criminal charges.

Of the three legal concepts impacting the criminal process, the traditional interpretation of the burden of proof rule may not apply to racial minority jurors. For the government's burden of proof is seen as part of the oppressive manipulations that are inherent in the discriminatory structures of criminal justice and court systems, the very barriers that racial and ethnic minorities feel that they have to overcome. While racial biases inherent in the criminal justice system lead to a greater scrutiny of the concepts of both presumed innocence and proof beyond a reasonable doubt in determining trial outcomes, then, the government taking on the burden of proof leads racial minorities to feel that a minority defendant may not receive a fair trial because of racially biased charges and evidence—so much so that the minority defendant must prove his or her innocence in order to be adjudicated not guilty.

At the other extreme, racial minorities who hold that a minority defendant may not receive a fair trial, regardless of the defendant's factual innocence or guilt, are more likely to endorse racially based jury nullification—the outright acquittal of minority defendants by disregarding the law, however powerful, as a racially orchestrated protest against racial discrimination in the criminal justice system.

Indeed, the acquittals by predominantly racial minority juries are on the rise. In the South Bronx where the jury pool is 80 percent African American or Hispanic, 47.6 percent of African American defendants and 37.6 percent of Hispanic defendants in felony cases were acquitted in 1995, compared with the national average of 17 percent (Velmen 1996). In other minority dominant cities, the overall acquittal rates were higher: 28.7 percent in Washington, D.C., for felony defendants in 1994, and 30 percent in Wayne County, Michigan which includes Detroit, in 1993 (Wilgoren 1995).

A racial divide still permeates the public perception of the Simpson verdict. A *Los Angeles Times* poll immediately after the verdict found that approximately three out of four respondents stated that race was the single most important influence in the trial and the jury verdict. A *CBS News* poll found 59 percent white respondents stated that the acquittal was wrong and 87 percent of African Americans said it was a correct verdict (Cockburn 1995; Cooper 1995). Postverdict analyses of three African-American Simpson jurors revealed that some jurors felt that the defendant might have murdered his exwife, Nicole, and Ronald Goldman, thus being guilty of the crime (Carlsen and Wildermuth 1995). Nevertheless, they felt that the government had failed to prove Simpson's guilt beyond the reasonable doubt necessary to secure a guilty verdict.

CONCLUSIONS

In criminal cases involving minority defendants, the advocates for jury nullification argue that despite overwhelming and powerful evidence of guilt, racial minority jurors should possess the moral obligation to acquit "guilty" defendants as a protest against racial discrimination in the criminal justice and court systems. While the rate of racial acquittals may be on the rise in criminal courts in large metropolitan jurisdictions, the present analysis shows that in a highly publicized criminal trial involving a member of racial and ethnic minorities, minority jurors are more likely to adhere to the strict application of criminal legal standards in their deliberative process.

Our empirical findings also suggest that, while biases in law enforcement raise questions of standards impacting reasonable doubt and proof beyond a reasonable doubt among white jurors, none of the three legal standards had statistically significant relations in determining the trial outcome. For racial minorities, by contrast, all three legal concepts, along with their acknowledgment of racial biases in the criminal justice system, show statistically significant impacts on their decision in the hypothetical, simulated Simpson verdict.

While advocates for racially based jury nullification reinforce the image of the lawlessness of minority jurors in America's criminal courts, as well as the public's concern about racial minorities' inclinations to disrespect and ignore the application of law, the present analysis show that, at least in a highly publicized criminal trial, involving a prominent minority defendant, minority jurors exhibit the opposite tendency—suggesting that racial minority jurors are indeed law abiding participants in criminal cases. Moreover, the fact that the O. J. Simpson jury was racially mixed and reached a unanimous decision in terms of announcing the final verdict may provide further evidence of the merit and benefits of empaneling a racially mixed jury in a racially sensitive trial. And so a critical analysis of the intertwined relationship between racial acquittal and affirmative jury selection to create racially mixed juries logically becomes the focus of the next chapter.

Chapter 8

JURY NULLIFICATION AND AFFIRMATIVE ACTION JURIES

In August 1991, the motorcade of the Lubavitcher Grand Rebbe Menachem Schneerson struck and killed seven-year-old Gavin Cato and injured another child, both African Americans (Kifner 1991a). Among those in the motorcade was Yosef Lifsh, a young Hassidic man, whose station wagon smashed into the children on the sidewalk. The killing of the child sparked three days of revolt by various groups living in the African American and Caribbean communities. During the melee, a visiting Jewish Hassidic student, Yankel Rosenbaum from Australia, was fatally stabbed in the Crown Heights section of Brooklyn, allegedly in retaliation for the death of Gavin Cato (Kifner 1991c).[1] Rosenbaum lived long enough to identify Lemrick Nelson Jr. an African American, as the stabber; and the police said that they found a bloody knife in Nelson's pocket.

Nelson faced a number of serious charges, and the case against him reached the stage of jury selection. While New York City had a 15.4 percent Jewish population in 1990, the jury selection process failed to produce a jury with a single Jewish member. The final jury included six African Americans, four Hispanics, and two whites (Ortner 1993).[2] During the criminal trial, Nelson's attorney, Arthur Lewis, argued that it was a "frame-up engineered by corrupt officers and a confession coerced from an emotionally disturbed youth," suggesting the possible conspiracy of the police, the medical examiner, and the medical experts, all colluding to frame the African American defendant (Gottlieb 1992). Then, in November 1992, the predominantly African American jury acquitted Nelson of all charges.[3] Eleven jury members then joined the post-verdict party with Nelson and his attorney to celebrate the acquittal (Labaton 1994).

The Crown Heights incidents had not only triggered violence, but the acquittal verdict also won strong approval from African American communities, largely because Gavin Cato's death symbolized the continuation of racial discrimination against minority groups in the criminal justice system. For instance, the district attorney's office concluded that the death of a seven-year-old African American child was merely accidental, not result of criminal negligence on the part of the driver; thus, no charges were brought against the Jewish rabbi. But the African American community reacted in anger because, at the scene of the accident, the Jewish driver was immediately cared for by emergency medical personnel and taken to the hospital before anything was done for the fatally wounded child (Kifner 1991b). The anger also reflected the long-standing perception that police gave Jewish community members preferential treatment. And the police asserted that because a large, angry African American crowd had assembled after the accident, they merely intended to take away the Jewish driver as quickly as possible to avoid a riot (Kifner 1991a).

Following the acquittal, racial unrest in the community broke out once again, a group of African Americans shouting, "Yay! Yay! . . . It's about time!" while a group of Hassidic Jews chanted the African American slogan, "No justice, no peace!" (McFadden 1992).[4] A study commissioned by Governor Mario Cuomo faulted African American Mayor David Dinkins for failure to take decisive law enforcement measures to restore order until after the third day of the riot in which one hundred twenty-nine were arrested and the damage was estimated as half million dollars (Chiles 1993). Members of the Hassidic community also filed a lawsuit, claiming injury due to the mayor's lack of awareness of the seriousness of the situation and his naive expectation that things would calm down if the police stayed uninvolved (Hazard 1993).

The racially charged atmosphere of the Crown Heights murder trial seemed to make jury verdict justice unattainable for the Jewish community. For the predominantly African American jury may have refused to convict the African American defendant, despite the prosecution's production of overwhelming evidence of guilt in the murder of the Jewish Hassidic student. Claiming that the defendant was being prosecuted for discriminatory reasons, the jury might well have nullified to avoid wrongful political persecution, reflecting on their common sense and community standards shared by many African American communities.

Yet, the jury verdict in the Crown Heights trial raised several critical issues impacting and elevating the debate over the jury's racial composition and its power to ignore the application of law. In the United States, a criminal jury may acquit a defendant, and such an acquittal is final and unreviewable by any court, including the United States Supreme Court. A judge can never vacate an acquittal, even in a case of a verdict which is clearly against the weight of the evidence. The prosecution can never successfully appeal a jury acquittal on grounds of judicial error or an erroneous jury determination. Complete lack of judicial control over a criminal jury's decision thus awards such juries the unreviewable power to acquit the defendant under most extreme circumstances. And the acquitted defendant can never be tried again for the same crimes, because of the legal shield against double jeopardy.[5] A jury's pronouncement of "guilty" or "not guilty" is made without official explanation by the jury, and the court cannot solicit or otherwise seek rational justification from the jury for the verdict.

No surprise, jury nullification has played a prominent role in the history of American jurisprudence, and we need to examine the logic and emotions that impact three types of jury nullification: (1) merciful acquittals, (2) vengeful convictions, and (3) racial acquittals.

JURY NULLIFICATION

Merciful Acquittals

In Colonial times, jurors frequently acquitted patriots charged with political crimes against the British Crown. Connecting past and modern times, typical examples of juries' merciful acquittals have involved political participants in the Boston Tea Party, under the Fugitive Slave Acts, as civil rights activists, and as opponents of America's involvement in the Vietnam War in 1960s and 1970s. In all these cases, criminal trial juries acknowledged defendants' deliberate violation of criminal codes, but returned verdicts of not guilty as a demonstration of their unwillingness to criminalize the defendants.

Such acquittals had a moral core. During the era of slavery, for instance, abolitionist northern juries often released defendants who harbored runaway slaves (Krooth, 1972). Similarly, jury nullification occurred in cases involving prohibition laws in the 1920s, as well as violations of draft registration laws and civil disobedience cases in the 1960s and early 1970s (Kalven and Zeisel 1966, 291–93). Political and civil rights activists were routinely acquitted by politically and socially concerned juries, illustrating the significant role that merciful jury nullification plays in a democratic system (Van Dyke 1977, 239-40).

More recently, merciful jury nullification has unsettled prosecutions involving abortion protesters, prostitution, and capital crime defendants (Scheflin and Van Dyke, 1980, 73). By nullifying the law and mercifully acquitting criminal defendants, juries have been led to exercise their own moral judgments of the merits or demerits of the evidence, independent of what the law requires. Merciful jury nullification is also recognized in cases where laws are too rigid or a statutory penalty is too harsh: the jury ameliorates the situation by convicting the defendants of a lesser crime in the conviction phase of criminal trials, or by mitigating the sentence when a jury is involved in the sentencing phase of capital trials.

Another aspect of merciful jury nullification involves mandatory sentencing laws, illustrating the jury's role in educating society on the changing landscape of what conduct is viewed as morally blameworthy, and to what extent the crime should be punished (Heumann and Cassack 1983, 353–54). Jurors also have failed to convict criminal defendants—performing a valuable check on the exercise of governmental power—when sentences are viewed as too stiff, punishments are considered too draconian, and when every third-time felony offense must go to trial because of California's three strikes law mandating twenty-five years to life imprisonment by the defendant's automatic agreement to plea bargain (Zimring, Kamin, and Hawkins 1999). In such cases, jurors are concerned with exactly what conduct the government seeks to punish and the extent of punishment a defendant deserves for alleged crimes.

Grand juries have also exercised the power of merciful jury nullification by refusing to indict, despite strong evidence of guilt, because the prosecution seemed politically motivated or the law in question appeared anachronistic or unpopular (Altman 1991). Thus, exercising its power of jury nullification, the jury has protected against excessive, unjust punishment and conviction.

Vengeful Convictions and Racial Acquittals

In the South, until quite recently, a more disturbing type of jury nullification—vengeful convictions—occurred when all-white juries disregarded exculpatory evidence to convict black defendants of crimes against whites. Vengeful convictions can be best illustrated in Scottsboro Boys' trials in Alabama in the 1940s, in which black defendants were convicted by all-white juries despite the overwhelming evidence of the defendants' innocence. The guilty verdict was seen as symbolic, a social and racialized message, perpetuating racial domination and superiority in the racially divided south (Braden 1965).

The O. J. Simpson verdict has been perceived by some as an example of the third type of jury nullification—racial acquittal or race-based jury nullification—in which the acquittal was depicted as an appropriate way for African Americans to respond to criminal injustices in Los Angeles' discriminatory judicial system that the jurors perceived as unfair, biased, and racist. With the courts, the police have been viewed as the controlling force in the minority community—the police state that impacts daily life of minority residents in the jurisdiction.

Ever since the videotaped beating of Rodney King by white officers of the Los Angeles Police Department (LAPD) was introduced into evidence in the trial of four white officers in 1991, the LAPD has been widely reviled as a corrupt and racist army of occupation in Los Angeles' African American communities (Fukurai, Butler, and Krooth 1994). The Simpson case further exposed the LADP, its officer Mark Furman, a racist perjurer, openly boasting of police brutality and fabricating evidence against African Americans. The Simpson jurors, nine of whom were African American, might have been outraged. While Simpson's lead attorney John Cochran denied it, many observers concluded that Cochran was implicitly advocating jury nullification in his closing statement, arguing that Simpson might be viewed by some as guilty, but the jurors had an overriding role in issuing a powerful statement about the continuing presence of racism within Los Angeles' criminal justice system (Chiang 1995a, 1995b).

There have been frequent race-based acquittals of southern white defendants by all-white juries in cases of violence against African Americans and civil rights activists (Moore 1973, 171; Scheflin and Van Dyke 1980, 90). In the South, all-white juries have self-righteously disregarded both ample and compelling proof of guilt in acquiting white defendants for crimes against blacks. Predominantly homogeneous, if not single-race, juries also acquitted criminal defendants in the Emmit Till murder trial in 1950s, the 1992 Crown Heights trial in New York, and neo-Nazi and skinhead trials in the 1980s in Greensboro, North Carolina—despite overwhelming evidence of their guilt (Fukurai, Butler, and Krooth 1993; Gottlieb 1992; Ortner 1993).

Though merciful acquittals had social and historical roots in Britain's hegemony over parts of North America, vengeful convictions have been a more recent expression of racial domination in America's Deep South and urban centers. Contemporary allegations of racial acquittal have centered on the issue of racial minorities' right to acquit minority defendants, despite overwhelming evidence of guilt. Most recent allegations of racial acquittals reported and analyzed by the mass media have involved cases in which most, if not all, jurors are members of minority communities adjudicating minority defendants.

Although the legal, moral, and political nature of jury nullification has been debated and its political and judicial implications have been examined by legal commentators and social scientists, past research has failed to examine the issue of the specific and critical relationship between the empaneled jury's racial balance and its potential acts of racial acquittal and jury nullification. The fact that the O. J. Simpson jury was racially mixed, and reached a unanimous decision in announcing the final verdict, may provide some evidence of the merit and benefits of empaneling a racially mixed jury in a racially sensitive trial. However, little information exists with regard to whether or not racially heterogeneous juries and racially diverse deliberative processes prevent or promote racial acquittals or other forms of jury nullification. Also unknown is the extent to which such decisions influence the perceived fairness and legitimacy of jury verdicts in race- or gender-based general communities.

In an extreme instance, what will be the social outcome when an all-minority jury or a racially mixed jury decides to racially acquit a minority defendant? How will the decision impact urban jurisdictions where the overwhelming majority of residents and potential jurors are racial minorities? Will the application of affirmative jury approaches ensuring the presence of white jurors in the final jury still lead to instances of jury nullification, thereby altering the public's perception of trial fairness, verdict legitimacy, and racial minorities' role in serving as trial jurors?

This chapter attempts to answer these matters by shedding critical and empirical light on the intertwined relationship between jury nullification and affirmative jury selection to create racially mixed juries. The main thrust of this chapter, then, is threefold: Part I discusses the relationship between jury nullification and affirmative action juries, examining whether affirmative jury structures might lead to, or prevent, instances of race-based jury nullification. Part II presents an analysis of the relation between race, jury nullification, and criminal justice concepts, and examines whether the possible use of affirmative jury selection for white jurors, as distinguished from racial minority jurors, would still lead to instances of jury nullification. Part III examines the legislative and judicial history of jury nullification, concluding that the application of affirmative jury selection would have significant consequences for the use of racially mixed juries in the public perceptions of trial fairness and verdict legitimacy. Finally, we also examine whether or not affirmative juries prevent the racially explicit forms of jury nullification, such as vengeful convictions and racial acquittals.

JURY NULLIFICATION AND AFFIRMATIVE ACTION JURIES

What is the essential link between the jury's ability to ignore the application of law and the function of proposed reforms of racially mixed juries created by race-conscious affirmative jury selection? This question is examined in table 8.1, showing the relationship between instances of jury nullification, socioeconomic variables, and potential jurors' racial backgrounds, suggesting that the following groups are more likely to support the jury's power to engage in nullification: (1) the young, (2) males, (3) the less educated, (4) nonwhites, and (5) individuals with black ancestry.

On the other side, those more likely to oppose jury nullification are self-identified whites, those with white ancestry and without black ancestry, the elderly, females, and the highly educated. Indeed, the relations between jury nullification and racial identity, age, gender, and education are found to be statistically significant (p.<.05).

With respect to the effect of attitudes towards affirmative action, affirmative jury structures, and different sets of judicial systems, table 8.2 shows that those who favor the use of affirmative jury selection to create racially mixed juries are more willing to engage in jury nullification (p.<.001). Specifically, 46.3 percent of those who support the use of mandated racial quotas to create racially mixed juries contend that the jury should have the power to ignore the law when they feel the application of the law is inappropriate. On the other hand, 76.3 percent of the opponents of affirmative jury selection seem to oppose the jury's power to engage in jury nullification (20.0 percent and 56.3 percent, for somewhat and strong disagreement, respectively). Another statistically significant relationship is found between jury nullification and views on the use of racial quotas, suggesting that 72.6 percent of those who feel that racial quotas are discriminatory opposed jury nullification (p.<.10).

None of the affirmative jury structures—supporters or opponents of the three affirmative models of racially mixed juries—showed a statistically significant relation with jury nullification, although supporters of the Hennepin model are more likely to oppose jury nullification and those who endorse the split medietate and social science jury structures are more likely to agree with the jury's power to engage in jury nullification. With respect to the public's preference for different judicial systems impacting jury nullification, those who believe that the

jury system is one of the nation's most democratic institutions are more likely to oppose jury nullification (p.<.10), suggesting that the jury as the emblem of democracy is not be equated with the jury's revolutionary role and power.

The above analyses focused on the so-called the bivariate relationship between jury nullification and the respective variables of affirmative action, affirmative jury structures, different judicial systems, and socioeconomic backgrounds. In order to simultaneously consider the effects of all these seemingly external factors on jury nullification, it is important to perform so-called multivariate analysis by incorporating all those factors in the same empirical model. Table 8.3 shows the result of the ordinary least square regression analysis of the effects of these socioeconomic, ideological, and attitudinal factors on jury nullification. Our analyses show that, in keeping socio-demographic and other attitudinal factors constant and neutral, viewpoints on the jury's power to engage in jury nullification is significantly supported by the following groups: (1) those who endorse affirmative action in jury selection to create racially mixed juries (p=.0003), (2) individuals who do not view the jury as one of the most democratic institution (p=.0246), (3) those who prefer the jury trial over the bench trial (p=.0901), (4) males (p=.0003), and (5) the less educated (p=.0007).

Some of these findings need further clarification and elaboration. First, while the bivariate analysis reveals the statistically significant effects of racial identity and ancestral factors on jury nullification, once all socio-demographic variables and attitudinal factors are incorporated and controlled in the multivariate analysis, race-specific factors no longer exert a significant influence on jury nullification, suggesting that one's racial identity and racial ancestry do not remain as a factor in predicting jury nullification. Second, jury nullification is specifically tied to the individual's perception of the specific use of affirmative, mandated racial quotas in jury selection to created racially mixed juries. Views on the other affirmative action policies and programs based on race or gender considerations do not exhibit statistically significant impacts on jury nullification, suggesting that the issue of the jury's power to engage in jury nullification has specific, intertwined relations with the affirmative jury selection method and the specific use of racial quotas, not with any other affirmative action programs or policies, regardless of whether they are race-specific or gender-conscious.

Third, contradictory views emerge with respect to the relation between jury nullification and individuals' perceptions of the jury's democratic function, as well as preference of a jury trial over a bench trial. While jury nullification is favored by those who fail to view the jury as one of the most democratic institutions, those who prefer the jury trial over the bench trial also support the jury's power to engage in jury nullification. This suggests that, for supporters of jury nullification, the jury trial may be seen as an institutional and procedural compromise between the bench trial system, where judges are sole decision makers, and the most idealized democratic institution, whatever it may be.

TABLE 8.2
Jury Nullification, Affirmative Action, Affirmative Juries, and Judicial Systems

Jury Nullification[1]	Affirmative Action						Attitudes on Affirmative Juries						Affirmative Jury Structures						Judicial Systems					
	Race[2]		Gender[2]		Jury***[3]		Match[4]		Fair[5]		Quota*[6]		Med.Ling.[7]		Hennepin[8]		Soc.Sci[9]		Jury*[10]		Bench[11]		Mixed.Trb[12]	
	Yes	No	Yes	No	Yes	No	Yes	No	Yes	No	Yes	No	Yes	No	Yes	No	Yes	No	Yes	No	Yes	No	Yes	No
Strongly Agree	19.1	20.0	19.2	7.1	25.5	13.3	18.7	21.0	17.4	18.9	18.6	8.5	21.6	18.2	17.3	33.3	17.9	21.1	19.1	20.3	17.4	20.5	20.2	17.9
Somewhat Agree	18.3	11.0	17.8	12.4	20.8	10.4	16.5	11.8	16.1	10.8	8.8	21.0	18.0	14.0	16.0	13.3	17.3	12.7	11.0	20.3	13.0	16.4	14.6	13.1
Somewhat Disagree	19.8	20.0	22.6	16.2	18.9	20.0	21.4	14.5	21.5	18.9	23.0	19.4	18.0	23.1	20.4	13.3	21.6	16.9	18.5	24.3	15.2	21.0	24.7	17.9
Strongly Disagree	42.7	49.0	40.4	54.3	34.9	56.3	43.4	52.6	45.0	51.4	49.6	41.1	42.3	44.6	46.2	40.0	43.2	49.3	51.4	35.1	54.3	42.1	40.4	51.2

Note: 1997 March Santa Cruz Community Survey (n=306).Statistical probabilities are based on a chi-square test of independence.

1. The question asks: "The jury should have the power to ignore the law when they feel the law is inappropriate."
2. "Please indicate whether you do or do not support affirmative action based on race." The identical question is asked for gender-based affirmative action.
3. "Racial quotas should be mandated to increase minority participation on juries."
4. "Trials should include African-American jurors when the defendant is African-American."
5. "Decisions reached by racially diverse juries are more *fair* than decisions reached by single race juries."
6. "Racial quotas to create racially mixed juries are discriminatory."
7. "If racially mixed juries are called for, they should be half majority and half minority jurors."
8. "The racial makeup of the jury should reflect that of the community."
9. "Some research says that without at least three minority jurors, group pressure may be simply too overwhelming. Thus if racially mixed juries are called for, juries should have at least three minority members."
10. "The jury is one of the most democratic institutions."
11. "The bench trial where a single judge makes a decision is better than the jury trial."
12. "Some European models which use input from both jurors and a judge to reach a verdict, are better than the American jury system which only relies on jurors."

* p<.10   ** p<.05   *** p<.01   **** p<.001

JURY NULLIFICATION AND CRIMINAL JUSTICE CONCEPTS

The previous chapter examined whether or not the verdict of "not guilty" in the O. J. Simpson trial was an instance of jury nullification by the predominantly African American jury. In such a highly publicized and racially charged criminal trial of a prominent African American defendant, our analysis demonstrated that African American jurors exhibited a greater propensity to engage in more stringent applications of criminal justice principles in the guilt determination phase of criminal proceedings—namely, the presumption of innocence and the standard of reasonable doubt. The question, however, still remains: Do racial minorities have a propensity to use jury nullification in other criminal trials that do not involve racial minority defendants or do not take place in a racially charged atmosphere? Similarly, concerning racial minorities' perceptions on affirmative jury selection to create racially mixed juries, what views will such juries take on their power of nullification?

"Bulls-Eye" Jury Selection in LA

Another matter that needs further exploration concerns urban jurisdictions where the overwhelming majority of residents are now becoming racial minorities: Will affirmative jury selection methods be applied in order to ensure the presence of white jurors in the final jury? Such remain the questions at Los Angeles Central Superior Court, the site of the O. J. Simpson and other prominent criminal cases in Los Angeles County—a place setting where the overwhelming majority of potential jurors at the jury panel stage of jury selection are African American.

Due to the LA's institution of the "bulls-eye" program—involving racially and socially discriminatory jury selection procedures, which draw potential jurors living closest to the courthouse—African American residents have historically dominated the downtown courthouse, despite the fact that African Americans, according to the 2000 United States Census, constituted only 9.8 percent of the county adult residents. But the underlying discriminatory effect of the bulls-eye selection system is well known—causing a significant deficit of their representation in all other thirty-plus municipal and superior courts in the jurisdiction. O. J. Simpson was able to obtain his racially mixed, criminal jury in L.A. Central Superior Courthouse in downtown Los Angeles. But the Simpson civil trial in Santa Monica Superior Court in suburban Los Angeles failed to include a single African American juror in its twelve-member jury.

If the affirmative jury selection method is to be applied in order to ensure a racially mixed jury in all Los Angeles courts, it also may be important to consider the possible use of mandated racial quotas to make sure that both white and minority-race jurors are included in the final jury. Though, historically, the two instances of jury nullification—merciful acquittals and vengeful convictions—had social and historical origins in either Britain's control over sections of the New World or white hegemony of the criminal justice and criminal court

TABLE 8.3

Jury Nullification, Socio-Demographic Variables, Affirmative Juries, and Judicial Systems: Ordinary Least Square Regression Analyses[1]

Variable	Regression Coefficient	Standard Error	Standaridized Coefficient	Critical Ratio	Significance Level
Affirmative Action					
Race[2]	−.020	.139	−.012	−.145	.8848
Gender[2]	.174	.130	.106	1.332	.1840
Jury[1]	.265	.072	.255	3.664	.0003
Attitudes on Affirmative Action[1]					
Race Matching	.102	.068	.097	1.482	.1396
Fair Decision	−.032	.068	−.028	−.468	.6400
Quota	−.004	.064	−.004	−.077	.9389
Affirmative Juries[1]					
Mediet. Ling.	−.073	.069	−.071	−1.064	.2882
Hennepin	−.033	.079	−.024	−.424	.6718
Soc. Science	−.091	.074	−.083	−1.221	.2231
Judicial Systems[1]					
Jury	−.148	.065	−.132	−2.261	.0246
Bench	−.128	.075	−.100	−1.701	.0901
Mixed Tribnl	.086	.075	.068	1.145	.2533
Socio-Demographic Factors					
Racial Identity[3]					
White	.159	.270	.041	.590	.5557
Racial Ancestry[4]					
White	.273	.293	.062	.931	.3527
Black	−.049	.381	−.007	−.131	.8957
Gender	.660	.179	.215	3.673	.0003
Age	.003	.005	.042	.699	.4853
Education[5]	.197	.057	.206	3.439	.0007

Intercept .817
R-Square .213

Note: 1997 March Santa Cruz Community Survey (n=306).

1. The variable are measured in terms of a five-point likert scale: (1) strongly agree, (2) somewhat agree, (3) not sure, (4) somewhat disagree, and (5) strongly disagree.
2. Race and gender questions on affirmative action are measured in terms of a three-point likert scale: (1) support, (2) not sure, and (3) do not support.
3. Racial identity is measured in terms of a dichotomous response: (0) nonwhite and (1) white.
4. Racial ancestry is measured in terms of a dichotomous response: (0) no and (1) yes.
5. Education is measured in terms of the following ordinal scale: (1) grade or elementary, (2) some high school, (3) high school diploma, (4) trade, technical, or vocational school, (5) some college, (6) college degree, (7) post college work, and (8) post college degree.

systems in the United States Deep South, the benefits of racially mixed juries may not be realized in urban courts, where white jurors who might otherwise appear in jury pools and jury boxes are excluded from criminal trials.

White-Collar Crimes and Criminals

Another important factor involves the extent to which potential jurors view the application of jury nullification in criminal cases involving white-collar criminals. Almost all of our focus so far has been on street and violent crimes involving racial and ethnic minority defendants. Yet, the socioeconomic and racial backgrounds of white-collar criminals are almost diametrically opposite to those of street criminals, who are more likely to be racial minorities, young, male, and those from lower socioeconomic echelons of society. The term, white-collar crimes, was first used by Sociologist Edwin H. Sutherland to cover nonviolent, non-street crimes, such as embezzlement, price fixing, antitrust violations, bribery, tax evasion, obstruction of justice, and fraud, including procurement fraud, stock fraud, fraud in government programs, investments, and other schemes (see generally, Coleman 1994). Due to the specific and more complex nature of the criminal charges filed against white-collar criminals and their resulting lengthy trials, the jury has been predominantly individuals who are more likely to be white, male, highly educated, and from higher socioeconomic classes. Such jurors are more likely to be lenient towards defendants of their own race, gender, educational status, and class. Thus, the application of affirmative action methods in white-collar criminal trials may be an important procedural mechanism to ensure the presence of racial minorities, effectively creating racially mixed juries, that may make quite different decisions. While the extent of media exposure and publicity in such criminal cases may not normally match that of racially sensitive criminal trials, affirmative jury selection may be useful to enhance the perceptions of verdict legitimacy and trial fairness in the eyes of marginalized segments of the general community.

The relationship between jury nullification, criminal justice concepts, affirmative inclusion of white jurors in racially mixed juries, and attitudes towards white-collar criminals and their trials are examined in table 8.4. There are a number of interesting and notable findings that emerged from the analysis. First, those who correctly understand criminal justice concepts are more likely to oppose jury nullification, suggesting on the other side that jury nullification is supported by potential jurors who are more likely to lack an understanding of criminal justice concepts. This finding may seem to support the media representation of the widely held image of jury nullification as the lawless and untamed action by incompetent minority jurors, who often misunderstand the basic criminal concepts of presumption of innocence, burden of proof, and reasonable doubt. A statistically significant relation is found between comprehending the meaning of the burden of proof and jury nullification, corroborating the link between the jurors' correct understandings of the concept and their strong opposition to jury nullification (p.<.01).

Second, affirmative action for whites is significantly related to their views on jury nullification (p.<.01). Almost half of the people who oppose affirmative action for whites also strongly oppose jury nullification (49.0 percent), while approximately 40 percent of those who support whites' affirmative selection generally endorse jury nullification (38.6 percent, i.e., 14.5 percent and 24.1 percent for definitely and somewhat agreeing with jury nullification). In urban courts where racial and ethnic minorities have begun to dominate jury pools and jury boxes in adjudicating minority defendants, such findings suggest that affirmative jury selection for whites and the creation of racially mixed juries may not always lead to the support for jury nullification. The opponents of affirmative action policies for whites are also strong opponents of the jury nullification, suggesting that "preferential treatment" for whites are not perceived to influence the jury's power and inclinations to either mercifully acquit or racially convict criminal defendants.

Third, those who endorse the equal treatment of both white-collar offenders and street criminals are more likely to support jury nullification (p.<.05). Almost all individuals who support preferred treatment for white-collar criminals oppose jury nullification (90.0 percent), suggesting that, because white-collar crimes are generally perceived to be nonviolent and less offensive than street crimes, the jury's ultimate power to negate and nullify the application of law is perceived to be less demanding or unimportant vis-à-vis jury nullification for more violent street criminals. Similarly, the type of crimes for which white-collar criminals are charged, such as income tax evasion, may not seem to jurors as remote from their own social and economic activities, especially compared to the alleged charges of more violent street crimes. The perception of the nonviolent nature of white-collar crimes may play a role in jurors' opposition to jury nullification.

Finally, views of jury nullification are not affected by the perceived influence of race on jury verdicts, or the discriminatory jury system, that may have led to the "not guilty" verdict in the O. J. Simpson trial. Nonetheless, those who believe that race has a significant impact on jury verdicts are more likely than others to support jury nullification (36.4 percent).

We have demonstrated in the previous chapter that the Simpson verdict may not have been an example of racial acquittal. Regardless of individuals' beliefs that the Simpson acquittal verdict was an inevitable result of the discriminatory, racialized jury system, the majority of potential jurors would oppose the jury's ultimate power to engage in jury nullification (65.3 percent and 69.5 percent, for "yes" and "no" for the Simpson verdict, respectively), supporting our view that the Simpson verdict was not an instance of jury nullification.

TABLE 8.4
Jury Nullification, Criminal Justice Concepts, White Jurors, and White-Collar Crimes

	Criminal Justice Concepts														
Jury Nullification[1]	Presumption of Innocence[2]		Presumption of Innocence[3]		Burden of Proof[4]		Reasonable Doubt[5]***		Aff. Action for Whites[6]***		White-Collar Crime[7]**		Race on Verdict[8]		Simpson Verdict[9]	
	Correct	Wrong	Correct	Wrong	Correct	Wrong	Correct	Wrong	Yes	No	Yes	No	Yes	No	Yes	No
Strongly Agree	13.0	12.4	11.2	15.4	11.4	13.1	9.9	14.4	14.5	8.2	20.0	5.0	13.3	9.6	11.6	9.7
Somewhat Agree	22.7	25.1	21.9	26.9	18.3	26.1	21.5	21.6	24.1	21.4	23.6	5.0	23.1	18.5	23.1	20.7
Somewhat Disagree	23.0	26.6	25.4	20.5	21.7	26.8	25.2	22.3	25.4	21.4	21.4	30.0	24.9	23.7	22.4	27.6
Strongly Disagree	41.2	36.0	41.4	37.2	48.6	34.1	43.3	41.6	36.0	49.0	35.0	60.0	38.6	48.1	42.9	41.9
Total[10]	99.9	100.1	99.9	100.0	100.0	100.1	99.9	99.9	100.0	100.0	100.0	100.0	99.9	99.9	100.0	99.9

Note: 1996–97 UC-Wide Survey (n=977). Statistical probabilities are based on a chi-square test of independence.

1. The question asks: "The jury should have the power to ignore the law when they feel the law is inappropriate."
2. "A person who has a criminal record and is accused of a serious crime is probably guilty."
3. "If the prosecution goes through the trouble of bringing someone to trial, the person is probably guilty."
4. "Regardless of what the law says, a defendant in a criminal trial should be required to prove his innocence."
5. "It is better for society to let some guilty people go free than to risk convicting an innocent person."
6. "If Whites had been historically discriminated against, they should be given preferential treatments."
7. "Corporations and their employees who endanger the public should be punished the same as street criminals."
8. "Trial outcomes are strongly influenced by the race of defendants or victims."
9. "Because of problems with our jury system, O.J. Simpson was not proven guilty."
10. Some totals did not reach 100.0% due to rounding errors.

* $p<.10$ ** $p<.05$ *** $p<.01$ **** $p<.001$

JUDICIAL AND LEGISLATIVE HISTORY OF JURY NULLIFICATION

Racially mixed juries and their impact on jury nullification have not been examined by the judiciary or legislatures. The United States Supreme Court first reviewed the jury's power to nullify the law in *Sparf and Hansen v. United States* (156 U.S. 51, 1895), declaring that in the federal system, there is no right to jury nullification. The Court stated that:

> [juries] have the physical power to disregard the law, as laid down to them by the court. But, I deny that . . . they have the moral right to decide the law according to their own notions or pleasure. On the contrary, I hold it the most sacred constitutional right of every party accused of a crime that the jury should respond as to the facts, and the court as to the law. . . . This is the right of every citizen, and it is his only protection. . . . Public and private safety alike would be in peril, if the principle be established that juries in criminal cases may, of right, disregard the law as expounded to them by the court and become a law unto themselves. . . . [T]he result would be that the enforcement of law against criminals and the protection of citizens against unjust and groundless prosecutions, would depend entirely upon juries uncontrolled by any settled, fixed, legal principles. (156 US 51 74, 101–102, 1895).

Thus, the Court's pronouncement in *Sparf and Hansen* established that there would be no right to jury nullification in the federal court system. Yet, the debate on jury nullification began to weaken in the midst of political controversies in the 1960s and 1970s.

United States v. Dougherty (473 F.2d 1113 [D.C., 1972]), a relatively recent federal case on jury nullification, involved nine Catholic clergy defendants, known as the "D.C. Nine," who ransacked the Dow Chemical offices in order to stop the production of napalm bombs. The defendants requested that the jury be told of their power to nullify the law, though the trial court refused and the court of appeals upheld the trial court's decision by a 2–1 vote (473 F.2d 1113 1130–37). Writing for the majority, upholding the trial court's decision, Judge Leventhal stated that jurors were already aware of their power to nullify the law and that requiring judicial instruction of the jury's right of nullification might alter the system in unpredictable ways. Thus, the court recognized the power of jury nullification, but not the jury's right to do so (1135). Dissenting, Judge Baselon criticized the court majority opinion as impinging the right of the jury to exercise its conscience in reaching a verdict, stating that: "Nullification is . . . a mechanism that permits a jury, as community conscience, to disregard the strict requirements of law where it finds that those requirements cannot justly be applied in a particular case" (at 1140).

In another Vietnam War era case, *United States v. Spock* (416 F.2d 165 [1st Cir.,1969]), the federal court also debated the jury's power of nullification. The trial court had attempted to eliminate the possibility of jury nullification by utilizing a verdict based on special interrogatories (180). This procedure was then contested on appeal to the First Circuit, which overturned the trial court decision, because it was considered to restrict the jury's right to render a verdict free from judicial control (181–182). By confining the court's holding to his narrow ground, the court avoided a controversial ruling that such special interrogatories were invalid because they prevented the possibility of jury nullification.

Without holding that federal juries have the power of nullification, appellate courts have nonetheless recognized the power of the jury to nullify the law in other cases, including *United States v. Burkhart* (501 F.2d 993[6th Cir., 1974]),[6] and *United States v. Boardman* (419 F.2d 110 [1st Cir.,1969]). Ever since the Supreme Court decided against jury nullification in the *Spart and Hansen* case in 1895, however, whether or not the jury has the power to nullify the law has not been considered by the Court, and there is no indication that the Court may consider it anytime soon.

The issues on the jury's power to nullify the law have also been debated in legislatures. Legislation has been introduced by statutes and constitutional amendments, requiring presiding judges to inform the jury of their right to nullify the law. A lobby organization called the Fully Informed Jury Association (FIJA) has also made considerable strides toward its goal of instructing the jury of their right to ignore the law and vote their conscience. FJIA is a nationwide grassroots, nonprofit educational organization, publishing and disseminating informational materials on the issue of jury nullification. Many state affiliate organizations have been formed, making media appearances and testifying at legislative hearings.[7]

In 1990 and 1991, seven states including Arizona, New York, Massachusetts, Louisiana, Tennessee, Texas, and Washington introduced legislative proposals or constitutional amendments that would require judges to inform the jury of their right to nullify the law and vote their conscience. The Arizona House of Representatives introduced the bill, HCR. 2015 in February 1991, requiring the judge to inform the jury that jurors have the right to judge the law, in addition to the jury's role as a fact-finder. While the House Judiciary Committee passed the bill unamended, the bill failed to obtain recommendation from the House Rules Committee and was not presented to the Senate. Thus far, none of the legislative proposals in other states have been enacted into law, though new and similar proposals are anticipated in some of those states.

In only two states, Maryland and Indiana, do the state constitutions currently require judges to inform jurors about their right to nullify the law. Article XV, Sec. 5 of the Maryland Constitution states: "In the trial of all criminal cases, the Jury shall be Judges of Law, as well as of fact, except that the Court may pass upon the sufficiency of the evidence to sustain a conviction." Maryland judges instruct the jury in the following way:

> Members of the jury, under the Constitution of Maryland, the jury in a criminal case is the judge of the law as well as the facts. Therefore, anything which I

may say about the law, including any instructions which I may give you, is merely advisory and you are not in any way bound by it. You may feel free to reject any advice on the law and to arrive at your own independent conclusions (Levine 1992, 102).

Similarly Art. I, Sec. 19 of the Indiana Constitution states that: "In all criminal cases whatsoever, the jury shall have the right to determine the law and the fact."

Given the current controversy over jury nullification and the public's concern about racial minorities' inclinations to disrespect and ignore the application of law, our research nonetheless reveals the opposite scenario—racial minorities are more likely to follow, yet be critical of, the strict application of legal principles in evaluating and assessing the credibility and validity of evidence presented in court.

CONCLUSIONS

The jury verdict in the O. J. Simpson trial raised public concerns over the jury's racial composition and the racial minority's power and opportunity to engage in jury nullification. Despite the importance of racially mixed juries and their impact on the perception of trial fairness and verdict legitimacy, little research has been done to examine whether or not racially heterogeneous juries and racially diverse deliberative processes may show a greater propensity to either prevent or promote instances of jury nullification. This chapter has thus attempted to shed critical light on the intertwined relationship between jury nullification and affirmative jury selection methods in creating racially diverse juries.

Empirical analyses reveal that jury nullification is viewed differently on the basis of potential jurors' age, gender, racial identity, racial ancestry, and education. With respect to the attitudes towards affirmative action, affirmative jury structures, and preference of different sets of judicial structures, those who support affirmative action in jury selection are most likely to endorse the jury's power to engage in jury nullification. Almost half of those who support the use of mandated racial quotas to create racially diverse juries believe that the jury should have the power to ignore the law when they feel the application of the law is immoral or inappropriate. Another important finding is that—though the bivariate analyses show significant influences of racial identity and ancestral factors on jury nullification—once all socio-demographic and attitudinal factors are incorporated and controlled in multivariate analyses, race-specific factors such as racial self-identity or racial ancestry are no longer significant factors in jury nullification. Rather, the issue of the jury's power to engage in jury nullification has specific, intertwined links to affirmative jury selection and the specific use of racial quotas to create racially mixed juries—not with regard to any other affirmative action programs—regardless of whether they are race-conscious or gender-specific.

Our analyses has also shown that jury nullification is more likely to be supported by those who do not hold a correct understanding of criminal justice concepts such as the presumption of innocence, the burden of proof, and reasonable doubt principles. This supports the media constructed image of lawless, incompetent minority jurors who are more likely to engage in jury nullification and acquittal of minority defendants, despite the overwhelming evidence of their guilt. A statistically significant relation was found between jurors' understanding the concept of the burden of proof and jury nullification, corroborating the relationship between jurors' correct understanding of criminal justice concepts and their strong opposition to jury nullification.

In comparing the patterns of jury nullification for street criminals and white-collar criminal defendants, our analysis reveals that those who endorse the equal treatment of both white-collar offenders and street criminals are more likely to support jury nullification, offering a privilege to white-collar criminals to be acquitted vis-à-vis street criminals—as white-collar crimes are generally perceived to be nonviolent and less criminally offensive than street crimes. Yet, the jury's power to engage in jury nullification for more violent street criminals is perceived by the public to equally as important as the jury's power to ignore the law for white-collar criminals.

Overall, our analysis suggests that views on affirmative jury selection through the use of mandated racial quotas reveal statistically significant relations with potential jurors' use of jury nullification. Attitudes or perceptions on other race-specific or gender-conscious affirmative action policies or programs failed to show statistically significant relations with the jury's power to engage in jury nullification. This suggests that supporters of racially mixed juries and affirmative jury selection—efforts to place a racially diverse group in the final jury—are most likely to endorse the jury's power to ignore the law when they feel the application of the law is inappropriate.

Chapter 9

RACE AND THE AFFIRMATIVE JURY

Conclusions

Handed down from the past, class and caste, race and gender, ethnicity and attributed national origins, together play a powerful role in the formation of racial hegemony and the racial state in the United States. Despite the illogic and fallacy of the premise that the human Homo species may be neatly divided and classified by racial categories, race relations and racial designations continue to serve as a powerful foundation of social divisions in our time. Racial hegemony and hierarchy have not only become deeply embedded in popular thinking, but also taken on institutional forms that may only be overturned by directly confronting and challenging them legally and by active *exposé,* leading to the retreat and transformation of both racialized ideas and their institutional permutations.

For the disenfranchised segments of the population, the only remaining shield may lie within the fold of the court system, though even here the best legal armor is the system of juries that still require great reforms and restructuring. And, as this study describes, the criminal jury is one place that these disenfranchised groups might look for relief and social reform: to install the racially mixed jury as a new mediating force in the heart of racial inequalities and inequities past—so much so that the traditional regime of prosecutors, police officers and judges, courts and juries, that once mediated law and order, are prevented from continuing their reign of imposing racial and legal inequities.

The potential for the democratic transformation of our legal system thus lies with the jury and its diversity, placed at the heart of the criminal justice system. Some might have said that the jury is the soul of our most democratic institutions, which in step says fairly little for the rights of disenfranchised racial and social groups. But even to play that role, the jury and its selection system will have to be drastically restructured, remodeled, and reshaped, top to bottom.

THE JURY AND THE POTENTIAL FOR DEMOCRACY

Today, after harshly criticized and attacked by the media and the public, the shortcomings, failures, and inequities of the jury system have led to the loss of much of its moral authority, respect, and legitimacy in our society. The persistent failure of juries to adequately represent racial minorities within particular jurisdictions, and the seemingly unjust verdicts that have been reached by racially unrepresentative juries, have brought on protest, questioning the legitimacy of the jury system, placing it under increasing suspicion. Systematic and significant underrepresentation of racial minorities in criminal trials has also led to the erosion of public trust in purported democratic and egalitarian principles embedded in the jury system.

Jury selection itself is often perceived to be a mystery that has been shrouded in obscure procedures and complicated legal language. At its most basic level, the selection of an accused's jury of peers should come from a community of individuals who may find resonance with the condition of the defendant in the social and cultural setting where the alleged offense took place. A problem, however, arises when such peers are purposefully or procedurally excluded, particularly in criminal cases when racial minorities are systematically screened and eliminated from serving on final juries.

To improve racial representation of the criminal jury, legal scholars and social scientists have long questioned racially discriminatory practices of peremptory challenges and their consequent unrepresentative makeup of final juries. These studies and recommendations, however, have their own shortcomings and limitations. For the call to eliminate peremptory challenges seems to reflect a mental frame seeking a quick or easy "fix," without mobilizing sufficient insight to face much deeper and more structured problems of institutionalized racism and skewed, racialized underrepresentation that actually begins at a much earlier stage of the jury selection process.

As demonstrated in chapter 6, the overwhelming majority of racial minorities have already been eliminated from jury service long before they report to the courthouse as potential jurors—that is, before they reach the jury panel stage of the selection process. A variety of procedural difficulties and structural biases impacting the jury selection system also remain in place, continuing to eliminate a significant proportion of racial minorities from jury service. Suggested reforms are also inadequate to rectify representative inequities; and the narrowly focused analyses of representative jury selection in voir dire—and the possible elimination of peremptory challenges as a reform measure—simply do not address much deeper problems inherent in the jury selection system itself.

What reforms, then, will bring about a more egalitarian method of selecting jurors? Our analysis substantiates that procedural remedies in the jury selection system may never lead to more racially representative and heterogeneous juries. While critical evaluations and identification of procedural biases and anomalies of the jury selection system are clearly needed and should be continued, more dramatic and courageous efforts are necessary to ensure the actual presence of racial minorities in the final jury. The implementation of this innovative and dramatic selection approach may be called for at this historical juncture, because the Supreme Court is reluctant to abolish peremptory challenges outright, raising the possibilities that legislatures will adopt a more creative mechanism to increase jury participation by racial minorities. Such a move towards using affirmative action in jury selection is a viable and promising alternative to current jury selection methods. Through such legislative action, affirmative jury structures with the use of affirmative peremptory inclusion of underrepresented groups in voir dire would together constitute the two integral parts of a positive and unfailing method to ensure the presence of racial minorities in the final jury.

In the remaining section of this final chapter, we focus on the distinguishing features and important characteristics of affirmative action mechanisms designed to create racially diverse juries. A cautionary note may be essential on the debates over affirmative action policies and programs. While the term, affirmative action, still stirs emotive sentiments among the public in the discourse about education, employment, and business contracting, the basic concept and application of affirmative action in jury selection is different from that in other contexts. By critically analyzing the distinguishing features of affirmative strategies in jury selection, we hope to make a strong and unapologetic case for a race-conscious, affirmative action mechanism to create racially diverse juries.

DISTINGUISHING FEATURES
OF AFFIRMATIVE ACTION IN JURY SELECTION

The features and characteristics of affirmative action in jury selection may be distinguished from race-conscious programs in other areas such as employment, contracting, and college admissions. For the distinct traits of affirmative jury selection methods are important to undo the specter of rejection and ambivalence that besets the contemporary discourse on race-specific affirmative action programs and policies elsewhere. Our research does not take positions in either rejecting or endorsing the affirmative action policies or programs in nonjury related areas. It is sufficient to note that an affirmative jury selection strategy is theoretically and functionally different from affirmative action programs in other areas.

The first distinctive characteristic of affirmative action in jury selection is that racial diversity in the makeup of the jury may be more important than racial diversity in other general contexts. This is because the jury performs a distinct task and judicial function shared only by the judge. The jury finds the facts, assigns criminal liability, and determines whether individuals should live or die in capital cases. The targets of affirmative action in other contexts such as admissions, hiring, contracting, and even the configuration, as well as the racial composition of, legislative districts, lack the distinguishing feature of the direct decision-making power vested in the jury.

Second, the beneficiary of affirmative jury selection policies is, by its nature, narrowly, personally, and individually tailored to the criminal defendant, unlike affirmative action programs in other areas. Racially mixed juries benefit the specific criminal defendant, not actual jurors in the jury box or members of excluded racial or ethnic groups in the community. Thus, the degree and extent of benefits and the notion of fairness awarded to each defendant will—or should —remain the same and constant across the spectrum of all such jury trials.

Opponents of affirmative action programs have argued that they have been denied a tangible benefit to which they are entitled based on skills and other meritocratic considerations, including their opportunities for college admissions, employment, and governmental contracts (Haney and Hurtado 1994, Fukurai, Butler and Krooth 1997). Jury selection and jury service is another matter, however, for it emphasizes little about merit and notions of entitlement based on personal proficiency or individual skills, and more about opportunity, participation, and fairness. Affirmative action in jury selection should not attempt to give special treatments to unqualified or marginally qualified individuals. Rather, affirmative jury selection is proposed only as a supplemental race-conscious mechanism to ensure broader racial and community participation in jury service.

Another distinct feature of affirmative jury selection is that a possible injury or harm imposed by affirmative action on the majority race does not directly translate into the special privilege or advantage to the minority race, particularly when jury service is considered more a hardship than a privilege. Some people equate the privilege of jury service to a century of litigation by minorities and women to obtain the right to vote (Glennon 1994; Amar 1995). Ever since *Strauder v. West Virginia* (100 U.S. 303, 1880), the Supreme Court has held a similar view, that the exclusion of blacks from jury service injures not only defendants, but also other members of the excluded class, for it denies the class of potential jurors the "privilege of participating equally . . . in the administration of justice" (100 U.S. at 308).

Jury studies reveal that the contemporary cost of jury service makes it look less like a privilege one fights for—such as voting, education, employment, or business opportunities. Instead, jury duty is perceived more like a hardship that one might prefer not to undergo (Fukurai, Butler, and Krooth 1991a; Dobbs 1992). Some studies show that citizens sometimes refuse to register to vote or to respond to jury questionnaires or summonses in hopes of evading jury duties (Brown 1994; Fukurai 1997). Similarly, the psychological trauma and disturbances experienced by some jurors in judging gruesome crime scenes in violent criminal cases may last a lifetime, creating even greater psychological stress and burdens for trial jurors (Kaplan and Winget 1992). Some psychological studies even compare jury service and its burden to combat duties, a kind of work that nobody desires (Golash 1986).

After spending nine months virtually with no outside contact, sequestered members of the O. J. Simpson jury were referred to as "prisoners," some commentators declaring that "prisoners in our jail . . . have a lot more liberties" ("Jury seclusion tough on O.J. deputies too" 1995). One poll found that, among seven hundred respondents who were asked: "If you were selected to serve on a jury, would you be happy to do it or would you rather not serve?" thirty-five percent of the respondents said that they preferred not to serve (King 1993a, 736, fn115).

So today's jury duties may be generally viewed as a hardship, not as a privilege. Evidence shows that more than one-third of citizens summoned for jury duty may ask for and receive excuses from jury service, often for personal and individualized hardship (Fukurai, Butler and Krooth 1993, 121–22). In addition to child care difficulties and transportation problems, excuses are also often granted for other economic and personal reasons (Fukurai, Butler, and Krooth 1993, 119–20). The Supreme Court stated: "The States are free to grand exemptions from jury service to individuals in case of special hardship or incapacity and to those engaged in particular occupations the uninterrupted performance of which is critical to the community's welfare" (*Taylor v. Louisiana, 419* U.S. 522 534, 1975). The hardship that jury duties entail thus provides the rationalization that jury service demands a heavy toll of economic, social, and personal sacrifice, as well as individual commitment.

There is another way of viewing affirmative mechanisms for jury selection, too. Professor Shelby Steele, a San Jose State University African American sociology professor and a strong opponent of affirmative action, has clearly noted that affirmative action programs are often thought to stigmatize members of racial minorities who are the beneficiaries of such race-specific preferences (Steele 1994). But it is less likely that racial minority jurors who are affirmatively selected to serve on the jury will suffer from such stigmatization as members of racially mixed juries. The perception of stigmatization and the accompanying psychological effects have no place in affirmative action jury selection methods. This is particularly true when jury service is perceived to be more a hardship than a privilege.

Affirmative action in other contexts has also been criticized on the basis that race-based privileges have resulted in mediocrity, suggesting that such racial diversities due to affirmative action lead to the decline of the work ethic or academic standards. Numerous studies on affirmative action in other contexts, however, suggest the opposite results and findings. In evaluating academic and work-related experiences, for example, past research shows that racial and ethnic diversity actually improves creativity, enhances performance, and increases productivity (Tien 1994; Connell and Nazario 1995; Decker 1995). Our research also substantiates that affirmative mechanisms for jury selection increase the perception of greater fairness and justice in jury deliberation and verdicts. Similarly, the presence of racial minorities certainly enhances the quality of jury deliberation and verdicts by forcing individual jurors of both majority and minority races to engage in viable and critical discussion concerning race-related issues and experiences.

Another criticism of affirmative action in other contexts is that the race-specific programs encourage minorities to exploit their own past victimization and consider it a purported justification for preference. To receive the benefits of preferential treatment, this perspective assumes that one must view oneself as a victim, implying that there is more power in minorities' past suffering than in present achievement. Professor Steele, for example, argued that the "liability of affirmative action comes from the fact that it indirectly encourages blacks to exploit their own past victimization as a source of power and privilege. . . . The obvious irony here is that we [African Americans] become inadvertently invested in the very condition we are trying to overcome" (Steele 1990, 118).

The affirmative mechanism in jury selection, however, addresses current discrimination that undercuts race-based decision-making practices in criminal court proceedings including jury deliberations, and it is not considered a compensatory program for past wrongs. The presence of racial minorities in the final jury also does not lead to purported justification for their preferential treatment in the jury box. Affirmatively chosen jurors are not treated any differently from other jurors because of their race or selection status.

Another distinctive feature of affirmative action in jury selection is that the use of racial quotas may prove less costly to both individuals and society than affirmative action in other contexts. Professor Vikram David Amar argues that the kinship between jury service and voting—in which race-based jury selection more broadly extends community participation in public affairs—and race-conscious measures and programs to promote civic participation together are easier to square with the Constitution than other affirmative action measures (Amar 1995). More speculatively, some may argue that affirmative action in creating racially mixed juries might have prevented a number of urban uprisings in 1980s and early 1990s conflicts that led to billions of dollars in damages, as well as extensive causalities.

The broader implication of affirmative action in jury selection will also help preserve and restore public confidence in, and the moral integrity of, the jury system. The racially diverse jury reaffirms the principle that the judgment of a person must be made according to the law or custom of that person's community, as well as by those who share in those customs, cultures, norms, and traditions. It follows that the strategy to remove the jury trial from its original jurisdiction by a change of venue—moving the trial to another jurisdiction where the case is tried by noncommunity members, as in the Rodney King assault trial against criminal police violence—may not offer a reasonable solution to criminal cases that involve highly sensitive issues of race and racism. For racially mixed juries then offer greater legitimacy to jury verdicts and advance the interest of society by enhancing public confidence in the fairness of jury proceedings.

There may be no racially neutral measure available to accomplish the same end as affirmative action policies in jury selection. Recognizing a right to a bench trial, for instance, would not accomplish the same goal. Judges may factor the race of both defendants and victims into their determination of guilt, not consciously, but unconsciously (Meyer and Jesilow 1997). Though judges may not let race affect their verdicts and decisions, a bench trial in itself is not a substitute for a racially neutral jury, and jury deliberations and decisions are often very different from those of judges. It is known, for example, that the rate of acquittals in jury trials is substantially higher than that of bench trials (Kalven and Zeisel 1966). Similarly, affirmative jury selection strategies may provide an important internal check in the criminal justice system to make sure the fair, proper, and just performance of police, prosecutors, judges, and even defense attorneys by empaneling racially diverse tribunals. As the minority-race jurors are shown to exhibit the greater propensity to apply stricter standards of presumption of innocence and reasonable doubt, race-specific affirmative selection may deter police, prosecutors, and other government agencies from pursuing racially discriminatory investigations, evidence gathering, trial preparations, and presentations.

Other possible remedies have been proposed as alternatives to affirmative strategies in order to eliminate racial bias from jury selection and adjudicating processes. One proposal is to educate jurors about the impact of racism on the jury verdicts (Herman 1993). In order to educate jurors to identify and neutralize their own unconscious biases, judges would be required to allow expert testimony on the impact of racism on jury verdicts, as well as provide juries a meaningful charge that they can consider the potential effects of prejudice and bias in jury deliberations. Such instructions still may not guarantee that trial jurors will either take such educational materials seriously or deliberate without their own conscious or unconscious biases and stereotypical images of the race, gender, or class backgrounds of defendants or their victims.

CONCLUSIONS

From the beginning, America has relied on racial divisions and distinctions to determine the allocation and distribution of economic resources, social opportunities, and legal rights to property and freedom. For more than two hundred years, the United States government has changed the legal definitions and the categorizations of race. White is the only racial category that survived from the initial 1790 government definition of race, while other racial categorizations have gone through dramatic changes. Many racial categories have been created, modified, destroyed, and recreated over the years. These different categorizations of racial groups have had varying impacts on our daily lives, socioeconomic prospects, as well as legal rights and opportunities. They have also shaped the jury system and altered the content and dynamics of jury deliberation proceedings and jury verdicts.

Our analysis provides empirical evidence that race is a social and political construction, not a fixed biological category. Critical examinations of "racial passing" and "statutory passing," for instance, exemplify the fluidity and flexibility of race, racial identity, and racial definitions. Since race has been used to determine the allocation and distribution of resources and legal opportunities, affirmative jury selection mechanisms are proposed to foster the redistribution and reallocation of the same resources and opportunities along racial lines. Affirmative action in jury selection is also seen as a social policy and legal reform measure to challenge the hegemony of "whiteness," undermining the privilege and social status, as well as discriminatory effects of "white advantages" in legal areas, including jury selection and jury service. The paradigm of a jury balanced equitably by the social construction of race under a mandatory formula may comprise in itself an intellectual standard that will eventually overcome and replace the opposite, socially reprehensible notion that race is an unalterable biological category that has been—and should continue to be—used as the conscious or unconscious subtext for the white-dominated composition of juries.

In the long history of the evolution of the jury system, there are several high points that impact the jury today. As we have seen, the jury de medietate linguae was utilized in England and the United States until fairly recently. Racial minorities such as Native Americans were once given the right to racially mixed juries that included the half of their tribal members as trial jurors. While the jury de medietate linguae was originally created out of financial and economic concerns in England, this affirmative mechanism provided the foundation for community-based jury proceedings and decisions. Our own surveys further support the perceived benefits of racially heterogeneous juries: jury deliberations and the resulting verdicts rendered by racially diverse juries are considered to be far fairer and more just than decisions reached by the single race juries.

These concepts are not commonly accepted, however. Such notions of fairness and legitimacy of the jury trial have been criticized because of recent instances of what are viewed as race-based jury deliberations and decisions. On the other hand, jury selection procedures that continue to eliminate a large proportion of racial and ethnic minorities have been questioned and scrutinized by some members of the public, as well as legal practitioners and legislatures. Nonetheless, proposed procedural remedies and race-neutral policies have so far been very ineffective in creating more racially heterogeneous and ethnically representative juries.

Our nation's court and jury system now faces a defining moment—to make changes long overdue, or to continue to lose faith and legitimacy in the eyes of marginalized segments of our community. The current methods of jury selection are woefully inadequate to deal with the continuing problem of underrepresentation of racial and ethnic minorities on juries. We have tried to demonstrate that affirmative methods in jury selection—peremptory inclusion of minority representatives in voir dire alongside jury structures with a racialized jury seat allocation—constitute the two integral parts for ensuring the presence of racial minorities in the final jury. We believe that such affirmative action in jury selection is a viable and promising jury alternative to current jury selection methods. And we foresee that the implementation of more deeply conceived selection approaches may become possible in the future—not only because the Supreme Court has erected a barrier by its reluctance to abolish peremptory challenges outright, but also because legislatures may be willing to adopt a more equitable path or mechanism to increase jury participation by racial and ethnic minorities. We believe, moreover, that proposed reforms and remedies cannot be left to either chance or the slow evolution of the legal apparatus.

Our proposal for race-conscious affirmative jury selection is certainly controversial and unsettling to some. But we believe that constructive debate and reasoned disputes about the application of affirmative jury selection will lead to even deeper social and political considerations surrounding the issue. With the public, legislatures, and the legal community discussing the question and its implications, we envision the successful emergence of a fair and just jury system and the institution of equitable selection procedures in representing the various racial and ethnic segments of our national community.

The need for racially and ethnically mixed tribunals became even clearer after September 11, 2001 when two hijacked U. S. commercial airplanes crashed into the World Trade Center, a third into the Pentagon, and a fourth into a field in Pennsylvania. The government immediately went on alert, President Bush signing executive orders, allowing the Justice Department, at its discretion, to pick up permanent residents and other non-citizens of Middle Eastern heritage and call military courts into session against them, possibly infringing on the civil and human rights of Arab and Islamic communities. (Washington, 2001; see also "Military Order of Nov. 13, 2001," 2001). Contrary to the Anglo-Saxon legal tradition, which relies on a jury of peers, military courts are designed to empanel juries more likely to convict, requiring only a two-thirds vote for conviction and being narrowly composed of six persons—three military judges and three select lay members affiliated with the military. While the American legal tradition requires open trials, military courts are conducted in camera, possibly breaching the bounds of constitutional traditions handed down over the last two centuries.

The government's predisposition to such measures revealed strong animosity toward Arab and Islamic communities. Even for criminal matters that fell outside suspicion of terrorist activities, racial motives and profiling exposed Arab and Islamic populations to legal harassment and government prosecution. While legal arguments used by defense attorneys may partly offset such harassment, only racially and ethnically mixed tribunals promise a means to ensure proper and fair treatment and proceedings. As this study has shown, these bodies would effectively reinstate juries de medietate linguae, reviving historic precedents used to redress unjust pasts when strong animosities led to the selective prosecution of foreigners and non-citizens such as Jews in medieval England and Native Americans in the New World.

In the great pendulum swing of history, the political denial of civil liberties and judicial rights of those charged with crimes against social order periodically reemerge. With increasing limitations on habeas corpus and with authoritarian secret trials, those trying to maintain trial fairness and verdict legitimacy need to fall back on tried methods and structures. Juries mixed by race and ethnicity—juries de medietate linguae—may become the prominent emblem of fairness and justice in our time.

Appendix A

SURVEY AND DATA BASE INFORMATION

O
ur book relies on a variety of data sets for empirical analyses, such as community-wide surveys (both individual and household surveys), census archival information (from the 1790 to 2000 censuses), college student surveys (University of California campuses), a college student experiment, and jury panel surveys (superior court jury panel studies). The following section explains each of these data sets in detail, including the year of the study, the nature of population to be studied, a sampling procedure for the selection of individuals or households, data collection procedures (mail surveys, interviews, and/or mass-administered surveys), questions and variables used in the questionnaire (open- and closed-ended questions and structured interviews), and statistical methods employed to analyze the data (bivariate and multivariate statistical models and analyses).

The data sets are classified into the following five types: (1) community-wide surveys (four county-level surveys); (2) a college student survey (a university-wide survey at different campuses of the University of California System); (3) jury panel surveys at superior courthouses (two surveys of reported jurors at the courthouse); (4) a college student experiment; and (5) United States censuses (from 1790 to 2000)

The data sets and surveys are explained in detail in a chronological order.

COMMUNITY SURVEYS (4 DATA SETS)

The 1986 Community Household Survey in Orange County, California (tables 6.1–6.3)

In 1986, Orange County, California, survey questionnaires were sent to potential jurors to examine the effect of jurors' socio-demongraphic and ideological backgrounds impacting their jury representation in the community. In order to obtain accurate estimates of the composition of racial and ethnic groups in the community, the statistical technique of cluster sampling with probabilities proportionate to size (PPS) was applied with the comprehensive list of all households in Orange County (see Fukurai and Butler 1991b for greater discussions of the sampling method). The original sample size of 2,175 households was then drawn from the California County Master Key List. Of the original sample, 1,500 were subsampled and the respondents were contacted by both mail and telephone interviews. Originally survey respondents were sent the questionnaire, and the initial mailing of the questionnaire resulted in 855 returns. The first follow-up resulted in 330 responses. The second follow-up, however, resulted in only nine returned questionnaires. The follow-up continued until the third mailings using certified mail. The certified mailings were then sent to 275 recalcitrant respondents, and fifty respondents returned the questionnaire. Finally, the remaining respondents were contacted by telephone.

Since the California County Master Key List did not provide the telephone number of potential jurors, the commercial directory called the Chris-Cross Directory (CCD) was used to identify the telephone number of recalcitrant respondents. The CCD provides both listed and unlisted telephone numbers according to residents' county addresses. The remaining thirty-one respondents were then contacted by telephone after their telephone numbers were identified by CCD. A total of 1,275 individuals responded to questions in the jury questionnaire regarding their demographic, socioeconomic, and attitudinal information (i.e., a response rate of 83.3 percent).

The research was funded by the Superior Court of Orange County. The entire survey took almost six months and the results were presented at the Santa Ana Superior Court in Orange County. The data identified socioeconomic, demographic, and ideological profiles of those who were placed on the master list for jury service.

The 1995 Community Survey in Santa Cruz, California (tables, 5.1–5.3, 5.5, 7.1–7.2)

In the spring of 1995, a telephone survey was conducted to examine the public's perception of the criminal justice system and criminal jury proceedings. The research site was Santa Cruz County, California. Modern sampling techniques (random digit dialing, or RDD) were employed to maximize the representativeness of the sample of adult respondents. The community survey included a number of questions and attitudinal measures concerning the criminal justice system, qualifications for jury participation, and the probable outcome of the Simpson trial.

In some respects, the survey differed from other studies in the degree to which we attempted to employ more elaborate questions concerning the fairness and legitimacy of jury proceedings, jury trials, and jury verdicts, as well as to explain to respondents the overall significance of the controversy over the O. J. Simpson trial and its effects on people's perceptions on the issue of crime and justice. Thus, within the limitations imposed by survey research methodology, we sought to have the respondents answer many of race-related questions in the general legal context that they might be posed as if they were jurors in court.

A total of 327 respondents were contacted and their responses were carefully coded, computerized, and analyzed.

Statistical Analytic Methods—LISREL (table 7.2)

In assessing our analytic model, we took advantage of the recent development of covariance structures and LISREL maximum-likelihood estimations to examine the overall goodness-of-fit test of the jury deliberation model (Joreskog and Sorbom 1985). The likelihood-ratio, chi-square statistic, and the likelihood-ratio indices, delta and rho, are employed in comparing fits in order to control for sample size (Bentler and Bonett 1980; Bollen 1989, 271–276). While failure to reject the null hypothesis may be taken as an indication that the model is consistent with the data, it is important to bear in mind that alternative models may also be consistent with the data (Fukurai and Butler 1991b; Joreskog and Sorbom 1985). Moreover, because the chi-square test is affected by sample size, it follows that (1) given a sufficiently large sample, an overidentified model may be rejected even when it fits the data well; and (2) when the sample size is small, one may fail to reject the null hypothesis even when the model fits the data poorly (Bollen 1989). Therefore, a general null model based on modified independence among variables is also proposed to provide an additional reference point for the evaluation of covariance structure models.

Two indices, delta and rho, are calculated in the following equations.

$$\Delta \ (\text{Delta}) = \frac{\text{chi-square (null)} - \text{chi-square (model)}}{\text{chi-square (null)}}$$

$$\rho \ (\text{Rho}) = \frac{\dfrac{\text{chi-square (null)} - \text{chi-square (model)}}{\text{df (null)} \qquad \text{df (model)}}}{\dfrac{\text{chi-square (null)}}{\text{df (null)}} - 1.0}$$

where df = degrees of freedom

The 1996 Pretrial Publicity Survey in Mendocino County, California (tables 4.3, 4.4)

In 1996, a random digit telephone survey was conducted by the Social Science Research Center at California State University, Chico, under the supervision and guidance of Professors Robert S. Ross and Edward J. Bronson at California State University, Chico. The survey was funded by the Mendocino Superior Court in Ukiah, California, with the purpose of examining the effect of prejudicial pretrial publicity concerning Eugene "Bear" Lincoln and his alleged crimes. From a preliminary report by a jury expert, it was clear that pretrial publicity was "extremely high" and prejudicial, with some 142 newspaper articles appearing in just the first ninety days following the shootings on April 14, 1995. Approximately four hundred fifty randomly selected residents of Mendocino County were contacted and their responses were computerized. The defense showed that a community survey indicated that 92.7 percent of a representative sample of eligible jurors already recognized the case.

The 1997 Community Survey in Santa Cruz, California (tables 3.1–3.3, 5.1–5.4, 8.1–8.3)

In the spring of 1997, a telephone survey was conducted in Santa Cruz, California, to examine the public's perception of the criminal justice system and criminal jury proceedings. Similar to the 1995 community survey, modern sampling techniques (random digit dialing, or RDD) were employed to maximize the representativeness of the sample of adult respondents. The survey included more than fifty questions of attitudinal measures on affirmative action in jury selection, as well as the respondents' understanding of the criminal justice system, jury participation, and the death penalty.

Since we were interested in accurately estimating the correct proportion of minorities to be represented in the sample, we needed to obtain a sufficient and optimum sample size for our study. The desired sample size was then estimated in the following fashion (Ott et al. 1992). The 1990 census information showed that the percentage of white adults in the county was 78 percent, suggesting that remaining 22 percent of all adults in the county were racial minorities. With a 95 percent confidence interval with error margins of plus or minus 5 percent, we inserted the following parameters into the equation to estimate the desirable sample size, n, necessary to achieve the desired confidence interval.

$$n = \frac{(1.96)^2 \; p^* q}{E^2}$$

where p=.22 and q=1-p = .78
E = .05 (error margins)

The estimate sample size was 264. After completing standardized procedures to insure interval validity of the survey, we obtained a total of 327 completed interviews, exceeding the required minimum sample size, and ensuring the 95 percent confidence interval and error margins of 5 percent.

COLLEGE STUDENT SURVEY (1 DATA SET)

UC-Wide Survey Sample (tables 2.3,–2.5, 8.4)

In 1996 and 1997, a representative group of college students at four University of California campuses (Berkeley, Irvine, Riverside, and Santa Cruz) were contacted to provide their responses to various questions involving racial quotas, racially mixed juries, and affirmative action in jury selection. The intent of the survey was to understand their knowledge about the controversy, and the debate surrounding the issue, of affirmative action, their understanding of the importance of racial impact on legal protections and social opportunities, and their opinions on the present and future status of affirmative action policies and programs. A total of 911 respondents were contacted and their responses were carefully coded, computerized, and analyzed. The survey was conducted by the research group called the Affirmative Action Research Group (AARG) (see Fukurai, Davies, Shin, Lum, and Shin 1997 for detailed discussions on AARGs research activities).

The analysis of the representative sample of UC students was specifically sought in order to examine racial identity, racial ancestry and respondents' views on affirmative action policies for a number of reasons. First, the University of California became the first-ever major institution of higher education in the United States to ban affirmative action programs. And because of students' greater awareness of the controversial issues surrounding affirmative action and their exposure to the hotly debated issue, their perceptions on race-conscious remedies provided important information for the success or failure of future affirmative action policies and programs.

Second, the 1996 passage of Proposition 209 ("California Civil Rights Initiative") and anti-affirmative action measure have powerfully affected the general population of California; and the 1995 University of California Regent's decision to ban affirmative action also took effect, including the elimination of both student affirmative action offices of all University of California campuses and race- or gender-based consideration in the admission of graduate students in 1997 and first-year undergraduate admissions in 1998. By considering a representative group of University of California students who already have been exposed to legal and extra-legal constraints of affirmative action, we were able to gain some important insights into the application and evaluation of different forms of affirmative action.

In order to enhance the external validity of the survey's empirical findings, a number of so-called blocking factors were incorporated in the statistical analysis, such as race, gender, and parental income which served as a proxy for social class. These variables were included in the analyses in order to provide empirical findings that were more likely to be generalized over larger and much broader populations.

Affirmative Action and Measurements

Four types of questions are used to examine the respondents' perception and attitude towards affirmative action programs and race-conscious remedies. In examining their views on admissions, hiring, and contracting, each respondent was asked: "Please check all areas in which you support affirmative action based on race," offering the following three distinct areas of affirmative action programs: "Admissions (Education)," "Hiring (Employment)," and "Contracting (Business)." When the respondent checked the specific area, then the response was coded as 1 and nonresponse was coded as 0.

With respect to the application of affirmative action in jury selection, the question asked for an "agree" or "disagree" response to the statement, "It is important to create affirmative mechanisms to ensure racially mixed juries." Because of the then recent urban uprisings triggered by the acquittal verdicts in racially sensitive trials such as the Rodney King beating trial in Los Angeles and the Lorenzo trial in Miami, Florida, this question examined the perception of possible uses of affirmative action in jury selection to ensure the presence of racial minorities in criminal trials that involved the highly sensitive and unmistakable element of race and racism. The response of "agreement" was coded as 1 and "disagreement" was coded as 0. These four areas of affirmative action programs were designed to examine the respondent's perceptions about race-based applications of affirmative action in eliminating racial inequality and discrimination in education, employment, business contracting, and jury selection.

Multiple Response Analysis (tables 2.3–2.4)

The statistical program called "SPSS" and its statistical option, "Multiple Response," is employed to examine the frequency and cross-tabulations of both racial identity and reported ancestral race. Since both self-identified race and ancestral race are coded in a dichotomous fashion, such as a "yes" or "no" response for each racial category, a special statistical program that can handle multiple, dichotomously coded responses is used as our empirical statistical tool. As the respondent can have one or more responses for his/her ancestral race, the program must be able to accommodate a varying number of responses for ancestral racial backgrounds. For example, each subject is only allowed to choose one specific racial group for his/her racial identity. However, for ancestral race, it is possible that some respondents may identify all six races as their ancestral roots and backgrounds, while some respondents may designate only one or two as ancestral race. Thus, in such multiple-response questions, the responses are coded as multiple-dichotomy variables that have one of two values: zero for "no," and one for "yes."

JURY PANEL SURVEY (1 DATA SET)

The 1996 Jury Panel Survey at the Superior Courthouse in Ukiah, Mendocino County, California (table 4.2)

From April 30,1996 to December 16, 1996, all prospective jurors who appeared at the Mendocino Superior Courthouse for jury service were asked to fill out the questionnaire to identify their racial and ethnic backgrounds. The 1996 Jury Panel Survey was conducted to examine the extent of Native Americans' jury participation at the Mendocino Superior Courthouse, evaluating the disparity of the Native Americans' composition in the community and in jury panels. In early 1996, the court gave the defense the permission to distribute a jury survey questionnaire at the courthouse in order to examine racial compositions of jury panels. The eight months survey identified racial and ethnic compositions of 2,042 potential jurors who appeared at the Mendocino Superior Courthouse.

Accurate Estimates of Native Americans in the Jurisdiction

The defense's fear of having an all-white Lincoln jury was well-founded. For example, the composition of Native Americans in Mendocino County is very small. According to the 1990 census, Native Americans comprised a mere 3.61 percent of the adult population in the jurisdiction. The 1990 census also undercounted Native Americans, especially on the Indian reservation. Although the proportion of eligible Native Americans reported by the 1990 census was adjusted and recomputed by incorporating other supplemental lists in obtaining an accurate estimate of Native American jurors in Mendocino County, the Indian proportion of the community residents was still small. Nevertheless, the defense attempted to show the court an accurate estimate of the Native Americans in the jurisdiction and to show the extent to which the existing source lists failed to include Indians who reside on the reservation.

Without an accurate estimate of Native American jurors in the jurisdiction, defense counsel could not accurately assess the extent of Native Americans' jury representativeness in the Superior Court. Tribal representative reports were supplied from the Bureau of Indian Affairs, including the list of ten federally recognized tribes and their full tribal membership. Incorporating the new information into the computation of Native American's proportional representation in the jurisdiction, approximately 5 to 6 percent of the adult populations in the county were found to be Native American, suggesting the 1990 United States Census underestimated the true Native American population in Mendocino County by 50 to 80 percent. Nevertheless, the Native Americans remained a very small percentage of the prospective jury pool in the jurisdiction.

COLLEGE STUDENT EXPERIMENT (1 DATA SET)

The 1997 College Student Experiment at the
University of California, Santa Cruz (table 4.5)

A total of eighty-three students at the University of California, Santa Cruz, participated in the jury experiment. Each participant was asked to act as both prosecuting and defending attorneys in selecting petit juries for the trial of a murder suspect under three different kinds of scenarios: (1) a white defendant with a white victim; (2) a black defendant with a white victim; and (3) a white defendant with a black victim. In each scenario, they were asked to select a group of three and six final jurors from the pool of prospective jurors who had the following racial and socioeconomic profiles: twenty-five males and twenty-five females; thirty whites, ten blacks, and ten Hispanic; twenty college-educated jurors and thirty jurors with high school education.

Similar to other studies, the race-related variables included the following two questions: (1) self-identified race, and (2) reported ancestral race. The responses were then numerically codified and entered into a statistical database to perform empirical analysis.

Thirty-nine percent of participants were male and 61 percent female. Fifty-nine percent of respondents identified as whites, while 40 percent identified as racial and ethnic minorities (3.6 percent blacks, 13.3 percent Hispanics, 14.5 percent Asian/Pacific Islanders, 8.4 percent others). Seventy-two percent of participants self-reported to share white racial ancestry, along with 7.2 percent black racial ancestry, 22.9 percent native American racial ancestry, 24.1 percent Hispanic racial ancestry, 22.9 percent Asian racial ancestry, and 12.0 percent other racial ancestry.

Trial Simulation (*Hoyt v. Florida*, 368 U.S. 64, 1961)

In the experiment, each participant was given the following trial background information. The scenario and case background reflects that of the Hoyt case that was reviewed by the U.S. Supreme Court in 1961. The Hoyt case was specifically chosen because of its race-neutral content and the question on the use of the affirmative jury selection method that specifically excluded women from serving on juries.

In the Hoyt case, the female defendant challenged the affirmative registration practice in Florida, that required women who wanted to serve on juries to go to the courthouse and formally register, whereas men were automatically registered and eligible for jury service. Because of this discriminatory practice, she argued that she had been denied her constitutional right to the due process of law.

The Hoyt case allowed us to critically cross-examine and make effective comparisons of the Court's opinions with those of the experimental participants. The scenario given to each experimental participant was the following:

A thirty-three-year-old [race] woman was charged with killing her [race] husband with a baseball bat while he slept because of his extra-marital affair with another woman and his repeated rejection of her efforts at a reconciliation.

They were divorced once twelve years ago, remarried, and had an eight-year-old son. The wife has had epilepsy since age twenty. Approximately a year-and-a-half prior to the homicide, the husband, an Air Force captain, was transferred to a new air force base, but the wife was not able to move to the base to be with or near her husband. For the first eight to nine months, the husband spent every weekend and all his leave time with his wife and son. The husband then began to change his habits, cutting his weekend visits short, failing to come home during his leaves, receiving strange telephone calls while at home, coming home with lipstick on his shirt, and washing his clothes immediately upon arrival at home, even at three or four o'clock in the morning.

Prior to the day of the homicide, she attempted repeatedly to contact him by telephone without success, and finally sent word the next day that their son was dying, hoping that this would bring her husband home. When he returned home the next day, she did everything in her power to reconcile any differences they may have had. That night she dressed in a sheer nightgown for the purpose of creating a love making atmosphere in which they could discuss their differences, but he ignored his wife, refusing to discuss any problems with her. At this juncture, because of his complete and final rejection of her efforts toward revitalizing their marriage, she became emotionally upset and struck him with a bat, numerous blows to the head inflicting injuries from which he died the next day. She was charged with first degree murder, but pleaded temporary insanity.

Race of both the victim and defendant were then systematically changed and switched in order to solicit participants' views on the most ideal racial and gender composition of the jury. Each participant was also asked to respond to a series of questions regarding their views on the criminal justice system, criminal concepts, affirmative action, as well as racial identity and backgrounds.

CENSUS INFORMATION

1790–2000 Censuses (table 2.1, 2.2)

We examined racial categories and statistics of United States censuses from 1790, the year that the first United States census was taken, to 2000, the most recent census available for analysis. The early Census Acts prescribed the inquiries in each decennial census, but the United States Government did not furnish uniform printed schedules until 1830. In 1790, for instance, the marshals submitted their returns in whatever form they found convenient (and sometime with added information); from 1800 to 1820, the government provided schedules of varying size and typeface. There are separate schedules for "taxed or untaxed Indians," depending on the census year. Supplemental data to racial breakdowns and statistical information between 1790 and 1990 also came from United States Bureau of Census (1993).

METHODOLOGICAL STRATEGIES ON HOW TO DETERMINE AND MEASURE RACE IN COURTROOMS

We have spent considerable space examining race and racial identity to set the framework for affirmative action reforms. Given the amorphous, fluid, and sometimes unsettling nature of race and racial identity, a critical analysis of race and racial identity constitutes the essential step to build an effective affirmative action program for jury selection in order to best empanel racially diverse tribunals in criminal trials.

Based on the discussion and examination of racial identity, we propose the following strategies for measuring race. First, in identifying one's race and racial identity, we should rely on the following two factors: (1) component racial identity, and (2) ancestral race. Component racial identity is similar to the elicitation used in the pre-2000 census, in which the respondent is asked to provide one and only one racial identity. The second factor measures one's racial, ancestral history, in which he or she is asked to check more than one ancestral background. This duality of racial questions is crucial because the race inquiry used in the year 2000 census only asks the respondent to check as many races as possible, without clearly and explicitly specifying that the identified race should reflect their actual racial identity, desired race, ancestral history, or something else.

As our analysis of racial identity and ancestry has indicated in chapter 2, a large proportion of individuals believe that they have more than one ancestral race. Yet, we also found that component racial identity and reported ancestral race are the two most important determinants and predictors of opinions and attitudes towards race-related issues and other matters, including affirmative action in jury selection and jurors' opinions on imposing the death penalty.

We believe that these two measurements are superior to the 2000 census question as they effectively control for historical artifacts in measuring race—for which racial identity is designed to provide the most current identity of one's race, while ancestral race provides the perceived and assumed genealogical history of one's race. Whether or not the identified racial ancestry truly reflects the genealogical backgrounds of one's race is neither crucial nor important, because today's racial categories are not the same as racial categories of the past, and there is no biologically measurable strategy to trace and determine one's racial background. Nevertheless, these two measurements of race (i.e., self-identity and ancestry) rely on the identical racial classification scheme as the most recent census question, making the racial data compatible with the most recent racial framework used by the federal government.

More elaborate designation of racial groups may also be used in actual criminal trials in identifying potential jurors, such as Chicano, Chicana, Mexicano, and Mexicana. But it is equally important to ensure that some of the affirmative action programs in jury selection rely on the same census category in order to secure crucial information about the desired number of jury seats to be allocated for certain racial groups. When the proportionate jury model is used to create racially diverse juries, for instance, racial distribution of jury seats may reflect the racial composition of the community. While individuals who identify themselves as Chicano may not feel that Hispanic is their racial or ethnic identity, the population composition is still available from the census data on the basis of the Hispanic populations or Mexican subpopulations in the jurisdiction.

In the final measurement of racial identity and ancestral race, reliance must be placed on self-identification and self-declaration by prospective jurors, not third-party observations of their race. As our analysis indicated, "other-identified race" may not always match the self-identified race. Self-identification of race is also compatible with that of the census procedure.

There are also procedural requirements that must be established in the courtroom so that the measurement of race and racial identity is collected and analyzed. Thus, it may become crucial for the judge to allow attorneys to distribute a short survey questionnaire prior to jury selection. As the distribution of questionnaires is often granted and routinely used in felony cases in most jurisdictions, the collection of racial and other relevant case-specific information by potential jurors should not pose major problems.

NOTES

CHAPTER 1: INTRODUCTION TO RACIALLY MIXED JURIES

1. Throughout the book, the term, black, will be used instead of other names such as African American, Afro-American, or Negro because of the governmental definition of race and racial classification specified in Directive 15 from the Office of Management and Budget in 1977, as well as its revision in 1998. Because of our empirical analysis involving various racial categories in subsequent chapters, the book relies on the federal governmental definition of race and racial classification.

2. The King jury members were not all white; ten whites, one Hispanic, and one Asian. However, after the defense's request for the change of venue was granted, the trial site moved from Los Angeles Central Superior Court, where the majority of prospective jurors were Blacks, to Simi Valley Superior Court, where approximately half of Los Angeles police officers lived. As a result, the King jury included three persons who were relatives of police officers and three jurors who were members of conservative national organizations including the National Rifle Association. With close associations with law enforcement agencies, those jurors were more likely to share the life experience and morals that may have been underlying factors in the crime in question. Furthermore, a racially mixed jury's verdict might have permitted both the minority and the white communities to focus on preventing and punishing crime and violence, among other common interests, rather than divisive questions of whether the racial composition of the jury diminished the fairness of the verdict. For greater discussions of jury deliberations and verdicts, see Hiroshi Fukurai and Edgar W. Butler (1994).

3. The case profile and the history of the Beckwith trial are largely based on the work of Maryanne Vollers (1995).

4. Eight Ku Klux Klan members were convicted of federal conspiracy charges in the case, but Mississippi never brought murder charges (Herbert 1994).

5. Medgar Evers' wife, Myrlie, had tried to establish a Nuremberg-type commission to investigate old civil rights atrocities, ones similar to the attempts by the Jews to pursue the Nazis after the war (Vollers 1995, 385).

6. While we would prefer terms such as civil disturbances, rebellions, or uprisings, the term, "riot," has been used in the manuscript in order to make it compatible with many reports of the urban uprisings and disturbances that have used the term riot.

7. Douglas L. Colbert (1990) discusses the racial make-up of juries and its influence on jury verdicts. Sheri Lynn Johnson (1985) discusses racial prejudice and its influence on the decision-making of criminal juries. The article, "Developments in the law" (1988), discusses the harm of minority underrepresentation on juries.

8. Colbert (1990) examined jury studies in showing that influence of race is minimized when the jury is racially mixed.

9. Jury members in the minority are far more likely to maintain their viewpoints and opinions if they are certain that at least one member of the jury agrees with them. See generally Richard S. Arnold (1993). Other jury studies, however, suggest that the quality of jury deliberations is suspect, especially in criminal cases and civil law suits that require the understanding of complexities and subtleties of the evidence (Pertnoy 1993, 630).

10. *Duren v. Missouri* (439 U.S. 357, 360, 1979), holding that the systematic exclusion of women from jury service violates the Constitution's fair cross section requirement.

11. *Georgia v. McCollum,* (112 S.Ct. 2348, 2357, 1992), recognizing that a defendant has a right to an impartial jury, but cannot disqualify a person as impartial based on race. See also *Taylor v. Louisiana* (419 U.S. 522, 538, 1975); *Ballad v. United States* (329 U.S. 187, 192–93, 1946); *Strauder v. West Virginia* (100 U.S. 303, 1880).

12. While Justice Thurgood Marshall was writing for only three justices, his sentiments echoed those of the Court in *Ballard v. United States* (329 U.S. 187, 193–194, 1946), and they are quoted approvingly by Justice White writing for the Court in *Taylor v Louisiana,* (419 U.S. 522, 532 n.12, 1975). In *Ballard* and *Taylor,* male defendants were challenging the exclusion of women; in Peters, a white defendant was challenging the exclusion of blacks. Thus, in each case, the Court felt obliged to explain how a defendant could be injured by the exclusion of a gender or racial group to which the defendant did not belong.

CHAPTER 2: DEFINING AND MEASURING RACE AND RACIAL IDENTITY

1. The class, "Race and Criminal Justice" (sociology 80I) was taught in the Fall Quarter of 1996 in Oaks College at the University of California, Santa Cruz.

2. People of Islamic backgrounds including those of Iranian and Iraqis heritage are also subject to social and racial discrimination in America (see generally *Saint Francis College v. Al-Khazraji,* 481 U.S.504, 1987).

3. This notion of "white" persons with "nonwhite" ancestors including black ancestry involves the analyses of racial transformation called "racial passing." Please refer to the discussion of those who "pass" as white in this chapter.

4. See the subsequent discussions on the analysis of the reliability and validity of race and racial classification.

5. Before determining racial categories for the 2000 census, a number of civil rights organizations, including the Association of Multi-Ethnic Americans which is a

national organization for people of multiracial multiethnic backgrounds, tried to pressure the Congress to adopt a multiracial checkoff list (McLead 1997).

6. Directive No. 15 provides the following racial categories and definitions. Revision to Directive No. 15 relies on almost identical racial categories and definitions except that two racial groups, Asian and Pacific Islanders, are now considered as separate racial categories. Racial groups and Hispanics as an ethnic group are defined by Directive No. 15 as follows: (1) *American Indian or Alaskan Native:* A person having origins in any of the original peoples of North America and who maintains cultural identification through tribal affiliations or community recognition: (2) *Asian or Pacific Islander:* A person having origins in any of the original peoples of the Far East, Southeast Asia, the Indian subcontinent, or the Pacific Islands. This area includes, for example, China, India, Japan, Korea, the Philippine Islands, and Samoa; (3) *Black:* A person having origins in any of the black racial groups of Africa; and (4) *Hispanic:* A person of Mexican, Puerto Rican, Cuban, Central or South American, or other Spanish culture or origin, regardless of race.

7. American society generally does not regard individuals with the origins in the Middle East or the North Africa as members of the racial majority. See *St. Francis College v. Al-Khazraji,* 481 U.S. 604, 1987 (in which a United States citizen born in Iraq brought a claim under Title VII (42. U.S.C. Sect., 1981), examining whether Arabs, who are taxonomically considered as white, are permitted to bring race discrimination claims under Sect. 1981).

8. According to 1990 data as reported in Maandstatiskiek van de Bevolking, Centraal Buro voor de Statistiek, March 1991 (see de Vries and Pettigrew 1994, 181, table 1), there were 204,000 Turks and 169,000 Moroccans, constituting 1.3 percent and 1.1 percent of the population in Netherlands. Their unemployment rate was 42 percent and 44 percent, the highest among four major ethnic minorities (27 percent for Surinamese, 23 percent for Antillians/Arubans, compared to only 13 percent for the Dutch).

9. The ruling also flies in the face of the previous industrial tribunal ruling in Glasgow in early 1997, holding that four airline stewards had no case in asserting that British Airways had discriminated against them because they were Scots (See Bowditch 1997).

10. The Burakumin are deemed to be outcasts and of a different race because their ancestors (up until the nineteenth century) were employed in professions that were considered ritually unclean, such as disposing of the dead, herding cattles, and tanning hides of dead animals (De Vos and Wetherall 1983, 337–340).

11. A critical examination of racial specification and classification becomes particularly important because almost every society adopts race-conscious solutions to solve incidents of past and present racial discrimination.

12. See *Technical documentation: Summary tape file 1, 1990 Census of population and housing,* at B–11.

13. Lisa Funderburg argues that "[s]ome population experts and multiracial support networks estimate that there are currently at least one million mixed-race people in this country" (Funderburg 1994, 11).

14. For greater discussions of interracial marriage and adoptions, see Ruth-Arlene Howe (1995).

15. Dean Cain, who played a superman on TV, is of Japanese, Irish, and Welsh background ("Netscape: Lois and Clark: The new adventures of superman," http://www.netgate.net/~asylum/dean.htm).

16. The figure shows the racial breakdown of the 1996–1997 first-year students at the four University of California campuses (Berkeley, Irvine, Riverside, and Santa Cruz).

17. Another important finding is that the level of racial mix is also generally higher for females than males, particularly the highest among self-identified black females (192.3 percent and 288.2 percent for black male and female, respectively).

18. For additional discussions of students' views and attitudes on affirmative action, see Hiroshi Fukurai and Darryl Davies (1997).

19. The respondent is a female student at the University of California, Riverside (UCR). Her parents' annual income was "7" ($50,000 to $79,000).

20. The respondent is a male student at the University of California, Riverside (UCR) whose parents' income was indicated as "4" ($15,000 to $24,999).

21. This student is from the University of California, Santa Cruz (UCSC) and his parents' income was indicated as "7" ($50,000 to $79,000).

22. She was enrolled at the University of California, Santa Cruz. Her parental income is "6" ($35,000 to $49,000), and both of her parents were college graduates.

23. The respondent is a female student at the University of California, Riverside (UCR), her parents' income is coded as "9" ($100,000 or more), her father has a post-college degree, and her mother has a college degree.

24. The respondent is a female student at the University of California, Santa Cruz (UCSC). She indicated that her parental income was "6" ($35,000 to $49,999) and both her parents had some college education.

25. One Native American scholar has argued that the "blood quantum" requirement is often misapprehended as a Native American's scheme to preserve their racial identification and increase their share of entitlements. This suggests that the tribal blood quantum requirements are "created by white American authorities to guarantee that the United States would remain a nation-state in the European mold rather than a confederation of free tribes consisting of Indians of European bloodline" (Toro 1995, 1234).

26. One white male student in the first author's "Law, Crime, and Social Justice" course (sociology 123 which was offered in Winter Quarter, 1997) exclaimed that it is a "hip" to have "Native American blood" after the first author presented the preliminary analyses of table 2.2 in the class in discussing the constructed nature of race and racial identity.

27. See United States Census (1980). Eurasians—self-identified whites with Asian ancestry and/or self-identified Asians with white ancestry—may not be subject to the "one-drop" rule as it has been applied to black descent. However, their racial identity still

remains unclear because Eurasians are often considered as white and often not accepted as their own ancestral members by Asian communities (Jenga 1995). There are also vexing identity questions for children of parents who are from different races. For instance, Chieko Saito (1993) described the particular identity problems of a twenty-six-year-old American born, Chinese-African American male, including a feeling of alienation from Chinese-American, African American, and white societies.

28. The deconstruction of racial categories reveals how the racialized meaning and definition of white, for example, are actively being part of nonwhite categories, suggesting that the seemingly binary opposition of white and "nonwhite" categories collapses. This method is called "deconstruction," in which the old system of racial oppositions or racial differences is destroyed by showing how the basic units of binary pairs of "white" and "nonwhite" distinctions contradict their own logic. See Jacques Derrida (1981) for more information on the method of deconstruction.

CHAPTER 3: RACIALLY MIXED JURIES AND AFFIRMATIVE ACTION

1. President Clinton considered the following four possible women for Attorney General, Janet Reno, Rya W. Zobel, Diana E. Murphy, and Linda A. Fairstein. See Neil A. Lewis (1993).

2. For example, in *Lamprecht v. FCC,* (958 F.2d 382, 1992), the opinion by Justice Clarence Thomas struck down an affirmative action program that gave women an advantage in the radio licensing process. The case involved that when Barbara Driscoll Marmet who applied for permission to build a radio station, the Federal Communications Commission (FCC) awarded her extra credit for being a woman. Jerome Thomas Lamprecht then argued that the FCC's policy deprived him of his constitutional right to the equal protection of the laws. The court agreed with the litigant, noting that

> When the government treats people differently because of their sex, equal-protection principles at the very least require that there be a meaningful factual predicate supporting a link between the government's means and its ends. In this case, the government has failed to show that its sex-preference policy is substantially related to achieving diversity on the airwaves. We therefore hold that the policy violates the Constitution (958 F.2d 382 398, 1992).

Justice Thomas was a member of the Second Circuit Court when the case was briefed and argued.

3. Transcript of Proceedings, *Minnesota v. Charles* (No. K0–92–1621) (Minn. 2d Jud. Dist. August 10, 1992). See also Stephanie Domitrovich (1994).

4. See HR 1182, 177th Gen. Assem., 1993 Reg. Sess. (1993). See notes 438–44 and accompanying texts for a discussion of the proposed legislation.

5. For greater discussions of the prejudice and animosity against the Jews in England, see Robert C. Stacey (1992).

6. For greater discussions of European legal treatments of the Jews, see Shael Herman (1992).

7. Although Jews played active roles in financing church activities, King Edward I not only hanged up to three hundred Jews, confiscating the assets of all other English Jews, but also expelled them from England (Johnson 1987, 212–13).

8. The history of the Jews in Christian Europe is one of insecurity, persecution, and expulsion. For instance, Jews were also expelled from France in 1306, and from Spain in 1492. For a greater description of Jews in Europe, see Dena S. Davis (1993). After the expulsion in England, from 1290 to 1656, no indigenous Jews and virtually no foreign Jews lived in England (Bush 1993).

9. Jury research indicates that "two centuries ago the Puritans of our Plymouth colony used now and then, out of policy, when they were trying a case relating to an Indian, to add Indians to the jury, as in a criminal case in 1682" (Thayer 1898, 307). See also Act of 1786, no. 1326, 4 Stat. S.C. 746 (conferring a right to a mixed jury); *Respublica v. Mesca,* 1 U.S. (1 Dall.) 73 (1783) (upholding a Pennsylvania defendant's right to a mixed jury); *Wendling v. Commonwealth,* (143 Ky. 587, 1911) (recognizing discretionary judicial authority to award a jury de medietate linguae); *People v. McLean,* 2 Johns. 380 (N.Y. Sup. Ct., 1807) (upholding a New York defendant's request for a trial de medietate linguae); *Richards v. Commonwealth,* 38 Va. (11 Leigh) 690 (1841) (holding that while a person has the right to a mixed jury, the court has complete discretionary authority to grant or deny the request).

10. 299 U.S. at 132–33 (citing *Crawford v. United States,* 212 U.S. 183, 1908).

11. *Commonwealth v. Richard Acen, Jr* and *Commonwealth v. Alberto Penabriel,* 396 MASS 472, 487 NE2D 189, 1986. In separate trials, defendants were tried and convicted in the Suffolk county Superior Court. Appeals were consolidated for purposes of briefing and oral argument in the appeals court. One defendant's application for direct appellate review was granted, and the second case was transferred to the Supreme Judicial Court on Court's own motion.

12. Id at 396 MASS 472, 473, 487 N.E.2D 189, 191.

13. Id at 396 MASS 472, 475, 479, 480, 487 N.E.2D 189, 191, 194, 195.

14. In California, Penal Code Sect. 888 covers the formation of the grand jury, and Sect. 903.4 requires that each jurisdiction or county appoint jury commissioners who are responsible for compiling lists of those qualified to serve as grand jurors. Section 903.3 also specifies that superior court judges shall examine the jury list submitted by jury commissioners, and may select "such persons, as in their opinion, should be selected for grand jury duty." However, Sect. 903.4 also allows judges to disregard these lists and select anyone from the county they find suitable and competent to serve as grand jurors. Section 903.4 specifically states:

> The judges are not required to select any names from the list returned by the jury commissioner, but may, if in *their judgment* the due administration of justice requires, make *all or any selections* from among the body of persons in the county suitable and competent to serve as grand jurors regardless of the list returned by the jury commissioner (emphasis added).

15. See *Ballew v. Georgia,* at 231–39, reviewing articles and studies critical of the six-person jury and refusing to uphold a five-person jury.

16. Sidney Lumet, the film's director, recently revealed that he "always felt *Twelve Angry Men* was romantic, and in a sense, unrealistic. I had no illusions even then. It's hard enough to find a jury with even a single unprejudiced person" (Margolick, 1989) For greater discussions of proposals and other methods to improve racial representation, see Stephanie Domitrovich (1994).

17. For greater discussions of the bill and other methods to improve racial representation, see Stephanie Domitrovich (1994).

18. The 1990 United States Census information shows that Santa Cruz County has the adult population of 175,030 (78.0% whites, 0.9% African Americans, 0.6% native Americans, 3.4% Asian and Pacific islanders, 17.0% Hispanics, and 0.1% other racial and ethnic groups).

19. The term, "quota," also has attained popular notoriety and "much of the attack [on quotas] has been an urgent appeal to alleviate the injustice worked upon the majority group which suffers the impact of the remedy" (Barnes 1995, 865).

CHAPTER 4: EUGENE "BEAR" LINCOLN AND THE NATIVE AMERICAN JURY

1. Jury research indicates that "two centuries ago the Puritans of our Plymouth Colony used now and then, out of policy, when they were trying a case relating to an Indian, to add Indians to the jury, as in a criminal case in 1682" (Thayer 1898, 307).

2. In his postverdict interview, Serra reflected his views on the bailiff's misconduct, arguing that:

During the process of jury selection, a sheriff standing outside the door of the courtroom told a prospective juror who was a potential leader, he said why, why, and I paraphrase, he said words to the effect, "Why are we even having this trial? Bear Lincoln has confessed." He whispered that into the ear of the juror, who went in and took the seat and was so outraged, he pointed and he said, "That man just told me that Bear Lincoln confessed. Is that right? Is that allowed?" He was outraged. And then that sheriff was brought in, and the judge said, "Identify the sheriff who said that," and he pointed his finger at him. And then thereafter what happened? They whitewashed it; they covered it up; nothing happened. They gave it to the Attorney General to investigate, and that office assigned it to an officer who was going on vacation for two weeks. And when that officer came back, someone else wasn't available. And so it trailed, and so it lagged, and finally we were given a little letter that the investigation has been completed, and the deputy made a mistake, but there was no criminal intention, and therefore, he is exonerated. Well, that is outrageous! . . . Why? Why didn't that happen? Ask yourself that, I'm sure you'll come up with a lot of meaningful answers (Wilson 1997a).

3. Wanda Bennet of Ukiah said "We just couldn't get beyond a reasonable doubt. . . . We started deliberating with the feeling that everyone involved had become caught up in a terrible tragedy," adding that the panel was troubled by a lack of physical

evidence to sort out what happened in two shootouts (Geniella 1997c). Dorene Burdick, a businesswoman from Mendocino, said, "[M]ost of us are outraged that this case was even brought to trial in the first place. They were on the lookout for an armed and dangerous Indian . . . and they had their triggers ready. . . . They created the war zone, and he [Lincoln] had every right to defend himself and flee for his life" (Snyder 1997b). Burdick also stated the earlier impressions that the jury was mostly swayed by reasonable doubt that "whitewashed the real strength of our decision. They called it a credibility contest. Well, it was no contest for us. . . . even if we are scoffed at as being a white and rural jury," adding that "this trial has brought at least five new activists to help the local Indian community in working to act as watchdogs over the justice system" (Snyder 1997b).

4. The 1989–90 figures were supplied by Ed Bronson, professor of political science at California State University, Chico.

CHAPTER 5: THE SIXTH AMENDMENT
AND THE RACIALLY MIXED JURY

1. The appellant, Raymond Wood convicted of petit larceny, argued a constitutional challenge to a federal statute that permitted federal employees to serve as jurors. Previously the Court of Appeals for the District of Columbia reversed the judgment of conviction. The Supreme Court, however, rejected the argument and affirmed the conviction.

2. The Court also held that "State courts enforcing similar requirements of state constitutions as to trial by jury have held that legislatures enjoy a reasonable freedom in establishing qualifications for jury service, although these involve a departure from common law rules. This principle was thus stated by the Court of Appeals of New York in *Stokes v. People*, 53 N.Y. 164, 173, 13, Am.Rep. 492: 'While the Constitution secures the right of trial by an impartial jury, the mode of procuring and impaneling such jury is regulated by law, either common or statutory, principally the latter, and it is within the power of the legislature to make, from time to time, such changes in the law as it may deem expedient, taking care to preserve the right of trial by an impartial jury' " (299 U.S. at 146).

3. See also *Goldberg v. Kelly,* 397 U.S. 254 271, 1970; see also *Marshall v. Jerric,* 446 U.S. 238 242, 1980, finding that the right to an impartial judge is inherent in the Due Process Clause.

4. The 1945 review specifically involved the application of, not the Sixth Amendment, but the Equal Protection Clause of the Fourteenth Amendment in evaluations of discriminatory jury selection procedures.

5. The defendant challenged the Sixth Amendment rather than the Equal Protection Clause of the Fourteenth Amendment, because of the question about whether the defendant would have standing to assert an equal protection claim as a white defendant. The court, however, held in *Powers v. Ohio,* 499 U.S. 400, 1991 that a white person does have standing to assert the equal protection rights of peremptory-challenged, black venire persons.

6. According to the 1990 United States Census information, blacks comprise 0.9 percent of the total adult population in Santa Cruz County, California (U.S. Bureau of Census, 1991)

7. The Court declared that "[n]either the jury roll nor the venire need be a perfect mirror of the community or accurately reflect the proportionate strength of every identifiable group" (e.g., *Swain v. Alabama*, 380 U.S. 202, 208, 1965).

8. Success rates of the same groups were only 16.9 percent and 13.3 percent, respectively, compared with whites (53.3 percent), women (30.0 percent), and men (33.3 percent). Batson remains a procedural option used almost exclusively by criminal defendants. Analyses also found that while it is relatively easy for a Batson complainant to establish a prima facie case, it is much more difficult ultimately to prevail on a Batson challenge (a success for criminal defendants was 15.8 percent, while prosecutors had an 84.6 percent success rate). Similarly, a very high percentage of successful Batson claims were concentrated in a few jurisdictions such as Alabama, Florida, Illinois, New York and Texas (58.7 percent of all successes) (Melilli 1996, 501–505).

9. See *United States v. Montgomery*, 819 F.2d at 851; however, the Eleventh Circuit Court of Appeals rejected this line of reasoning in *Fleming v. Kemp* 794 F.2d 1478 (11th Cir., 1986), and United States v. David, 803 F.2d 1567 (11th Cir. 1986); see also *United States v. Vaccaro*, 816 F.2d 443, 457 (9th Cir., 1987); *Fields v. People*, 732 P.2d 1145, 1158 n.20 (Colo. 1987).

10. Section 21 of the Magna Carta also provides that "Earls and barons shall not be amerced save through their peers, and only according to the measures of the offense." Another translation of the Magna Carta also uses "equals" rather than "peers." For example, the Sect. 39 states: "No free man shall be seized or imprisoned, or stripped of his rights or possessions, or outlawed or exiled, or deprived of his standing in any other way, nor will we proceed with force against him, or send others to do so, except by the lawful judgment of his equals or by the law of the land" (Davis 1989).

11. The Court quoted *Strauder v. West Virginia*, 100 U.S. 303, 35, 1880.

12. The jury comprised of the broadly defined peers may lead to two distinct forms of groups for the judicial decision-making system. First, the jury can deny participatory opportunities to the judge, prosecutors, or other governmental officials and administrators from serving as members of the jury. Many states still give automatic exemptions from jury service to judges, prosecutors, police officers, or other governmental officials who play a vital function in the criminal justice system, suggesting that a jury of the broadly defined peers do not necessarily include and equate them as their equals. On the other hand, the inclusion of the professional judges as members of the broadly defined equals or peers may lead to a judicial decision-making process and judicial structure other than the jury system or the jury decision-making body.

Since the history of American juries reflects the member of the jury of peers functioning as fact-finders and community spokespersons, a judicial system based on the bench trial or the mixed tribunal systems may also be recognized as alternative judicial structures to the jury system, because the professional judge, for example, is regarded as a member of the decision makers within the broadly defined equals or peers. Research has shown, however, that few seriously argue for the abolition of the jury system or such trials (Fukurai and Davies 1997).

13. Professor Toni M. Massaro, for example, distinguishes the following two terms which are closely related, but are distinctly different: (1) empathy and (2) sympathy. "The idea behind the peer concept . . . is to assure empathy, not sympathy, for the accused. . . . Sympathy . . . suggests an affinity or relationship with another such that the feelings, volitions, or ideas of another are shared or mutually experienced. Sympathy is a form of shared caring and will incline one to reach a particular result without regard to applicable neutral standards" (1986, 552).

14. Another example of narrowly defined peers can be also seen in the Court's review in *Hoyt v. Florida,* (368 U.S. 57, 1961). A woman was convicted of killing her husband with a baseball bat. She was driven to murder her husband by his adultery and rejection of her. As a defense, she pleaded temporary insanity. However, an all male jury convicted her of second degree murder. She challenged the affirmative registration practice in Florida, which required women who wanted to serve on juries to go to the courthouse and formally register, whereas men were automatically registered and eligible to jury service. The affirmative registration certainly limited women's jury participation. In Hillsborough County, where the crime was committed, of the 114,000 registered voters, approximately 46,000 were female. However, only 220 women had volunteered for jury duty through affirmative registration (*Hoyt v. Florida,* 368 U.S. 57 65, 1961). The defense argued that not only did the jury panel fail to represent the community, but the jury also failed to include her peers, that is, women. However, the Court denied her claim, stating that:

> the jury selection in Florida has given women an absolute exemption from jury duty based solely on their sex, no similar exemption obtaining as to men. . . . Despite the enlightened emancipation of women from the restrictions and protections of bygone years, and their entry into many parts of community life formerly considered to be reserved to men, woman is still regarded as the center of *home and family life* (*Hoyt v. Florida,* 368 U.S. 57 64, 1961) (emphasis added).

15. The proposal such as affirmative peremptories (or affirmative inclusion) shows that race or gender is no longer the key identifier for the selection of empathetic jurors. See chapter 4 for our discussion of peremptory inclusive methods. For extended discussions of affirmative peremptories, see also Donna J. Meyer (1994) and Deborah Ramirez (1995).

CHAPTER 6: SHORTCOMINGS OF PROCEDURALLY BASED REMEDIES

1. These are the actual phrases specified in jury qualification questionnaires sent out by the jury commissioner's office of Orange County, California.

2. Again the jury qualification questionnaire specifically uses the phrases as specified in the main text.

3. Again, the probability is based on an one-tailed test, assuming that whites are more likely than racial minorities to be selected to serve on juries.

4. The 1994 report of the New York Jury Project recommends that for the first three days of service, employers are required to pay their juror-employees $40, the same as the federal rate. Thereafter, for longer trial commitment, the court may pay $40 per day unless the employer continues to compensate the employee for the remainder of jurors' service (McMahon 1994, 98). Similarly the American Bar Association recommends that employers be required to pay jurors' salaries for the first three days of jury service (ABA 1993, 135). In order to balance the organizational inequities in firms' jury leave policies, the New York Jury Project recommends that unemployed jurors and those who work for employers with fewer than nineteen employees should receive $40 per day from the state beginning with the first day of jury service (98–99).

5. Currently, thirty-eight states exclude from jury service persons who are incompetent "by reason of physical or mental ability to render satisfactory jury service" ; thirty-nine states also exclude persons who cannot read, speak, and/or understand the English language; and twelve exclude persons of unsound mind or who are insane or adjudicated incompetent (Bleyer, McCarty, and Wood 1995, 250).

6. See table 11, "Citizenship status of the foreign-born population: 1890 to 1950 and 1970 to 1990," Source: U.S. Bureau of the Census (Internet release date: March 9, 1999)," http://www.census.gov/population/www/documentation/twps0029/tab11.html.

CHAPTER 7: JURY NULLIFICATION AND THE MINORITY-DOMINANT CRIMINAL JURY

1. Nancy J. King (1996) also provides interesting elaborations of different views of jury nullification between two of the most prominent legal scholars on this subject, Jeffrey Abramson and Paul Butler.

2. Public surveys show that the understanding of presumed innocence may have been influenced by pervasiveness of media scrutiny in the Simpson trial. For instance, the 1994 Time/CNN pretrial poll indicated that the pervasive media scrutiny of the Simpson case led 69 percent of African Americans to believe that Simpson would not receive a fair trial because the media's general tone already assumed Simpson's guilt; only 37 percent of whites felt the same way. Similarly the finding showed that only 24 percent of African Americans thought that all races were treated in the same way by the criminal justice system, with 50 percent of whites feeling the same way. The Gallup poll commissioned by the American Bar Association in October 1994 found that 80 percent of survey respondents believe that celebrities receive favorable treatment in the courts (DeBenedictis 1994). The 1995 January poll conducted by the Associated Press found that 57 percent of respondents said that the Simpson criminal charges were true or probably true, while only 18 percent said that they were not true or probably not true (Carlsen 1995). The 1995 May California Survey also found that 75 percent felt that Simpson was guilty: 78 percent of white respondents believed Simpson's guilt while 50 percent of African Americans felt so, up from findings of its previous survey. Another Harris poll found that 61 percent of white respondents thought that the defendant was guilty, while 68 percent of African Americans said "not guilty." While results for whites were virtually unchanged from the 1994 Gallup poll, only 8 percent of African Americans said that the

defendant was guilty, down from 16 percent in the earlier poll (Noble 1995). Another poll finding also indicated that the pervasive media publicity of the Simpson trial caused the public interest in serving on juries to drop more than 50 percent after the Simpson trial began (Curriden 1995). The pervasive public scrutiny and intense media coverage of the trial thus exerted significance influence on potential jurors' perceptions for the possibility for a fair trial and their assessment of the presumption of innocence.

3. Thomas Riordan (1994) argues that racial bias and police brutality were the status quo throughout the LAPD, and that disciplinary actions for police officers have been nonexistent (709–710).

4. Josephine Chow (1992) also argues that although the LAPD's policy against racism disapproves of racially and ethnically oriented remarks, referring to such messages as inappropriate, the policy has not been enforced (898).

The Independent Commission led by Warren Christopher also found that in Los Angeles there were a significant number of officers who repetitively misuse force and persistently ignore the written policies and guidelines of the department regarding force. The commission reported:

> The problem of excessive force in the LAPD is fundamentally a problem of supervision, management, and leadership. What leaps out from the Department's own statistics—and is confirmed by LAPD officers at the command level and in the rank and file—is that a "problem group" of officers use force, and are the subject of complaints alleging excessive or improper force, far more frequently than most other officers. Yet, the evidence obtained by the Commission shows that this group has received inadequate supervisory and management attention (Christopher 1991, 32).

CHAPTER 8: JURY NULLIFICATION AND AFFIRMATIVE ACTION JURIES

1. Because of the negligence of medical personnel at the hospital who failed to notice a second knife wound on his body, Rosenbaum would probably have lived. For greater details, see John Kifner (1991c).

2. The post-verdict interviews revealed that the jurors believed that "the police were not honest" (McFadden 1992).

3. The perception that political pressure has driven the efforts to reprosecute Nelson was compounded, however, when District Attorney Charles J. Hynes announced his candidacy for New York State Attorney General in January 1994, raising suspicion about his motive to persuade United States Attorney General Reno to conduct a federal prosecution after he unsuccessfully prosecuted in state court. Hynes was also joined by Representative Charles Schumer (D.-NY) to convince Reno to spend more time outlining what many have said would be an extremely difficult civil rights case (Hellmann 1994, 149, fn26)

4. Nelson subsequently moved to Georgia and was convicted of slashing a schoolmate in a separate, criminal trial, and he was also the subject of a federal prosecution for violating Rosenbaum's civil rights under 18 U.S.C. Sect. 245(b)(2)(B) which requires that

federal prosecutors would have to show that the murder was due to the victim's religion and in connection with his use of a "public facility." See generally Francis A. McMorris (1994). See also *United States v Nelson,* Cr. No. 94–823 (EDNY, 1994). For more recent information on the further development of the case, see Karen Freifeld (2002).

   5. See United States Constitution Amend. V ("nor shall any person be subject for the same offence to be twice put in jeopardy of life or limb").

   6. Cert. denied, 420 U.S. 946, 1975.

   7. See generally the FIJAs home page, "Official FIJA Web Site," at http://www.fija.org.

BIBLIOGRAPHY

"100 year old clan feud is behind 3 Mendocino County killings." 1995. *San Francisco Chronicle*, 17 April, c14.

ABA. 1993. Committee on Jury Standards Relating to Juror Use and Management. Chicago, IL: American Bar Association.

Abramson, Jeffrey. 1994. *We, the Jury: The Jury System and the Ideal of Democracy.* New York: Basic Books.

————. 1995. "After the O.J. Trial: The Quest to Create a Color-blind Jury." *Chronicle of Higher Education,* 3 November, B1.

Abu-Jamal, Mumia. 1991. "Teetering on the Brink: Between Death and Life." *Yale Law Journal* 100: 993–1003.

Adrian, Jeremy. 1992. "Fear eats the soul in little Tehran: Arrests of Illegal Iranian Aliens in Tokyo, Japan." *Businessweek,* n 3585, (October 5): 30d.

Altman, Lawrence J. 1991. "Jury Declines to Indict a Doctor Who Said He Aided in a Suicide." *New York Times,* 27 July, A1.

Altman, Tracey L. 1986. "Note, Affirmative Action: A New Response to Peremptory Challenge Abuse." *Stanford Law Review* 38: 800–812.

Alschuler, Albert W. 1989. "The Supreme Court and the Jury: Voir Dire, Peremptory Challenges, and the Review of Jury Verdicts." *University of Chicago Law Review* 56: 153–233.

Amar, Akhil Reed. 1984. "Note: Choosing Representatives by Lottery Voting." *Yale Law Journal* 93:1283–1308.

————. 1991. "The Bill of Rights as a Constitution." *Yale Law Journal* 100:1131–1210.

Amar, Vikram David. 1995. "Jury Service as Political Participation Akin to Voting." *Cornell Law Review* 80: 203–259.

Archer, Dane, Les Chun, Chris De La Ronde, Veronica Fiske, Chris Heavey, Jon Hussey, Bonita Iritani, Sung Hae Kim, Terre Meyerhoff, and Catherine Smith. 2001. "A Code for Thematic Violence: A New Application of Content Analysis." Santa Cruz: University of California.

Arnold, Richard S. 1993. "Trial by Jury: The Constitutional Right to a Jury of Twelve in Civil Trials." *Hofstra Law Review* 22:1-35.

Associated Press. 2000. "Presidential Candidates React to Diallo Verdict." *Nation and World,* 26 February.

Babbie, Earl. 1995. *The Practice of Social Research.* Belmont, CA: Wadsworth Publishing Company.

"Baishin seido ga sutaato." 1963. *Ryukyu Shinpo,* 20 March, evening news edition.

Baldus, David C., George Woodworth, and Charles A. Pulaski, Jr. 1990. *Equal Justice and the Death Penalty: A Legal and Empirical Analysis.* Boston, MA: Northeastern University Press.

Barber, Jeremy W. 1994. "The Jury is Still Out: The Role of Jury Science in the Modern American Courtroom." *American Criminal Law Review* 31: 1225–1252.

Barnes, Richard L. 1995. "Quotas as Satin-lined Traps." *New England Law Review* 29: 865–882.

Barringer, Felicity. 1989. "Mixed-race Generation Emerges But Is Not Sure Where It Fits." *New York Times,* 24 September, p.22.

Bedau, Hugo Adam and Michael L. Radelet. 1987. "Miscarriages of Justice in Potentially Capital Cases." *Stanford Law Review* 40: 21–179.

Berke, Richard L. 1993. "Clinton Picks Miami Woman, Veteran State Prosecutor, to be His Attorney General; The Third Choice; President Appears Eager to Move Past Turmoil of Baird and Wood." *New York Times,* 12 February, A1.

Bell, Derrick. 1980. *Race, Racism and American Law.* Boston, MA: Little, Brown.

———. 1989. "Xerces and the Affirmative Action Mystique." *George Washington Law Review* 57: 1595–1613.

Bentler, Peter M., and Douglas G. Bonett. 1980. "Significance Tests and Goodness of Fit in the Analysis of Covariances Structure." *Psychological Bulletin* 88:588–606.

Bleyer, Kristi, Kethryn S. McCarty, and Erica Wood. 1995. "Access to Jury Service for Persons with Disabilities." *Mental and Physical Disability Law Reporter* 19: 249–254.

Blum, Andrew. 1995. "Poll: More Lawyers See O.J. Walking." *National Law Journal,* 27 February, A1.

Blum, David. 1980. "Jury System is Found Guilty of Shortcomings in Some Complex Cases." *Wall Street Journal,* 9 June, p. 1.

Bollen, Kenneth A. 1989. *Structural Equations With Latent Variables.* New York: A. John Wiley and Sons.

Bonora, Beth and Elissa Krauss. 1993. *Jurywork: Systematic Techniques.* New York: Boardman.

Booth, William. 1993. "Law Officer Is Acquitted in Florida." *Washington Post,* 29 May, A1.

———. 1994. "Jackson, Miss.: The City Time Remembers—Has It Really Changed Since the Murder of Medgar Evers?" *Washington Post,* 11 February at B1.

Bowditch, Gillian. 1997. "Scots and English Are Different Races, Tribunal Decides," *London Times,* 29 March, p.4.

Braden, Ann. 1965. "The Southern Freedom Movement in Perspective." *Monthly Review* 17:3.

Brest, Paul. 1987. "Affirmative Action and the Constitution: Three Theories." *Iowa Law Review* 72: 281–285.

Brown, Cynthia L. 1994. "A Challenge to the English-language Requirement of the Juror Qualification Provision of New York's Judiciary Law." *New York Law School Law Review* 39: 479–510.

Brown, Darryl K. 1994. "The Role of Race in Jury Impartiality and Venue Transfers." *Maryland Law Review* 53: 107–156.

Bush, Jonathan A. " 'You're Gonna Miss Me When I'm Gone': Early Modern Common Law Discourse and the Case of Jews." *Wisconsin Law Review* (1993): 1225–1285.

Butler, Paul. 1995a. "Racially Based Jury Nullification: Black Power in the Criminal Justice System." *Yale Law Journal* 105: 677–725.

———. 1995b. "Black Jurors: Right to Acquit?" *Harper's Magazine* 291: 11.

California Jury Instructions: Criminal (CALJIC), 5th ed. 1988. St. Paul, MN: West Publishing.

Callahan, Mary. 1997. "Throng of Supporters Cheers Verdicts." *Press Democrat,* 24 September.

Cammack, Mark. 1995. "In Search of the Post-positivist Jury." *Indiana Law Journal* 70: 405-489.

Carlsen, William. 1995. "Most in Poll Think O.J. Did It: Public Interest in Murder Case." *San Francisco Chronicle,* 20 January, A3.

Carlsen, William and John Wildermuth. 1995. "O.J. Calls In, While Jurors Speak Out Simpson Tells CNN of 'Misrepresentations.' " *San Francisco Chronicle,* 5 October, A1.

Cavalli-Sforza, L. Luca, Paolo Menozzi, and Aloberto Piazza. 1994. *The History of Geography of Human Genes.* Princeton, N.J.: Princeton University Press.

Cecil, Joe S., E. Allan Lind, and Gordon Bermant. 1987. *Jury Service in Lengthy Civil Trials.* Federal Judicial Center.

Chiang, Harriet. 1995a. "Lawyers Say Swift Decision Bodes Ill for O.J." *San Francisco Chronicle,* 3 October, A1.

———. 1995b. "O.J. Backlash Worries Defense Attorneys." *San Francisco Chronicle,* 5 October, A3.

———. 1997. "O.J. Jury Forced to Start Over: Asian Alternate Replaces Dismissed Black Juror." *San Francisco Chronicle,* 1 February, A1.

Chiles, Nick. 1993. "Critical Moments in Crown Heights." *Newsday,* 20 July, p. 80.

Chow, Josephine. 1992. "Sticks and Stones Will Break My Bones, But Will Racist Humor? A Look Around the World at Whether Police Officers Have a Free Speech Right to Engage in Racist Humor." *Loyola of Los Angeles International and Comparative Law Journal* 14: 851–901.

Christopher, Warren. 1991. *Report of the Independent Commission on the Los Angeles Police Department.* LA: Independent Commission.

Clark, Lewis. 1975. *The Grand Jury, the Use and Abuse of Political Power.* New York: Quadrangle/New York Times Book Co.

Clary, Mike. 1993. "Miami on Edge as Ex-Policeman's Retrial to Begin." *Los Angeles Times,* 8 May, A14.

Cocke, A. K. 1979. "Constitutional Law—Sixth Amendment Right to Trial by Jury—Five Jurors Are Not Enough." *Tennessee Law Review* 46: 847–864.

Cockburn, Alexander. 1995. "White Rage: The Press and the Verdict." *Nation* 261: 491–493.

Coke, Tanya E. 1994. "Lady Justice May be Blind, But Is She a Soul Sister? Race-neutrality and the Ideal of Representative Juries." *New York University Law Review* 69: 327–386.

Colbert, Douglas L. 1990. "Challenging the Challenge: Thirteenth Amendment as a Prohibition Against the Racial Use of Peremptory Challenges." *Cornell Law Review* 76:1–128.

Coleman, James William. 1994. *The Criminal Elite: The Sociology of White-Collar Crime.* New York: St. Martin's Press.

Connell, Rich and Sonia Nazario. 1995. "How Well Does It Work? A Visit to America's Factories and Offices, Based on a Times Analysis, Shows Affirmative Action Has Produced Striking, If Uneven Results That Have Helped Fuel Debate Over Who Benefits—and at . . . ," *Los Angeles Times,* 10 September, A1.

Constable, Marianne. 1994. *The Law of the Other.* Chicago, IL: University of Chicago Press.

Contemporary Social Issues in Los Angeles: A Panel Discussion-Final Report. 1992. Santa Cruz: University of California, Social Science Division.

Cooper, Marc. 1995. "Jury's Still Out: White Americans' Reactions to the O.J. Simpson Double Murder Trial Verdict." *Nation* 261: 488.

Crewdson, John. 1980. "10 Die in Miami Riot: Arson and Looting Persist for 2nd Day." *New York Times,* 19 May, A1.

Crispell, Diane. 1993. "Interracial Children Pose Challenge For Classifiers." *Wall Street Journal,* 27 January, B1

Curriden, Mark. 1995. "No one Agrees on Whether the System is Broken, but Everyone is Trying to Change It." *ABA Journal* 81: 72–76.

Davis, Godfrey. 1989. *Magna Carta.* London: British Library.

Davis, Dena S. 1993. "Ironic Encounter: African-Americans, American Jews, and the Church-state Relationship." *Catholic University Law Review* 43:109–141.

De Vos, George A., and William O. Wetherall. 1983. *Japan's Minorities: Burakumin, Koreans, Ainu and Okinawans.* London: Minority Rights Group.

de Vries, Sijiera and Thomas F. Pettigrew. 1994. "A Comparative Perspective on Affirmative Action: Positieve Aktie in the Netherlands." *Basic and Applied Social Psychology* 15: 179–199.

DeBenedictis, Don J. 1994. "The National Verdict." *ABA Journal,* October, p. 53.

Decker, Cathleen. 1995. "Most Back Anti-bias Policy But Spurn Racial Preferences." *Los Angeles Times,* 30 March, A1.

Derrida, Jacques. 1981. *Dissemination.* Chicago, IL: University of Chicago Press.

Deutsch, Linda. 1995. " 'Mountain of Evidence' May Not Overcome Gaps, Miscues and a Charismatic O.J. Simpson." *San Francisco Examiner,* 17 July.

"Developments in the law: Race and the Criminal Process." 1988. *Harvard Law Review* 101:1472–60.

Dillon, Sam. 1996. "Don't be a Stranger, says Mexico to Emigres in the U.S." *New York Times,* 10 December, A5.

DiPerna, Paula. 1984. *Juries on Trial: Faces of American Justice.* New York: Dembner Books.

Dobbs, Marjorie O. 1992. "Note: Jury Traumatization in High Profile Criminal Trials: A Case for Crisis Debriefing?" *Law and Psychology Review* 16: 201.

Domitrovich, Stephanie. 1994. "Fury Source Lists and the Community's Need to Achieve Racial Balance on the jury." *Duquesne Law Review* 33:39–103.

Dripps, Donald A. 1987. "The Constitutional Status of the Reasonable Doubt Rule." *California Law Review* 75:1665–1718.

Drizin, Steven A., and Stephen K. Harper. 2000. "Old Enough to Kill, Old Enough to Die." *San Francisco Chronicle* 16 April, P1.

Dustin, Dan. 1986. *How to Avoid Jury Duty: A Guilt Free Guide.* La Mesa, CA: Mockingbooks.

Ellers, Elizabeth. 1993. "Vision: A Plan for the Future of California's Courts." *Southern California Law Review* 66: 2183–2197.

Elliott, Jeff. 1995. "The Dark Legacy of Nome Cult." Albion Monitor, 2 September.

———. 1997. "Bitter Victory." *Albion Monitor,* 4 October.

Equal Employment Opportunity Commission. 1992. *Standard Form 100 Instruction Booklet 5.* Washington, DC: The Commission.

"Extradition Ordered in Evers Murder Case." 1991. *Los Angeles Times,* 4 June, A21.

FACTS (Families to Amend California's Three-Strikes). 2000. "Latest Statistics." http://www.facts1.com/general/stats.htm#4,076.

Fagan, Jeffrey and Garth Davies. 2000. "Street Stops and Broken Windows: Terry, Race, and Disorder in New York City," *Fordham Urban Law Review* 28:457–504.

Fahringer, Herald Price. 1995. " 'And Then There Were None': The Fate of Peremptory Challenges in New York." *Saint John's Journal of Legal Commentary* 10:291–302.

Farber, Daniel A., and Suzanna Sherry. 1997. *Beyond All Reason: The Radical Assault on Truth in American Law.* New York: Oxford University Press.

Finkel, Norman J. 1995. *Commonsense Justice: Jurors' Notions of the Law.* Cambridge, MA: Harvard University Press.

Fisher, Marc. 1993. "Germans Link Deaths to Far-Right Climate." *Washington Post,* 4 June, A20.

Flowers, Roberta K. 2000. "An Unholly Alliance: The Ex-parte Relationship Between the Judge and the Prosecutor." *Nebraska Law Review* 79:251–292.

Ford, Christopher A. 1994. "Administering Identity: The Determination of 'Race' in Race-Conscious Law." *California Law Review* 82: 1231–1285.

Freifeld, Karen. 2002. "Feds' Move Outrages Rosenbaums." *Newsday,* 9 March, A11.

Fuenfrios, Guillermo. 1993. "The Emergence of the New Chicano." In *Aztlan: An Anthology of Mexican American Literature.* (Edited by Luis Valdez and Stan Steiner). New York: Knopf.

Fukurai, Hiroshi. 1994. "Racial Empowerment in Grand Jury Indictment: Race, the Jury, and the Challenges of Social Control." A Paper presented at the 1994 annual meeting of American Society of Criminology in Miami, Florida.

———. 1996. "Race, Social Class, and Jury Participation: New Dimensions for Evaluating Discrimination in Jury Service and Jury Selection." *Journal of Criminal Justice* 24:71–88.

———. 1997. "A Quota Jury: Affirmative Action in Jury Selection." *Journal of Criminal Justice* 25:477–500.

———. 1999a. "The Representative Jury Requirement: Jury Representativeness and Cross-Sectional Participation From the Beginning to the End of the Jury Selection Process." *International Journal of Comparative and Applied Criminal Justice* 23: 55–90.

———. 1999b. "Social Deconstruction of Race and Affirmative Action in Jury Selection." *La Raza Law Journal* 11:17–68.

———. 2000. "Where Did Hispanic Jurors Go? Racial and Ethnic Disenfranchisement in the Grand Jury and the Search for Justice." *Western Criminology Review* 2, n. 2: http://wcr.sonoma.edu/v2n2/fukurai.html.

———. 2001. "Critical Evaluations of Hispanic Participation on the Grand Jury: Keyman Selection, Jury Mandering, Language, and Representative Quotas." *Texas Hispanic Journal of Law and Policy* 5: 7–39.

Fukurai, Hiroshi and Edgar W. Butler. 1991a. "Organization, Labor Force, and Jury Representation: Economic Excuses and Jury Participation." *Jurimetrics* 32: 49–69.

———. 1991b. "Computer-aided Evaluations of Racial Representation in Jury Selection." *Computers, Environment and Urban Systems* 16: 131–155.

———. 1994. "Sources of Racial Disenfranchisement in the Jury and Jury Selection System." *National Black Law Journal* 13:238–275.

Fukurai, Hiroshi and Darryl Davies. 1997. "Affirmative Action in Jury Selection: Racially Representative Juries, Racial Quotas, and Affirmative Juries of the Hennepin Model and the Jury De Medietate Linguae." *Virginia Journal of Social Policy and the Law* 4:645–681.

Fukurai, Hiroshi, Edgar W. Butler, and Richard Krooth. 1991a. "Where Did Black Jurors Go? A Theoretical Synthesis of Racial Disenfranchisement in the Jury System and Jury Selection." *Journal of Black Studies* 22, no. 2: 196–215.

———. 1991b. "A Cross-sectional Jury Representation or Systematic Jury Representation? Simple Random and Cluster Sampling Strategies in Jury Selection." *Journal of Criminal Justice* 19: 31–48

———. 1993. *Race and the Jury: Racial Disenfranchisement and the Search for Justice.* New York: Plenum Press.

———. 1994. "The Rodney King Beating Verdicts." In *The 1992 Los Angeles Riots and Rebellion.* Edited by Mark Baldassare. 73–102. CO: Westview Press.

Fukurai, Hiroshi, Darryl Davies, Anne Shin, Belinda Lum, and Michael Shin. 1997. "The Ironies of Affirmative Action: Empirical Analyses of UC Students' Views on Fallacies and Problems of Affirmative Action." *California Sociologist* 24: 71–88.

Funderburg, Lisa. 1994. *White, Other: Biracial Americans Talk About Race and Identity.* New York: W. Morrow and Co.

Geniella, Mike. 1997a, " Deputy's Wife Breaks Silence." *Press Democrat,* 3 October.

———. 1997b. "Verdicts for Lincoln Mystify Prosecutor." *Press Democrat,* 1 October.

———. 1997c. "'We Just Couldn't Get Beyond a Reasonable Doubt'." *Press Democrat,* 30 September.

———. 1997d. "Bear Lincoln Acquitted on Murder Charges." *Press Democrat,* 24 September.

———. 1998. "Mendocino D.A. Upset Creates Stir." *Press Democrat,* 5 November.

Gilbert, M. Shanara. 1993. "An Ounce of Prevention: A Constitutional Prescription for Choice of Venue in Racially Sensitive Criminal Cases." *Tulane Law Review* 67: 1855–1944.

Glennon, Robert Jerome. 1994. "The Jurisdictional Legacy of the Civil Rights Movement." *Tennessee Law Review* 61: 869–932.

Golash, Deirdre. 1986. "Race, Fairness, and Jury Selection." *Behavioral Science and the Law* 10:155–177.

Gold, James H. 1984. "Voir Dire: Questioning Prospective Jurors on their Willingness to Follow the Law." *Indiana Law Journal* 60: 163–190.

Goldberg-Ambrose, Charole. 1997. *Planting Tail Feathers: Tribal Survival and Public Law 280.* Los Angeles, CA: American Indian Studies Center, University of California, Los Angeles.

Goldman, John J. "Four Officers Acquitted in New York Shooting Death." *LA Times,* 26 February.

Goldman, Olivia Q. 1994. "The Need for an Independent International Mechanism to Protect Group Rights: A Case Study of the Kurds." *Tulsa Journal of Comparative and International Law,* 2: 44–89.

Gottleib, Martin. "Emotions Rise on U.S. Inquiry in Crown Heights." *New York Times,* 9 November, B1.

Goyer, Doreen S., and Eliane Domschke. 1983. *The Handbook of National Population Censuses.* Westport, CT: Greenwood Press.

Graber, Mark A. 1997. "Desperately Ducking Slavery: Dred Scott and Contemporary Constitutional Theory." *Constitutional Commentary* 14: 271–318.

Gross, Charles. 1908. *Select Cases Concerning the Law Merchant.* London: B. Quaritch.

Gunnison, R. B. 1995. "Wilson Sues His Own State: New Attempt to Halt Affirmative Action." *San Francisco Chronicle* 11 August, A1.

Haney, Craig and Aida Hurtado. 1994. "The Jurisprudence of Race and Meritocracy: Standardized Testing and 'Race-Neutral' Racism in the Workplace." *Law and Human Behavior* 18: 223–248.

Haney-Lopez, Ian F. 1994. "The Social Construction of Race: Some Observations on Illusion, Fabrication, and Choice." *Harvard Civil Rights-Civil Liberties Law Review* 29: 1–62.

———. 1996. *White by Law: The Legal Construction of Race.* New York: New York University Press.

Hans, Valerie and Neil Vidmar. 1986. *Judging the Jury.* New York: Plenum Press.

Hansen, Mark. 1993a. "New Trial for White Supremacist? Defense Claims Retrial in 30-Year-Old Murder Case Would Be Unconstitutional." *ABA Journal* 79:21.

Hansen, Mark. 1993b. "Third Trial Allowed: White Supremacist Loses Appeal." *ABA Journal* 79:26.

Harris, Cheryl. 1993. "Whiteness as Property." *Harvard Law Review* 106: 1709–1791.

Harrison, Eric. 1995. "New Facts on '66 Slaying of Rights Leader Reach Light of Day: FBI Releases Sealed Documents on Unsolved Murder of Vernon Dahmer—Family Has Been Seeking Retrial of Klansmen Who Escaped Conviction." *Los Angeles Times* 26 April, A5.

Hastie, Reid. 1993. *Inside the Juror: The Psychology of Juror Decision Making.* Cambridge, MA: Cambridge University Press.

Hastie, Reid, Steven Penrod, and Nancy Pennington. 1983. *Inside the Jury.* Cambridge, MA: Harvard University Press.

Hazard, Geoffrey C. 1993. "Some Say Mayor Dinkins' Questionning Was Typical. That May Be the Problem." *National Law Journal* 16:15.

Heimann, Mark. 1995. "'Bear' Lincoln Surrenders." *Albion Monitor,* 19 August.

Heiser, Robert. 1974. *The Destruction of California Indians.* Lincoln, NE: University of Nebraska Press.

Hellmann, Kevin J. 1994. "The Fallacy of Dueling Sovereignties: Why the Supreme Court Refuses to Eliminate the Dual Sovereignty Doctrine." *Journal of Law and Policy* 2:149–185.

Herbert, Bob. 1994. "Freedom Summer '94: Remembering 1964 Civil Rights Activists James Chaney, Michael Schwerner, and Andrew Goodman." *New York Times,* 26 June, E17.

Herman, Shael. 1992. "Legacy and Legend: The Continuity of Roman and English Regulation of Jews." *Tulane Law Review* 66: 1781–1851.

Herman, Susan N. 1993. "Why the Court Loves Batson: Representation-reinforcement, Colorblindness, and the Jury." *Tulane Law Review* 67: 1807–1853.

Heumann, Milton and Lance Cossak. 1983. "No-So-Blissful Ignorance: Informing Jurors About Punishment in Mandatory Sentencing Cases." *American Criminal Law Review* 20:343–360.

Hoffman, Morris, B. 1997. "Peremptory Challenges Should Be Abolished: A Trial Judge's Perspective." *University of Chicago Law Review* 64: 809–871.

Holding, R. 1995. "Prop. 187 Debates Goes on in Court: No Sign From Judge on Ruling." *San Francisco Chronicle,* 27 July, A 13.

Howe, Ruth-Arlene, W. 1995. "Redefining the Transracial Adoption Controversy." *Duke Journal of Gender Law and Policy* 2: 131–164.

Hubert, Cynthia. 1995. "O.J. Furman on Sidelines as Defense Winds Up Case." *San Francisco Examiner,* 8 September.

Japanese Federation of Bar Associations (JFBA). 1992. *Okinawano Baishin Saiban (Jury Trials in Okinawa).* Tokyo: Takachiho Shobo.

Jenga, Matsu Saito. 1995. "Finding Our Voices, Teaching Our Truth: Reflections on Legal Pedagogy and Asian American Identity." *Asian Pacific American Law Journal* 3: 81–93.

Joe, Jennie. 1991. "The Delivery of Health Care to American Indians: History, Policies, and Prospects." In *American Indians: Social Justice and Public Policy.* Edited by Donald E. Green and Thomas V. Tonnesen. Milwaukee, WI: University of Wisconsin System, Institute on Race and Ethnicity.

Johnson, Paul. 1987. *A History of the Jews.* New York: Harper and Row.

Johnson, Alex M. 1996. "Destabilizing Racial Classifications Based on Insights Gleaned From Trademark Law." *California Law Review* 84: 887–952.

Johnson, Clarence. 1995. "S.F. Board Urges Caution on '3-Strikes': D.A. Advised to Use Discretion in Prosecutions." *San Francisco Chronicle,* 11 July, A18.

Johnson, Sheri Lynn. 1985. "Black Innocence and the White Jury." *Michigan Law Review* 83: 1611–1708.

Joreskog, Karl G., and Dag Sorbom. 1985. *LISREL VI: Analysis of Linear Structural Relationships By the Method of Maximum Likelihood.* Chicago, IL: National Educational Resources.

"Jury Chosen in 3d Evers Trial." 1994. *New York Times,* 27 Jan, A12.

"Jury Seclusion Tough on O.J. Deputies Too." 1995. *San Francisco Examiner,* 23 April, A1.

Kajita, Takamichi. 1995. "Characteristics of the Foreign Workers Problem in Japan: To an Analytical Viewpoint." *Hitotsubashi Journal of Social Studies* 27:1–26.

Kalven, Harry, Jr., and Hans Zeisel. 1966. *The American Jury.* Boston, MA: Little, Brown and Co.

Kaplan, Stanley M., and Carolyn Winget. 1992. "The Occupational Hazards of Jury Duty." *Bulletin of the American Academy of Psychiatry and the Law* 20:325–333.

Karst, Kenneth L. 1995. "Myths of Identity: Individual and Group Portraits of Race and Sexual Orientation." *UCLA Law Review* 43: 263–369.

Kawashima, Yasuhide. 1986. *Puritan Justice and the Indian: White Man's Law in Massachusetts, 1630–1763.* Middletown, CT: Wesleyan University Press.

Kaye, David. 1980. "And Then There Were Twelve: Statistical Reasoning, the Supreme Court, and the Size of the Jury." *California Law Review* 68: 1004.

Keele, Lucy M. 1991. "An Analysis of Six vs. 12-Person Juries." *Tennessee Bar Journal,* Jan.-Feb.: 32–40.

Kerr, Norbert L., and Robert J. MacCoun. 1985. "The Effects of Jury Size and Polling Method on the Process and Product of Jury Deliberation." *Journal of Personality and Social Psychology,* 48, no. 2: 349–363.

Kifner, John. 1991a. "A Boy's Death Ignites Clashes in Crown Heights." *New York Times,* 21 August, B1.

———. 1991b. "Clashes Persist in Crown Heights For 3d Night in Row." *New York Times,* 22 August, B1

———. 1991c. "Stabbing Victim's Brother Seeks Answers." *New York Times,* 11 November, B3.

King, James D. 1994. "Political Culture, Registration Laws, and Voter Turnout Among the American States." *Publius* 24: 115–127.

King, Nancy J. 1993a. "Racial Jurymandering: Cancer or Cure? A Contemporary Review of Affirmative Action in Jury Selection." *New York University Law Review* 68:707–776.

———. 1993b. "Post Conviction Review of Jury Discrimination: Measuring the Effects of Juror Race on Jury Decisions." *Michigan Law Review* 92: 63–130.

———. 1994. "The Effect of Race-Conscious Jury Selection on Public Confidence in the Fairness of Jury Proceedings: An Empirical Puzzle (Symposium on bias in justice administration." *American Criminal Law Review* 31: 1177–1201.

———. 1996. "Book Review: We, the Jury, by Jeffrey Abramson." *Cumberland Law Review* 26: 165–175.

Klarman, Michael. 1991. "An Interpretive History of Modern Equal Protection." *Michigan Law Review* 90: 213–318.

Klein, Richard. 1986. "The Emperor Gideon Has No Clothes: The Empty Promise of the Constitutional Right to Effective Assistance of Counsel." *Hastings Constitutional Law Quarterly* 13: 625.

Knutson, Lawrence. 2000. "Rights Leaders to March Against Police Brutality." *Nation and World,* 25 May.

Koch, Adrienne and William Peden. 1944. *The Life and Selected Writings of Thomas Jefferson.* New York: The Modern Library.

Komives, Paul and Peggy Blotner. 1991. "Loss and Restoration of Civil Rights Affecting Disqualification for Federal Jury Service." *Michigan Bar Journal* 70: 542–561.

Kotler, Martin. 2000. "Social Norms and Judicial Rulemaking: Commitment to Political Process and the Basis of Tort Law." *Kansas Law Review* 49: 65–134.

Krooth, Richard. 1972. *"Sojourner truth," Wisconsin Patriot.* Madison, WI: Wisconsin Alliance Press.

———. 1995. *Mexico, NAFTA and the Hardship of Progress.* Jefferson, NC: McFarland and Co.

Krooth, Richard and Minoo Moallem. 1995. *The Middle East: A Geographical Study of the Region in New Global Era.* Jefferson, NC: McFarland and Co.

Labaton, Stephen. 1994. "Reno to Take Over Inquiry in Slaying in Crown Heights." *New York Times,* 25 January, A1.

Ladner, Robert A. 1981. "The Miami Riots of 1980: Antecedent Conditions, Community Responses and Participant Characteristics." *Research in Social Movements, Conflicts and Change* 4:171–214.

LaFraniere, Sharon. 1990. "Murder Charge Filed in Evers Case." *Washington Post,* 19 December, A1.

Laufer, William S. 1995. "The Rhetoric of Innocence." *Washington Law Review* 70: 329–421.

Lauter, David. 1993. "Miami Prosecutor is Atty. Gen. Choice." *Los Angeles Times,* 12 February, A1.

Lempinen, Edward W., and Pamela Burdman. 1996. "Measure to Cut Back Affirmative Action Wins." *San Francisco Chronicle,* 6 November, A1.

Levine, James P. 1992. *Juries and Politics.* Pacific Grove, CA: Brooks/Cole Pub. Co.

Lewis, Neil A. 1993. "4 More Women Are Being Considered for Attorney General." *New York Times,* 11 February, A16.

Lipton, Jack. 1983. "Racism in the Jury Box: The Hispanic Defendant." *Hispanic Journal of Behavioral Sciences* 5: 275–290.

Ludwikowski, Rett R. 1995."Fundamental Constitutional Rights in the New Constitutions of Eastern and Central Europe." *Cardozo Journal of International and Comparative Law* 3:73–162.

Magna Carta: *Exemplification of 1215.* 1995. London: The British Library Board.

Mann, Nyta. 1994. "What Race Wars?" *New Statesman and Society* 7:12–13.

"Many Jurors Consider Deep Pockets and Ignore Presumption of Innocence." 1993. *National Law Journal,* 15, 22 Feb., S 12.

Marcus, Rebecca. 1994. "Racism In Our Courts: The Underfunding of Public Defenders and Its Disproportionate Impact Upon Racial Minorities." *Hastings Constitutional Law Quarterly* 22: 219–267.

Margolick, David. 1989. "Again, Sidney Lumet Ponders Justice." *New York Times,* 31 December, V. 139.

Marion, Samara. 1999. "Justice by Geography? A Study of San Diego County's Three Strikes Sentencing Practices From July-December 1996." *Stanford Law and Policy Review* 11:29–41.

Massaro, Toni M. 1986. "Peremptories or Peers?—Rethinking Sixth Amendment Doctrine, Images, and Procedures." *North Carolina Law Review* 64: 501–564.

McCall, Andrew. 1979. *The Medieval Underworld.* London: H. Hamilton.

McDougall, Harold. 1970. "The Case For Black Juries." *Yale Law Journal* 79: 531–550.

McFadden, Robert D. 1992. "Teen-ager Acquitted in Slaying During '91 Crown Heights Melee." *New York Times,* 30 October, A1.

McKinney, Bill. 1993. "Representation: Should Juries Have More Blacks?" *Erie Morning News,* 13 January, C1.

McLead, Ramon G. 1997. "Tiger Woods: An Emblem for Census Issue Calls For a Multiracial Category on Form Gaining Momentum." *San Francisco Chronicle,* 24 April, A4.

McMahon, Colleen. 1994. *The Jury Project: Report to the Chief Judge of the State of New York.* New York: The Jury Project.

McMorris, Frances A. 1994. "High Hurdles for U.S. Probe on Race Riot." *National Law Journal* 16:8.

McShane, Larry. 1999. "Trial in N.Y. Police Shooting Moved." *Nation and World,* 17 December.

Melilli, Kenneth J. 1996. "Batson in Practice: What We Have Learned About Batson and Peremptory Challenges." *Notre Dame Law Review* 71: 447–503.

Mello, Michael. 1995. "Defunding Death: Challenging Racial Bias in the Application of the Death Penalty." *American Criminal Law Review* 32: 933–1012.

Mendocino Superior Court. 1996. *The Jury Panel Survey at the Superior Courthouse.* Ukiah, Mendocino County, CA.

Meyer, Donna J. 1994. Note: A New Peremptory Inclusion to Increase Representative and Impartiality in Jury Selection." *Case Western Reserve University* 45: 251–289.

Meyer, Jon'a and Paul Jesilow. 1997. *Doing Justice in the People's Court.* Albany, NY: State University of New York Press.

"Miami Still Shows Scars of Rioting." 1980. *Newsweek,* 15 December, 20.

"Military Order of Nov. 13, 2001: Detention, Treatment, and Trial of Certain Non-Citizens in the War Against Terrorism." 2001. *Federal Register* 66 (222): 57831–57836.

"Mississippi May Reopen Klan Killing." 1995. *New York Times,* 2 April, 18(L).

Montgomery, Paul L. 1980. "Anger Long in Rising Among Miami Blacks." *New York Times,* 19 May, A1.

Moore, Lloyd E. 1973. *The Jury, Tool of King's Palladium of Liberty.* Cincinnati, CT: W. H. Anderson Co.

Mori, Hiromi. 1997. *Immigration Policy and Foreign Workers in Japan.* London: Macmillan.

Morse, Rob. 1997. "In Cablinasia, Crustaceans and Kayo rule." *San Francisco Examiner,* 23 April, A2.

Moses, Ray E. 1997. "The Last Word." *Champion* 21:55–60.

Myrdal, Gunnar. 1944. *An American Dilemma: The Negro Problem and Modern Democracy.* New York: Harper and Brothers.

Mydans, Seth. 1992a. "Officers' Assault Trial Nears Opening." *New York Times,* 2 March.

———. 1992b. "Los Angeles Policemen Acquitted in Taped Beating." *New York Times,* 30 April.

"Native Man Framed for Police Murder." 1997. http://kafka.uvic.ca/~vipirg/SISIS/emerg/may08bea.html#overview, May 8 (last revised May 12, 1998).

Nei, Masatoshi and Arun Roychoudhury. 1982. "Genetic Relationship and Evolution of Human Races." *Evolutionary Biology* 14: 1–16.

Nevius, C. W. 1997. "O'Meara, Tiger are Neighbors, Fishing Buddies." *San Francisco Chronicle,* 3 February, E4.

Nishimuro, Kunio. 1995. "Interpreting Justice: Foreigners and Crime in Japan." *Look Japan* 41: 4–7.

Noble, Kenneth B. 1995. "The Simpson Defense: Source of Black Pride." *New York Times,* 6 March, A8.

Nunn, Kenneth. 1995. "The Trial as Text: Allegory, Myth, and Symbol in the Adversarial Criminal Process—A Critique of the Role of the Public Defender and a Proposal for Reform." *American Criminal Law Review* 32: 743–822.

"O.J. Simpson case: A Legal Aberration." 1995. *San Francisco Chronicle,* 7 October, A18.

Office of the Hennepin County Attorney. 1992. *Final Report: Task Force on Racial Composition of the Grand Jury.* Minneapolis, MN: Hennepin County Attorney.

Okrent, Daniel. 2001. "Background Check: Was Babe Ruth Black? More Important, Should We Care?" *Sports Illustrated,* May 7: 27.

Oldham, James C. 1983. "The Origins of the Special Jury." *University of Chicago Law Review* 50: 137–213.

Omi, Michael. 1997. "Racial Identity and the State: The Dilemmas of Classification." *Law and Inequality: A Journal of Theory and Practice.* 15: 7–23.

Omi, Michael and Howard Winant. 1986. *Racial Formation in the United States: From the 1960s to the 1980s.* New York: Routledge and Kegan Paul.

Ooms, Herman. 1996. *Tokugawa Village Practice: Class, Status, Power, Law.* Berkeley, CA: University of California Press.

Ortner, William G. 1993. "Jews, African-Americans, and the Crown Heights Riots: Applying Mutsuda's Proposal to Restrict Racist Speech." *Boston University Law Review* 73: 897–918.

Ott, R. Lyman, Larson, Richard, Cynthia Rexroat, and William Mendenhall. 1992. *Statistics: A Tool for the Social Sciences.* Belmont, CA: Duxbury Press.

Packer, Herbert L. 1968. *The Limits of the Criminal Sanction.* Stanford, CA: Stanford University Press.

Patterson, Orlando. 2001. "Race by the Numbers." *New York Times,* 8 May, A27.

Payson, Kenneth E. 1996. "Check One Box: Reconsidering Directive No. 15 and the Classification of Mixed Race People." *California Law Review* 84: 1233–1291.

Perea, Juan F. 1992. *"Hernandez v. New York." Hofstra Law Review* 21: 1–61.

Pertnoy, Leonard. 1993. "The Juror's Need to Know vs. the Constitutional Right to a Fair Trial." *Dickinson Law Review* 97: 627–654.

Pite, David F. 1980. "Rage in Miami a Warning?" *U.S. News and World Report,* 2 June, p. 19.

Piven, Francis Fox and Richard A. Cloward. 1988. *Why Americans Don't Vote.* New York: Pantheon Books.

Porter, Bruce and Marvin Dunn. 1985. *The Miami Riot of 1980: Crossing the Bounds.* Lexington, MA: D.C. Heath and Co.

Potash. 1973. "Mandatory Inclusion of Racial Minorities in Jury Panels." *Black Law Journal* 3:80–92.

Potter, Harold. 1958. *Potter's Historical Introduction to English Law and Its Institutions.* London: Sweet and Maxwell.

"Presumed innocent." 1992. *National Review* 44:17.

Quinley, Harold E., and Charles Y. Glock. 1972. *Anti-Semitism in America.* New York: Free Press.

"Rage at Verdict." 1980. *Miami Herald,* 18 May, A32.

Ramirez, Deborah. 1994. "The Mixed Jury and the Ancient Custom of Trial by Jury De Medietate Linguae: A History and a Proposal for Change." *Boston University Law Review* 74: 777–818.

———. 1995. "Multicultural Empowerment: It's Not Just Black and White Anymore." *Stanford Law Review* 47: 957–992.

Raskin, Jamin B. 1993. "Legal Aliens, Local Citizens: The Historical, Constitutional and Theoretical Meanings of Alien Suffrage." *University of Pennsylvania Law Review* 141: 1391–1470.

Rich, Frank. 1995. "The Second Wind: Public Anger Over O.J. Simpson Verdict." *New York Times,* 14 October, p. 15.

Riordan, Thomas. 1994. "Copping An Attitude: Rule of Law Lessons From the Rodney King Incident." *Loyola of Los Angeles Law Review* 27: 675–733.

Robinson, V. 1993. "'Race,' Gender, and Internal Migration Within England and Wales." *Environment and Planning* 25: 1453–1465.

Rohter, Larry. 1993. "Miami Police Officer Is Acquitted in Racially Charged Case." *New York Times,* 29 May, 1, 5.

Roper, Robert T. 1980. "Jury Size and Verdict Consistency: A Line Has to be Drawn Somewhere." *Law and Society Review* 1414: 977–995.

Ryoko, Mike. 1991. "Read My Lips, No Quota for Court." *Chicago Tribune,* 2 July, 3.

St. John, Craig, Mark Edwards, and Deeann Wenk. 1995. "Racial Differences in Intraurban Residential Moblity." *Urban Affairs Review* 30: 709–729.

Saito, Chieko. 1993. "A Case of Biracial Identity and Confusion." In *Transference and Empathy in Asian American Psychotherapy.* Edited by Jean Lau Chin, Joan Huser Liem, MaryAnna Domokos-Cheng Ham, and George K. Hong. Westport, CT: Praeger.

Saks, Michael J. 1977. *Jury Verdicts: The Role of Group Size and Social Decision Rule.* Lexington, MA: Lexington Books.

Sampson, Robert J., and Dawn Jeglum Bartusch. 1998. "Legal Cynicism and (Subcultural?) Tolerance of Deviance: The Neighborhood Context of Racial Differences." *Law and Society Review* 32: 777–800.

Saragoza, Alex M., Concepcion R. Juarrez, Abel Valenzuela Jr., and Oscar Gonzalez. 1992. "History and Public Policy: Title VII and the Use of the Hispanic Classification." *La Raza Law Journal* 5:1–27.

Sauer, Kristen K. 1995. "Informed Conviction: Instructing the Jury About Mandatory Sentencing Consequences." *Columbia Law Review* 95: 1232–1272.

Scheflin, Alan W. 1972. "Jury Nullification: The Right To Say No." *California Law Review* 45: 168.

Scheflin, Alan W. and Jon Van Dyke. 1980. "Jury Nullification: The Contours of a Controversy." *Law and Contemporary Problems* 43: 1–120

Schafmann, Sigrid. 2001. "Women in United Germany." Ph.D. diss., Golden Gate University, Public Policy Administration.

Scott, Philip B. 1989. "Jury Nullification: An Historical Perspective on a Modern Debate." *West Virginia Law Review* 91: 389–432.

Seabrook, Jeremy. 1992. "Land of Broken Toys: Racism in Liverpool, England." *New Statesman and Society* 5: 16–17.

Sheriff Abuse Hearing. 1991. LA: Los Angeles County Sheriff's Department.

Silvergate, Harvey A. 1995. "Simpson Jury Sends a Subtle Message on Race." *National Law Journal* vol. 18: 16 October, A21.

Simon, Rita J. 1992. "Jury Nullification, or Prejudice and Ignorance in the Marion Barry Trial." *Journal of Criminal Justice* 20: 261–266.

Small, Stephen. 1994. *Racialized Barriers: The Black Experience in the United States and England in the 1980s.* NY: Routledge and Kegan Paul.

Smith, Abbe. 1998. " 'Nice Work If You Can Get It,' Ethical Jury Selection in Criminal Defense." *Fordham Law Review* 67:523–568.

Smith, Louis N. 1993. "Final Report of the Hennepin County Attorney's Task Force on Racial Composition of the Grand Jury." *Hamline Law Review* 16: 879–921.

Smothers, Ronald. 1994a. "No Testimony by Defendant in '63 Slaying: Defense in Evers Killing Ends Its Presentation." *New York Times,* 4 February, A7.

———. 1994b. "White Supremacist is Convicted of Slaying Rights Leader in '63: Beckwith 73, Gets Life Sentence for Killing Medgar Evers." *New York Times,* 6 February, 1(N), 1(L).

Snyder, George. 1994. "Change of Venue Asked in Polly Slaying Trial." *San Francisco Chronicle*, 7 December. 1994.

———. 1995. "Not Guilty Plea in Slaying on Mendocino Reservation." *San Francisco Chronicle*, 1 September, A21.

———. 1996. "Families Sue Cops Over Manhunt at Reservation." *San Francisco Chronicle*, 1 June, A19.

———. 1997a. "Judge Orders Jury Tampering Probe in Murder Case." *San Francisco Chronicle*, 27 June, A23.

———. 1997b. "Mendocino Acquittal Explained: Juror Said Cop Shooting Was in Self-Defense." *San Francisco Chronicle*, 3 October, A17.

Sowell, Thomas. 1983. *The Economics of Politics of Race: An International Perspective*. New York: W. Morrow.

Stacey, Robert C. 1992. "The Conversion of Jews to Christianity in Thirteenth-century England." *Speculum: A Journal of Medieval Studies* 67:263–283.

Steele, Shelby. 1990. *The Content of Our Character: A New Vision of Race in America*. New York: St. Martin's Press.

———. 1994. "A Negative Vote on Affirmative Action." In *Debating Affirmative Action: Race, Gender, Ethnicity, and the Politics of Inclusion*. Edited by Micholaus Mills, 37–47. New York: Delta Book.

Stevens, Amy. 1992. "Defendant May Be Tried For Third Time in Death of Civil Rights Leader." *Wall Street Journal*, 5 August, B6(W), B5(E).

Strawn, D., and Buchanan, R. 1977. "Jury Seabrook, Jeremy. 1992. "Land of Broken Toys: Racism in Liverpool, England." *New Statesman and Society* 5: 16–17.

Stuart, Reginald. 1984a. "Policeman in Miami Is Acquitted by Jury in Slaying of Black." *New York Times*, 16 March, A1, col. 1.

———. 1984b. "Police Occupy Tense Areas in Miami After 300 Arrests." *New York Times*, 17 March, 6, col.1.

Susman, Amelia, 1976. *The Round Valley Indians of California: An Unpublished Chapter in Acculturation in Seven (or Eight) American Indian Tribes*. Berkeley, CA: University of California, Department of Anthropology, Contributions of the University of California Archaeological Research Facility, no. 31.

Takagi, Dana. 1992. *The Retreat from Race*. New Brunswick: Rutgers University Press.

Takaki, Ronald. 1987. *From Different Shores: Perspectives on Race and Ethnicity in America*. New York: Oxford University Press.

Talbot, David. 1990. "The Ballad of Hooty Croy." *Los Angeles Times*, 24 June, magazine, 16.

Thayer, James B. 1892. "The Jury and Its Development (pt.1)." *Harvard Law Review* 5: 249–288.

———. 1898. *A Preliminary Treatise on Evidence at the Common Law*. Boston, MA: Little, Brown, and Company.

Tien, Chang-Lin. 1994. "Diversity and Excellence in Higher Education." In *Debating Affirmative Action: Race, Gender, Ethnicity, and the Politics of Inclusion*. Edited by Micholaus Mills, 237–246. New York: Delta Book.

Tienda, Marta and Leif Jensen. 1988. "Poverty and Minorities: A Quarter-century Profile of Color and Socioeconomic Disadvantage." In *Divided Opportunities: Minorities, Poverty, and Social Policy*. Edited by Gary D. Sandefur and Marta Tienda, 23–61. New York: Plenum Press.

Tiersma, Peter Meijes. 1995. "Dictionaries and Death: Do Capital Jurors Understand Mitigation?" *Utah Law Review* 1995: 1–49.

Tindale, R. Scott, James H. Davis, David A. Vollrath, Dennis H. Nagao, and others. 1990. "Asymmetrical Social Influence in Freely Interacting Groups: A Test of Three Models." *Journal of Personality and Social Psychology* 58:438–449.

Tocqueville, Alexis de. 1994. *Democracy in America.* New York: Knopf.

Tomforde, Anna. 1994. "Neo-Nazi Hate Shifts from Turks to Jews." *The Guardian,* 28 May, 13.

Tooby, John and Leda Cosmides. 1990. "On the Universality of Human Nature and the Uniqueness of the Individual: The Role of Genetics and Adaptation." *Journal of Personality* 58: 17–67.

Toro, Luis A. 1995. "'A People of Distinct From Others'": Race and Identity in Federal Indian Law and the Hispanic Classification in OMB Directive No. 15." *Texas Tech Law Review* 26: 1219–1274.

Truyol, Berta E. H. 1994. "Building Brides—Latinas and Latinos At the Crossroad: Realities, Rhetoric and Replacement." *Columbia Human Rights Law Review* 25:369–433.

Twining, William. 1990. *Rethinking Evidence: Exploratory Essays.* Oxford, UK: Blackwell.

Tyler, Tom R. 2001. "Trust and Law Abidingness: A Proactive Model of Social Regulation." *Boston University Law Review* 81: 361–406.

U.S. Department of Commerce. 1991. *Technical Documentation: Summary tape tile 1—1990 Census of Population and Housing.* Washington D.C.: Bureau of the Census.

———. 1993. *200 Years of U.S. Census Taking: Population and Housing Questions,* 1790–1990. Washington D.C.: Bureau of the Census.

U.S. Department of Justice. 2000. *Prisoners in 1999.* Washington, D.C.: Office of Justice Programs, Bureau of Justice Statistics.

Van Dyke, Jon. 1983. "Jury trial." In *Encyclopedia of Crime and Justice.* Edited by Sanford H. Kadish. New York: Free Press.

———. 1977. *Jury Selection Procedures: Our Uncertain Commitment to Representative Panels.* Cambridge, MA: Ballinger Publication Co.

———. 1970. "The Jury As a Political Institution." *Catholic Law* 16: 224.

Velmen, Gerald F. 1996. "Why Some Juries Judge the System: Black Jurors Know What Color Makes a Difference in Arrest and Sentencing, Thus Jury Nullification." *Los Angeles Times,* 24 January, B9.

Vollers, Maryanne. 1995. *Ghosts of Mississippi: The Murder of Medgar Evers, the Trials of Byron de la Beckwith, and the Haun.* Boston, MA: Little, Brown.

Ward, Keith A. 1995. " 'The Only Thing in the Middle of the Road Is a Dead Skunk and a Yellow Stripe': Peremptory Challenges—Take 'Em or Leave 'Em." *Texas Tech Law Review* 26: 1361–1392.

Washington, Robin. 2001. "War on terrorism: Lawyers raise red flags over military tribunals." *Boston Herald,* 15 November, p. 5.

Weinstein, Jack B. 1993. "Considering Jury 'Nullification': When May and Should a Jury Reject the Law to Do Justice." *American Criminal Law Review* 30: 239–254.

Whitney, Craig R. 1992. "Caldron of Hate: A Special Report—East Europe's Frustration Finds Targets. Immigrants." *New York Times,* 13 November, A1.

Wilgoren, Jodi. 1995. "Anger Over Verdicts Sparks Wave of Grass-Roots Protest." *Los Angeles Times,* 12 October, A20.

Williams, Patricia J. 1991. *The Alchemy of Race and Rights.* Cambridge, MA: Harvard University Press.

Williamson, Joel. 1980. *New People: Miscegenation and Mulattos in the United States.* New York: Free Press.

Wilson, Nicholas. 1995a. "Round Valley Reservation Triple Slayings Lead to Charges of Police Cover-up and Harassment." *Albion Monitor,* 16 May.

———. 1995b. "Judge Quashes Indictment of Bear Lincoln, New Charges Filed." *Albion Monitor,* 5 December.

———. 1996. "Change of Venue Sought for Bear Lincoln Trial: Newspaper Editor Defies Subpoena." *Albion Monitor,* 16 March.

———. 1997a. "Spying, Jury Tampering Questions Raised in Bear Lincoln Trial." *Albion Monitor,* 8 July.

———. 1997b. "Stage Set as Trial Opens with All-white Jury." *Albion Monitor,* 29 July.

———. 1997c. "DA's Lone Surprise." *Albion Monitor,* 24 August.

———. 1997c. "Prosecutor Fails to Unseat Juror." *Albion Monitor,* 24 August.

———. 1997e. "The Trail of Blood Detailed." *Albion Monitor,* 21 September.

———. 1998. "Mendocino Enviros Should Oppose DA Massini." *Albion Monitor,* 24 June.

———. 1999. "Bear Lincoln Case Finally Over." *Albion Monitor,* 26 April.

Wishman, Seymour. 1986. *Anatomy of the Jury: The System on Trial.* New York: Times Books.

Wright, Luther Jr. 1995. "Who's Black, Who's White, and Who Cares: Reconceptualizing the United States's Definition of Race and Racial Classification." *Vanderbilt Law Review* 48: 513–569.

Zack, Naomi, 1995. "Introduction: Microdiversity v. Purity." In *American Mixed Race: The Culture of Microdiversity.* Edited by Naomi Zack. Lanham, MD: Rowman and Littlefield Publishers.

Zimring, Franklin, Sam Kamin, and Gordon Hawkins. 1999. *Crime and Punishment in California: The Impact of Three Strikes and You're Out.* Berkeley, CA: Institute of Government Studies Press, University of California, Berkeley.

Zinzun, Michael. 1992. "Is Your Police Breeding Racism? Part 3." In *A Message to the Grass-Roots.* Pasadena 56 Channel Access.

INDEX

Absolute disparity, 105, 106, 155, 156
Acquittal, 1, 7, 71, 87, 95, 100, 101, 118,
    123, 198; jury nullification and 197, 198,
    199, 202, 221, 229; in Miami trials 13, 14;
    in Simpson trial 176, 178, 179, 183, 185,
    186, 193, 194, 195, 196. *See also* Merciful
    acquittal; Racial acquittal; Vengeful
    conviction
Affirmative action, 23, 37, 38, 41, 58, 61 62,
    217–21, 228, 229, 232, 233, 238, 239; in
    education, employment and business
    contracting 19, 51, 52, 53; in Holland 30;
    political appointment and 61; racial identity/
    ancestry and 44–51; racial passing and 37,
    38, 53, 55; University of California and 122.
    See also Affirmative action in jury selection
Affirmative action in jury selection, 18, 19, 21,
    23, 41, 60, 73, 74–89, 92, 123, 125, 136,
    137, 147, 148, 149, 150, 217; civic
    participation and 220; criminal concepts and
    221; distinguished features of 217–21;
    fairness and 217–18; four types of xi, xii,
    90–91; hardship and 218–19; Hennepin
    County model and 69–70; jury de medietate
    linguae and 65–69; jury education and 221;
    jury nullification and 197–214; in Lincoln
    trial 92, 102, 103, 111, 113, 114–15, 117;
    quality of deliberation and verdict in 15–17;
    racial identity/ancestry and 44–51, 74–88;
    social science model and 70–72. *See also*
    Affirmative action, Racially mixed juries
Affirmative action juries. *See* Hennepin
    County model; Jury de medietate linguae;
    Social science model
Affirmative jury selection. *See* Affirmative
    action in jury selection
Affirmative jury structure. *See* Affirmative
    action in jury selection; Hennepin County
    model; Jury de medietate linguae; Social
    science model
Affirmative peremptory inclusion. *See*
    Peremptory inclusion

Afghan refugees, 21–22.
Agassi, Andre, 21
Age, 82, 170, 232; affirmative action juries
    and 74, 76; excuses and 158; jury
    nullification and 202, 213; master files and
    152, 167, 168
African American. *See* Blacks
Aliens, 154; jury de medietate linguae and 64,
    65, 67, 68, 69; jury qualifications and 170–
    171
All-white jury, xi, 1, 8, 10, 12, 13, 71, 87,
    90–91, 97, 98, 102, 107, 111, 123, 133,
    139, 142, 145, 230. *See also* Whites;
    Whiteness
Altman, Tracey, 117
Alvarez, Luiz, 12
America's Most Wanted, 107
American Bar Association (ABA), 171, 245
Arab, 57, 223, 237
Asian. *See* Asian and/or Pacific Islanders
    (API)
Asian and/or Pacific Islanders (API), 16, 21,
    24, 25–28 (Table 2.1), 29, 30, 32, 33, 35,
    36, 38, 39, 58, 155, 231, 235, 238–39, 241;
    affirmative action and 44–51, 55; affirma-
    tive action juries and 73–83, 115, 129;
    birth/death certificate discrepancy and 34;
    criminal justice concepts and 181; cross
    section and 134; Directive No. 15 and 237;
    in England 30; impartial jury and 129; jury
    of one's peers and 140, 144; racial identity/
    ancestry and 41–44; residential mobility
    and 152. *See also* Race; Racial identity

Bangladesh, 30
Banks, Dennis, 99
Barnett, Ross, 8
Barry, Marion, 142
Bell, Derrick, 87
Bench trial, 140, 147, 204, 221, 243
Bill of Rights, 68, 125, 170
Black Codes, 62

Blacks, xii, 1–2, 24, 25, 29, 177, 237; affirmative action and 47–51; affirmative action juries and 74–83; capital punishment and 191; change of venue and 3; cross section and 134, 135; impartial jury and 129; jury nullification and 143; jury of one's peers and 139–142; peremptory challenges and 137; racial identity/ancestry and 41–44; residential mobility of 152; victims and 6, 7, 10, 11, 12, 13, 15. *See also* Race; Racial identity
Blanchard, Allan, 13
Bradley, Bill, 1
Bradley, Tom, 1
Britton, Eugene, 94
Britton, Justin, 93
Britton, Neil, 94
Broadly defined peers, 139–40, 143, 147, 243. *See also* Narrowly defined peers; Peers
Bronson, Edward J., 226
"Bulls Eye" jury selection, 206–8
Burakumin, 31, 237
Burden of proof, x, xii, 166, 167, 178, 179, 180, 181–82, 183, 184, 187, 190, 191, 194, 208, 214; in Lincoln trial 107; measurements of 186. *See also* Presumption of innocence; Reasonable doubt
Bureau of Indian Affairs, U.S., 55–56, 96, 104, 230
Bush, George H.W., 1, 61
Bush, George W., 223
Butler, Paul, 178, 245

California Jury Instruction, 183
Capital punishment, 6, 51, 71, 233; Beckwith trial and 7; erroneous imposition of 6, 87
Cato, Gavin, 197
Challenges for cause, 16, 114, 127, 136, 154, 173; peremptory inclusion and 117, 119. *See also* Peremptory challenges; Voir dire
Chaney, James, 10
Change of venue, ix, 2–3, 87, 113, 220, 235; in Lincoln trial 97, 102, 107–11 (Table 4.3); in Miami trials 13–14. *See also* Jury selection procedures
Checks and balances, x, 16, 17, 19, 131, 221; jury nullification and 177, 199, 200
Chicago Jury Project, 183
Chinese, 24, 29, 33, 237, 239
Chi-square statistics, 226
Christopher Commission, 192, 246. *See also* Los Angeles Police Department (LAPD)
Christopher, Warren, 246
Citizens Against Racism, 63
Civil Rights Act, 7
Civil trials, 206
Civil War, 2, 62

Clinton, Bill, 61, 239
Cochran, Johnnie, 176, 200
Coffery, John, 1
Cohen, Lawrence, 63
Comparative disparity, 105, 106, 155, 156, 157
Cross-section criteria, xii, 126, 129, 133–36, 146, 151, 155; Supreme Court rulings affecting 18, 131–33
Crown Heights trial. *See* Nelson, Lemrick
Croy, Patric "Hooty," 95
Cuomo, Mario, 198

Davis, Bob, 94, 97, 100, 101
Davis, Phyllis, 101
Davis, Richard Allen, 93
de la Beckwith, Byron, 4, 14, 235; in trials 7–11
de Tocqueville, Alexis, 146
Death penalty. *See* Capital punishment
Deconstruction, 22, 41, 59, 239; racial identity/ancestry and 51–58. *See also* Race; Racial identity
DeJong, Phil, 100
Delmar, Vernon, 10
Dennis, Delmar, 9
Denny, Reginald 63
Diallo, Amadou, 1, 3, 15, 140
Dickson, Clarence, 1
Diggs, Ira, 11
Dinkins, David, 198
Directive No. 15 (1977), 29–30, 32, 34–36, 59, 235, 237
District attorney. *See* Prosecutors
Drivers Motor Vehicle (DMV) lists, 3, 103, 111, 151, 152, 153, 154, 155–58, 167, 168, 174. *See also* Registration of Voters (ROV) lists; Source lists

Education, 16, 30, 31, 47, 48, 51, 231, 238; affirmative action and xiii, 19, 23, 30, 47, 51, 55, 74–83, 217, 218, 221, 229; impartial jury and 129; jury nullification and 202, 208, 213; jury of one's peers and 139–43; jury selection and 158–69; peremptory inclusion and 83–88, 118
Employment, 129, 158; affirmative action and xiii, 19, 23, 30, 47, 51, 55, 74–83, 217, 218, 221, 229; cross section and 133–38; impartial jury and 126–29; jury nullification and 202, 208, 213; jury of one's peers and 139–43; jury selection and 158–69; peremptory inclusion and 83–88, 118
English language proficiency, 154, 159, 167, 173–74, 245
Equal Employment Opportunity Commission (EEOC), 34, 38

Ethnicity, xi, 29, 38, 52, 87, 144, 176, 215. *See also* Race; Racial identity

Fifth Amendment, 182
Fill–it–up quota methods. *See* Hennepin County model; Peremptory inclusion
Fonda, Henry, 71
Founding Fathers, 125
Fourteenth Amendment: due process clause of 181, 182; equal protection clause of 62, 136, 170, 173, 181, 193, 242
Fully Informed Jury Association (FIJA), 212, 247
Furman, Mark, 200

Gender, 58, 64, 128, 129, 228; affirmative action juries and 74, 76, 115; criminal justice concepts and 107; jury nullification and 202; jury selection and 125, 169; in Lincoln trial 107; racial identity/ancestry and 44
Gilbert, M. Shanara, 87
Golden, John, 124
Goldman, Ronald, 143, 195
Goodman, Andrew, 10.
Grand jury, 1; in Beckwith trials 7, 9; Hennepin County model and 69–70; jury nullification and 200; jury qualifications and 154, 240; in Lincoln trial 96, 98; in Okinawa 69, 170, 171
Gupta, Nalini, 99

Hallinan, Terence, 122
Hanlon, William, 11
Hennepin County model, xi, 62, 64, 69–70, 71, 89, 114, 115, 202; affirmative action juries and 76–83; peremptory inclusion and 120, 123; public perceptions of 72–74. *See also* Jury de medietate linguae; Social science model
Hennepin jury model. *See* Hennepin County model.
Henry III, 65
Henry IV, 65
Hindu, 29
Hispanics, 3, 14, 69, 74; cross section and 134, 135; ethnicity and 29; impartial jury and 129; language proficiency and 173–74; legal resident aliens and 171; legally defined felons and 171–72; "quasi-racial category" and 37; passing and 38–40, 57, 60, 221; peremptory challenges and 137; residential mobility and 152; Spanish surnames and 39. *See also* Race
Hobby, James, 8, 9
Humburg, Dan, 99
Hung jury, 8, 10, 70–71, 179; in Lincoln trial 102, 123; peremptory inclusion and 118–19; social science model and 71

Hussein, Saddam, 21, 29
Hypodescent rules ("one-drop of blood" hypothesis), 21, 33, 38, 43, 44, 52–53, 55, 56, 59. *See also* Blacks; Racial identity

Illinois Pattern Instructions (IPI), 182
Immigration and Naturalization Service (INS), 70
Impartial jury, 2, 10, 15, 17, 125, 126–27, 146, 167, 236, 242; as a group concept 128–29. *See also* Burden of proof; Reasonable doubt
Income, 209, 228, 238; jury selection and 150, 152, 156, 158–66, 174; racial identity/ancestry and 47–51. *See also* Socio-economic factors
India, 30, 237
Iran, 21, 30, 57, 236
Iraq, 21, 29, 30, 57, 236, 237
Islam, 223, 236

Japan, 24, 29, 30, 31, 237, 238; Okinawa in 69, 170
Jefferson, Thomas, 90
Jews, 235, 240; jury de medietate linguae and 64, 65–66, 138, 239; in Nelson trial 142, 197–98
Johnson, Nevell, 12–13
Johnson, Sheri Lynn, 71
Jury de medietate linguae, 65–69, 223: in American colonies 63–64, 67–68; in British colonies 68–69; in England 63–64, 65–67; ideal racial compositions and 115; in Lincoln trial 114–15; Massachusetts Declaration of Rights and 68; Native Americans and 90; public perceptions of 72–74, 76–83; Supreme Court rulings on 68; Thomas Jefferson and 90. *See also* Hennepin County model; Racially mixed jury; Social science model
Jury foreperson, x, 2, 4, 16; in Lincoln trial 101
Jury nullification, xii, xiii, 73, 76, 87, 176, 177, 179, 191–95, 197–214; affirmative action juries and 202–5, 213–14; criminal justice concepts and 181–85, 187–90, 206, 208–10; history of 211–13; jury of one's peers and 143–46; in Nelson trial 197–98; Supreme Court rulings on 211. *See also* Acquittal
Jury qualification criteria, 2–3, 154, 166, 168; felony convictions and 171–73; jury de medietate linguae and 66; language proficiency and 173–74; legal resident aliens and 170–71; peremptory inclusion and 117–18, 120. *See also* Jury selection procedures

Jury selection procedures, 2–5, 149–75, 216–
   17; affirmative jury selection and 149;
   diagram (Figure 1.1) of 5; eight stages of
   2–6; jury qualification and 154; seven
   checkpoints in 153–55; socio-economic
   factors and 158–66; Supreme Court rulings
   on 64
Jury Selection and Service Act of 1968, 121
Jury tampering, 99, 241

Kadafi, Moammar, 21, 29
King, Martin Luther, 13
King, Rodney, 1, 6, 13, 63, 142, 144, 192,
   200, 220, 229, 235; change of venue and
   2–3, 13
Klaas, Polly 93
Korea, 29
Ku Klux Klan, 2, 8, 10, 101, 192, 235
Kurds, 30

Legal cynicism, 4, 6, 179
Lifsh, Yosef, 197
Lincoln, Eugene "Bear," 91–102; affirmative
   action juries and 114–15; defense strategies
   for 102–11, 123–24; J. Tony Serra and 98,
   99, 124, 241; peremptory inclusion and 91,
   111–13, 115–20, 123; progressive
   legislation/court action and 121–23
Lincoln, Pat, 96
LISREL maximum-likelihood estimations, 226
Lloyd, Clement Anthony, 13–14
Los Angeles Police Department (LAPD), 142,
   191–92, 200, 246
Los Angeles Times, 195
Lozano, William, 13
Lumet, Sidney, 71

Madison, James, 90
Magna Carta, 68, 138, 243
Marshall, Thurgood, 18, 61
Marston, Lester, 97–98
Massaro, Toni M, 127, 244
McDougall, Harold, 86–87
McDuffie, Arthur, 11
Melilli, Kenneth J., 137, 170
Merciful acquittal, 87, 199–200, 201, 206,
   209. See also Acquittal; Racial acquittal
Mexican, 39, 122, 171, 234; ethnicity and 29,
   30, 237; racial category and 29, 59. See
   also Hispanics
Mexico, 31, 38
Miami trials, 1, 7, 11–14, 63, 142, 229
"Military Order of November 13, 2001," 223
Miller, Dennis, 94, 100
Mixed Tribunal, 140, 141 (Table 5.3), 147.
   See also Bench trial

Morgan, Peggy, 9
Morrero, Alex, 11
Mulatto. See Blacks
Myrdal, Gunnar, 37

Narrowly defined peers, 139, 140–48, 244.
   See also Broadly defined peers; Peers
National Center for Health Statistics, 35
National Jury Project, 181
National Voter Registration Act, 151
Native Americans, xi, 21, 24–25, 34, 222,
   238, 241; affirmative action juries and 67;
   in Lincoln trial 90–124; racial identity/
   ancestry and 29, 41–44, 45 (Table 2.3). See
   also Jury; Race; Racial identity
Naturalization Act, 67
Nelson, Lemrick, 142, 197, 198, 201, 246–47

O'Connor, Elizabeth Day, 88
Octoroon. See Blacks
Office of Management and Budget (OMB),
   29, 36, 235
Okinawa, 69, 170–71. See also Japan
Okrent, Daniel, 20
"One-drop of blood" hypothesis. See also
   Hypo-descent rules

Pakistan, 30
Pardo, Joyce, 100
Passing, 22, 36–41, 43–44, 52; affirmative
   action and 53–55; blacks and 37, 44, 236;
   Hispanics and 38–40, 57, 60, 221; racial
   immobility and 60. See also Statutory
   passing
Patterson, Orlando, 20
Peers, xii, 10, 65, 72, 126, 129, 138–46, 177,
   216, 243–44; jury de medietate linguae
   and 65, 68; in Lincoln trial 111, 119;
   peremptory inclusion and 92. See also
   Broadly defined peers; Narrowly defined
   peers
Peltier, Leonard, 94
Pennsylvania "jury peer representation" bill, 72.
Peremptory challenges, x, 3, 4, 16, 39–40, 72,
   92, 113, 127, 132, 154, 173; affirmative
   action juries and 83–88; in Lincoln trial 98,
   100, 107, 111, 113; in Miami trials 12, 13;
   peremptory inclusion and 91, 117–18, 123;
   racial representation and 136–37, 170, 216,
   223, 242
Peremptory inclusion, xii, 19, 91, 92, 122,
   123, 149, 175, 217, 223; cross section and
   136–38; Hennepin County model and 120–
   21; jury of one's peers and 145; jury
   selection criteria and 118–19, 120–21;
   Lincoln trial and 113, 115–20. See also

Affirmative action in jury selection;
Peremptory challenges
Perry, Bill, 13.
Peters, Arylis, 94, 96
Peters, Byron, 93
Peters, Leonard "Acorn," 94, 96
Presumption of innocence, x, xii, 142, 166,
167, 180–81, 182, 184, 187, 190–91,
193–95, 208, 221, 245–46; in Lincoln trial
107; measurements of 186. *See also* Burden
of proof; Reasonable doubt
Prince, Dan, 9
Proportional jury. *See* Hennepin County model
Prosecutors, ix, xi, 16, 17, 131, 177, 180, 193,
221, 243, 247; in Beckwith trials 7, 9, 10;
jury of one's peers and 139, 142; in
Lincoln trial 98, 99–100, 101; in Miami
trials and 11, 12–13; peremptory challenges
and 136–37, 170; in Simpson trial 194

Qualification questionnaires. *See* Jury
qualification criteria
Quadroon. *See* Blacks
Quarter jury. *See* Social science model
Quota, xii, 64, 70, 72, 73, 74, 77, 78–88, 113,
202, 213, 220, 228, 241; Hennepin County
model and 120–21; Supreme Court rulings
on 88

Race, 1, 20–60; biological construction of 24;
deconstruction of 51–58; Eurocentric
notions of 24; impartiality and 129;
measurement of 21, 233–34; political
construction of (Table 2.1) 25–28; social
construction of 20–21, 22, 221; as
unreliable and invalid concept 32–41; white
hegemony and 221–22; white identity and
20–21. *See also* Racial identity
Racial acquittal, 178, 185, 194, 195, 196,
200–2. *See also* Acquittal; Jury nullification; Merciful acquittal; Vengeful
conviction
Racial ancestry 22, 31, 33, 213; affirmative
action and 44–51, 53–55; measurement of
41–44, 233–34; racial identity and 41–44.
See also Racial identity
Racial identity, 20, 190–91: affirmative action
and 44–51; as cultural construct 21–23, 59–
60; deconstruction of 51–58; in England,
30; in Europe 30; illusion of 20–23;
internal inconsistency and 32–34; in Japan
30; lack of verification for 34–35; passing
and 36–41; racial ancestry and 41–51;
racial immobility and 43, 60; "rule" of
hypodescent ("one-drop of blood"
hypothesis) and 21, 33, 38, 43, 44, 56; U.S.

government and 24, 25–28 (Table 2.1), 29,
30. *See also* Asian and/or Pacific Islanders
(API); Blacks; Hispanics
Racial passing. *See* Passing; Statutory passing
Racial profiling 1, 6, 223. *See also* Prosecutors; Race; Racial identity
Racial quota. *See* Quota
Racial riot, 18, 235; in Albany 15; in England
66; in Miami 11, 12, 13, 14; in New York
198
Racially mixed jury 17–18; affirmative action
juries and 63–65, 74–77, 78–83; in
Beckwith trials and 9; benefits of 2, 16–
17, 87–88; checks and balances and 16,
17, 131, 221; democratic elements of 125–
26; Hennepin County model and 69–70;
jury de mediate and 65–69; jury of one's
peers and 139–46; in Miami trials 14;
peremptory challenges and 83–88; social
science model and 70–72. *See also*
Affirmative action in jury selection; Jury
de medietate linguae; Hennepin County
model; Social science model
Racially mixed persons, 37, 56, 238–39;
racially mixed marriage and 35
Reasonable doubt, x, xii, 182–84, 187–95,
206, 208, 214, 221, 242; in Lincoln trial
97, 100, 101; measurements of 186;
peremptory inclusion and 119. *See also*
Burden of proof; Presumption of innocence
Registration of Voters (ROV) lists, 3, 103,
111, 150, 151, 152, 153, 155–58, 167, 168,
174. *See also* Drivers Motor Vehicle
(DMV) lists
Reiley, Mark, 9
Reno, Janet, 11, 12, 61
Revision to Directive No. 15 (1998), 29, 32,
36, 59, 235, 237. *See also* Directive No. 15
(1977)
Ross, Robert S., 226
Round Valley Indian Reservation, 92, 94, 96,
97–98, 102, 104 (Table 4.1)
Ruth, Babe, 20

San Francisco Police Department, 95
Santa Cruz community survey, 72, 182, 184,
185, 225, 227
Santa Monica Superior Court, 143, 206. *See
also* Simpson, O.J.
Sassamon, John, 67
Schneerson, Menachem, 197
Schwerner, Michael, 10
Scottsboro Boys' case, 143, 200
Serra, J. Tony, 95–96, 98–99, 124, 241
Seventh Amendment, 129
Simmons, Cora Lee, 102

Simpson, Nicole Brown, 143, 195
Simpson, O.J., xii, 73, 140, 206, 213, 225, 245; acquittal and 176–96, 209; in civil trial 143, 206; criminal jury and 201, 218; jury nullification and 200, 206. *See also* Jury nullification; Santa Monica Superior Court
Sixth Amendment, xii, 17, 68, 125–48, 173, 174, 180, 193, 242
Slaves, 31, 62, 199; Native Americans as 98; U.S. Census and 24. *See also* Blacks
Smith, Abbe, 149
Social construction of race. *See* Blacks; Race; Racial identity
Social science model, xi, 62, 65, 70–72, 91, 202; in Lincoln trial 102, 114–15, 117, 118, 121; public perceptions of 72–74, 76–83. *See also* Jury de medietate linguae; Hennepin County model
Socio-economic factors, 83, 86–88, 92, 208, 221, 225, 231; affirmative action and 47–51; impartial jury and 128; jury nullification and 202, 204; jury of one's peers and 140–42; jury selection and 2, 63, 156–69. *See also* Income
Source lists, 2, 3, 70, 150–51, 152, 153–54, 156–57, 166, 174; Native Americans and 102, 230. *See also* Drivers Motor Vehicle (DMV) lists; Jury selection procedures; Registration of Voters (ROV) lists. *See also* specific types
Split jury. *See* Jury de medietate linguae
Sri Lanka, 30
State of Maryland Constitution, 212–13
State of Indiana Constitution, 213
Statutory passing, 60, 221. *See also* Hispanics; Passing
Steele, Shelby, 219
Supreme Court, U.S., ix, 2, 17–18, 61, 62, 231, 242; cognizable status and 113; Hispanics and 39; impartial jury and 129; jury nullification and 211; Native Americans and 113; peremptory challenges and 136, 169–70, 217; presumption of innocence and 180; race and 24; reasonable doubt and 182–83. *See also* specific cases of, in Table of Cases
Susman, Amelia, 98
Sutherland, Donald, 208

Telephone registration lists, 111. *See also* Source lists
Thomas, Clarence, 61
Three strikes law, 48, 122, 172, 199

Till, Emmit, 201
Tribal lists, 103–4, 230. *See also* Source lists
Tripp, Alvin, 101
Tuso, Jim, 95
Type I and Type II errors, 183

Unaminity rule, 170, 178, 182; wrongful convictions and 71
Undeliberables, 153, 154
University of California, Santa Cruz Human Resources, 36
University of California (UC) wide survey, 41, 228, 231, 238
Urban Institute, 171
Utility company lists, 113. *See also* Source lists

Vanoven, Shellie, 101
Vengeful conviction, xiii, 199, 200–2; affirmative action juries and 87; in Lincoln trial 98. *See also* Acquittal; Jury nullification; Merciful acquittal; Racial acquittal
Voir dire, 2, 3, 16, 113, 127, 149, 175, 216: in Beckwith trials 7; impartial jurors and 127; jury selection and 3–4, 154, 157, 168, 173; in Lincoln trial 97–98; peremptory inclusion and 19, 115–21. *See also* Peremptory challenges
Voting Rights Act, 151

Walker, Bill, 8
Watts, Michael, 11
Welfare recipient lists, 111. *See also* Source lists
Whites 1, 20–22, 24, 56–57, 221, 237; affirmative action and civil issues (Table 2.5) and 44–51; as desired race 36, 43–44; four different groups of 206, 215–16; racial identity of 20–21, 44; social fabrication and 57, 60. *See also* Passing; Race; Racial identity
White-collar crime, 208–10, 214
White-dominated jury. *See* All-white jury
Whiteness, 48, 56–57, 222; passing and 54–55; privilege of 36, 37, 43, 58. *See also* Race; Passing; Whites
Williams, Aaron, 101
Wilson, Pete, 95
Women. *See* Gender.
Wright, Don, 11
Wrongful conviction, 71, 87–88

Z-test statistics, 155, 156, 157, 166, 167; in Lincoln trial 105